Contributors:

Walter Berns
Alexander M. Bickel
Reo Christensen
Victor B. Cline
Harry Clor
Steven Courrier
Roger G. Croft
Emily S. Davidson
Robert E. Fitch
Irving Kristol
Robert M. Liebert
Paul J. McGeady
Blaine McLaughlin
John M. Neale
Norman Podhoretz
Alberta Siegel
Jesse L. Steinfeld
Ernest van den Haag
Fredric Wertham
James Q. Wilson

WHERE DO YOU DRAW THE LINE?

An Exploration into Media Violence,
Pornography, and Censorship

Edited by Victor B. Cline

Brigham Young University Press

9/01   J. Doe/gift

Library of Congress Cataloging in Publication Data

Cline, Victor B   comp.
    Where do you draw the line?

    Includes bibliographies.
    1. Mass media--Censorship.   2.   Violence in mass
media.   3.   Sex in mass media.   4.   Censorship--United
States.   I.   Berns, Walter Fred, 1919-   II.   Title.
P96.C4C58   363.3'1'0973   74-9670
ISBN 0-8425-0986-0
ISBN 0-8425-0974-7 (pbk.)

Library of Congress Catalog Card Number: 74-9670
International Standard Book Number: 0-8425-0986-0 (hardback)
                                        0-8425-0974-7 (paperback)
© 1974 Brigham Young University Press. All rights reserved
Brigham Young University Press, Provo, Utah 84602
Printed in the United States of America
74 4.5Mp   .5Mh   1454

Contents

Preface

Over the centuries, many men and women have given their lives and in small increments have paved the way for the establishment of free societies such as ours. Few would deny that our civilization is built on the bodies of many martyrs and on the sacrifices of individuals who, unable to tolerate tyranny, opposed it in any form.

Because truth and justice in political and social affairs are often difficult to determine immediately, it is generally conceded that they are best arrived at by free and open discussion. It is additionally conceded that free and unrestrained discussion is not only a legitimate outlet for dissent, but also that it greatly reduces the likelihood of more violent forms of social protest.

Freedom of speech, as embodied in the First Amendment to the United States Constitution, has origins dating back to other forms of government: the participatory democracy of Greece's city states; the later development of Roman codes and institutions based on a "universal natural law," where all men were seen as equal; the still later Magna Charta of 1215; the Edict of Nantes (1598); France's Declaration of the Rights of Man and the Citizen (1789); as well as our own Constitution with its first ten amendments. These all represent tumultuous milestones in the development of our free society.

Since "free speech" represents such a vital element in the development as well as the preservation of our free society, can we ever compromise on the issue?

Does the First Amendment to the Constitution really mean what it says: "Congress shall make no law ... abridging the freedom of speech or the press?"

As Norman Podhoretz, editor of *Commentary* magazine, has put it, this is not an easy question to respond to:

Whenever I am forced to think seriously about freedom of speech and the problems it poses, I instantly find myself getting depressed. I tend to take an absolutistic position on freedom of speech, roughly on the ground that restricting it seems on the whole to entail more odious consequences than letting it run entirely wild. Yet I know . . . the absolutist position is highly vulnerable on a theoretical plane—and it is increasingly hard to defend wholeheartedly in the face of certain concrete results ("Living with Free Speech," this volume).

This dilemma, facing many thoughtful people in our society, along with possible consequences, is frequently scrutinized in two areas: media violence and pornography.

These two issues have received much attention in recent years from behavioral scientists and morality groups, ordinary citizens and PTAs, countless juries, and three presidential commissions.

Recent research suggests, for example, that behavioral scientists have finally established a causal relationship between some children's exposure to TV violence and increased aggressive behavior. This could be interpreted as meaning that some TV programs (and movies) may constitute a "clear and present danger" to some of their younger viewers. If so, does this justify editing (a polite word for censoring) the content of such programs? What about the rights of adult viewers? But then, are some adults also "harmed" by the violence they witness?

What about the elimination of cigarette advertising on TV—is this not a form of censorship? Is it not a violation of the First Amendment in fact and spirit? Do not cigarette manufacturers have free speech protection, too? Is the harm caused by cigarette advertising sufficient to justify this type of suppression of speech?

On the other hand, if this is truly a free society, do not the majority have rights, through their elected representatives, to enact legislation controlling cigarette advertising, TV or movie violence, live sex on stage or whatever—if this were seen to be in the best interest of society generally? For example, is filmed or live sexual sado-masochism in a public theater a form of free speech?

Where does one draw the line on free speech? Or does one ever draw that line? Should one draw such a line? It is the intention of this book to push these issues as hard and as far as possible—to discomfort the reader, never allowing him to "get off the hook" or to avoid facing the dilemmas created by either total license or excessive censure, regarding the open expression of ideas and the free depiction of images and behavior in the various media.

The "state of the art," according to scientific knowledge about "effects," is here presented in the aforementioned areas of violence in the media and pornography. The tough, thorny issues of censorship, freedom of speech, and public morality, as well as the current thinking of the courts on these matters are also tackled with considerable zeal by many commentators.

Victor B. Cline

Acknowledgments

I express my deep appreciation and indebtedness not only to William F. Prokasy, Stewart Proctor, Arvo van Alstyne, and Raymond Gauer for reading portions of the manuscript and offering many helpful suggestions but also to Irwin Altman for his critique of the pornography-effects section.

I am grateful to editor Louise Hanson for her generous and helpful consultation and her encouragement as I organized this book.

On behalf of the publisher, I express gratitude also to the following authors and organizations for granting permission to use the indicated copyright material: Alexander Bickel's "The 'Uninhibited, Robust, and Wide-Open' First Amendment" and Norman Podhoretz's "Living with Free Speech: A Response to Alexander M. Bickel," both reprinted from *Commentary* by permission, copyright © 1972 the American Jewish Committee; Walter Berns's "Democracy, Censorship, and the Arts" and Harry Clor's "Obscenity and Freedom of Expression," both reprinted from *Censorship and Freedom of Expression,* copyright © 1971, Public Affairs Conference Center, Kenyon College; James Q. Wilson's "Violence, Pornography, and Social Science," *The Public Interest,* No. 22 (Winter 1971), pp. 45-61, copyright © National Affairs, Inc., 1971; Fredric Wertham's "School for Violence, Mayhem in the Mass Media" from *A Sign for Cain,* copyright © Macmillan Publishing Co., 1966; Reo Christenson's "Censorship of Pornography, Yes" from *The Progressive,* copyright © September, 1970; Victor Cline et al. "The Desensitization of Children to TV Violence," copyright © 1973 the American Psychological Association, *J. of Pers. and Soc. Psychology,* September, 1973, Vol. 27, No. 3; and Irving Kristol's "The Case for Liberal Censorship," March 28, 1971, *New York Times,* by permission of the author, copyright © 1971.

Where Do You Draw the Line? An Introduction

I don't know why middle-aged men have to be protected from reading about [pornographic] activities that are too rigorous for them to take part in, but the "fig leafers" are out to do it. I haven't read anything to indicate that the books peddled in "adult bookstores" or the movies shown at the skin theaters have been turning people into "Jack the Rippers." Yet the tight-lipped censors are convinced that such material changes otherwise calm men into fiends.

Mike Royko, 14 July 1973, *Chicago Daily News.*

Nobody has been forced to see or read a single pornographic scene in these past years of permissiveness. It has been a matter of personal taste, good or bad, which is exactly where it should be left in a free country. There is a reasonable chance that the "average person" whom the attorney general is so eager to protect will be treated in the future to perhaps the most obscene act any respecter of our Constitution can conjure: policemen with mauls breaking down the door to a hall on a university campus to enforce censorship. There is no way a court, a legislature, or an attorney general can decide for an entire state what is acceptable to see or read and what is not. Nor can they do so for a city, a ward, and particularly not for an individual.

Ernest B. Ferguson, 12 July 1973, *Los Angeles Times.*

Vicious acts of war, racism, starvation, and the systematic cruelty of poverty are the real obscenities—not pornography.

Adele T. Buxbaum, 18 April 1971, letter to *New York Times.*

The First Amendment to our Constitution evolved out of many centuries of struggle for man's free agency. The majority of the world's population live in essentially totalitarian states where individual freedoms are sharply limited. The present freedoms we enjoy in speech and expression were not easily won. The blood of many martyrs over the centuries was only a partial price paid for the free society which so many of us now so casually enjoy.

The frequent attempts by self-appointed censors to suppress what people might read or see or say because it might be bad for some individuals or have certain alleged negative consequences has its roots in antiquity. Even Socrates urged the censoring of the writers of fiction to protect the young.

Most, though not all, libertarians agree, however, that there are still a few limits or exceptions to free speech as free speech. Speech that creates a "clear and present danger" such as yelling fire in a crowded theater probably should be limited or constrained; conspiracy, engaging in speech that amounts to an obstruction of justice (e.g., Watergate), and false advertising might be other examples. For most people there does not exist a great deal of concern about "loss of liberties" through constraints on this type of speech.

With the dramatic recent change in social attitudes and possibly behavior in the area of human sexuality and with the decline of religion as an effective voice and significant moral and socializing agent in our society, the issue of censorship of pornography has in recent years been repeatedly challenged in the courts and has been a matter of continuing public debate. This debate led to the establishment of a national commission to assess the influence of erotica and to suggest to the Congress what might be done about it.

The question which has repeatedly been raised with great vigor by many thoughtful citizens is, "Why should pornography be exempt from the First Amendment guarantees of free speech?" Or as actress Shirley MacLaine recently expressed it, "As a citizen I resent being told what I can or cannot see, read, or enjoy. These choices belong to me. Not to the FBI or the Justice Department" (7 May 1973, *Newsweek*).

Interestingly, most of those individuals who wish to censor erotic materials show little concern about violence in the media, despite its proven harmful effects, especially on young viewers; their interest appears limited to erotic materials and sexual morality. Should not concern be shown, however, for other types of morality—such as honesty and ethical conduct? Yet nobody has ever censored something because it promoted selfishness or dishonesty. In a similar way, those who are concerned about media violence and its effects on the viewer seem to have little concern about erotica.

When Joe Steinman, national sales manager for Boxoffice International, was asked (Rotsler, 1973), "Are sex films harmful to anyone?" He responded, "No . . . [but] violence is. If there is any tendency to emulate what is on the screen, well which is worse—to go home and make love to your wife or your girl friend, or to kill someone?" Columnist Mike Royko (1973) comments further on this issue:

How did Americans develop such a great affection for .45 caliber pistols and such a great fear of genitalia? On the Fourth of July, a recent immigrant from Yugoslavia sat in his suburban Chicago apartment shooting a pistol out his window not knowing where the bullets might go. The police said he wasn't trying to shoot anybody—he thought that Americans celebrated their independence anniversary by shooting guns. One of the bullets struck a little boy, who said a few words to his father, then fell dead. The immigrant had bought the gun at a suburban gun shop. He had no trouble buying it. In our country, guns are as easy to buy as milkshakes. Had his interest been pornography and had he spent the day reading dirty books, that little boy would be alive.

With the companion issue of violence depicted in the arts and media, the recent Surgeon General's Report, finding a causal relationship between witnessing TV violence and increased aggressive behavior in some children, could suggest a "clear and present danger." If the same danger is present in the use of pornography, which at least some research suggests, then we have a clear conflict between the censor (who argues that pornography is essentially harmful not only to the individual but also to public morality) and the libertarian who upholds free speech with no compromise. This obviously raises some tough, thorny questions and issues. Is there a point where one may draw a line that most people can agree upon in the public display of violence and eroticism—especially if "harm" is a legitimate issue? But then who would draw the line? Whom would we trust to judge?

In the countless books and articles which address themselves to this question, at least thirty-six significant arguments express well the viewpoint in opposition to censorship. While the arguments vary in detail, their crux will be summarized here without comment or response as to their logic, their veracity, or their validity. Some apply equally to pornography and violence and to "free expression" generally, while others apply more to one than the other.

1. You can't legislate morality. And even if you could, it would be an inappropriate function of government, especially in a pluralistic society such as ours where so many culturally different subgroups espouse many diverse values and points of view.

2. The censoring of erotica or violence (or anything else) in any of the arts would necessarily mean banning many great works of art and literature, and this would be intolerable in a free society. Permitting the occasionally vulgar or that which is in poor taste is not too great a price to pay, for that would allow and encourage the great work of art or genius without fetters and constraints. Our society would be enriched overall by such a policy.

3. Censorship laws create crimes without victims. If you send a man to jail for selling a forbidden book or picture or for showing an illegal cinema (which consenting adults have chosen to expose themselves to) we have a "crime" without any victim. This is illogical and tyrannical.

4. The First Amendment to the Constitution of the United States un-

equivocally suggests that any censorship law is unconstitutional. The wording is clear and unambiguous: Congress shall make no law . . . abridging the freedom of speech or of the press. Thus it is inappropriate for the government to tell any citizen what he can say, see, hear, or read. And to permit punishment for ideas that are offensive to some is totally unacceptable. The prime function of the First Amendment is to keep debate open to liberal-minded as well as staid people.

5. The real obscenities in life are not pornographic books or films but rather war, poverty, prejudice, pollution, and the like.

6. Erotica suggests a uniting of the sexes, of love, of pleasuring and giving to someone else. Sexual imagery, no matter how explicit, merely reflects a universal life function. This is not bad, but good. Only those with sexual hangups and neuroses (which many censors appear to have) will be afraid of the human body and human sexuality and oppose its dissemination to those adults who choose to have it. To deny sex is to deny life. To reject art is to impoverish yourself, rejecting pleasure and growth. To accept sex and art together is to advance oneself, to be positive instead of negative.

7. What is pornography? It is a question beyond definition—almost by definition. It cannot be defined. What is pornographic to one man is mildly risqué to another. Obscenity is in the eye (or groin) of the beholder. Because it is a variable concept this means that its definition is mercurial and constantly shifting depending on ever-changing times, tastes, and morals as well as individual differences. And if you can't define it, it's impossible to legislate against it. No law can be so precisely framed as to indicate what this will-o'-the-wisp is so as to provide a clear guilt. And every man should be able to know with certainty when he is committing a crime. No such certainty exists in the obscenity area.

8. Only one short step separates the censorship of literature and the arts from the censorship of political thought. We can't take that chance. When you set a precedent and allow some censorship, it can easily spread to other kinds of material. Censorship is the hallmark of an authoritarian regime. A society can be strong only when it is truly free.

9. There is no really conclusive evidence that erotic or even violent imagery or words ever harmed anybody. No girl was ever seduced by a book or received physical injury from same (unless it was dropped on her head or thrown at her).

10. Seeing erotic or violent images is probably cathartic and therapeutic. It provides a vicarious outlet for our aggressive and sexual impulses. This could help keep a "rapist off the street," drain his impulses so that he won't commit an antisocial act; in other words this type of material may render some people less socially dangerous by providing a fantasy release for aggressive and sexual impulses, thereby proving beneficial to mankind.

11. If you do enact censorship laws, you have nobody who is really qualified to act as censor. This would include Mrs. Grundy, the Citizens'

4

Puritan League, the PTA president, the district judge, or the vice squad officer; for all of these people will necessarily possess special biases, points of view, and possible neurotic hangups. And what if their biases are different from yours or mine? Why should they censor what I read or see? Won't this mean that censorship will necessarily always be capricious, arbitrary, and variable—depending on who is doing the censoring? And is this tolerable in a free society? There are some individuals who become excited by seeing lingerie ads in the Sears-Roebuck catalog. Should they be censors? But if not they, then who?

12. Censorship always and invariably interferes with the creativity of the artist, writer, sculptor, film producer, playwright, and others. It creates a repressive climate that is antithetical to creativity. This is intolerable and should not be permitted. The artist as creator must necessarily challenge common beliefs and cultural values, for the creative process identifies new relationships out of which come new meanings; and this is good.

13. Even though the majority should rule, they shouldn't be allowed to legislate their prejudices in areas and issues dealing with free speech and expression. Even unpopular ideas and material in poor taste, even shoddy things should have the opportunity of being presented and being accepted or rejected in a free marketplace. The Constitution protects coarse expression as well as refined, and vulgarity no less than elegance.

14. The enjoyment and personal use of erotica or violent imagery is a private, not a public act, and as such is not a matter for the state to involve itself in. The Supreme Court's ruling (Stanley v. Georgia) supports this position and suggests the corollary, that one should have the right to purchase this kind of material if he chooses.

15. Materials (in film, art, and books) reflecting moral heresy (even erotica and violence) should enjoy the same freedom of expression as that reflecting political heresy and unorthodoxy. The rights of the best of men are secured only as the rights of the vilest and most abhorrent are protected.

16. The most outrageously immoral, intolerant, and obscene act is that of someone censoring what consenting adults wish to read or view.

17. Pornography and violence (in images or words) help people overcome their fear of sexuality (or violence) through the process of desensitization. Exposure to this material helps one overcome sexual hangups and neuroses. It demythologizes sex and helps one laugh at it, producing a more healthy view of it.

18. When you censor something, you invest it with a special "forbidden fruit" aura; you make it tempting and prurient. This actually creates a morbid interest in the material—not a healthy one. You artificially create a desire for it.

19. If we abandon censorship, works of art and "trash" can legitimately compete on their true merits, not on contrived prurience. This would be healthy and good for society.

20. Art can be both pornographic and violent and a great work of art at the same time. To censor this material would mean a loss to our society and a rejection of a possible work of great talent or genius.

21. Pornography is a boon to the lonely, the sexually confused, and the hopelessly ugly. In fantasy it gives them some relief from their sexual frustrations.

22. Sex and violence are a part of life. If you censor these in the arts or hide them, you are hypocritically denying extremely important aspects of living and life. You are creating a distorted and untrue vision of man. You are being artistically and aesthetically dishonest about human experience.

23. By abolishing taboos (eliminating censorship), you liberate the human spirit and free the man. You abolish guilt about sex and violence. But by censorship you indirectly make people feel guilty about sex, you create neuroses, and you may make people sick.

24. Censorship never really works. In a democracy, people see and read what they wish despite what the law says. Just as during prohibition, if you pass a law which everybody violates, it creates an attitude or climate of indifference toward the law and a disrespect which could generalize to other legitimate and valid laws.

25. The government should not enforce widely held moral or religious beliefs which inveigh against communication of sexual stimuli merely on the ground that it is evil, bad, or wrong. This is private morality and is not the province of governmental intrusion or interference. It may be a legitimate area of concern of parent, priest, or teacher, but never of the government. To suppress a book in the interest of the prevailing sexual morality strikes as deep into the First Amendment as the dictator's knife can go.

26. Public opinion is a much better force to deal with pornography and violence than oppressive censorship laws. A majority of the citizens by their public disapproval could keep this sort of thing in check and within tolerable bounds in our society.

27. The less power the police and state have over our private lives the better.

28. If we ignore pornography—let it take its course, people will soon tire of it, and its novelty will wear off. They'll satiate. Pornography will tend to go away, or at least its interest to the general public will greatly diminish. It is better that we deal with it this way than through repressive legislation.

29. Censorship stifles social change and progress by impeding ideological change, which tends to preserve or "freeze" the present morality via the powers of the state.

30. Censorship limits the student's education. It leaves him with a distorted and jaundiced view of society. It suggests that we do not trust his judgment. How can we expect to produce a free, reasoning person who can make his own decisions, understand his culture, and live compassionately with his fellow man if we censor vital elements of his culture and human experience?

31. Censors are a far greater danger to society than the works they attack or seek to proscribe. To vest a few fallible men—prosecutors, judges, and jurors with the vast power of literary and artistic censorship—to convert them into moral police—is to make them despots.

32. Censorship laws to protect children will not work because children can always get older persons to buy the forbidden material for them. And there is nothing in the Constitution that gives the Supreme Court the right to water down the First Amendment to protect young people. To censor material because it is supposedly deleterious to youth is to burn the house to roast the pig.

33. If it is argued that whatever excites sexual longing and interest may possibly produce sexual misconduct, then perfumes, hot pants, and brief bathing suits will have to be banned along with obscenity.

34. Paternalistic guardianship by the government (e.g., "papa knows best") of the thoughts of grown-up citizens enervates their spirit, keeps them immature, makes conformists out of them, and creates a crippling dependence on the state or on others to do their thinking for them. This is undesirable in a democracy.

35. One never hears a judge, a prosecutor, a censor, or a moralist declare that *their* moral fiber has been injured by looking at a dirty picture, a movie, or a book. It's always someone else's moral fiber for which anxiety is felt. It's always "they" who get damaged.

36. Control of improper *conduct,* not of expression, is the proper function of government.

Legislative and Court Approved Limitations on "Free Speech"

Supreme Court Justices William O. Douglas and Hugo Black have been inclined, with but few exceptions, to take the more libertarian view in their voting record on First Amendment issues. They have tended to regard free speech as free speech, not to be tampered with. However, the majority of the court has tended in most cases not to go along with them.

The legislative arm of the government as well as the majority of state and federal courts have always felt that there were certain types of speech and expression which society has a right to restrict, censor, or protect itself from. At the present time there are at least eighteen areas where free speech can be limited, prohibited, or in some way "censored" because this censorship is viewed as in the best interest of our society. This, in effect, means that the First Amendment has itself been "amended" a number of times by the courts and legislatures with the approval and sanction in most cases of the majority of the populace. These "amendments" include the following:

1. False advertising. It is illegal to fraudulently misrepresent merchandise for sale. The courts have unfailingly upheld the rights of the legislative branch of government to pass legislation prohibiting and penalizing this type

of "speech" or expression. Within recent years government agencies protecting the consumer have been particularly vigilant, requiring advertisers to cease and desist with regards to promotions of a great many products.

2. Speaking a prayer, reading from the Bible, or giving instruction in religious matters. These things are prohibited in public schools because of the separation of church and state clause contained in the First Amendment itself. The Supreme Court has indicated that the First Amendment, in effect, has its own implied exception to free speech in the "religion clause." In a sense, therefore, the First Amendment has a built-in contradiction, at least regarding court interpretation of its meaning.

3. Libel, slander, defamation of character. In general the courts have held that false and defamatory statements about an individual are not protected by the First Amendment's free speech clause. In fact, one can be prosecuted for engaging in "group libel" (e.g., slandering an ethnic, religious, or racial group such as Negroes or Jews). However, public officials have less recourse to redress in this area than do ordinary citizens and tend to be more vulnerable to defamatory or scurrilous attacks than others.

4. Saying words which amount to a conspiracy or an obstruction of justice.

5. Sedition. This might include words that suggest or that plan for the violent overthrow of our government.

6. Words that tend to create a "clear and present danger," such as yelling "fire" in a crowded theater and making inflammatory remarks which might incite a riot. It would be a jury's duty to decide such issues.

7. Using words that constitute offering a bribe (say, of a government official).

8. Words that threaten social harm because they advocate illegal acts.

9. Words (from a loudspeaker) at 3:00 a.m. in a residential neighborhood, disturbing the peace.

10. A public address in the middle of Main Street at high noon, which as a consequence interferes with the orderly movement of traffic.

11. Being in contempt of court. The judge may send you to jail if either your behavior or your speech is inappropriate.

12. Committing perjury under oath.

13. Television cigarette advertisements.

14. Saying words or giving information which have been classified (e.g., secret) by the government.

15. Obscenity. While the Supreme Court has repeatedly affirmed that obscenity is not a protected form of speech, it has permitted local communities to form their own criteria of what is and is not permitted, as long as these criteria include appeal to prurient interest and lack of redeeming artistic, scientific or literary value.

16. Copyright violations.

17. Pretrial publicity which might interfere with a defendant's opportunity to secure a fair trial by his peers.

18. U.S. Government employees engaging in political speech or activity (prohibited by the Hatch Act, 1939, 1940).

Thus, despite the commitment to free speech in the Constitution's First Amendment, the legislatures and courts have never hesitated to find numerous exemptions and exceptions. And these exceptions undoubtedly reflect the will of the people, each exception representing a trade-off between the perceived harm (as in perjury, libel and false advertising) of totally unrestrained speech and the advantages and protection of a few carefully legislated exceptions. The basic notions that we are free to communicate any ideas we wish and to propagandize to influence our fellow citizens on various courses of action still remain relatively intact and unendangered. Because of the constantly shifting values of many individuals in our society, controls over pornography and media violence could be seen as a gray middle area where an overwhelming consensus as to how to deal with it does not exist. The real issues here involve deciding "where to draw the line." Some libertarians suggest that if it can be proved that pornography causes social harms, they would object less to censorship of it. However, in the area of media violence, where harm has been proven, they are strangely silent.

All of this means, in sum, that these issues will be resolved—as they should be—through continuing vigorous public debate, then in the legislatures and courts of the land.

Reference

Rotsler, William.
1973.   Contemporary Erotic Cinema. New York: Ballantine Books.

CENSORSHIP VERSUS FREEDOM OF SPEECH

*So many new ideas are at first
strange and horrible though ultimately
valuable that a very heavy responsibility rests upon those who would
prevent their dissemination.*
            J. B. S. Haldane

Introduction

In his general introduction to this volume, Victor Cline has listed traditional arguments against censorship, noting, however, that in our body of law we have with some unanimity made a few important exceptions to free speech (e.g., when we prohibit it, as in perjury, false advertising, and in similar instances).

In the first chapter of this section, then, Robert Fitch discusses the effects of violence and pornography on the arts. Walter Berns follows with a discussion on the consequences of the failure to distinguish between the justified and the unjustified employment of obscenity in the arts—according to law.

In the final chapter, Irving Kristol makes a powerful case for using limited censorship when society sees that it is in its best interest.

The Impact of Violence and Pornography on the Arts and Morality

Robert E. Fitch

Any discussion of censorship in relation to violence and pornography in the media has to face up to four questions. Do literature and the arts have an effect on morals? What do violence and pornography do to the arts? What is a definition of violence and of pornography? What can be done about it? None of these questions can be formulated or answered with scientific precision. Aristotle told us a long time ago that no questions of morals or of politics can be dealt with scientifically. However, because of their importance, they do require the exercise of good judgment in responsible decision making. The outcome of the inquiry must be a series of functional generalizations which are pragmatically feasible and which appeal to our common sense.

1. Do Literature and the Arts Affect Morals?

By this time we ought to know that, if we want to consider the interaction between the arts and morals, we need waste no more time on commissions set up to conduct sociological surveys of the matter. Within the past decade there have been several such commissions to investigate violence, rioting, and pornography, both in and outside the media. They all have a common feature: the unconvincingness of their conclusions. In part this is

Robert E. Fitch, born in Ningpo China in 1902, has studied at Yale, Union Theological Seminary, Columbia University, and the University of Paris. He received his Ph.D. in 1935 at Columbia. For a number of years he was dean of the Pacific School of Religion at Berkeley. He has authored over a hundred magazine and journal articles as well as nine books on such topics as *The Decline and Fall of Sex, Odyssey of the Self-Centered Self,* and *Of Love and of Suffering.* He is currently in half-hearted retirement at Walnut Creek, California—but continues to lecture, write, and travel a great deal.

because their observations are unable to establish any one-to-one correlations. Again, it is because no survey of the human scene is able to manipulate its materials so as to employ what Mill called the experimental method of difference. Most important of all are the antecedent value judgments of the surveyors. Indeed, if one knows in advance from what ideological sector of society the commissioners come, it is not too difficult to predict just what will be the outcome of their investigations.

Let us begin, instead, with the observation that all artists are evangelists. Every artist has a message or a vision that he must communicate. This vision may have no necessary connection with what we get from the professional moralist or politician. But then again there may be astonishing identities. If the artist has no such compelling vision, if he is merely a mechanic for hire, then there is no good reason why he should talk about the civil liberty of freedom of expression. But even as a mechanic for hire, he is communicating some sort of message or vision; and, depending on the quality and timeliness of his craftsmanship, he is making an impact on the mind and the morals of others.

We tend to think that the vision of the artist has to do chiefly with beauty and with truth, so that Keats speaks for all of the breed in his *Ode on a Grecian Urn* when he declares that beauty is truth and truth beauty. Yet it is Shakespeare's Antonio in *Twelfth Night* who tells us that virtue is beauty. In any case, there are great artists whose motivation is consciously moral. These are satirists like Hogarth, Daumier, and much of the time Goya; or, again, Jonathan Swift, Voltaire, Samuel Butler, and at his best, Aldous Huxley. Some of the great writers of comedy belong here, too. The ethical intent is unmistakable in Aristophanes and in Moliere, though I do not find it in the humorous episodes in Shakespeare. Alfred Harbage has said that Shakespeare was moral without being a moralist, and that some of our modern artists are moralists without being moral. Certainly in much contemporary poetry, painting, theater, and fiction there is an intolerable preachiness, in which sanctimony increases in direct proportion to obscenity.

In our Western culture the first great thinker to insist on the impact of the arts on morals was Plato. In his ideal republic there is to be censorship of every kind of literature. The reason why a poet like Homer is to be excluded is that Homer, whose writings provided the Bible of the Greeks, portrayed the gods as irrational and immoral. Plato did not want such examples set before his young people. There were also to be restrictions on the kind of musical instruments admitted and on the tunes and rhythms that might be rendered. The lax, the effeminate, and the convivial must be shut out; and only those airs that promote martial vigor or calm and dignity of temper may be used. What we have in Plato can be found essentially in Confucius. The principle on which these two agree lay behind the practice of the Puritans and is axiomatic in the organization of all totalitarian societies. We may in every case repudiate such absolute controls; but can we really reject an assumption that comes to us from such diverse cultures and in such diverse times and places?

Charles McCabe, whose column "The Fearless Spectator" appears daily in the *San Francisco Chronicle,* is a man-about-town who would never be listed with snoopers and censors. Yet recently he has complained that, as he walks down Broadway to his favorite hangout for lunch, his attention is assaulted from every direction by the barkers for the topless and bottomless joints that abound in that area. He finds that their behavior is "intrusive and offensive." Indeed, that is precisely the case—not just on Broadway in San Francisco and on Times Square in New York City—but wherever such freedom of expression is allowed. By a kind of Gresham's Law in art and in ethics, whereby the bad drives out the good, violence and pornography gradually intrude upon the novel, the theater, the movies, the television, the streets of the city, even the erstwhile quiet retreats of the college campus, until, in their brazen offensiveness, if they do not find a victim in the individual, they will make a victim of society, and so corrupt and pollute the quality of the life we all lead.

2. *What Effect Have Violence and Pornography on the Arts?*

Apart from the problem in morals, there is an important one in aesthetics. The historical record makes it abundantly clear that when violence and pornography take over in the novel, in the theater, and in painting, there is a consequent degradation of those arts.

Certainly it is a mistaken assumption that good entertainment is impossible without resort to violence and obscenity. Fortunately I had already learned this lesson at the time I had to assume the responsibility for the "Happy Hour" performances on board an attack transport in World War II. One of my teachers was William Shakespeare. There is only one of the four-letter words in all his plays, and it appears a total of four times. This is the four-letter word for urinating. And in spite of the frankness in jesting about sexual relations, which is in accord with the proprieties of the Elizabethan era, no irregularities *in conduct* are tolerated here. My other teacher was that durable comedian Ed Wynn, with whom I had some association while he was connected with the Ziegfeld Follies. To be sure "the most beautiful girls in the world" were on parade in those Follies; but the script and the dialogue were under the control of the famous humorist, and, as he once pointed out to me, there was never anything like a "dirty joke" or anything that could not be seen and heard by the whole family together.

For a contemporary example of what violence and pornography can do to a work of art one might take the Hefner-Polanski production of *Macbeth.* Here the witches appear in the nude, and Lady Macbeth does her sleep-walking in the nude. To be sure the impact of this is neither erotic nor pornographic. The witches are simply made repulsive as they lose their aura of

17

supernatural significance. Lady Macbeth without a nightie is made physically absurd while she loses her meaning of terror and mental confusion. Also, three deaths, which occur offstage in the original, are portrayed in vivid, gory, and horrifying detail before our eyes: the execution of the first Thane of Cawdor, the murder of King Duncan, the slaying in combat of Macbeth. So we get to enjoy our violence: but miss Shakespeare's point that the deep repentance of the first traitor Cawdor is in contrast to the nonrepentance of the traitor who inherits his title; miss Shakespeare's emphasis, not on the death of Duncan, but on what is happening to the mind and spirit of Macbeth at that moment; then miss what should be the sharper impact of the deaths on stage of Banquo and later of Lady Macduff and her children, as Shakespeare is ready to make plain that Macbeth is now no better than a "butcher"; and finally miss the point of the religious and ethical values in the triumph of Malcolm at the time of the death of Macbeth. This is our modern method of degrading the vision of the artist.

One can see the beginnings of the same sort of thing in the theater that comes to the fore at the end of Shakespeare's career. *Two Noble Kinsmen* is partly his writing and partly the work of Fletcher. In the third scene of the third act there is an episode where Palamon and Arcite drink a toast "to the wenches we have known in our days! The Lord Steward's daughter . . . The Marshall's sister. . . ." and then brag with obscene jests about their conquests. Any amateur disciple of the Bard of Avon who is at all acquainted with the preceding thirty-six plays knows that this sort of thing simply cannot belong to the canon. This is not the healthy and robust handling of sex that belongs to Shakespeare, who is never really divorced from the chivalrous attitude toward women. This is the point at which sex turns into a smirk and a snigger, with an innuendo of naughtiness and obscenity, to tickle the jaded palates of a super-sophisticated audience of the courtly élite. It is the kind of sex which takes over in the period just before the Puritans, and again in the Restoration period, in a theater which, curiously enough, at the same time becomes increasingly decorous and restrained in the matter of death and violence.

The first impact of violence and pornography in fiction and in the theater, and perforce in the movies and on the television screen, is the triumph of sensationalism. All other meanings give way to the meanings of the shock of novelty and of the novelty of shock. There are those who would speak in defense of the senses and say that these organs are also entitled to their expression and fulfillment in the arts. However, it just does not work out that way. Sensationalism, when it is given free rein, always leads to satiety, tedium, torpor, and impotence. What sets out to be a catering to the senses ends up by being an occlusion of their powers. This is because we are people, not pigs, and have to take our sex and violence as human beings who are endowed with a free will and are capable of reason and of love.

Indeed, the incursion of violence and of pornography into the arts today is as much a symptom as a cause of the whole movement toward the current celebration of the meaninglessness of life. *King Lear* has been objected to, chiefly by French critics, because of all its madness and violence. But in a rendering of Lear by Paul Scofield, under the direction of Peter Brook, on the stage of Stratford-upon-Avon, England, even that madness and that violence fell upon a cold eye and an inert ear; because, as critics as diverse as Kenneth Tynan and Robert Speaight and Walter Kerr pointed out, this play was suddenly a philosophic farce, a drama of despair rather than a drama of redemption, the tale of an infinite emptiness in which there can be neither great passions nor tragic consequences according to this new creed; all that the artist can talk about, as Samuel Beckett once affirmed, is "The Mess"— the bottomless Slough of Despond in which we are all bemired.

During that brief period when we are still "getting a kick" out of our violence and our pornography, it may appear that everything is very much alive. Actually the arts involved are on the way to destroying themselves. It is a false tradition which says that the theater after Shakespeare was killed off by the Puritans. The theater then, like the American theater and movies today, was deeply engaged in the business of committing suicide. All that the Puritans did was to go backstage, drag out a stinking corpse, and give it decent burial.

3. *What is a Definition of Violence and of Pornography?*

So far this inquiry has proceeded without any sharp definitions. Perhaps the time has come to be more clear and more precise about what we are discussing. Let us begin with the axiom that there is nothing in our human nature or human behavior which is a subject matter automatically alien to any of the arts. This does not mean that any art can treat of any part of our humanity. There are technical limitations to any craft, although these limits are to be determined experimentally and not by antecedent authority. I used to believe that there were some things that could be adequately rendered only by the theater or by the opera and not by the ballet—for instance, the death of Socrates, or the crucifixion of Christ—but after seeing on stage the resourceful creativity of the Joffrey Ballet, I am not so sure any longer of such limits. Nevertheless, there are differences in what can be done with opera, ballet, theater, movies, music, painting, sculpture, architecture, and television.

As for the rendering of violence in the arts, it is not quite the same affair as violence in daily life. Ordinarily violence means injury to persons or to property. In a more subtle and significant sense it is any act which prevents a person—whether a human being or an institution—from fulfilling its natural functions. But neither of these forms of violence is relevant to the arts. There is a third kind of violence, which is the use of force in excess of or apart from the ends to be achieved. In the ordinary sense war is always a form of violence. But pillage and rapine are disapproved of by military authorities because they destroy military discipline and because they are in excess of and apart from the military ends to be achieved—indeed, may even be hurtful to those same military ends.

It is in a similar manner that we have to think about violence and pornography in the arts. It is not the act, the episode, the portrait which in itself has an invidious character. Rather it is the relationship of this particular item to the larger intent of the artist. Here we have to recognize the difference in impact between the arts in their psychological distance or psychological proximity. What we read in a book, no matter how inflammatory its intent, can be held at a relative distance. The minute the word is spoken, rather than read, it comes closer to us. The radio and the lecture platform are more intrusive, if not more intimate, than the book. But the minute we combine the visual with the auditory, as on the stage, or in the movies, or in television, the impact is more direct and inescapable. And when one of these comes into our own hearth and home, then it is getting as close to us as anything in the arts can get.

Now one may be as leary as was John Dewey about imposing fixed ends on any human enterprise; but unless there is some regard for ends, we have neither an art nor an enterprise but only a bustle and a blur and a blob. The theater, the movies, and television are arts that deal directly with our humanity. But what is a human being? The classical Greeks made intelligence central; Jews and Christians focus on love and justice: both traditions emphasize freedom and responsibility. Man, at the very least, is a creature capable of reason, of love and justice, and of free and responsible choice and decision.

One can see now the superior values of Restoration drama in England in the period after Cromwell: it knew little of love and of justice, but it did keep intelligence alive. It is the achievement of much contemporary drama that it deletes the intelligence as well. And if man is portrayed as a creature still capable of choice, then the choices he makes are merely in the satisfaction of cruder appetites for money, or power, or lust. In this pattern the means of life become the ends of life, and the sexual, the scatological, and the sado-masochistic become the whole meaning of our humanity. That these things are a part of us, who will presume to deny? That they are the whole of us, who will wish to affirm?

Another way to get at the problem is to raise the question of Truth. One critic has said of Tennessee Williams that he is "addicted to the embroidering lie," and that too many of his plays give the "effect of painful falsity." The critic in this instance is Mary McCarthy, who is about as sophisticated an observer as one might wish, and who in her own novels and short stories is scarcely hampered by conventional standards of morality. But what is this "lie," what is this "falsity" which she finds in Tennessee Williams? Incidentally she makes no such complaint about Eugene O'Neill—although she is oppressed by the prosiness of his prose, in contrast to the occasional bursts of lyrical utterance in the other author. The "lie" in Tennessee Williams, which grows large after his first few plays, is the conviction that what he is giving us is the full measure of our humanity, along with a growing desire on his part to celebrate and to glorify this subhumanity. Eugene O'Neill, a deeply troubled but *in truth* a great dramatist, can portray evil realistically, but he does not bow down to it or worship it.

Another way to get at the problem is to inquire after the larger frame of reference of a work of art. In Swift's *Gulliver's Travels* there is talk of urination and of excretion; in Ophelia's mad ravings there is an explicit sexuality; both in Rabelais and in Martin Luther there is often a peasant coarseness of expression; in Goya's painting, "The Shooting of May Third," there is an intense concentration on the brutality and inhumanity of war; in Voltaire's *Candide* there is an interminable succession of rape, assault, hangings, killings, burnings, and mutilations; in the Bible, as much as in Shakespeare, there are innumerable scenes which, if taken by themselves and isolated from the larger context, might be viewed as salacious, sadistic, incestuous, crudely pornographic, or intolerably bestial and cruel. But it takes a deliberately prurient mind to find offense in these passages, because they are never ends in themselves, and they all point to meanings in the larger frame of our humanity.

To refuse to discuss these questions of what is it to be human? what is truth in art? what is the larger frame of reference of meanings? is not to escape the basic issue at all. What we do then is simply to surrender to current clichés. Thus any amount of shabby and meretricious writing and playwriting will be justified because it is "brave" and "honest," or because, ah, yes indeed, it is so courageously "truthful!" If it gives us an inundation of ordure, we are told that this is a necessary part of the great "literature of protest." If it is wanton in violence and in the breach of all moral decencies, it takes on a halo of holiness because it is so righteously "antibourgeois" or it is a blow against the "Establishment." If it is sufficiently blatant in being "anticonformist," then it is automatically noble and gracious, just as surely as we know that what conforms to custom and convention must be evil and ugly. And so, because we disdain to wrestle with ultimate questions of the Good, the True, and the Beautiful, we succumb to superficial and transient orthodoxies, and make ourselves the prisoners of a sterile secular creedalism which has no regard for either art or ethics.

4. *What Can We Do About It?*

Obviously our first obligation in such a situation is to keep alive a discussion of ultimate values that may be flexible and inclusive at the same time that it is forthright, incisive, and unequivocating. But if we are to move beyond discussion into the arena of action in the public domain, then we must resort to the law.

Here at the very beginning we should be aware that there are limits to what can be accomplished by laws. A good example is the whole enterprise of attempting to outlaw Communism in a free society. I am not talking about Communism as a body of doctrine: this must always be open to free inquiry and discussion. I am talking about Communism as an organized, disciplined movement for the deliberate subversion of all constituted orders and liberties. The dilemma immediately becomes apparent: where you can outlaw Communism, you need not; where you need to outlaw Communism, you can't. In the great English-speaking republics—Great Britain, the United States, Canada, Australia, New Zealand—and in some other democracies, it might be possible to pass and to enforce such a law; but it would be a superfluity. In some of the Latin republics, notably France and Italy, but also including some countries in South America, it might be thought desirable to have such a law, but it would be difficult to enact such legislation and impossible to enforce it. A law is not some magical device for social reform which is automatically the bearer of its own warrant and its own efficacy. A law is rooted in the *Volksgeist,* in the spirit and temper of the people.

In a free society a law is an instrument of reason and of right, resting on the consent of the majority and exercising force against a minority that is negligent, or recalcitrant, or subversive. To call it an instrument of reason is to acknowledge our Hellenic and Roman heritage: Aristotle said that law is intelligence without passion. To call it an instrument of right is to acknowledge our Hebrew-Christian heritage: the laws of God, the laws of nature, the laws of human nature, are interrelated. To say that it rests upon consent is to accept the tradition of English Common Law: custom is the expression of implicit consent; decisions by courts which establish precedents, and enactments by legislature are expressions of explicit consent. The latent force behind any law is that consent; but force may become overt when consent is challenged by a minority. The minority, of course, is a floating minority. All of us at some time or other belong to a negligent minority. Some of us occasionally are part of a deliberately recalcitrant minority. A very few become members of a consciously subversive minority.

Part of our problem in the United States today is that the meanings of reason, of right, of consent, and of force are obscured, distorted, debased, and even turned upside down. With regard to reason, there are those who, if one would speak up against smut or obscenity, will tell us that the *real* obscenities in American life are poverty, racial injustice, the violation of the environment, and war: and so they speak the truth, not to promote action, but to cut the nerve of all discriminating and effective actions. With regard to right, there are free spirits who would change the marriage vow from "so long as ye both shall live" to "so long as ye both shall love," and then undertake, with Bertrand Russell, to demonstrate the transitoriness of true love. With regard to force, there are alleged liberals so inebriated with the anarchies of our times that they will undertake to justify violence, of any sort in any situation, to bring about proposed changes. With regard to consent, there are those who, under the pretense of insisting on the consent of the governed, make a big to-do about "participatory democracy," and then, having rigged their public meetings with ratios and quotas, surrender all governance into the hands of a vigorous and highly vocal few; such that when recently, by these devices, a candidate for president of the United States was nominated by one of our major political parties, that same candidate was repudiated at the polls by the rank and file of his own party because that rank and file had not really been allowed to participate in his selection and because what masqueraded as a democratic process was in reality a usurpation by a tyrannical minority.

The heart of the political process is to be found in the folkways and in the religious traditions of a people. If these are not sound, then nothing else can be sound. The focal institutions are the home, the church, and the school. In our time the schools mean much more than the public schools through the eighth grade or the twelfth grade. They include the community colleges, the four-year colleges, and the universities which are attended by increasing numbers of young people and of adults. If the pervasive mood and temper in the home, the church, and the school is relativist, permissive, impressionist, existentialist, such that there is no regard for norms and standards in literature and the arts any more than in morals and manners, then chaos is king. But if, as I believe, there still exists in the bosoms of the great majority of the American people a conviction that there are objective though multiple distinctions between the "clean" and the "unclean"—the right and the wrong, the true and the false, the beautiful and the ugly—then there is a foundation for effective action in the public domain.

At the same time our courts may need to be reminded that no sort of liberty is an absolute right. There are limits to liberty that reside in the moral order itself. As both St. Paul and Plato understood, liberty carried to the point of license results in anarchy for the individual and for society: in the first case, it results in becoming a slave to passion; in the second case it eventuates in tyranny. Liberty is limited by other competing values—such as equality; it is limited by the price we are willing to pay for it; it is limited, as both Shakespeare and Edmund Burke knew, by the need for a framework of law and order within which true liberties can flourish. Increasing limits to liberty are set by the growth of codes of professional ethics—among clergy, lawyers, doctors, teachers, bankers—which choose to be more restrictive of freedom than the courts may be. To freedom of expression there have been limits of libel and slander, of participating in treason, of the overt act (one has the right to dissent, not the right to disrupt), of the "clear and present danger," of the right of the press to try a case in its columns before it has been tried in the courts. There have also been limits to free speech and to free behavior with a view to protecting public decency.

Communities should have the right to determine what makes up public decency without interference from the courts except where the most basic constitutional rights and liberties are obviously threatened. Of course what the community can do will depend upon the most intimate and the most recurrent practices and beliefs of the community itself. It may be impossible to outlaw prostitution in some Latin countries; it is possible to outlaw it in most American communities; it is superfluous to outlaw it among primitive tribesmen in Africa since they do not know the meaning of the thing. A pornographic flick like "Deep Throat" may be shut down in New York City while it runs in three theaters simultaneously in San Francisco. One state of the Union may be extremely permissive about prostitution, but much stricter about pornography in the media partly because the second enterprise distracts too much business from the first. In effect, each community will get pretty much what it really wants if no artificial controls from the courts are imposed upon it. This protects the principle of consent, even though the principles of reason and of right may suffer for the moment.

In a democratic society there is no way to coerce the consent of the majority. And it is part of the education, part of the growing pains, of a free society, that people must learn to enlighten and to rectify their consent until it comes more closely in accord with standards of reason and of right. If they cannot learn that lesson, then it matters little whether they succumb to an evil within or are overwhelmed by an evil from without.

In any case we have some basic assumptions, some clear principles, to guide conduct. Literature and the arts most certainly have an important impact on morals. Violence and pornography assuredly are deleterious to the arts themselves. The leading questions we must always keep in mind, and which must be a part of continuing inquiry and debate, are: what is distinctively human about human beings? what is truth or falsehood in the arts? what is the larger frame of reference, or what is the kingdom of ends, to which a work of art belongs? What sort of censorship in a given community is functional and feasible? When is legislation helpful, or impotent, or harmful; and to what extent can laws be designed, not just to curb the ugly and the evil, but to be liberators of excellence?

Democracy, Censorship, and the Arts

Walter Berns

I

The case against censorship is very old and very familiar. Almost anyone can formulate it without difficulty. One has merely to set the venerable Milton's *Areopagitica* in modern prose, using modern spelling, punctuation and examples. This is essentially what the civil libertarians did in their successful struggle with the censors. The unenlightened holder of the bishop's imprimatur, Milton's "unleasur'd licencer" who has never known "the labour of bookwriting," became the ignorant policeman or the bigoted school board member who is offended by *Mrs. Warren's Profession,* or the benighted librarian who refuses to shelf *The Scarlet Letter,* or the insensitive customs official who seizes *Ulysses* in the name of an outrageous law, or the Comstockian vigilante who glues together the pages of every copy of *A Farewell to Arms* she can find in the bookstore. The industrious learned Milton, insulted by being asked to "appear in Print like a punie with his guardian and his censors hand on the back of his title to be his bayle and surety," was replaced by Shaw, Hawthorne, Joyce or Hemingway, and those who followed in their wake, all victims of the mean-spirited and narrow-

Walter Berns is professor of political science at the University of Toronto. Formerly he taught at Louisiana State University and at Yale, Cornell, and Colgate. He has been both a Rockefeller and a Fulbright Fellow. In the mid-1960s he was chairman of Cornell's Department of Government.

Earlier, he studied at the University of Iowa and at Reed College and the London School of Economics and Political Science. He obtained his M.A. and Ph.D. degrees at the University of Chicago in 1951 and 1953 respectively.

He has authored three books and eighteen articles in various journals. These have tended to focus on First Amendment issues, due process of law, world government, law and behavioral science, and reform of the American party system.

minded officials who were appointed, or in some cases took it upon themselves, to judge what others should read, or at least not read. The victory of truth when it grapples with falsehood became the victory of "enduring ideas" in the free competition of the market. With these updated versions of old and familiar arguments the civil libertarians have prevailed.

They prevailed partly because of the absurdity of some of their opposition, and also because of a difficulty inherent in the task their opponents set for themselves. The censors would proscribe that obscene, and even assuming, as our law did, that obscene speech is no part of the speech protected by the First Amendment to the Constitution and may therefore be proscribed without violation of the Constitution, it is not easy to formulate a rule of law that distinguishes the nonobscene from the obscene. Is it the presence of four-letter words? But many a literary masterpiece contains four letter words. Detailed descriptions of sexual acts? James Joyce provides these. Words tending to corrupt those into whose hands they are likely to fall? But who is to say what corrupts, or, for that matter, whether anything corrupts or, again, what is meant by corruption? Is it an appeal to the "prurient interest" or a work that is "patently offensive"? If that is what is meant by the obscene, many a "socially important work," many a book, play, or film with "redeeming social value" would be lost to us. The college professors said so, and if college professors do not know the socially important, who does? Be that as it may, they succeeded in convincing the Supreme Court, and the result was the complete rout of the "forces of reaction." To the college professors, therefore, as well as to the "courageous" publishers and the "public-spirited" attorneys who had selflessly fought the cases through the courts, a debt of gratitude is owed by the lovers of Shaw, Hawthorne, Joyce and Hemingway—and others too numerous to detail here. In the same spirit one might say that never has there been such a flourishing of the arts in this country.

Astonishingly, the editors of the *New York Times* disagree, and in an editorial printed on April 1, 1969, under the heading "Beyond the (Garbage) Pale," they expressed their disagreement in language that we have been accustomed to read only in the journals of the "reactionary right."

The explicit portrayal on the stage of sexual intercourse is the final step in the erosion of taste and subtlety in the theater. It reduces actors to mere exhibitionists, turns audiences into voyeurs and debases sexual relationships almost to the level of prostitution.

It is difficult to see any great principle of civil liberties involved when persons indulging themselves on-stage in this kind of peep-show activity are arrested for "public lewdness and obscenity"— as were the actors and staff of a recently opened New York production that, in displaying sodomy and other sexual aberration, reached the reductio ad obscenum *of the theatrical art. While there may be no difference in principle between pornography on the stage, on the screen and on the printed page, there is a difference in immediacy and in direct visual impact when it is carried out by live actors before a (presumably) live audience.*

The fact that the legally enforceable standards of public decency have been interpreted away by the courts almost to the point of no return does not absolve artists, producers or publishers from all responsibility or restraining in pandering to the lowest possible public taste in quest of the largest possible monetary reward. Nor does the fact that a play, film, article or book attacks the so-called 'establishment,' revels in gutter language or drools over every known or unknown form of erotica justify the suspension of sophisticated critical judgment.

Yet this does not seem to be just what has been suspended in the case of many recent works, viz. one current bestseller hailed as a "masterpiece," which, wallowing in a self-indulgent public psychoanalysis, drowns its literary merits in revolting excesses of masturbation and copulation.

The utter degradation of taste in pursuit of the dollar is perhaps best observed in films, both domestic and foreign such as one of the more notorious Swedish imports, refreshingly described by one reviewer unafraid of being called a "square" as "pseudopornography at its ugliest and least titillating and pseudosociology at its lowest point of technical ineptitude."

Far from providing a measure of cultural emancipation, such descents into degeneracy represent caricatures of art, deserving no exemption from the laws of common decency merely because they masquerade as drama or literature. It is preposterous to banish topless waitresses when there is no bottom to voyeurism on the stage or in the movie houses.

In the end, however, there may be an even more effective answer. The insensate pursuit of the urge to shock, carried from one excess to a more abysmal one, is bound to achieve its own antidote in total boredom. When there is no lower depth to descend to, ennui will erase the problem.[1]

This must be reckoned an astonishing statement because in the liberal world for which the *Times* speaks it has not been customary—on the contrary, it has been quite unfashionable—to cast any doubt on the wisdom of the anticensorship policy so long pursued by the leaders of this world. Now suddenly the *Times,* contrary to what its readers expect of it and even to the general tenor of its own drama and literary pages, registers its misgivings. This is not what they wanted to happen. In their struggle against the censor they did not mean to defend "the explicit portrayal of sexual intercourse" on the stage or in films; they did not have in mind "sodomy and other sexual aberrations." They intended to protect the freedom of the arts from bigoted censors; they were defending *Ulysses* when the customs laws would have excluded it from the country, and sensitive foreign films, such as *Les Amants*, from Ohio's laws; but they certainly did not intend to establish a place for "revolting excesses of masturbation and copulation."

Nine months later one of the country's principal foes of censorship checked in with the same disclaimer. *Ulysses*, yes, said Morris Ernst, but "sodomy on the stage or masturbation in the public arena," no! Although it never appeared to figure with any prominence, or figure at all for that matter, in the arguments that had made him one of the foremost civil liberties lawyers in the country, Ernst now insists that he had always made it clear that he "would hate to live in a world with utter freedom." He deeply resents "the idea that the lowest common denominator, the most tawdry magazine, pandering for profit . . . should be able to compete in the marketplace with no restraints." The free marketplace has become the dirty marketplace, and Ernst wants no part in it and no responsibility for it.[2]

But surely this was inevitable? Pornography and the taste for it are not new phenomena. What is new is the fact that it can display itself openly in the marketplace, so to speak, whereas in the past it had been confined by the laws to the back alleys, or to the underworld, where its sales were limited not by a weakness of the potential demand but rather by the comparative inaccessibility of the market. Prodded by the civil libertarians, the Supreme Court made pornography a growth industry by giving it a license to operate in the accessible and legitimate market, thereby bringing buyer and seller together. True, the Court did not directly license *Oh! Calcutta!* or *Che!* but so long as the Court is consistent these works are certain to benefit from the licenses given *Les Amants* and *Fanny Hill* and the others. Consider the state of the law developed on their behalf. So long as a work is not "*utterly* without redeeming social value" (and the emphasis is the Supreme Court's),* it cannot be proscribed even if it is "patently offensive" and is found by a jury to appeal to a "prurient interest." All that is needed to save any work from the censor, or the police, is some college professor willing to testify as to its "social value" or "social importance," and there is no shortage of such

2. The *New York Times*, 5 January 1970, p. 32. Whatever Ernst now says he used to say, or meant all along, what we remember from his is on the printed page, and there he said that "censorship of the theater is truly an anomaly"; and there he scoffed at the idea that a book, any book, could be "corrupting (whatever that may mean)"; and there he insisted that censorship could be justified only if it could be demonstrated that a "causal relationship" existed "between word or picture and human behavior," and that such a relationship had never been demonstrated "in the field of obscenity."! In fact, he added, "the indications seem to be to the contrary." Morris L. Ernst and Alan U. Schwartz, *Censorship: The Search for the Obscene* (New York: The Macmillan Company, 1964), pp. 142, 200, 250-51.

*Berns's article was written before the June 1973 Supreme Court ruling (Miller v. California) that did away with the "redeeming social value" test of pornography.

professors with such testimony. Indeed, the work has not been written, staged or filmed that cannot find its champions among the professors.[3]

It was not supposed to turn out this way. Some invisible and benign hand was supposed to operate in this market too, and guarantee the triumph of the true and the beautiful. "People," said Justice William O. Douglas in one of the obscenity cases only a couple of years ago, "are mature enough to pick and choose, to recognize trash when they see it, to be attracted to the literature that satisfies their deepest need, and . . . to move from plateau to plateau and finally reach the world of enduring ideas." This is the liberal faith and the *Times* shared it, and it is worth noting that even in its distress it refuses to forsake it altogether. The editors express their disgust with what has happened, but they must know that this will be unavailing with those who are themselves disgusting. Certainly the "artists, producers [and] publishers . . . pandering to the lowest public taste in quest of the largest possible monetary reward" are not going to forego this reward simply because some fainthearted libertarians, even on the *Times*, look upon their work as disgusting. "I paid to see filth and I want filth," said the woman from Connecticut by way of protesting a showing of an expurgated *I Am Curious (Yellow)*. She paid to see filth and, no matter what the *Times* says, there will always be "artists, producers [and] publishers" to see to it that she gets her money's worth. That is why there used to be laws against filth, because the legislators who wrote these laws knew full well the fruitlessness of relying on admonition or expressions of disgust. The *Times* does not call for the refurbishment of these laws, but appeals instead to the "laws of common decency," as if these so-called laws had not passed into desuetude with the demise of the statute laws that constituted their foundations. So it is that, in the end, they return to the old liberal faith in an invisible hand that will provide our salvation: "When there is no lower depth to descend to, ennui will erase the problem."

---

3. "LONG BEACH, Calif. Jan 13 [1970] (AP)—Four nude models—two male, two female—postured before the coeducational sociology class of 250 persons.

"On movie screens, lesbian and heterosexual couples went through acts of lovemaking.

"Sound systems blared recordings by the Beatles and from the rock musical 'Hair.' "

"Two hours after the class ended yesterday, California State College suspended its teachers, Marion Steele, 31 years old, and Dr. Donald Robertson, 29, for thirty days without pay. Further action was threatened.

"Mr. Steele and Dr. Robertson said they had staged the show to ridicule what they called America's prudishness about sex as contrasted with its toleration of what they considered such 'glaring obscenities' as the Vietnam war, violence on television and pollution of air and water.

" 'This produces hangups and keeps millions from enjoying genuine sexual pleasure and makes our entire world obscene,' Dr. Robertson told the class." The *New York Times,* 14 January 1970, p. 11.

Such a conclusion is pitifully inadequate, but it is an accurate reflection of the thinking that has been done on this issue during our time. Neither the *Times* nor Morris Ernst has a grasp of the principle with which—or even a suitable vocabulary in which—to challenge the powerful orthodoxy that has long governed the public discussion of censorship and the arts. To be a liberal is to be against censorship or it is to be nothing—or so it has been thought—and after a career spent arguing against it, it is not easy to formulate an argument in its favor. They deserve our gratitude nevertheless, for, although they leave it undefined, their disclaimers do have the merit of acknowledging that there is something wrong with things as they are, and there *is* a problem. The respectability attached to their names makes it easier to reexamine this problem.

II

Just as it is no simple task to formulate a rule of law that distinguishes the nonobscene from the obscene, it is still more difficult to distinguish the obscene from the work of genuine literary merit. In fact, it is impossible, and our failure to understand this may be said to be a condition, if not a cause, of our present situation. Our laws proscribe obscenity as such and by name, and we are unwilling to admit that great literary and dramatic works can be, and frequently are, obscene. In combination these two facts explain how it came about that we now have, with the sanction of the law, what is probably the most vulgar theatre and literature in history. The paradox is readily explained. The various statutes making up the law have made obscenity a criminal thing, and our judges assume that if a work of art is really a work of art, and not vulgar rubbish, it cannot be obscene. Thus, Judge Woolsey, in his celebrated opinion in the *Ulysses* case, recounts how he had asked two literary friends whether the book was obscene within the legal definition, which he had explained to them, and how they had both agreed with him that it was not. But of course *Ulysses* is obscene. Not so obscene as an undoubted masterpiece, Aristophanes' *Assembly of Women,* for example, which would not be a masterpiece—which would not be anything—were its obscenity removed, but obscene nevertheless. The trouble stems from the fact that the Tariff Act of 1930 would exclude "obscene" books from the country, and Judge Woolsey, being a sensible man, did not want this to happen to *Ulysses.* So he fashioned a rule to protect it. But the same rule of law protects *The Tropic of Cancer,* because according to the rule's necessarily clumsy categories, the latter is no more obscene than the former, however it compares on another scale and whatever the distances separating its author, Henry Miller, and James Joyce as poets. Eventually, and for the same reason, the protection of the law was extended to *Trim, MANual,* and *Grecian Guild Pictorial,* the homosexual magazines involved in a case before the Supreme Court in 1962, and then to *Fanny Hill.* At this point, if one ignores the *Ginzburg* aberration and the recent children's cases,[4] the censors seem to have given up, and we have—well, anything that anyone will pay to see or read. Thus, having begun by exempting the work of art from the censorship laws, we have effectively arrived at the civil libertarian's destination; the case where the Supreme Court throws in its hand and concludes that there is no such thing as obscenity. If *Oh! Calcutta!* is not obscene, what is?

Underlying this unfortunate development is the familiar liberal idea of progress. Rather than attempt to inhibit artists and scientists, the good polity will grant them complete freedom of expression and of inquiry, and will benefit collectively by so doing. What is good for the arts and sciences is good for the polity: this proposition has gone largely unquestioned among us for 200 years now. The case for censorship rests on its denial, and can be made only by separately examining its parts. What is good for the arts and sciences and what is good for the polity? The case for censorship arises initially out of a consideration of the second question.

The case for censorship is at least as old as the case against it, and, contrary to what is usually thought today, has been made under decent and democratic auspices and by intelligent men. To the extent to which it is known today, however, it is thought to be pernicious, or, at best, irrelevant to the enlightened conditions of the twentieth century. It begins from the premise that the laws cannot remain indifferent to the manner in which men amuse themselves, or to the kinds of amusement offered them. "The object of art," as Lessing put the case, "is pleasure, and pleasure is not indispensable. What kind and what degree of pleasure shall be permitted may justly depend on the law-giver."[5] Such a view, especially in this uncompromising form, appears excessively Spartan and illiberal to us; yet Lessing was one of the greatest lovers of art who ever lived and wrote.

We turn to the arts—to literature, films, and the theatre, as well as to the graphic arts which were the special concern of Lessing—for the pleasure to be derived from them, and pleasure has the capacity to form our tastes and

---

4. In *Ginzburg* v. *United States,* 383 U.S. 463 (1966), the Supreme Court upheld the conviction because Ginzburg had employed "pandering" in the advertising of his obscene wares, a rule never applied in the past and inapplicable in the future. The next year it resumed its habit of reversing obscenity convictions, although the publications involved were at least as offensive as anything Ginzburg published. *Redrup* v. *New York,* 386 U.S. 767 (1967). States have been permitted to prohibit the sale of obscenity to minors, *Ginzberg* v. *New York,* 390 U.S. 629 (1968), but, on the other hand, not to classify films with a view to protecting minors—not, at least, with a "vague" ordinance. *Interstate Circuit, Inc. v. Dallas,* 390 U.S. 676 (1968). Mr. Justice Douglas would not prohibit the sale of obscenity even to children; he says, and he ought to know, that most juvenile delinquents are over fifty.

5. *Laocoon* (New York: Noonday Press), ch. 1, p. 10.

thereby to affect our lives, and the kind of people we become, and the lives of those with whom and among whom we live. Is it politically uninteresting whether men and women derive pleasure from performing their duties as citizens, parents, and spouses or, on the other hand, from watching their laws and customs and institutions ridiculed on the stage? Whether the passions are excited by, and the affections drawn to, what is noble or what is base? Whether the relations between men and women are depicted in terms of an eroticism wholly divorced from love and calculated to destroy the capacity for love and the institutions, such as the family, that depend on love? Whether a dramatist uses pleasure to attach man to what is beautiful or what is ugly? We may not be accustomed to thinking of these things in this manner, but it is not strange that so much of the obscenity from which so many of us derive our pleasure today has an avowed political purpose.[6] It would seem that these pornographers know intuitively what liberals—for example, Morris Ernst—have forgotten, namely, that there is indeed a "causal relationship . . . between word or pictures and human behavior." At least they are not waiting for behavioral science to discover this fact.

The purpose is sometimes directly political and sometimes political in the sense that it will have political consequences intended or not. This latter purpose is to make us shameless, and it seems to be succeeding with astonishing speed. Activities that were once confined to the private scene—to the "ob-scene," to make an etymological assumption—are now presented for our delectation and emulation in center stage. Nothing that is appropriate to one place is inappropriate to any other place. No act, we are to infer, no human possibility, no possible physical combination or connection, is shameful. Even our lawmakers now so declare. "However plebian my tastes may be," Justice Douglas asked somewhat disingenuously in the *Ginzburg* case, "who am I to say that others' tastes must be so limited and that others' tastes have no 'social importance'?" Nothing prevents a dog from enjoying sexual intercourse in the marketplace, and it is unnatural to deprive man of the same pleasure, either actively or as voyeurs in the theatre. Shame itself is unnatural, a convention devised by hypocrites to inhibit the pleasures of the body. We must get rid of our "hangups."

But what if, contrary to Freud and to what is generally assumed, shame is natural to man in the sense of being an original feature of human existence, and shamelessness unnatural in the sense of having to be acquired? What if the beauty that we are capable of knowing and achieving in our lives with each other derives from the fact that man is naturally a "blushing creature," the only creature capable of blushing. Consider the case of voyeurism, a case that, under the circumstances, comes quickly to mind. Some of us—I have even known students to confess to it—experience discomfort watching others

6. *Che!* and *Hair,* for example, are political plays. See also note 3, this chapter.

on the stage or screen performing sexual acts or even the acts preparatory to sexual acts, such as the disrobing of a woman by a man. This discomfort is caused by shame or is akin to shame. True, it could derive from the fear of being discovered enjoying what society still sees as a forbidden game. The voyeur who experiences shame in this sense is judging himself by the conventions of his society and, according to the usual modern account, the greater the distance separating him from his society in space or time, the less he will experience this kind of shame. This shame, which may be denoted as concealing shame, is a function of the fear of discovery by one's own group. The group may have its reasons for forbidding a particular act, and thereby leading those who engage in it to conceal it—to be ashamed of it—but these reasons have nothing to do with the nature of man. Voyeurism, according to this account, is a perversion only because society says it is, and a man guided only by nature would not be ashamed of it.

According to another view, however, not to be ashamed—to be a shameless voyeur—is more likely to require explanation, for voyeurism is by nature a perversion.

Anyone who draws his sexual gratification from looking at another lives continuously at a distance. If it is normal to approach and unite with the partner, then it is precisely characteristic of the voyeur that he remains alone, without a partner, an outsider who acts in a stealthy and furtive manner. To keep his distance when it is essential to draw near is one of the paradoxes of his perversion. The looking of the voyeur is of course also a looking at and, as such, is as different from the looks exchanged by lovers as medical palpitation from the gentle caress of the hand.[7]

From this point of view, voyeurism is perversion not merely because it is contrary to convention but because it is contrary to nature. Convention here follows nature. Whereas sexual attraction brings man and woman together seeking a unity that culminates in the living being they together create, the voyeur maintains a distance; and because he maintains a distance, he looks at, he does not communicate; and because he looks at, he objectifies, he makes an object of that with which it is natural to join. Objectifying, he is incapable of uniting and therefore of love. The need to conceal voyeurism—

---

7. Erwin W. Straus, *Phenomenological Psychology* (New York: Basic Books, 1966), p. 219. I have no doubt that it is possible to want to observe sexual acts for reasons unrelated to voyeurism. Just as a physician has a clinical interest in the parts of the body, philosophers will have an interest in the parts of the soul, or in the varieties of human things which are manifestations of the body and the soul. Such a "looking" would not be voyeurism and would be unaccompanied by shame; or the desire to see and to understand would require the "seer" to overcome shame. (Plato, *Republic,* 439e). In any event, the case of the philosopher is politically irrelevant, and aesthetically irrelevant as well.

the concealing shame—is a corollary of the protective shame, the shame that impels lovers to search for privacy and for an experience protected from the profane and the eyes of the stranger. The stranger is "at odds with the shared unity of the [erotic couple], and his mere presence tends to introduce some objectification into every immediate relationship."[8] Shame, both concealing and protective, protects lovers and therefore love. And a polity without love—without the tenderness and the charming sentiments and the poetry and the beauty and the uniquely human things that depend on it and derive from it—a polity without love would be an unnatural monstrosity.[9]

To speak in a manner that is more obviously political, such a polity may even be impossible, except in a form unacceptable to free men. There is a connection between self-restraint and shame and therefore a connection between shame and self-government or democracy. There is therefore a danger in promoting shamelessness and the fullest self-expression or indulgence. To live together requires rules and a governing of the passions, and those who are without shame will be unruly and unrulable; having lost the ability to restrain themselves by observing the rules they collectively give themselves, they will have to be ruled by others. Tyranny is the mode of government for the shameless and self-indulgent who have carried liberty beyond any restraint, natural and conventional.

Such was the argument made prior to the twentieth century, when it was generally understood that democracy, more than any other form of government, requires self-restraint, which it would inculcate through moral education and impose on itself through laws, including laws governing the manner of public amusements. It was the tyrant who could usually allow the people to indulge themselves. Indulgence of the sort we are now witnessing did not threaten his rule, because his rule did not depend on a citizenry of good character. Anyone can be ruled by a tyrant, and the more debased his subjects the safer his rule. A case can be made for complete freedom of the arts among such people, whose pleasures are derived from activities divorced from their labors and any duties associated with citizenship. Among them a theatre, for example, can serve to divert the search for pleasure from what

8. Straus, *Phenomenological Psychology*, p. 221.

9. It is easy to prove that shamefulness is not the only principle governing the question of what may properly be presented on the stage; shamefulness would not, for example, govern the case of a scene showing the copulating of a married couple who love each other very much. That is not intrinsically shameful—on the contrary—yet it ought not to be shown. The principle here is, I think, an aesthetic one: such a scene is dramatically weak because the response of the audience would be characterized by a prurience and not by a sympathy with what the scene is intended to portray, a beautiful love. This statement can be tested by joining a collegetown movie audience; it is confirmed unintentionally by a defender of nudity on the stage; see note 12, this chapter.

the tyrant regards as more dangerous or pernicious pursuits.[10]

Such an argument was not unknown among thoughtful men at the time modern democracies were being constituted. It is to be found in Jean-Jacques Rousseau's *Letter to M. d'Alembert on the Theatre*. Its principles were known by Washington and Jefferson, to say nothing of the antifederalists, and later on by Lincoln, all of whom insisted that democracy would not work without citizens of good character; and until recently no justice of the Supreme Court and no man in public life doubted the necessity for the law to make at least a modest effort to promote that good character, if only by protecting the effort of other institutions, such as the church and the family, to promote and maintain it. The case for censorship, at first glance, was made wholly with a view to the political good, and it had as its premise that what was good for the arts and sciences was *not* necessarily good for the polity.

There was no illusion that censorship laws would be easy to administer, and there was a recognition of the danger they represented. One obvious danger was that the lawmakers will demand too much, that the Anthony Comstocks who are always present will become the agents of the law and demand not merely decency but sanctity. Macaulay stated the problem in his essay on Restoration Comedy (mild fare compared to that regularly exhibited in our day):

It must, indeed, be acknowledged, in justice to the writers of whom we have spoken thus severely, that they were to a great extent the creatures of their age. And if it be asked why that age encouraged immorality which no other age would have tolerated, we have no hesitation in answering that this great depravation of the national taste was the effect of the prevalence of Puritanism under the Commonwealth.

To punish public outrages on morals and religion is unquestionably within the competence of rulers. But when a government, not content with requiring decency, requires sanctity, it oversteps the bounds which mark its proper functions. And it may be laid down as a universal rule that a

10. The modern tyrant does not encourage passivity among his subjects; on the contrary, they are expected by him to be public-spirited: to work for the State, to exceed production schedules, to be citizen soldiers in the huge armies, and to love Big Brother. Indeed, in Nazi Germany and the Soviet Union alike, the private life was and is discouraged, and with it erotic love and the private attachments it fosters. Censorship in a modern tyrannical state is designed to abolish the private life to the extent that this is possible. George Orwell understood this perfectly. This severe censorship that characterizes modern tyranny, and distinguishes it sharply from premodern tyranny, derives from the basis of modern tyrannical rule: both of utopian theory. The modern tyrant parades as a political philosopher, the heir of Nietzsche or Marx, with a historical mission to perform. He cannot leave his subjects alone.

*government which attempts more than it ought will perform less. . . . And so
a government which, not content with repressing scandalous excesses,
demands from its subjects fervent and austere piety, will soon discover that,
while attempting to render an impossible service to the cause of virtue, it has
in truth only promoted vice.*

The truth of this was amply demonstrated in the United States in the Prohibition era, when the attempt was made to enforce abstemiousness and not,
labels to the contrary, temperance. In a word, the principle should be not to
attempt to eradicate vice—the means by which that might conceivably be
accomplished are incompatible with free government—but to make it difficult, knowing that while it will continue to flourish covertly, it will not be
openly exhibited. And that was thought to be important.

It ought to be clear that this old and largely forgotten case for censorship
was made by men who were not insensitive to the beauty of the arts and the
noble role they can play in the lives of men. Rousseau admitted that he
never willingly missed a performance of any of Molière's plays, and did so in
the very context of arguing that all theatrical productions should be banned
in the decent and self-government polity. Like Plato he would banish the
poets, yet he was himself a poet—a musician, opera composer, and novelist—
and demonstrated his love for and knowledge of poetry, or as we would say,
the arts, in his works and in his life. But he was above all a thinker of the
highest rank, and as such he knew that the basic premise of the later liberalism is false. A century later John Stuart Mill could no longer conceive of a
conflict between the intrinsic and therefore legitimate demands of the
sciences and the intrinsic and therefore legitimate demands of the polity;
whereas Rousseau had argued that the "restoration" of the arts and sciences
did not tend to purify morals, but that, on the contrary, their restoration
and popularization would be destructive of the possibility of a good civil
society. His contemporaries were shocked and angered by this teaching and
excluded Rousseau from their society; if we were taught by them and more
directly by Mill and his followers—Justice Douglas, for example—we might
tend to dismiss it as the teaching of a madman or fool. Are we, however, still
prepared to stand with Mill and his predecessors against Rousseau to argue
that what is good for science is necessarily good for civil society?

III

In practice censors have acted out of an unsophisticated concern for
public morality, with no concern for the arts and with no appreciation of
what would be sacrificed if their policy were to be adopted. Their opponents
have resisted them out of a sophisticated concern for the freedom of expression, but with no concern for the effect of this on public morality. It would
appear that concern for public morality requires censorship and that concern
for the arts requires the abolition of censorship. The law developed by our
courts is an attempt to avoid this dilemma by denying that it exists. But with

what results? Rousseau predicted there would be not only a corruption of public morality but a degradation of the arts. His case for censorship appears only at first glance to be made wholly with a view to protecting the simple and decent political order from corruption at the hands of literature and the theatre; it was in fact also a case made with a view to preventing the corruption of the arts themselves. The popularization would be their degradation. To deny the tension between politics and the arts is to assume that the subject requires no governing, that what is produced by writers and dramatists may be ignored by the law in the same manner that the production of economic goods and services was once said to be of no legitimate concern of the law. The free market will be permitted to operate, with the result that what appears in print and on the stage will be determined by the tastes operating in that market, which in a democracy will be a mass market. The law will no longer attempt to influence this market; having denied the distinction between the nonobscene and the obscene, it will in fact come to deny the distinction between art and trash. This is what has happened. Justice Douglas, who told us that the "ideal of the Free Society written into our Constitution . . . is that people are mature enough . . . to recognize trash when they see it," also denies that anyone, mature or immature, can define the difference between art and trash. "Some like Chopin, others like 'rock and roll.' Some are 'normal,' some are masochistic, some deviant in other respects . . . But why is freedom of the press and expression denied them? When the Court today speaks of 'social value' does it mean a 'value' to the majority? . . . If a publication caters to the idiosyncracies of a minority, why does it not have 'social importance'?"[11] To him, whether a publication has "social value" is answered by whether anyone wants to read it, which is to say any publication may have "social value." It is all a question of idiosyncratic taste: some like Chopin, some like rock and roll; some are normal—or as he writes it, "normal"—and some masochistic or deviant—or, as he ought to have written it, "deviant." These statements of course make nonsense of his business of ascending "from plateau to plateau and finally reach[ing] the world of enduring ideas"; because if everything has value, and if there is no standard by which to judge among them, then there is no upward or downward, no "plateau" higher than another "plateau," no art or trash, and, of course, no problem. Art is now defined as the "socially important," and this, in turn, is defined by Douglas as anything anyone has a taste for.

It is true that Douglas is uniquely vulgar for a Supreme Court justice, but his colleagues have not been far behind him on the substantive issue. In principle they acknowledge the category of socially "important" publications and productions, but they do not depend on an educated critical

11. Ginzburg v. United States, 383 U.S. 463, 489-490 (1966). Dissenting opinion.

judgment to define it. They simply accept the judgment of any literary hack willing to testify, which amounts to transferring the mass market to the courtroom. It was solemnly said in testimony that *Fanny Hill* is a work of social importance, which was then elaborated as "literary merit" and "historical value," just the sort of thing to be taught in the classroom (and, as Douglas argued, in sermons from the pulpit). Another "expert witness" described it as a work of art that "asks for and receives a literary response." Its style was said to be "literary" and its central character, in addition to being a whore, an "intellectual," which is probably understood to be the highest praise within the power of these experts to bestow. An intellectual, the court was then told, is one who is "extremely curious about life and who seeks . . . to record with accuracy the details of the external world"—in Fanny's case, such "external details" as her "physical sensations."

Censorship, undertaken in the name of the public necessity to maintain the distinction between the nonobscene and the obscene, has the secondary effect of lending some support to the distinction between art and trash. At a minimum it requires a judgment of what is proper and what is improper, which is to say a judgment of what is worthy of being enjoyed and what is unworthy, and this has the effect of at least supporting the idea that there is a distinction to be made and that the distinction is important. Our law as announced by the judges of our highest court now denies this, explicitly in the case of Douglas and implicitly in the case of his colleagues making up the rest of the Court's majority. The law has resigned in favor of the free mass market, and it has done so not because the free market is seen as a mechanism best calculated to bring about a particular result (for example, the material wealth desired by the *laissez-faire* economists) but because it attaches no significance to the decision the market will make. The popularization of the arts will not lead to their degradation because there is no such thing as degradation.

The *New York Times* does not agree with this when it calls for "sophisticated critical judgment" to save us from the pile of muck that now passes for art. But the "sophisticated critical judgment" of its own drama and book pages praised the very works condemned in the editorial; besides, much of this market is impervious to "sophisticated critical judgment." This is confirmed in the *Times* itself in a piece printed a few months later on the first page of the Sunday drama section: "Nobody yet knows how to control the effect of nudity for a production's purposes, but producers encourage it anyhow. Why? The explanation, I should think is obvious: sex, as always, is good box office."[12] Exactly, it was the law, not the critics, that kept the

12. The *New York Times,* January 18, 1970. The author of this piece, Martin Gottfried, a man of "sophisticated critical judgment" presumably—after all, the *Times* printed him—defends *Che!* and the others, and ends up with a very sophisticated defense of a

strip tease and the "skin flick" confined to the illegitimate theatre, and it is foolish to think, or to have thought, that the critics alone will be able to keep them there, or in fact, from flourishing in the legitimate theatre. That game is caught, as Lincoln would have put it. What remains at large, un-answered, is whether "sophisticated critical judgment" can preserve artistic tastes in another part of the same theatre, or whether there will be any "sophisticated critical judgment." To ask this is to wonder whether the public taste—or at least a part of the public taste—can be educated, and educated with no assistance from the law. This is an old question; to ask it is to return to Rousseau's quarrel with Voltaire and the Enlightenment, and to Tocqueville and John Stuart Mill—in short, to the beginnings of modern democracy where, in political philosophy, the question re-ceived thematic treatment.

The principle of modern democracy is the natural equality of all men, and the problem was to find some way of preventing this principle from be-coming all-pervasive, and especially from invading the arts and sciences them-selves. Stated otherwise, the problem was to find a substitute for the aristo-cratic class which had formerly sustained the arts and sciences, some basis on which, or some citadel from which, the arts and sciences could resist public opinion. The constitutional principle of freedom of speech and press would, perhaps, protect them from hostile political passions, but this institutional device would not protect them from the much more subtle danger, corrup-tion by public opinion, of coming to share the public's taste and of doing the public's work according to the public's standards. One solution, it was hoped by some, would be the modern university, which, as Allan Bloom has re-cently written, was to be "a center for reflection and education independent of the regime and the pervasive influence of its principles, free of the over-whelming effect of public opinion in its crude and subtle forms, devoted to the dispassionate quest for the important and comprehensive truths."[13] Tenure and academic freedom would protect the professors of the arts and sciences, and thereby protect the arts and sciences themselves, and the stu-dents would be educated in the principles of the arts and sciences and their tastes formed accordingly. The education of the public's taste in the arts, which will prevent the popularization of the arts from becoming the cause of their degradation, must take place in the universities if it is to take place at all.

But the so-called expert witnesses who testified in the obscenity cases

---

homosexual rape scene from a production entitled *Fortune and Men's Eyes,* done, of course, in the nude and apparently leaving nothing to the imagination. His principle is that "no climactic scene, in any play, should happen offstage. . . ."

13. "The Democratization of the University," in Robert A. Goldwin (ed.), *How Democratic is America?* (Chicago: Rand McNally, 1971).

came from the universities. *Fanny Hill*'s champions were university professors, and not, by any means, in minor institutions. To rely on the professors to provide the "sophisticated critical judgment" or to educate the tastes of the mass market, or any part of it, is to ignore what is going on in the universities. Several years ago Cornell paid $800 to a man to conduct (lead? orchestrate? create?) a "happening" on campus as part of a Festival of Contemporary Art. This happening consisted of the following: a group of students was led to the city dump where they selected the charred remains of an old automobile, spread it with several hundred pounds of strawberry jam, removed their shirts and blouses, and then danced around it, stopping occasionally to lick the jam. By 1970 standards this was not especially offensive; it was silly, as so many "college boy" antics have been silly. What distinguishes it from goldfish swallowing and panty raids is that it was conducted under official university auspices and with the support and participation of professors.

The call for a "sophisticated critical judgment" is merely a variety of the general call for education, which libertarians have customarily offered as an alternative to the policy of forbidding or punishing speech. It is an attractive alternative, attractive for its consistency with liberal principles as well as for its avoidance of the difficulties accompanying a policy of censorship; unfortunately, in the present intellectual climate, education in this area is almost impossible. Consider the case of the parent who wants to convince his children of the impropriety of the use of the four-letter verb meaning to copulate. At the present time the task confronting him is only slightly less formidable than that faced by the parent who would teach his children that the world is flat. Just as the latter will have to overcome a body of scientific evidence to the contrary, the former will have to overcome the power of common usage and the idea of propriety it implies. Until recently propriety required the use of the verb "to make love,"[14] and this delicacy was not without purpose. It was meant to remind us—to *teach* us, or at least to allow us to be taught—that, whereas human copulation can be indistinguishable from animal copulation generally, it ought to be marked by the presence of a passion of which other animals are incapable. Now, to a quickly increasing extent, the four-letter verb—more "honest" in the opinion of its devotees—is being used openly and therefore without impropriety. The parent will fail in his effort to educate because he will be on his own, trying to teach a lesson his society no longer wants taught—by the law, by the language, or by the schools. Especially by the schools. When in 1964 the University of California at Berkeley could not find a reason to censure the students for whom "free

14. That this is not merely the product of English or American "puritanism" is proved by, for example, the French *faire l'amour* and the Italian *fare-all'amore,* as well as the fastidious German *mit einem liebeln.*

speech" meant the brandishing of the four-letter verb on the placards, it not only made legitimate what had been illegitimate, but announced that from that time forward it would not attempt to teach its students anything contrary to their passions—sexual, political, or, with reference to drug use, physiological. What became true then at Berkeley is now true generally. The professors have nothing to teach their students. The younger ones have joined the students and have come to share their tastes and their political passions; the older ones are silent, and together they are in the process of abdicating to the students their authority to govern the universities, to enforce parietals, to prescribe the curriculum, and even their right to teach them. Critical judgment is being replaced by "doing your own thing," which is what Justice Douglas was talking about, and this being so, it is doubtful, to say the least, whether the universities will be able to educate the tastes of anyone. And if this is not done in the universities, where can it be done?[15] Where in the midst of all the vulgarity and this incessant clamor for doing one's own thing can be found a refuge for the arts? There can be no "sophisticated critical judgment" without it.

IV

One who undertakes to defend censorship in the name of the arts is obliged to acknowledge that he has not exhausted his subject when he has completed that defense. What is missing is a defense of obscenity. What is missing is a defense of the obscenity employed by the greatest of our poets—Aristophanes and Chaucer, Shakespeare and Swift—because it is impossible to believe, it is unreasonable to believe, that what they did is indefensible; and what they did, among other things, was to write a good deal of obscenity. Unfortunately, it would require a talent I do not possess to give a sufficient account of it.

They seemed to employ it mainly in comedy, but their purpose was not simply to make us laugh. Comedy, according to Aristotle,[16] makes us laugh at what is ludicrous in ugliness, and its purpose is to teach, just as tragedy teaches by making us cry before what is destructive in nobility. The latter imitates what is higher, the former what is lower, but they are equally

---

15. In a number of universities, students are permitted to receive course credit for "courses" taught by themselves to themselves. Not surprisingly, it was left to Cornell to carry this to its absurd extreme. In May, 1970, the Educational Policy Committee of the College of Arts and Sciences voted 5-2 to grant "three credit hours to ten students who had 'taught' themselves a course in children's literature"—including not only *Alice in Wonderland*, but *Pinocchio, Where the Wild Things Are,* and *Now We Are Six*. "The students claimed that it is one of the jobs of a university to remedy deficiencies in kindergarten education. In any case, as one of the two dissenters later reported to the full faculty, "whether the books had ever been read to them remains unclear." Cornell *Chronicle,* 1970 June 4.

16. *Poetics,* 1449a-35.

serious; Aristotle discussed both, and Shakespeare, for example, was a comic as well as a tragic poet.

Those aspects of his soul that make man truly human and distinguish him from all other beings—higher or lower in the natural order of things—require political life. And no great poet ever denied this. Man's very virtues, as well as their counterparts, his vices, require him to be governed and to govern; they initiate demands that can be met only in political life, but the poet knows with Rousseau that the demands of human virtue cannot be fully met in political life because they transcend political life. The poet knows the beauty of that order beyond the polity; he reminds us that there is an order outside the conventional and that we are part of that natural order, as well as of the conventional. Shakespeare knows with Rousseau that there is a tension between this natural order and the conventional or legal order, and his purpose is to resolve it, at least for some men, at the highest possible level. They must first be shown that the conventional world is not the only world—that beyond Venice there is Belmont[17]—and here is where obscenity may play a part. It can be used to ridicule the conventional. But it is used in the name of the natural, that order outside the conventional according to which the conventional may be criticized and perhaps, if only to an extent, reformed. Obscenity in the hands of such a poet can serve to *elevate* men, elevate them, the few of them, above the conventional order in which all of us are forced to live our mundane lives. Its purpose is to teach what is truly beautiful—not what convention holds to be beautiful—and to do so by means of pleasure, for obscenity can be pleasurable.

Shakespeare expresses this conflict between nature and law in Edmund's soliloquy at the beginning of Act I, Scene 2, of *King Lear:*

> Thou, Nature, art my goddess; to thy law
> My services are bound, Wherefore should I
> Stand in the plague of custom, and permit
> The curiosity of nations to deprive me,
> For that I as some twelve or fourteen moonshines
> Lag of a brother? Why bastard? Wherefore base?
> When my dimensions are as well compact,
> My mind as generous, and my shape as true,
> As honest madam's issue? Why brand they us
> With base? with baseness? bastardy? base, base?
> Who, in the lusty stealth of nature, take
> More composition and fierce quality
> Than doth, within a dull, stale, tired bed,

17. See the chapter on "The Merchant of Venice" in Allan Bloom with Harry V. Jaffa, *Shakespeare's Politics* (New York: Basic Books, 1964).

Go to th' creating a whole tribe of fops
Got 'tween asleep and wake? Well, then,
Legitimate Edgar, I must have your land.
Our father's love is to the bastard Edmund
As to th' legitimate. Fine word, *'legitimate'!*
Well, my legitimate, if this letter speed,
And my invention thrive, Edmund the base
Shall top th' legitimate. I grow; I prosper.
Now, gods, stand up for bastards.

This serves to illustrate a theme to which great poets address themselves—what is right by law and what is right by nature—and in the development of which the obscenity in comedy has a legitimate and perhaps even
noble role to play. When it is so used it is fully justified, especially because
great poetry even when it is obscene is of interest only to a few—those who
read it primarily for what is beyond its obscenity, that towards which
obscenity points. But when obscenity is employed as it is today, merely in
an effort to capture an audience or to shock without elevating, or in the
effort to set loose idiosyncratic "selfs" doing their own things, or to bring
down the constitutional order, it is not justified, for it lacks the ground on
which to claim exemption from the law. The modern advocates of obscenity
do not seem to be aware of this consequence of their advocacy. They have
obliterated the distinction between art and trash, and in so doing they have
deprived themselves of the ground on which they might protest the law.
What possible argument could have been used against the police had they
decided to arrest the participants in the Cornell "happening" for indecent
exposure, or against a law forbidding these festivals of contemporary "art"?
In this generous world the police must be accorded a right to do their "own
thing" too, and they would probably be able to do it with the support of the
majority and therefore of the law. In a world of everyone doing his own
thing, the majority not only rules but can do no wrong, because there is no
standard of right and wrong. Justice Douglas sees his job as protecting the
right of these contemporary "artists" to do their own thing, but a thoughtful
judge is likely to ask how an artistic judgment that is wholly idiosyncratic
can be capable of supporting an objection to the law. The objection, "*I* like
it," is sufficiently rebutted by the response, "*We* don't."

How to express in a rule of law this distinction between the justified and
the unjustified employment of obscenity is no simple task. That I have argued
and that I willingly concede. I have also argued that it cannot be done at all
on the premise from which our law has proceeded. I have, finally, tried to
indicate the consequences of a failure to maintain the distinction in the law:
not only will we no longer be able to teach the distinction between the
proper and the improper, but we will no longer be able to teach—and will
therefore come to forget—the distinction between art and trash. Stated

otherwise, censorship, because it inhibits self-indulgence and supports the idea of propriety and impropriety, protects political democracy; paradoxically, when it faces the problem of the justified and unjustified use of obscenity, censorship also serves to maintain the distinction between art and trash and, therefore, to protect art and, thereby, to enhance the quality of this democracy. We forgot this. We began with a proper distrust of the capacities of juries and judges to make sound judgments in an area that lies outside their professional competence; but led by the Supreme Court we went on improperly to conclude that the judgments should not be made because they cannot be made, that there is nothing for anyone to judge. No doubt the law used to err on occasion; but democracy can live without *Mrs. Warren's Profession,* if it must, as well as without *Fanny Hill*—or to speak more precisely, it can live with the error that consigns *Mrs. Warren's Profession* to under-the-counter custom along with *Fanny Hill.* It remains to be seen whether the true friend of democracy will want to live in the world without under-the-counter custom, the world that does not know the difference between *Mrs. Warren's Profession* and *Fanny Hill.*

The Case for
Liberal Censorship

Irving Kristol

Being frustrated is disagreeable, but the real disasters in life begin when you get what you want. For almost a century now, a great many intelligent, well-meaning and articulate people—of a kind generally called liberal or intellectual, or both—have argued eloquently against any kind of censorship of art and/or entertainment. And within the past ten years, the courts and the legislatures of most Western nations have found these arguments persuasive—so persuasive that hardly a man is now alive who clearly remembers what the answers to these arguments were. Today, in the United States and other democracies, censorship has to all intents and purposes ceased to exist.

Is there a sense of triumphant exhilaration in the land? Hardly. There is, on the contrary, a rapidly growing unease and disquiet. Somehow, things have not worked out as they were supposed to, and many notable civil libertarians have gone on record as saying this was not what they meant at all. They wanted a world in which *Desire Under the Elms* could be produced, or *Ulysses* published, without interference by philistine busybodies holding public office. They have got that, of course; but they have also got a world in which homosexual rape takes place on the stage, in which the public flocks during lunch hours to witness varieties of professional fornication, in which Times Square has become little more than a hideous market for the sale and distribution of printed filth that panders to all known (and some fanciful) sexual perversions.

Irving Kristol, born in New York City in 1920, graduated from City College in 1940. From 1947 to 1952 he was managing editor of *Commentary* Magazine; from 1953 to 1958 he was co-founder and editor (along with Stephen Spender) of *Encounter* Magazine; from 1959 to 1960 he was editor of *The Reporter* Magazine; from 1961 to 1969 he was executive vice president of Basic Books, Inc., a New York publishing house; in 1969 he was appointed Henry R. Luce Professor of Urban Values at New York University, a

But disagreeable as this may be, does it really matter? Might not our unease and disquiet be merely a cultural hangover—a "hangup," as they say? What reason is there to think that anyone was ever corrupted by a book?

This last question, oddly enough, is asked by the very same people who seem convinced that advertisements in magazines or displays of violence on television do indeed have the power to corrupt. It is also asked, incredibly enough and in all sincerity, by people (e.g., university professors and school teachers) whose very lives provide all the answers one could want. After all, if you believe that no one was ever corrupted by a book, you have also to believe that no one was ever improved by a book (or a play or a movie). You have to believe, in other words, that all art is morally trivial and that, consequently, all education is morally irrelevant. No one, not even a university professor, really believes that.

To be sure, it is extremely difficult, as social scientists tell us, to trace the effects of any single book (or play or movie) on an individual reader or any class of readers. But we all know, and social scientists know it too, that the ways in which we use our minds and imaginations do shape our characters and help define us as persons. That those who certainly know this are nevertheless moved to deny it merely indicates how a dogmatic resistance to the idea of censorship can—like most dogmatism—result in a mindless insistence on the absurd.

I have used these harsh terms—"dogmatism" and "mindless"—advisedly. I might also have added "hypocritical." For the plain fact is that none of us is a complete civil libertarian. We all believe that there is some point at which the public authorities ought to step in to limit the "self expression" of an individual or a group, even where this might be seriously intended as a form of artistic expression, and even where the artistic transaction is between consenting adults. A playwright or theatrical director might, in this crazy world of ours, find someone willing to commit suicide on the stage, as called for by the script. We would not allow that—any more than we would permit scenes of real physical torture on the stage, even if the victim were a willing masochist. And I know of no one, no matter how free in spirit, who argues

position he still holds; he is also co-editor, along with Nathan Glazer, of *The Public Interest* Magazine.

A member of both the National Council on the Humanities and the Council on Foreign Relations, he is also a Fellow of the American Academy of Arts and Sciences. He has been appointed as a member of the Board of the Corporation for Public Broadcasting.

Kristol has written more than sixty articles, which have been published in the *New York Times* Magazine, *Harper's, Atlantic Monthly, Foreign Affairs, Fortune, Commentary, Encounter, The Public Interest,* and others.

He is co-editor, along with Daniel Bell, of *Confrontation: The Student Rebellion and the University,* published in 1969, and *Capitalism Today,* published in 1971. A collection of his essays, entitled *On the Democratic Idea in America* was published in 1972.

that we ought to permit gladiatorial contests in Yankee Stadium, similar to those once performed in the Colosseum at Rome—even if only consenting adults were involved.

The basic point that emerges is one that Professor Walter Berns has powerfully argued: no society can be utterly indifferent to the ways its citizens publicly entertain themselves.[1] Bearbaiting and cockfighting are prohibited only in part out of compassion for the suffering animals; the main reason they were abolished was because it was felt that they debased and brutalized the citizenry who flocked to witness such spectacles. And the question we face with regard to pornography and obscenity is whether . . . they can or will brutalize and debase our citizenry. We are, after all, not dealing with one passing incident—one book, or one play, or one movie. We are dealing with a general tendency that is suffusing our entire culture.

I say pornography and obscenity because, though they have different dictionary definitions and are frequently distinguishable as "artistic" genres, they are nevertheless in the end identical in effect. Pornography is not objectionable simply because it arouses sexual desire or lust or prurience in the mind of the reader or spectator; this is a silly Victorian notion. A great many nonpornographic works—including some parts of the Bible—excite sexual desire very successfully. What is distinctive about pornography is that, in the words of D. H. Lawrence, it attempts "to do dirt on sex. . . . It is an insult to a vital human relationship."

In other words, pornography differs from erotic art in that its whole purpose is to treat human beings obscenely, to deprive human beings of their specifically human dimension. That is what obscenity is all about. It is light years removed from any kind of carefree sensuality—there is no continuum between Fielding's *Tom Jones* and the Marquis de Sade's *Justine.* These works have quite opposite intentions. To quote Susan Sontag: "What pornographic literature does is precisely to drive a wedge between one's existence as a full human being and one's existence as a sexual being—while in ordinary life a healthy person is one who prevents such a gap from opening up." This definition occurs in an essay defending pornography—Miss Sontag is a candid as well as gifted critic—so the definition, which I accept, is neither tendentious nor censorious.

Along these same lines, one can point out—as C. S. Lewis pointed out some years back—that it is no accident that in the history of all literatures obscene words—the so-called "four-letter words"—have always been the vocabulary of farce or vituperation. The reason is clear; they reduce men and women to some of their mere bodily functions—they reduce man to his

---

1. This is as good a place as any to express my profound indebtedness to Walter Berns's superb essay, "Pornography vs. Democracy," in the winter, 1971, issue of *The Public Interest.*

animal component, and such a reduction is an essential purpose of farce or vituperation.

Similarly, Lewis also suggested that it is not an accident that we have no offhand, colloquial, neutral terms—not in any Western European language at any rate—for our most private parts. The words we do use are either (a) nursery terms, (b) archaisms, (c) scientific terms, or (d) a term from the gutter (i.e., a demeaning term). Here I think the genius of language is telling us something important about man. It is telling us that man is an animal with a difference: he has a unique sense of privacy, and a unique capacity for shame when this privacy is violated. Our "private parts" are indeed private, and not merely because convention prescribes it. This particular convention is indigenous to the human race. In practically all primitive tribes, men and women cover their private parts; and in practically all primitive tribes, men and women do not copulate in public.

It may well be that Western society, in the latter half of the 20th century, is experiencing a drastic change in sexual mores and sexual relationships. We have had many such "sexual revolutions" in the past—and the bourgeois family and bourgeois ideas of sexual propriety were themselves established in the course of a revolution against 18th-century "licentiousness"—and we shall doubtless have others in the future. It is, however, highly improbable (to put it mildly) that what we are witnessing is the Final Revolution which will make sexual relations utterly unproblematic, permit us to dispense with any kind of ordered relationships between the sexes, and allow us freely to redefine the human condition. And so long as humanity has not reached that utopia, obscenity will remain a problem.

One of the reasons it will remain a problem is that obscenity is not merely about sex, any more than science fiction is about science. Science fiction, as every student of the genre knows, is a peculiar vision of power: what it is really about is politics. And obscenity is a peculiar vision of humanity: what it is really about is ethics and metaphysics.

Imagine a man—a well-known man, much in the public eye—in a hospital ward, dying an agonizing death. He is not in control of his bodily functions, so that his bladder and his bowels empty themselves of their own accord. His consciousness is overwhelmed and extinguished by pain, so that he cannot communicate with us, nor we with him. Now, it would be, technically, the easiest thing in the world to put a television camera in his hospital room and let the whole world witness this spectacle. We don't do it—at least we don't do it as yet—because we regard this as an obscene invasion of privacy. And what would make the spectacle obscene is that we would be witnessing the extinguishing of humanity in a human animal.

Incidentally, in the past our humanitarian crusaders against capital punishment understood this point very well. The abolitionist literature goes into great physical detail about what happens to a man when he is hanged or electrocuted or gassed. And their argument was—and is—that what happens is shockingly obscene, and that no civilized society should be responsible for perpetrating such obscenities, particularly since in the nature of the case there must be spectators to ascertain that this horror was indeed being perpetrated in fulfillment of the law.

Sex—like death—is an activity that is both animal and human. There are human sentiments and human ideals involved in this animal activity. But when sex is public, the viewer does not see—cannot see—the sentiments and the ideals. He can only see the animal coupling. And that is why, when men and women make love, as we say, they prefer to be alone—because it is only when you are alone that you can make love, as distinct from merely copulating in an animal and casual way. And that, too, is why those who are voyeurs, if they are not irredeemably sick, also feel ashamed at what they are witnessing. When sex is a public spectacle, a human relationship has been debased into a mere animal connection.

It is also worth noting that this making of sex into an obscenity is not a mutual and equal transaction, but is rather an act of exploitation by one of the partners—the male partner. I do not wish to get into the complicated question as to what, if any, are the essential differences—as distinct from conventional and cultural differences—between male and female. I do not claim to know the answer to that. But I do know—and I take it as a sign which has meaning—that pornography is, and always has been, a man's work; that women rarely write pornography; and that women tend to be indifferent consumers of pornography.[2] My own guess, by way of explanation, is that a woman's sexual experience is ordinarily more suffused with human emotion than is man's, that men are more easily satisfied with autoerotic activities, and that men can therefore more easily take a more "technocratic" view of sex and its pleasures. Perhaps this is not correct. But whatever the explanation, there can be no question that pornography is a form of "sexism," as the Women's Liberation Movement calls it, and that the instinct of Women's Lib has been unerring in perceiving that, when pornography is perpetrated, it is perpetrated against them, as part of a conspiracy to deprive them of their full humanity.

But even if all this is granted, it might be said—and doubtless will be said—that I really ought not to be unduly concerned. Free competition in the cultural marketplace—it is argued by people who have never otherwise had a kind word to say for laissez-faire—will automatically dispose of the problem. The present fad for pornography and obscenity, it will be asserted, is just that, a fad. It will spend itself in the course of time, people will get

---

2. There are, of course, a few exceptions—but of a kind that prove the rule. *L'Histoire d'O,* for instance, written by a woman, is unquestionably the most *melancholy* work of pornography ever written. And its theme is precisely the dehumanization accomplished by obscenity.

bored with it, will be able to take it or leave it alone in a casual way, in a "mature way," and, in sum, I am being unnecessarily distressed about the whole business. The *New York Times,* in an editorial, concludes hopefully in this vein:

In the end . . . the insensate pursuit of the urge to shock, carried from one excess to a more abysmal one, is bound to achieve its own antidote in total boredom. When there is no lower depth to descend to, ennui will erase the problem.

I would like to be able to go along with this line of reasoning, but I cannot. I think it is false, and for two reasons, the first psychological, the second political.

The basic psychological fact about pornography and obscenity is that it appeals to and provokes a kind of sexual regression. The sexual pleasure one gets from pornography and obscenity is autoerotic and infantile; put bluntly, it is a masturbatory exercise of the imagination, when it is not masturbation pure and simple. Now, people who masturbate do not get bored with masturbation, just as sadists don't get bored with sadism, and voyeurs don't get bored with voyeurism.

In other words, infantile sexuality is not only a permanent temptation for the adolescent or even the adult—it can quite easily become a permanent self-reinforcing neurosis. It is because of an awareness of this possibility of regression toward the infantile condition, a regression which is always open to us, that all the codes of sexual conduct ever devised by the human race take such a dim view of autoerotic activities and try to discourage autoerotic fantasies. Masturbation is indeed a perfectly natural autoerotic activity, as so many sexologists blandly assure us today. And it is precisely because it is so perfectly natural that is can be so dangerous to the mature or maturing person, if it is not controlled or sublimated in some way. That is the true meaning of Portnoy's complaint. Portnoy, you will recall, grows up to be a man who is incapable of having an adult sexual relationship with a woman; his sexuality remains fixed in an infantile mode, the prison of his autoerotic fantasies. Inevitably, Portnoy comes to think, in a perfectly infantile way, that it was all his mother's fault.

It is true that, in our time, some quite brilliant minds have come to the conclusion that a reversion to infantile sexuality is the ultimate mission and secret destiny of the human race. I am thinking in particular of Norman O. Brown, for whose writings I have the deepest respect. One of the reasons I respect them so deeply is that Mr. Brown is a serious thinker who is unafraid to face up to the radical consequences of his radical theories. Thus, Mr. Brown knows and says that for his kind of salvation to be achieved, humanity must annul the civilization it has created—not merely the civilization we have today, but all civilization—so as to be able to make the long descent backwards into animal innocence.

What is at stake is civilization and humanity, nothing less. The idea that "everything is permitted," as Nietzsche put it, rests on the premise of nihilism and has nihilistic implications. I will not pretend that the case against nihilism and for civilization is an easy one to make. We are here confronting the most fundamental of philosophical questions, on the deepest levels. But that is precisely my point—that the matter of pornography and obscenity is not a trivial one, and that only superficial minds can take a bland and untroubled view of it.

In this connection, I might also point out those who are primarily against censorship on liberal grounds tell us not to take pornography or obscenity seriously, while those who are for pornography and obscenity, on radical grounds, take it very seriously indeed. I believe the radicals—writers like Susan Sontag, Herbert Marcuse, Norman O. Brown and even Jerry Rubin—are right, and the liberals are wrong. I also believe that those young radicals at Berkeley, some five years ago, who provoked a major confrontation over the public use of obscene words, showed a brilliant political instinct. Once the faculty and administration had capitulated on this issue—saying: "Oh, for God's sake, let's be adult: what difference does it make anyway?"—once they said that, they were bound to lose on every other issue. And once Mark Rudd could publicly ascribe to the president of Columbia a notoriously obscene relationship to his mother, without provoking any kind of reaction, the Students for a Democratic Society (SDS) had already won the day. The occupation of Columbia's buildings merely ratified their victory. Men who show themselves unwilling to defend civilization against nihilism are not going to be either resolute or effective in defending the university against anything.

I am already touching upon a political aspect of pornography when I suggest that it is inherently and purposefully subversive of civilization and its institutions. But there is another and more specifically political aspect, which has to do with the relationship of pornography and/or obscenity to democracy, and especially to the quality of public life on which democratic government ultimately rests.

Though the phrase, "the quality of life," trips easily from so many lips these days, it tends to be one of those clichés with many trivial meanings and no large, serious one. Sometimes it merely refers to such externals as the enjoyment of cleaner air, cleaner water, cleaner streets. At other times it refers to the merely private enjoyment of music, painting, or literature. Rarely does it have anything to do with the way the citizen in a democracy views himself—his obligations, his intentions, his ultimate self-definition.

Instead, what I would call the "managerial" conception of democracy is the predominant opinion among political scientists, sociologists and economists, and has, through the untiring efforts of these scholars, become the conventional journalistic opinion as well. The root idea behind this "managerial" conception is that democracy is a "political system" (as they say) which can be adequately defined in terms of—can be fully reduced to—its mechanical arrangements. Democracy is then seen as a set of rules and procedures, and nothing *but* a set of rules and procedures, whereby majority rule and minority rights are reconciled into a state of equilibrium. If everyone follows these rules and procedures, then a democracy is in working order. I think this is a fair description of the democratic idea that currently prevails in academia. One can also fairly say that it is now the liberal idea of democracy par excellence.

I cannot help but feel that there is something ridiculous about being this kind of a democrat, and I must further confess to having a sneaking sympathy for those of our young radicals who also find it ridiculous. The absurdity is the absurdity of idolatry—of taking the symbolic for the real, the means for the end. The purpose of democracy cannot possibly be the endless functioning of its own political machinery. The purpose of any political regime is to achieve some version of the good life and the good society. It is not at all difficult to imagine a perfectly functioning democracy which answers all questions except one—namely, why should anyone of intelligence and spirit care a fig for it?

There is, however, an older idea of democracy—one which was fairly common until about the beginning of this century—for which the conception of the quality of public life is absolutely crucial. This idea starts from the proposition that democracy is a form of self-government, and that if you want it to be a meritorious polity, you have to care about what kind of people govern it. Indeed, it puts the matter more strongly and declares that, if you want self-government, you are only entitled to it if that "self" is worthy of governing. There is no inherent right to self-government if it means that such government is vicious, mean, squalid, and debased. Only a dogmatist and a fanatic, an idolater of democratic machinery, could approve of self-government under such conditions.

And because the desirability of self-government depends on the character of the people who govern, the older idea of democracy was very solicitous of the condition of this character. It was solicitous of the individual self, and felt an obligation to educate it into what used to be called "republican virtue." And it was solicitous of that collective self which we call public opinion and which, in a democracy, governs us collectively. Perhaps in some respects it was nervously over-solicitous—that would not be surprising. But the main thing is that it cared, cared not merely about the machinery of democracy but about the quality of life that this machinery might generate.

And because it cared, this older idea of democracy had no problem in principle with pornography and/or obscenity. It censored them—and it did so with a perfect clarity of mind and a perfectly clear conscience. It was not about to permit people capriciously to corrupt themselves. Or, to put it more precisely: in this version of democracy, the people took some care not to let themselves be governed by the more infantile and irrational parts of themselves.

I have, it may be noticed, uttered that dreadful word, "censorship." And I am not about to back away from it. If you think pornography and/or obscenity is a serious problem, you have to be for censorship. I'll go even further and say that if you want to prevent pornography and/or obscenity from becoming a problem, you have to be for censorship. And lest there be any misunderstanding as to what I am saying, I'll put it as bluntly as possible: if you care for the quality of life in our American democracy, then you have to be for censorship.

But can a liberal be for censorship? Unless one assumes that being a liberal *must* mean being indifferent to the quality of American life, then the answer has to be: yes, a liberal can be for censorship—but he ought to favor a liberal form of censorship.

Is that a contradiction in terms? I don't think so. We have no problem contrasting *repressive* laws governing alcohol and drugs and tobacco with laws *regulating* (i.e., discouraging the sale of) alcohol and drugs and tobacco. Laws encouraging temperance are not the same thing as laws that have as their goal prohibition or abolition. We have not made the smoking of cigarettes a criminal offense. We have, however, and with good liberal conscience, prohibited cigarette advertising on television, and may yet, again with good liberal conscience, prohibit it in newspapers and magazines. The idea of restricting individual freedom, in a liberal way, is not at all unfamiliar to us.

I therefore see no reason why we should not be able to distinguish repressive censorship from liberal censorship of the written and spoken word. In Britain, until a few years ago, you could perform almost any play you wished—but certain plays, judged to be obscene, had to be performed in private theatrical clubs which were deemed to have a "serious" interest in theater. In the United States, all of us who grew up using public libraries are familiar with the circumstances under which certain books could be circulated only to adults, while still other books had to be read in the library reading room, under the librarian's skeptical eye. In both cases, a small minority that was willing to make a serious effort to see an obscene book could do so. But the impact of obscenity was circumscribed and the quality of public life was only marginally affected.[3]

I am not saying it is easy in practice to sustain a distinction between liberal and repressive censorship, especially in the public realm of a democracy, where popular opinion is so vulnerable to demagoguery. Moreover, an

3. It is fairly predictable that someone is going to object that this point of view is "elitist"—that, under a system of liberal censorship, the rich will have privileged access to pornography and obscenity. Yes, of course they will—just as, at present, the rich have privileged access to heroin if they want it. But one would have to be an egalitarian maniac to object to this state of affairs on the grounds of equality.

acceptable system of liberal censorship is likely to be exceedingly difficult to devise in the United States today, because our educated classes, upon whose judgment a liberal censorship must rest, are so convinced that there is no such thing as a problem of obscenity, or even that there is no such thing as obscenity at all. But, to counterbalance this, there is the further, fortunate truth that the tolerable margin for error is quite large, and single mistakes or single injustices are not all that important.

This possibility, of course, occasions much distress among artists and academics. It is a fact, one that cannot and should not be denied, that any system of censorship is bound, upon occasion, to treat unjustly a particular work of art—to find pornography where there is only gentle eroticism, to find obscenity where none really exists, or to find both where its existence ought to be tolerated because it serves a larger moral purpose. Though most works of art are not obscene, and though most obscenity has nothing to do with art, there are some few works of art that are, at least in part, pornographic and/or obscene. There are also some few works of art that are in the special category of the comic-ironic "bawdy" (Boccaccio, Rabelais). It is such works of art that are likely to suffer at the hands of the censor. That is the price one has to be prepared to pay for censorship—even liberal censorship.

But just how high is this price? If you believe, as so many artists seem to believe today, that art is the only sacrosanct activity in our profane and vulgar world—that any man who designates himself an artist thereby acquires a sacred office—then obviously censorship is an intolerable form of sacrilege. But for those of us who do not subscribe to this religion of art, the costs of censorship do not seem so high at all.

If you look at the history of American or English literature, there is precious little damage you can point to as a consequence of the censorship that prevailed throughout most of that history. Very few works of literature—of real literary merit, I mean—ever were suppressed; and those that were, were not suppressed for long. Nor have I noticed, now that censorship of the written word has to all intents and purposes ceased in this country, that hitherto suppressed or repressed masterpieces are flooding the market. Yes, we can now read *Fanny Hill* and the Marquis de Sade. Or, to be more exact, we can now openly purchase them, since many people were able to read them even though they were publicly banned, which is as it should be under a liberal censorship. So how much have literature and the arts gained from the fact that we can all now buy them over the counter, that, indeed, we are all now encouraged to buy them over the counter? They have not gained much that I can see.

And one might also ask a question that is almost never raised: how much has literature lost from the fact that everything is now permitted? It has lost quite a bit, I should say. In a free market, Gresham's Law can work for books or theater as efficiently as it does for coinage—driving out the good, establishing the debased. The cultural market in the United States today is being pre-empted by dirty books, dirty movies, dirty theater. A pornographic novel has a far better chance of being published today that a non-pornographic one, and quite a few pretty good novels are not being published at all simply because they are not pornographic, and are therefore less likely to sell. Our cultural condition has not improved as a result of the new freedom. American cultural life wasn't much to brag about twenty years ago; today one feels ashamed for it.

Just one last point which I dare not leave untouched. If we start censoring pornography or obscenity, shall we not inevitably end up censoring political opinion? A lot of people seem to think this would be the case—which only shows the power of doctrinaire thinking over reality. We had censorship of pornography and obscenity for 150 years, until almost yesterday, and I am not aware that freedom of opinion in this country was in any way diminished as a consequence of this fact. Fortunately for those of us who are liberal, freedom is not indivisible. If it were, the case for liberalism would be indistinguishable from the case for anarchy; and they are two very different things.

But I must repeat and emphasize: what kinds of laws we pass governing pornography and obscenity, what kind of censorship—or, since we are still a federal nation—what kinds of censorship we institute in our various localities may indeed be difficult matters to cope with; nevertheless the real issue is one of principle. I myself subscribe to a liberal view of the enforcement problem; I think that pornography should be illegal and available to anyone who wants it so badly as to make a pretty strenuous effort to get it. We have lived with under-the-counter pornography for centuries now, in a fairly comfortable way. But the issue of principle, of whether it should be over or under the counter, has to be settled before we can reflect on the advantages and disadvantages of alternative modes of censorship. I think the settlement we are living under now, in which obscenity and democracy are regarded as equals, is wrong: I believe it is inherently unstable; I think it will, in the long run, be incompatible with any authentic concern for the quality of life in our democracy.

Comments and Conclusions

As a citizenry, we have the obligation to see that the law functions for our common good to the greatest extent possible. Limitations exist, of course, as Fitch mentions. However, in a free society, law rests upon the consent of the majority. If the traditions of a people are sound, their laws will also be.

Thus, if a majority of the people are convinced that a distinction can be made between that which is obscene and transient and that which is uplifting and enduring, their laws will ultimately reflect that conviction.

As Kristol observes, "Very few works of literature—of real literary merit, I mean—ever were suppressed; and those that were, were not suppressed for long." This is an example of that kind of democratic evolvement which justifies both our form of government and our laws.

THE
LAW

The Law is the standard and guardian of our liberty;
It circumscribes and defends it;
But to imagine liberty without law—
  is to imagine every man with a sword in his hand
to destroy him, who is weaker than himself.

                                   E. H. Clarendon

Introduction

As long as free men have lived in democratic societies, tension and conflict have accompanied the question of where to draw the line on the printed and the spoken word and on freedom of expression in the arts.

The law is the formal repository of the societal concensus on this question.

In our first chapter in this section, in a brilliant, rousing way, Alexander Bickel presents the dilemmas that are inherent in our "uninhibited, robust, and wide-open" First Amendment to our Constitution. He shows the fascinating contests between the written law and the judiciary, the juries, and the plaintiffs and defendants—all against the background of the First Amendment. And the issues again and again are: How far can you go? Where do you draw the line on free speech? What kinds of consequences are you willing to tolerate?

Norman Podhoretz, editor of Commentary magazine, published by the American Jewish Committee, responds to Bickel—in the role of an avowed liberal and "free speecher" as he, too, wrestles with the First Amendment. Is there a point where you draw a line and say, "Enough—this is going too far; that should be prohibited"?

New York attorney Paul McGeady then focuses on the evolution of obscenity control legislation. He brings us up to the 1973 Supreme Court landmark "Miller" decision which has so incensed some civil libertarians.

The "Uninhibited, Robust, and Wide-Open" First Amendment

Alexander M. Bickel

In 1964 the Supreme Court decided New York Times Co. v. Sullivan, an important and novel decision of great consequence in the law of the First Amendment.

Among other things, the Court declared the Sedition Act of 1798 unconstitutional, better than a century-and-a-half after its expiration. Justice delayed, but not denied.

In a more contemporary frame of mind, the Court reversed a judgment in a libel action granted by the Alabama courts to the police commissioner of Montgomery against the *New York Times.* The Times had printed some inaccurate statements about the Commissioner in a fund-raising advertisement for Dr. Martin Luther King, who in turn had run afoul of the commissioner in the course of some demonstrations. The Court held that the First Amendment prevents a public official from recovering damages for a defamatory falsehood relating to his official conduct, unless he proves that the false statement about him was made with actual knowledge that it was false, or with reckless disregard of whether it was false or not; in other words, with malice. Such a rule, historically quite a new departure, was necessary, the Court said, in order to carry out "a profound national commitment to the principle that debate on public issues should be uninhibited, robust, and wide-open," and should be allowed to include even "vehement, caustic, and

Alexander M. Bickel is Chancellor Kent Professor of Law and Legal History at Yale University Law School. He obtained his law degree in 1949 from Harvard University, where he was also case editor of the Harvard Law Review. He worked for the Department of State as a law officer and later became a law clerk to Supreme Court Justice Felix Frankfurter. In addition to his law school affiliation at Yale, he is also a member of the history department. His writing interests have frequently focused on the Supreme Court, administrative law, Constitutional law, and legislation.

sometimes unpleasantly sharp attacks on government and public officials."

To require that debate, however uninhibited, robust, wide-open, vehement, caustic, and unpleasantly sharp, be truthful in its factual assertions would dampen the vigor, and limit the variety, of public debate—certainly limit the variety. It would deprive First Amendment rights, said Justice Brennan for the Court, of necessary breathing space. Knowing that they might have to prove their assertions to a jury, would-be critics of official conduct might be deterred from making assertions they fully believed to be true. For we all know that few statements, however true, can be proved to be a mathematical certainty; we know that juries exercise judgment, which is fallible and may be prejudiced, and that, in any event, trials are fearfully expensive. As a litigant, Judge Learned Hand once said, "I should dread a lawsuit beyond almost anything else short of sickness and death.

The lesson of New York Times Co. v. Sullivan—that the First Amendment guarantees the right to publish falsehood—was well learned by a Republican Congressman who voted in the summer of 1971, quite rightly in my judgment, against a resolution that would have cited President Stanton of CBS for contempt of Congress for refusing to make available to Congress editorial matter used in connection with a broadcast called, "The Selling of the Pentagon." "The First Amendment," said the Congressman, perhaps unfairly but with acute appreciation of the constitutional position, "guarantees CBS the right to lie, and they exercise it frequently."

The right of the decision in New York Times v. Sullivan is as interesting as its substance. To borrow the Court's phrase in Sullivan, only of late has the First Amendment played, as in Sullivan, an "uninhibited, robust, and wide-open" role in our law. And the total career, robust or otherwise, of the First Amendment as part of the law of the Constitution encompasses little more than half a century. Of course the First Amendment has been in the Constitution and has had pride of place in the Bill of Rights since 1791, so what we may think of as its admonitory career is quite long. But its legal career in court decisions is a matter, essentially, of the past half century.

In England and in the colonies in the 18th century, and in the United States in the administration of President John Adams, there was a great deal of turmoil and a great deal of legal maneuvering about freedom of speech, and more particularly of the press. This constitutes the background and the earliest environment of the First Amendment. But in England, and the more so in the United States, an easy and uncontested freedom of speech and of the press prevailed through the 19th century. During this period, the First Amendment was legally an unquestioned assumption.

I have no wish to romanticize the 19th century. Locally, especially around the critical contradiction of slavery, there were infringements of freedom of speech. Abolitionist speakers were sometimes dealt with harshly by law in the South and in parts of Northern and Border states. And mobs and other private forces, abetted from time to time in informal fashion by public force, imposed their own episodic constraints, sometimes violently. So did one or another military commander in the Civil War and Reconstruction periods. But there were no systemic, and certainly no nationwide, legal constraints.

Government was, of course, altogether during this century very far from the ubiquitous presence that it is now. The late Zechariah Chafee, Jr., the first great scholar of the First Amendment, tells us that "the (then) prevailing doctrine of laissez faire was extended to the field of discussion. The outstanding representative of the liberty of the time was John Stuart Mill." It seemed "odd" to Chafee "to link together the legal restrictions on business and wealth enacted by collectivists at the opening of the 20th century and the Sedition laws enacted against collectivists" just about contemporaneously, after the long century of consensus and freedom. Yet Chafee recognized the common impulse behind the social and economic legislation and the restrictions on freedom of speech, both of which the 20th century ushered in. The impulse proceeded from social unrest. The movement for industrial justice disturbed the consensus and gave rise to government action regulating industry on the one hand and constricting freedom of speech and of the press on the other. Then followed judicial decisions testing the reach of the First Amendment.

Chafee thought it unfortunate that during the 19th century, "freedom of speech was a cherished tradition, but remained without specific (legal) content." In this we may consider that Chafee was mistaken. For law can never make us as secure as we are when we do not need it. Those freedoms which are neither challenged nor defined are the most secure. In this sense, for example, it is true that the American press was freer before it won its battle with the government over the Pentagon Papers in 1971 than after its victory. Before June 15, 1971, through the troubles of 1798, through one civil and two world wars, and other wars, there had never been an effort by the federal government to censor a newspaper by attempting to impose a restraint prior to publication, directly or in litigation. That spell was broken, and in a sense freedom was thus diminished.

But freedom was also extended in that the conditions in which government will not be allowed to restrain publication are now clearer and perhaps more stringent than they have been. We are, or at least we feel, freer when we feel no need to extend our freedom. The conflict and contention by which we extend freedom seem to mark, or at least to threaten, contraction; and in truth they do, for they endanger an assumed freedom, which appeared limitless because its limits were untried. Appearance and reality are nearly one. We extend the legal reality of freedom at some cost in its limitless appearance. And the cost is real.

Chafee held that the First Amendment "protects two kinds of interest in speech. There is an individual interest, the need of many men to express their opinions on matters vital to them if life is to be worth living. . . ." Secondly, Chafee wrote, there is "a social interest in the attainment of truth, so that the country may not only adopt the wisest course of action but carry it out in the wisest way."

Now, the interest in truth of which Chafee spoke is not inconsistent with the First Amendment's protection of demonstrable falsehood, for as I have indicated, men may be deterred from speaking what they believe to be true because they may fear that it will be found to be false, or that the proof of its truth will be too expensive. Moreover, the individual interest that Chafee mentioned has its truth-seeking aspect. Yet the First Amendment does not operate solely or even chiefly to foster the quest for truth, unless we take the view that truth is entirely a product of the marketplace and is definable as the perceptions of the majority of men, and not otherwise. The social interest that the First Amendment vindicates is rather, as Alexander Meiklejohn emphasized, the interest in the successful operation of the political process, so that the country may better be able to adopt the course of action that conforms to the wishes of the greatest number, whether or not it is wise or is founded in truth.

Discussion, the exchange of views, the ventilation of desires and demands—these are, of course, crucial to our politics. And so, for much the same reasons, is the effectiveness of the decisions reached by the political process, that is to say, the effectiveness of law embodying the wishes of the greatest number, or at any rate, of their chosen representatives. It would follow that the First Amendment should protect and indeed encourage speech so long as it serves to make the political process work—so long, that is, as it seeks to achieve objectives through the political process, by persuading a majority of voters; but not when it amounts to an effort to supplant, disrupt, or coerce the process, as by overthrowing the government, by rioting, or by other forms of violence; and not also when it constitutes a breach of an otherwise valid law, a violation of majority decisions embodied in law.

There would be considerably less of a problem with the First Amendment if we could distinguish with assurance between speech and conduct, as the late Justice Black and Justice Douglas have sometimes tried to persuade us that we can. Only conduct, their argument has run, can overthrow the government, be violent, hurt someone or something. Speech cannot. That, however, is unfortunately not so.

Very little conduct that involves more than one person is impossible without speech. Speech leads to it, merges into it, is necessary to it. That is the point of Holmes's famous metaphor: "The most stringent protection of free speech would not protect a man in falsely shouting fire in a theater, and causing a panic." It was Holmes also, in the course of a truly fervent defense of free speech, in the dissent in the Gitlow case, who said: "Every idea is an incitement. It offers itself for belief and if believed it is acted on unless some other belief outweighs it or some failure of energy stifles the movement at its birth."

There are, then, problems. I have mentioned two. One is the problem of speech which is not discussion forming part of the political process, but which is aimed at dispensing with it, or at a disruption of it, a coercion of it by violence. Second, there is the problem of speech which is aimed at, or otherwise involves, the violation of a valid law or procedure; speech that has no general purpose to supplant the political process but that refuses to accept its operation or its outcome in a given instance. Here I have in mind counseling, or inciting to, disobedience of law—perfectly peaceable disobedience, but disobedience. I have in mind also speech or assembly that involves a breach of laws or procedures which safeguard the public peace and tranquility, or some other public interest—laws or procedures whose validity would not be questioned except as they are violated in the course of engaging in speech or assembly.

That aspect of the first problem—the problem with efforts to supplant or coerce the political process—which is embraced in the historic concept of seditious speech, is dealt with, and perhaps solved as well as may be, by the clear-and-present danger test that Holmes formulated better than half a century ago. The solution is in terms of a judgment, as Holmes often liked to say, of proximity and degree: a pragmatic judgment, drawing a distinction between speech that carries a high risk of disruption, coercion, or violence, and speech that carries no, or less, risk. This judgment is generalized loosely into the clear-and-present-danger formula, under which speech is protected unless it constitutes, in the circumstances, an intentional incitement to imminent forbidden action.

Since it is perfectly true, as Holmes said, that every idea is an incitement, society would enjoy very little freedom of heated, passionate, or emotional discourse, or altogether of radical discussion, unless this distinction were drawn and enforced. Shortly before Holmes first formulated the clear-and-present-danger test, Judge Learned Hand wrote: "Detestation of existing policies is easily transformed into forcible resistance of the authority which puts them into execution, and it would be folly to disregard the causal relation between the two. Yet to assimilate agitation . . . with direct incitement to violent resistance is to disregard the tolerance of all methods of political agitation which in normal times is a safeguard of free government." Recently, in Watts v. United States, the Supreme Court dealt with an alleged violation of a statute making it a crime to threaten the life of the president. Watts had said at a public rally that he had been classified 1-A, and: "I am not going. If they ever make me carry a rifle, the first man I want to get is LBJ." The Court held that this was "political hyperbole" rather than intentional incitement, and could not form the basis of a criminal prosecution. Political speech, said the Court, is often "vituperative, abusive, inexact." Watts's pronouncement was no more than a crude and offensive statement of opposition to President Johnson.

The clear-and-present-danger test as originally formulated by Holmes also purported to solve the second of the problems I have mentioned—the problem of speech which does not incite to violence or any other coercion of the political process, but merely to the violation of an otherwise valid law or procedure. Our political process, however, is too dependent on registering intensity of feeling as well as majority wish, the former of which it cannot do through the ballot box; it has too many stages of decision-making before laws are ultimately held valid, and too many stages of law-formation which often render law provisional only; and on the other hand it results by now in a very pervasive government and makes numerous laws and regulations of vastly differing orders of importance—the process is, in sum, too complex, diverse, and resourceful to subsume an unvarying duty to obey all laws. Simple application of the clear-and-present-danger test to forbid all speech which constitutes an intentional incitement to break a law, or all speech which by itself or through its by-products, as in the form of assembly, or of marching, or of handing out leaflets, involves a breach of rules or procedures safeguarding an otherwise valid public interest, would be an anomalous and unrealistic result. It would rest on a snapshot of the political process that showed it as consisting of discussion and voting and nothing else. That is not the whole process, not nearly. It would not work if it were; it would not generate the necessary consent to government and would not be stable. We cannot, therefore, as a society, be held to put that kind of store by the duty to obey.

Consequently, quite early, in Whitney v. California, Brandeis, with Holmes concurring, drew some further distinctions and made occasion for additional judgments of proximity and degree. The fact that speech is likely to result in some violation of law was not enough, he said, to justify its suppression. "There must be the probability of serious injury to the state." And Brandeis gave a very interesting example, calling to mind an ancient and persistent form of civil disobedience: speech that creates an imminent danger of organized trespass on unenclosed, privately-owned land. It would be unconstitutional, he suggested, to prohibit such speech, despite the imminent danger it presented, because the harm to society which the prohibition would seek to avert would be "relatively trivial."

Subsequent cases have required government to show not merely a rational, otherwise valid, interest in support of a law or procedure that is endangered or actually violated by speech or by activity attending speech, but a "compelling interest." As the Court said in 1939, in Schneider v. State, when speech or assembly breaks or threatens to break a law, "the delicate and difficult task falls upon the courts to weigh the circumstances and to appraise the substantiality of the reasons advanced in support of" the law in question. Hence, the ultimate formulation of the clear-and-present-danger test, by Judge Learned Hand, is that the courts must ask "whether the gravity of the evil, discounted by its improbability, justifies such invasion of free speech as is necessary to avoid the danger."

The nature and gravity of the evil, its gravity as well as its proximity, thus form part of the judicial judgment. One may ask by what warrant courts decide that some valid laws passed by a legislature are less important than other ones and may be endangered or disobeyed. Someone must [decide], however, unless each and every legitimate but utterly trivial public interest is to prevail over the interest in what Meiklejohn called those activities of communication by which we govern. Hence courts do so decide. And we have thus built into the system a kind of domesticated form of civil disobedience.

It is this aspect of the First Amendment that the Pentagon Papers-New York Times case of 1971 illustrated and developed. The case can be viewed in another light, as I shall show. And it had other features. It was a prior restraint case. Prior restraints are traditionally disfavored—and in circumstances such as those of the Pentagon Papers publication, with very good reason—even where an attempt might be allowed to regulate the same sort of speech through the *in terrorem* effect of a subsequent sanction. Again, the case involved a question of statutory construction and a problem of the separation of powers. Passing these features, the essence of the government's complaint was that publication of the Pentagon Papers violated a public interest in the confidentiality of government documents, an interest which the executive order establishing the classification system, and also, the government contended, the Espionage Act were intended to safeguard. The Espionage Act raised the question of statutory construction to which I have referred, and the attempt to apply executive order concerning classification of documents, not internally within the executive branch of government, but externally to private persons and entities gave rise to the problem of separation of powers. Assuming, however, that the government had prevailed on either or both of these points—assuming, that is, acceptance of the government's argument that the public interest in confidentiality of government documents was embodied in valid and applicable law, either in the executive order or in the Espionage Act or both—there remained the issue whether the given injury to this public interest was in the circumstances grave enough to justify a restriction on speech, or too trivial to justify it.

Justice Harlan took the position that the weighing of the gravity of the injury was in this instance not for the judges to undertake because when the injury is to the nation's foreign relations, as it was plausibly alleged to be, judges should, he thought, simply accept the president's assessment of its gravity. The government did not really contend for this much, and no other Justice seemed prepared to concede it. Rather the government tried to persuade the judges themselves that the breach of confidentiality constituted, in the circumstances, a grave and not merely probable, but immediate injury. The injury was prolongation of the Vietnam war by providing the enemy with helpful information and embarrassment to the United States in the conduct of diplomatic affairs.

Now, as to the war, there was a question of immediacy, and indeed of causal connection between publication and the feared injury. The discount for improbability was heavy. There was actually nothing more than a tendency, if that, and the bad-tendency test in seditious speech cases is precisely what the clear-and-present-danger doctrine displaced, as its very formulation indicates. It required a high probability instead. As to the claim of embarrassment in the conduct of diplomatic affairs, however, an immediate causal connection was reasonably clear. Here the gravity of the injury was squarely in issue. And it was held insufficient. The predilection for in-system civil disobedience prevailed.

The clear-and-present-danger doctrine, then, as it has evolved beyond its original formulation, makes room for what used to be called seditious speech and for a measure of necessary in-system civil disobedience. It gives fair satisfaction, even though it places a bit more reliance in the discretion and prudence of judges than either voluptuaries of liberty or judicial conservatives find altogether comfortable. The underlying broad principle is that the First Amendment protects the political process and a right of self-expression consistent with its requirements. But other, fundamental difficulties remain, which the clear-and-present-danger test rather tends to sweep under the rug. Obviously the political process is not what we pursue everywhere, for purposes of all decision making, or always. There are times when we do not, and places where we do not, and times when the need for self-expression is also not a dominant interest. Equally obviously, not all the results that the political process might attain are acceptable.

Thus a criminal trial to a jury does not operate on the rules of the political process or as a forum for self-expression, and if a witness, therefore, should wish to recite some hearsay evidence to the jury, we stop him. We forbid him to speak. We might also, and we should, as Justice Black intimated, although in dissent, in Cox v. Louisiana, stop a speaker from assailing a trial by haranguing a crowd on the courthouse lawn while the trial is proceeding. "Government under law as ordained by our Constitution is too precious, too sacred," said Justice Black, "to be jeopardized by subjecting the courts to intimidatory practices that have been fatal to individual liberty and minority rights wherever such practices have been allowed to poison the steams of justice." What is meant by intimidatory practices is public opinion impinging too proximately and too directly on the trial. Only a year later, in 1966, in Adderley v. Florida, Justice Black, now in the majority, indicated that the grounds of a jail were also no place for free expression of views. The democratic political process is not the method by which we conduct trials, it is not what prevails within a jail or around it, and where it does not prevail, the First Amendment should not protect speech that in other circumstances would be protected. Faculties that just a few years ago felt embarrassed to exclude students from their deliberations might have remembered that. A university is also not governed by the democratic political process. And of course we recognize times when that process is suspended even in places where ordinarily it does rule. Hence curfews, hence martial law.

In approaching the other and greater difficulty—unacceptable results that the political process, with free speech as a principal component, might reach, or unacceptable acts that speech might counsel its hearers to engage in—one wants to be extremely careful not to be understood as following the teaching of Herbert Marcuse. But that does not mean that the problem shouldn't be stated and faced. Take, for example, the advocacy—not the intentional incitement, which the clear-and-present-danger test does allow us to reach—but the advocacy of genocide. Or, to recall what is more familiar, suppose, more minimally, a speech as in Beauharnais v. Illinois, decided in 1952, which urged the segregation of Negroes on the ground that they are all given to rape, robbery, knives, guns, and marijuana. Or the speech in Brandenburg v. Ohio, decided in 1969: "I believe the nigger should be returned to Africa, the Jew returned to Israel." Or the speech in a case of the early 1950's, Kunz v. New York: "All the garbage that didn't believe in Christ should have been burnt in the incinerators. It's a shame they all weren't." Or Jerry Rubin urging the young to go home and kill their parents, or other talk looking with favor on murder, rape, fire, and destruction.

Writing in Kunz v. New York, not long after his experience as prosecutor at the Nuremberg trials, the late Justice Robert H. Jackson said: "Essential freedoms are today threatened from without and within. It may become difficult to preserve here what a large part of the world has lost—the right to speak, even temperately, on matters vital to spirit and body. In such a setting, to blanket hateful and hate-stirring attacks on races and faiths under the protections for freedom of speech may be a noble innovation. On the other hand, it may be a quixotic tilt at windmills which belittles great principles of liberty. Only time can tell. But I incline to the latter view. . . ."

Passing for the moment the question whether there are greater dangers in trying to define and control the sort of speech I have been reciting than in risking that it will achieve the results it advocates, one may allow such speech on one of two premises: either the cynical premise that words don't matter, that they make nothing happen and are too trivial to bother with; or else on the premise taken by Justice Brandeis in Whitney v. California that "discussion affords ordinarily adequate protection against the dissemination of noxious doctrine."

As to the first premise, it is inconsistent with the idea of a First Amendment; if speech doesn't matter, we might as well suppress it, because it is sometimes a nuisance. As to the second, we have lived through too much to believe it. To be sure, Justice Brandeis adhered to the clear-and-present-danger test, and conceded, therefore, that in circumstances of emergent danger we can stop speech. But we know, as Justice Brandeis may have allowed himself to forget, that speech can attain unacceptable ends even if it does not have the qualities of incitement, and even if it comes from people who lack the intent to achieve those ends.

Disastrously, unacceptably noxious doctrine can prevail, and can be made to prevail by the most innocent sort of advocacy. Holmes recognized as much in the passage in the Gitlow dissent in which he said that every ideal is an incitement. He went on: "Eloquence may set fire to reason." In the Gitlow case itself he saw neither incitement nor eloquence, and no chance of present conflagration, no clear and present danger. Yet he did admit that all ideas were an incitement and that they carried the seed of future dangers as well as benefits. His answer was this: "If in the long run the beliefs expressed in proletarian dictatorship are destined to be accepted by the dominant forces of the community, the only meaning of free speech [—the only—] is that they should be given their chance and have their way."

If in the long run the belief, let us say, in genocide is destined to be accepted by the dominant forces of the community, the only meaning of free speech is that it should be given its chance and have its way. Do we believe that? Do we accept it?

Even speech which advocates no idea can have its consequences. It may inflict injury by its very utterance, as the Court said a generation ago, in the Chaplinsky case, of lewd or profane or fighting words. More, and equally important, it may create a climate, an environment in which conduct and actions that were not possible before become possible. It is from this point of view that the decision in the Watts case, in which the Court passed off as political hyperbole an expressed intention to shoot the president, is perhaps dubious. We have been listening for years now—the level of it in the universities is happily on the decline—to countless apocalyptic pronouncements and to filthy and violent rhetoric and have dealt with them as speech, as statements of a position, of one side of an issue, to which we may respond by disagreeing, while necessarily accepting by implication the legitimacy of the statement, the right of the speaker to make it.

To listen to something on the assumption of the speaker's right to say it is to legitimate it. There is a story—I cannot vouch for its accuracy, but I found it plausible—of a crowd gathered in front of the ROTC building at a university some years ago. At this university, as elsewhere in this time, some members of the faculty and administration had undertaken to discharge the function of cardinal legate to the barbarians, going without the walls, every so often, to negotiate the sack of the city. On this occasion, with the best of intentions, members of the faculty joined the crowd and participated in discussing the question whether or not to set fire to the building. The faculty, I gather, took the negative, and I assume that none of the students arguing the affirmative could have been deemed guilty of inciting the crowd. The matter was ultimately voted upon, and the affirmative lost—narrowly. But the negative taken by the faculty was only one side of a debate which the faculty rendered legitimate by engaging in it. Where nothing is unspeakable, nothing is undoable.

This is also the problem with obscenity. The question about obscenity is not whether books get girls pregnant, or sexy or violent movies turn men to crime. To view it in this way is to try to shoehorn the obscenity problem into the clear-and-present-danger analysis, and the fit is a bad one. Books, let us assume, do not get girls pregnant: at any rate, there are plenty of other efficient causes of pregnancy, as of crime. We may assume further that it is right to protect privacy, and that we have no business, therefore, punishing anyone for amusing himself obscenely in his home. But the question is, should there be a right to obtain obscene books and pictures in the market, or to foregather in public places—discreet, but accessible to all—with others who share a taste for the obscene? To grant this right is to affect the world about the rest of us, and to impinge on other privacies and other interests, as those concerned with the theater in New York have found, apparently to their surprise. Perhaps each of us can, if he wishes, effectively avert the eye and stop the ear. Still, what is commonly read and seen and heard and done intrudes upon us all, wanted or not, for it constitutes our environment.

The problem is no different from that raised by the physical environment, or by indecent exposure, by boisterous drunkenness, rampant prostitution, or public lovemaking. Yet the same Supreme Court which during the past decade has decreed virtually unlimited permissiveness with regard to obscenity has not construed the Constitution so as to forbid the placing of legal restraints on architectural designs, for example, or on indecencies of public behavior. Nor is the Court very likely to tell us that fostering heterosexual marriage while not countenancing homosexual unions, which is what the legal order does, of course, is unconstitutional. The assigned reason is that the First Amendment throws special safeguards around speech and other forms of communication, which are relevant to obscenity, but does not protect conduct. But the point is absurd. There is no bright line between communication and conduct. The effect, in the segment of both that we are here considering, is surely the same. What is a live sex show, communication or conduct?

I state these problems without having a general solution to offer. They are uninhibited, robust, and intractable, although so far as obscenity, at least, is concerned, the Supreme Court could well have permitted some inhibitions of the robuster forms of it without needing to confront the ultimately intractable dilemma I shall pose presently. The argument for resolving these problems by extending protection to speech except as the clear-and-present-danger formula would authorize very limited suppression is stated by Holmes in the dissent in Abrams v. New York: "Persecution for the expression of opinions seems to me perfectly logical. If you have no doubt of your premises or your power and want a certain result with all your heart you naturally express your wishes in law and sweep away all opposition." To allow opposition by speech, Holmes continues, indicates either that you think the speech does not matter, or that you doubt your power or your premises. He goes on: "But when men have realized that time has upset many fighting faiths, they may come to believe even more than they believe the very foundations of their own conduct that the ultimate good desired is better reached by free trade in ideas—that the best test of truth is the power of the thought to get itself accepted in the competition of the market, and that truth is the only ground upon which their wishes safely can be carried out." This is the point at which one asks whether the best test of the idea of proletarian dictatorship, or segregation, or genocide is really the marketplace, whether our experience has not taught us that even such ideas can get themselves accepted there, and that a marketplace without rules of civil discourse is no marketplace of ideas, but a bullring.

The theory of the truth of the marketplace, Holmes concluded, expressing, one may believe, more his own view than that of the Philadelphia Convention, "is the theory of our Constitution. It is an experiment, as all life is an experiment." But the theory of the truth of the marketplace, determined ultimately by a count of noses—this total relativism cannot be the theory of our Constitution, or there would be no Bill of Rights in it and certainly no Supreme Court to enforce it. It amused Holmes to pretend that if his fellow citizens wanted to go to hell in a basket, he would help them. It was his job, he said. Sometimes he did, to be sure, and sometimes it was his job as a judge. But not his sole job, and not always. And Holmes knew that, too. He had what he called his "can't helps," and he knew that the framers of the Constitution had had theirs, and somewhere in the combination of his "can't helps,"—of the framers', of his fellow judges', and of those of other leaders of opinion—were to be found the values to the society. If his fellow citizens wanted to consign these values to hell, perhaps they could do so, but it was not Holmes's job to help them.

"I do not know what is true," said Holmes. "I do not know the meaning of the universe." His biographer, the late Mark DeWolfe Howe, wondered whether our stomachs are "strong enough to accept the bitter pill which Holmes tendered us." They had better be, no doubt. We had better recognize how much a random confusion is human activity, and that there is no final validity to be claimed for truths. If we allow ourselves to be engulfed in moral certitudes we will march to self-destruction from one Vietnam and one domestic revolution—sometimes Marcusean and often not—to another. But we do need, individually and as a society, some values, some belief in the foundations of our conduct, in order to make life bearable. If they, too, are lies, they are, as Holmes's great contemporary, Joseph Conrad, thought them, true lies; if illusions, then indispensable ones. To abandon them is to commit moral suicide.

Yet whom are we to trust as the custodians and enforcers of those few beliefs which constitute the foundations of our conduct? Passing majorities of the moment? That is the marketplace, which the First Amendment may enjoin us to guard, but not to trust, certainly not to trust to govern access to itself. Whom then? Electorally irresponsible courts? It is one thing to rely on them to keep the marketplace open, another to permit them to close it, even though we do trust our courts to guard some values against majoritarian subversion. We have no answer to these questions, and that is the real reason why we prefer, so often, to err on the side of permissiveness. But we should know also that we err—on the right side, perhaps, but we err.

Actually, ambiguity and ambivalence, not the theory of the truth of the marketplace, as Holmes would have had us think, is, if not the theory, at any rate the condition of the First Amendment in the law of our Constitution. Nothing is more characteristic of the law of the First Amendment—not the rhetoric, but the actual law of it—than the Supreme Court's resourceful efforts to cushion rather than resolve clashes between the First Amendment and interests conflicting with it. The Court's chief concern has been with process, with procedural compromises (using the term in a large sense), and with accommodations that rely on the separation and diffusion of power. A great deal of freedom of speech can flourish in a democratic society which naturally shares, or accepts from its judges or other pastors, a minimal definition of the good, the beautiful, the true, and the properly civil. A great deal of freedom of speech can flourish as well, for a time, at any rate, in a society which accepts the proposition of bullring, or marketplace, truth. We are neither society. We have tended to resemble the latter, of late, and we have more freedom than the former might enjoy, and than we enjoyed in the 19th century, but we are actually more nearly the former. Freedom of speech, with us, is a compromise, an accommodation. There is nothing else it could be.

The devices of compromise and accommodation that are perhaps in commonest use go by the names of vagueness and overbreadth. The Court will not accept infringements on free speech by administrative or executive action, and if the infringement occurs pursuant to a statute, the Court will demand that the statute express the wish of the legislature in the clearest, most precise, and narrowest fashion possible. Essentially what the Court is exacting is assurance that the judgment that speech should be suppressed is that of the full, pluralist, open political process, not of someone down the line, representing only one or another particular segment of the society—and assurance that the judgment has been made closely and deliberately, with awareness of the consequences and with clear focus on the sort of speech that the legislature wished to suppress.

An accommodation relying on the diffusion and separation of powers is what the Pentagon Papers-New York Times case also amounts to in the end. Not long after the case was decided, in September, 1971, the president invoked what is called *executive privilege* to deny the Senate Foreign Relations Committee access to certain documents bearing on long-range plans for foreign military assistance. This was but one of numerous invocations of executive privilege, on the part of this and previous presidents, and whatever the merits of this particular invocation of it, there is little doubt of the president's authority, in general, to safeguard the privacy of executive deliberations by classifying documents and withholding them from Congress, and of course from the public. Yet under the New York Times case, if a newspaper had got hold of these documents without itself participating in a theft of them, although somebody else might to its knowledge have stolen them, it could have published them with impunity. And if someone stole these documents and brought them to Senator Fulbright, he could use them and read them on the floor of the Senate if he chose, thus making them public, and there would be no recourse against him because of the immunity the Constitution grants to members of Congress in respect of statements on the floor, or for the matter of that, in committee.

Now this, to say the least, is a paradox. The government is entitled to keep things private, but with few exceptions involving the highest probability of very grave consequences, it may not do so effectively. It is severely limited as to means, being restricted, by and large, to enforcing security at the source. Members of Congress as well as the press may publish materials that the government wishes to, and is entitled to, keep private. It is a disorderly situation surely. But if we ordered it, we would have to sacrifice one of two contending values—privacy or public discourse—which are ultimately irreconcilable. If we should let the government censor as well as withhold, that would be too much dangerous power, and too much privacy. If we should allow the government neither to censor nor to withhold, that would provide for too little privacy of decision making, and too much power in the press and in Congress. So we are content with the pulling and hauling, because in it lies the maximum assurance of both privacy and freedom of information. Not full assurance of either, but maximum assurance of both.

Madison knew the secret of this disorderly system, indeed he invented it. The secret is the separation and balance of powers, men's ambition joined to the requirements of their office so that they push those requirements to the limit, which in turn is set by the contrary requirements of another office, joined to the ambition of other men. This is not an arrangement whose justification is efficiency, logic, or clarity. Its justification is that it accommodates power to freedom and vice versa. It reconciles the irreconcilable.

Madison's conception of the separation and diffusion of powers was intragovernmental, but the First Amendment, as the Pentagon Papers case demonstrated, extends it beyond government, so that it prevails not only among the institutions of government but also between them and the private sector. The First Amendment offers us no formula describing the degree of freedom of information that is consistent with necessary privacy of government decision making. Rather as the Supreme Court applied it, it ordains an unruly contest between the press, whose office is freedom of information and whose ambition is joined to that office, and government, whose need is often the privacy of decision making, and whose servants are ambitious to satisfy that need. This is not to say that we can get along without any restraint or self-discipline on the part of government and the press in the discharge of their respective offices and in the ambitious pursuit by each of its interest. Not at all. But it is the contest that serves the interest of society as a whole, which identifies neither with the interest of the government alone, nor of the press.

The upshot in our system is that a whole series of defensive procedural entrenchments and an obstacle course of the diffusion of powers and functions lie between the First Amendment and claims adverse to it. Hence the direct, ultimate confrontation is rare, and when it does occur, limited and manageable. We thus contrive to avoid most judgments that we do not know how to make.

Living with Free Speech: A Response to Alexander M. Bickel

Norman Podhoretz

Whenever I am forced as I have been by Alexander M. Bickel to think seriously about freedom of speech and the problems it poses, I instantly find myself getting depressed. I tend to take an absolutistic position on freedom of speech, roughly on the ground that restricting it seems on the whole to entail more odious consequences than letting it run entirely wild. Yet I know that the absolutist position is very hard to uphold against the arguments Mr. Bickel recites. And not only is the absolutist position highly vulnerable on the theoretical plane; it is increasingly hard to defend wholeheartedly in the face of certain of its concrete results, the most vivid of which is the spread of hard-core pornography. As it happens, I myself am not as troubled by this particular phenomenon as many libertarians are, but I do have my own favorite horrible examples. The main one is the truly astonishing privilege enjoyed since the Sullivan case by the press and television to libel with impunity, to lie with impunity, and with equal impunity to invade the privacy of anyone whose privacy they choose to invade.

Being a writer and a magazine editor, I share in that privilege and perhaps I should be grateful for it. Nevertheless, I cannot help wondering why the media should be entitled to unchecked power when no other institution, whether public or private, is deemed by any respectable body of opinion to be so entitled. Indeed, the very people who protest most loudly against any attempt by the government to interfere with the freedom of newspapers or

Norman Podhoretz graduated from Columbia University in 1950 and at the same time secured a B.H.L. degree from the Jewish Theological Seminary. He has also studied at Hamilton College and Cambridge University. At the present time he is editor-in-chief of *Commentary*, a magazine published by the National Jewish Committee.

He is the author of the *Commentary Reader, Making It*, and *Doings and Undoings, the Fifties and After*. New York City is his home.

television networks to say or do whatever it may please—or profit!—them to do are also the ones most loudly demanding that the government should interfere more and more with the freedom of other private corporations to do whatever it may please or profit *them* to do.

I very much doubt that this contradiction can be resolved satisfactorily in theory. But of course an American need not resolve it in theory; he need only cite the First Amendment—"Congress shall make no law . . . abridging the freedom of speech, or of the press"—and he need only point out that no similar prohibition so unambiguously protects the freedom of any other economic enterprise. The *New York Times,* in short, is protected, but General Motors is not. And, in truth, in the presence of such plain language as the First Amendment uses, there is no escaping the force of the late Hugo Black's famous insistence that when the Constitution says "Congress shall make no law . . . abridging the freedom of speech, or of the press," it means that Congress shall make no law abridging the freedom of speech, or of the press.

As Mr. Bickel shows, there were restrictions on freedom of speech that even Black was willing to impose, not because he was a hypocrite or more than ordinarily inconsistent, but because it is virtually impossible to tolerate absolute freedom of speech under any and all circumstances. Still, no sooner does one acknowledge this than the inexorable clarity of that language rises up to haunt one again: "Congress shall make no law . . . abridging the freedom of speech, or of the press." What can be done with words like these? When in another clause of the First Amendment the Constitution forbids "an establishment of religion," or when in the Eighth Amendment it prohibits "cruel and unusual punishment," the way is left wide open to judicial interpretation. Does federal aid to parochial schools violate the prohibition against an establishment of religion or not? Is the death sentence for murder cruel and unusual punishment or not? The answers are by no means obvious, and both the negative and the positive are reasonably consistent with the language of the Constitution. But no such vagueness attaches to the clause dealing with freedom of speech and the press. Thus although there are good reasons for restricting those freedoms under certain circumstances—in wartime, for example, or in Holmes's crowded theater where, he decreed, the First Amendment does not protect the right to cry "Fire!"—the words of the Constitution themselves cannot be convincingly read to admit of any restriction.

It would seem to me, then, that so long as we continue to honor the First Amendment, we will continue to be burdened as a political community with more freedom of speech than may well be good for us to live with, assuming that it is even humanly possible. In this respect Americans, commanded to accept absolute freedom of speech, may be compared with Christians commanded to turn the other cheek: neither can succeed in obeying but both are required to try, and both will be led uneasily into casuistry whenever it becomes necessary to sin against the clear sense of the injunction.

However, precisely because we must try to be absolutists where freedom of speech is concerned, it is all the more important to maintain as firm a distinction as we can between speech and other forms of behavior not singled out by the Constitution for privileged protection. Mr. Bickel is certainly right when he observes that the effort to draw "a bright line between communication and conduct" often falls into absurdity. But surely there *is* a line in reality between verbal and nonverbal behavior, wavering and fuzzy though it may generally be. To hurl an obscenity at a policeman, for instance, is speech; to hurl a rock at him is not and neither is spitting in his face. Yet we hear it claimed on the one side that the First Amendment does not extend to the former, and we hear it claimed on the other side that actions like the latter are a kind of speech and hence protected by the First Amendment. Well, distinctions can always be blurred, but I for one would like to see more energy devoted by the courts and everyone else to keeping the line between verbal and nonverbal behavior clear even if, as Mr. Bickel says, there can never be any hope of always keeping it bright.

Obscenity Law and the Supreme Court

Paul J. McGeady

I. Introduction

On June 21, 1973, the Supreme Court of the United States handed down a landmark decision establishing new guidelines in the area of obscenity legislation and control. The key case was Miller v. California (41 L.W. 4925). Hereafter, whenever obscenity control laws are discussed on countless TV shows, in books and magazines, in law journals, as well as in ordinary conversation—the focus will be on Miller, just as before it was on Roth, the previous landmark decision in 1957 which had such a great impact on obscenity law in America. Rather than start with a discussion of Miller, I prefer to relegate the new court opinions to their chronological point in time, at the end of the discussion, in order to help the reader better understand their true meaning by first reviewing the prior history and cases from which they emerged.

I will attempt to make this chapter meaningful to both those versed in the law (hence a number of footnotes and references have been included*) as well as to the ordinary layman.

Laws controlling obscenity represent a fascinating study of our legal fabric because, to a great extent, they are a reflection of our values and moral

Paul J. McGeady is an attorney in New York City. He is a member of the New York State and American Bar Associations. He was appointed by former Mayor Wagner to a commission to study the problem of pornography in New York City. McGeady is a graduate of Fordham University Law School.

*Two sources for the reference material in this chapter, available at university law schools, in law offices, and in many urban libraries are 1) West Publishing Company Reporter System and 2) The Lawyers' Cooperative Publishing Company Supreme Court Reports.

customs, which are now going through a period of great challenge and change. Both legislation and judicial rulings in this area have, with great frequency, been marked by ambiguity, confusion, contradictions, and much controversy. So let's first look at what the law was before the Miller case.

II. The Rule before Miller

The Law proscribed obscenity. The difficulty was in defining it, or more properly—in understanding the definition. Yet, the definition of obscene material, as given to us by the United States Supreme Court in the case of Roth v. United States[1], appeared reasonably clear. Roth said:

> "Obscene Material is material
> which deals with sex in a manner
> appealing to prurient interest."

The Court assists those of us who may have difficulty with the phrase, "material . . . appealing to *prurient* interest" by telling us in a footnote that this means "material having a tendency to excite lustful thoughts."[2]

Now, it appears quite obvious to all of us that there has been a plethora of material meeting this definition, available, displayed, sold, and viewed in the last five years. How could this be if the Supreme Court said such material was obscene and illegal? To answer that question, we shall have to begin at the beginning, go on to the end, and then stop. In our progression we shall observe that the Supreme Court set out a ruler in Roth in 1957 to measure obscenity to conform to its definition. This ruler was successfully applied by the courts and legislatures until 1966 when the Fanny Hill[3] case was decided. In that case, three of the Justices attempted to add a new dimension to the Roth rules not present in the original case. This was the suggestion that in addition to prurient interest appeal, the jury or judge must separately determine that the disputed material was "utterly without redeeming social value." While there was no Court opinion in Fanny Hill and while the opinion of three out of nine justices creates no law,[4] many lower courts and legislators were misled into believing that it was a Supreme Court opinion and that this new dimension was a necessary, constitutional part of the Roth test. Since only a "modicum" of social value was required, those who desired to create an obscene work or motion picture and stay within the law needed only add a dash of "value" to redeem it. Such an approach to obscenity, quite obviously would, and almost did, effectively scuttle Roth and any effective control of obscenity.

1. 354 U.S. 476, 1 L. Ed. 2d. 1498 (1957)
2. F.N. 20. 354, U.S. 487, 1 L. Ed. 2d 1508 (1957)
3. *Memoirs of a Woman of Pleasure* v. Attorney General of Massachusetts, 383 U.S. 413, 16 L. Ed. 2d 1. (1966)
4. Cf. F.N. 12, infra.

III. The Hicklin Test

Until interred by Roth in 1957, many of the American courts had adopted the test for obscenity set down by the English Courts in Reginia v. Hicklin. In that case, the Court stated:

The test of obscenity is this, whether the tendency of the matter charged as obscene is to deprave and corrupt those whose minds are open to such immoral influences, and into whose hands a publication of this sort may fall.[5]

As we shall see, this rule was later considered incompatible with the freedom of expression permitted in the United States and was gradually eroded during the period 1933 through 1957. While it was in effect, however, and without evaluating other influences, the United States, it would appear, was a remarkably "clean" country.[6] This can also be observed from the number of reported obscenity decisions during the last 100 years.

From 1870 to 1929, approximately two obscenity cases were reported in the law books per year. In 1970, more than 70 cases were reported. This is an increase of over 3,000%.

The Hicklin rule, as may be observed, was attuned to the most susceptible person and could be violated by the presence of isolated passages or episodes of erotica. The first judge to seriously question its continued applicability was Judge Learned Hand, in United States v. Kennerly,[7] a 1913 Federal District Court case. In that case, while applying the Hicklin rule, Judge Hand asked rhetorically, "Should not the word obscene be allowed to indicate the present critical point in the compromise between candor and shame at which the community may have arrived here and now?"

In 1930 in United States v. Dennett,[8] it was held that serious instruction relating to sex matters did not violate the federal obscenity statute.

It was not until the case of United States v. One Book Called Ulysses, however, that the validity of Hicklin was directly contradicted. In that case, the Federal District Court in 1933 stated that the appeal to lust would not be judged by its effect on the most susceptible person (such as a child) but, "on a person with average sex instincts." On affirming this case, on appeal in 1934, the Circuit Court further repudiated as much of the Hicklin rule that permitted the work to be condemned solely because of isolated passages and stated:

5. L. R. 3 Q. B. 360 (1868)
6. "American Literature has been fairly clean"—statement of N.Y. Ct. of Appeals, Judge Cran, in Halsey v. N.Y. Society for the Suppression of Vice. 234 N.Y. 14 (1922)
7. 209 F. 119 (1913)
8. 39 F. 2d 564 (2d Cir.) (1930)

The question in each case is whether the publications, taken as a whole, have a libidinous effect ... the effect of the book as a whole is the test ... we believe the proper test of whether a book is obscene is its dominant effect.[9]

In 1954, American Civil Liberties Union v. Chicago quoted the cases which had rejected the Hicklin rule and applied them to motion pictures:

We hold ... that a motion picture is obscene ... if when considered as a whole, its calculated purpose or dominant effect is substantially to arouse sexual desires, and if the probability of this effect is so great as to outweigh whatever artistic or other merits the film may possess. In making this determination the film must be tested with reference to its effect upon the normal, average person. ...[10]

IV. The Roth Case

Roth v. United States and Alberts v. California were two appeals heard together and decided on June 24, 1957.[11] Roth was charged with violating the Federal Act and Alberts the state statute. Roth and Alberts both contended that obscenity was protected free speech. A *majority* of the Supreme Court voiced its opinion through Justice Brennan, who, quoting from a prior Supreme Court case, said:

There are certain well-defined and narrowly limited classes of speech, the prevention and punishment of which have never been thought to raise a constitutional problem. These include the lewd and obscene. ... It has been well observed that such utterances are no essential part of any exposition of ideas, and are of such slight social value as a step to truth that any benefit that may be derived from them is clearly outweighed by the social interest in order and morality.

The Court then set down the test for obscenity as follows:

Whether to the average person, applying contemporary community standards, the dominant theme of the material taken as a whole appeals to the prurient interest.

The Court indicated in a footnote that it formulated its test from the later cases including *Ulysses* and the American Civil Liberties Union.

9. 5 F. Supp. 182, Affld. 72 F. 2d 705 (2d Cir.) (1934)
10. 121 N.E. 2d 585 (Sup. Ct. Ill) (1954)
11. Note 1, supra.

The Court then specifically approved the lower court's charge to the jury in Roth on the test for obscenity:

... the test is not whether it would arouse sexual desires or sexual impure thoughts in those comprising a particular segment of the community, the young, the immature or the highly prudish or would leave another segment, the scientific or highly educated or the so-called worldly-wise and sophisticated, indifferent and unmoved ... the test in each case is the effect of the books, pictures and circulars upon all those whom it is likely to reach. In other words, you determine its impact upon the average person in the community. The books, pictures and circulars must be judged as a whole in their entire context, and you are not to consider detached or separate portions in reaching a conclusion. You judge the circulars, pictures and publications ... by present-day standards of the community. You may ask yourself does it offend the common conscience of the community by present-day standards of the community; ... in determining that conscience you are to consider the community as a whole, young and old, educated and uneducated, the religious and irreligious—men, women and children.

The Roth case told us that the test for judging a publication was as follows:

(1) It is to be viewed as if it were judged by the person in the community who is designated as the average person.

(2) Assuming such a person viewed it, he must apply the moral standards of the community as to whether there is a permissible or shameful depiction of sexuality.

(3) If it is by such standards a shameful depiction of sexuality, does the dominant theme of the material judged as a whole appeal to pruriency?

If when so viewed and so judged the dominant effect does appeal to pruriency, then it is obscene and may be proscribed.

In its discussion of the fact that obscenity (while an utterance) was not protected under the First Amendment, the Court stated:

All ideas having the slightest social importance ... have the full protection of the guaranties ... But, implicit in the history of the First Amendment is the rejection of obscenity as utterly without redeeming social importance.

This passing statement was seized upon by some of the Supreme Court Justices in the cases subsequent to Roth and was the cause of an unfortunate twisting of the meaning of Roth by some other judges and courts.

This twisting of meaning arose by requiring in those cases that the trier of the fact find (in addition to the test set down in Roth) as an additional test that the material was "utterly without redeeming social value." Roth, however, stood for the proposition that once such material was found obscene under Roth, it was deemed to be inherently without social importance without further inquiry. It is without social importance *because* it meets the definition of what is obscene propounded in Roth.

V. Fanny Hill

This was a 1966 case properly known as: A Book Named *Memoirs of a Woman of Pleasure* v. Attorney General of Massachusetts.

In a proceeding instituted in a Massachusetts state court by the State Attorney General, the book commonly known as "Fanny Hill" was declared obscene. On appeal, the Supreme Court reversed this ruling. The Court Reporter, at 16 L. Ed. 2d 1, states:

The . . . members of the Court . . . did not agree upon an opinion [emphasis supplied].

Justices Brennan, Warren, and Fortas stated that the Massachusetts court erred in holding that a book need not be "unqualifiedly worthless before it can be deemed obscene," and they qualified their opinion: (16 L. Ed. 2d 5)

Three elements must coalesce: it must be established that (a) the dominant theme of the material taken as a whole appeals to a prurient interest in sex; (b) the material is patently offensive because it affronts contemporary community standards relating to the description or representation of sexual matters and (c) the material is utterly without redeeming social value. . . .

Even on the view of the court below, that Memoirs possessed only a modicum of social value, its judgment must be reversed [emphasis supplied].

Justice Clark's opinion appears at 16 L. Ed. 2d 18:

While there is no majority opinion in this case, there are three justices who import a new test into that laid down in Roth [emphasis supplied] *namely that "a book cannot be proscribed unless it is found to be utterly without redeeming social value." I agree with my Brother White that such a condition rejects the basic holding of Roth and gives the smut artist free rein to carry on his dirty business. My vote in that case—which was the deciding one for the majority opinion—was cast solely because the Court declared the test of obscenity to be: "whether to the average person, applying contemporary community standards, the dominant theme of the material taken as a whole appeals to prurient interest." I understood that test to include only two constitutional requirements: (1) the book must be judged as a whole, not by its parts; and (2) it must be judged in terms of its appeal to the prurient interest of the average person, applying contemporary community standards.*

Indeed, obscenity was denoted in Roth as having "such slight social value as <u>*a step to truth that any benefit that may be derived . . . is clearly outweighed*</u> <u>*by the social interest in order and morality"*</u> [emphasis supplied by Justice Clark]. *Moreover, in no subsequent decision of this court has any "utterly without redeeming social value" test been suggested much less expounded. The first reference to such a test was made by my Brother Brennan in* <u>*Jacobelis v. Ohio*</u> *. . . seven years after Roth in an opinion joined only by Justice Goldberg. . . .*

Justice White, in his opinion at 16 L. Ed. 2d 29, stated:

In <u>*Roth v. United States*</u> *. . . the Court held a publication to be obscene if its predominant theme appeals to the prurient interest in a manner exceeding customary limits of candor. Material of this kind, the Court said, is "utterly without redeeming social importance" and is therefore unprotected by the First Amendment.*

To say that material within the Roth definition of obscenity is nevertheless not obscene if it has some redeeming social value is to reject one of the basic propositions of the Roth case—that such material is not protected because it is inherently and utterly without social value.

If "social importance" is to be used . . . obscene material, however far beyond customary limits of candor, is immune if it has any literary style, if it contains any historical references or language characteristic of a bygone day, or even if it is printed or bound in an interesting way. Well-written, especially effective obscenity is protected; the poorly written is vulnerable.

A fortiari, if the predominant theme of the book appeals to the prurient interest as stated in Roth, but the book nevertheless contains here and there a passage descriptive of character, geography, or architecture, the book would not be "obscene" under the social importance test. I had thought that Roth counseled the contrary: that the character of the book is fixed by its predominant theme and is not altered by the presence of minor themes of a different nature. The Roth court's emphatic reliance on the quotation from Chaplinsky . . . means nothing less:

<u>*"Such utterances are no essential part of any exposition of ideas, and are of*</u> <u>*such slight social value as a step to truth that any benefit that may be*</u> <u>*derived from them is clearly outweighed by the social interest in order and*</u> <u>*morality"*</u> [emphasis supplied by White].

In my view, "social importance" is not an independent test of obscenity but is relevant only to determine the predominant prurient interest of the ma-

terial, a determination which the court or the jury will make based on the material itself and all the evidence of the case, expert or otherwise.

Commissioners Morton A. Hill, Winfrey C. Link, and Charles H. Keating, Jr., of the President's Commission on Obscenity and Pornography, adopted the following commentary on Fanny Hill:

It is to be noted that there is no court opinion in Fanny Hill and the opinion of three judges out of nine does not constitute a precedent requiring any court or legislature to follow their suggestions. It is not the law of the land.

Where the members of the Court . . . reach a decision but cannot . . . by a majority agree on the reason; therefore, no point of law is established by the decision and it cannot be a precedent covered by the stare decisis rule.[12]

Roth, on the other hand, is a Supreme Court opinion and it does not use the social value phrase as part of its test for obscenity. Once the Roth test is applied to a disputed work and it is judged to be "obscene," then Roth conclusively presumes the material to be utterly without redeeming social importance. Roth says obscenity may have social value, but that value is outweighed by the social interest in morality. Three justices in Fanny Hill say if it has any social value, it is not obscene. This contradicts Roth in an essential manner and is in error. The charge to the jury approved in the Roth case did not have a "social value" or "social importance" test or phrase. Since Roth is still the only *Supreme Court opinion* focusing on the definition of obscenity, then no social value "test" need be given to any jury nor be made part of any statute. If it were a necessary charge, Roth would have insisted upon it.[13]

VI. Kois v. Wisconsin, a 1972 Reiteration of Pure Roth Test

While the Supreme Court has frequently indicated since 1957 that Roth is the standard, it did not until the Miller case (1973) directly face and excise the Fanny Hill accretion. The only real Supreme Court opinion *other than Miller* since Roth touching the fundamentals of its definition was the June, 1972, per curian opinion rendered in Kois v. Wisconsin[14] where the Court appeared to signal the acceptance of Justice White's statement in Fanny Hill:

---

12. 29 *Amer. Jurisprudence* 2d Sec. 195 "Courts", quoting U.S. v. Pink, 315 U.S. 203, 86 L. Ed. 796 (1941); to same effect is Hertz v. Woodward, 218 U.S. 205, 213-214.

13. *Cf.* The Report of the Commission on Obscenity and Pornography, pp. 449-450.

14. 92 S. Ct. 2245 (1972)

Social importance is not an independent test of obscenity, but is relevant only to determine the predominant prurient interest of the material.[15]

In Kois, the Court reiterated the pure Roth definition of obscenity without the Fanny Hill accretion and then said:

In this case, considering the poem's content . . . we believe that it bears some of the earmarks of an attempt at serious art. While such earmarks are not inevitably a guarantee against a finding of obscenity . . . this element must be considered in assessing whether the "dominant" theme of the material is to prurient interest . . .

We may conclude from this case that as Justice White says, "Social Importance" or "attempts at serious art" must be an element to be weighed in determining the dominant theme. Such an approach rejected the Brennan-Warren-Fortas Fanny Hill approach: 16 L. Ed. 2d 6:

The Supreme Judicial Court erred in holding that a book need not be "unqualifiedly worthless before it can be deemed obscene." A book cannot be proscribed unless it is found to be utterly without redeeming social value. . . . The social value of the book can neither be weighed against nor cancelled by its prurient appeal or patent offensiveness. Hence, even on the view of the Court below that Memoirs possessed only a modicum of social value, its judgment must be reversed. . . .

It seems plain that the Brennan-Warren-Fortas concept in Fanny Hill contradicted not only Roth, the first pronouncement of the Supreme Court, but also Kois its latest, prior to Miller.

It should also be noted that the Supreme Court in Roth quoted the American Civil Liberties Union case (referred to later in this writing), as a case that helped formulate its rule. In the American Civil Liberties case, the Court, as may be seen above, weighed the lustful arousal against artistry to determine dominant effect.

There were other pre-Miller Supreme Court cases since Roth other than Kois, but all of them were concerned with procedural questions or periferal areas of the definition. We appeared to be at the point where a reiteration and further clarification of Roth by the Supreme Court would restore some semblance of control over the obscenity problem. Kois v. Wisconsin signaled that intent.

15. See Justice White, above (Fanny Hill opinion)

VII. Supreme Court Consideration of Obscenity Problems Other Than the Definition of Obscenity

The problems that appeared on the docket of the United States Supreme Court at Miller time (1973) were a reflection of the panoply of difficulties and complexities surrounding this subject.

Among the questions awaiting clarification were the following:

1. When can the federal district courts intervene in state court proceedings?
2. Can advertising obscenity be proscribed?
3. Are community standards national, state, or local?
4. May materials found not obscene in other cases and jurisdictions be introduced for comparison?
5. May obscenity strictures be applied against consenting adults?
6. Must the prosecution introduce expert testimony on the elements of obscenity?
7. Can "obscene" speech be proscribed?
8. Are prior adversary hearings necessary before a film or other allegedly obscene material may be seized?
9. May nuisance statutes be applied to "adult" bookstores and motion picture theaters?
10. Is "social value" an independent test of obscenity?

At all events, many cases awaited decision. Some important ones involving "social value," "prior adversary hearings," "consenting adults," and "community standards" were argued and, ripe for decision, were on the top of the decision docket. They were eagerly awaited, but the momentous question was whether or not Roth, if reaffirmed in its pure form, was adequate to constitutionally inhibit the depiction of explicit graphic sex on TV, in motion pictures, and in magazines and books? There was a general turning toward Congress and the state legislature, and many thought that perhaps there the ultimate answer *might* be found. Before Congress could act, however, Miller was decided.

VIII. The New Tests for Obscenity: Miller v. California

On June 21, 1973, in a historic pronouncement, the Supreme Court of the United States decided to meet head-on the issue of defining obscenity in a manner that would minimize obscuration and misunderstanding and bring order out of the chaotic misconceptions prevailing in the post Fanny Hill period. That day it decided Miller v. California[16] and related cases and gave the United States a new frame of reference for deciding obscenity cases.

16. 41 L. W. 4925 (U.S. Sup. Ct. 1973)

These decisions will, without doubt, inhibit the flow of hard-core pornography and restore the right of the "community" to be protected if it chooses from offensive assaults on its standards of morality in the sexual field.

1. The New Standards

In the Miller case, Marvin Miller had been convicted of violating the Penal Code of the State of California in distributing obscene matter. Miller had conducted a mass mailing to advertise the sale of erotically illustrated books and was specifically convicted for having sent some of these unsolicited advertisements to a restaurant in Newport Beach, California. The brochures described four books and, while containing some printed matter, primarily consisted of pictures and drawings explicitly depicting men and women engaging in a variety of sexual activities, with genitals often prominently displayed.

Chief Justice Burger, speaking for a majority of the Court, spoke:

Since the Court now undertakes to formulate standards more concrete than those in the past, it is useful for us to focus on two of the landmark cases in the somewhat tortured history of the Court's obscenity decisions. In Roth v. United States, 354 U.S. 476 (1957) the Court sustained a conviction under a federal statute punishing the mailing of "obscene, lewd, lascivious, or filthy" materials. The key to that holding was the Court's rejection of the claim that obscene materials were protected by the First Amendment. Five justices joined in the opinion stating:

"*Implicit in the history of the First Amendment is the rejection of obscenity as utterly without redeeming social importance. . . . This is the same judgment expressed by this Court in Chaplinsky v. New Hampshire . . .*

'*that . . . such utterances are no essential part of any exposition of ideas, and are of such slight social value as a step to truth that any benefit that may be derived from them is clearly outweighed by the social interest in order and morality'* " [emphasis by Court in Roth opinion].

Nine years later in Memoirs v. Massachusetts, 383 U.S. 413 (1966), the Court veered sharply away from the Roth concept and with only three Justices in the plurality opinion, articulated a new test of obscenity. . . .

While Roth presumed "obscenity" to be "utterly without redeeming social value," Memoirs required that to prove obscenity it must be affirmatively established that the material is "utterly without redeeming social value." Thus even as they repeated the words of Roth, the Memoirs plurality pro-

duced a drastically altered test that called on the prosecution to prove a negative, i.e., that the material was "utterly without redeeming social value"—a burden virtually impossible to discharge under our criminal standards of proof. . . .

Apart from . . . Roth . . . no majority of the Court has at any given time been able to agree upon a standard. . . ."

The case we now review was tried on a theory that the California Penal Code . . . approximately incorporates the three stage Memoirs test. . . . But now the Memoirs test has been abandoned as unworkable by its author and no member of the court today supports the Memoirs formulation. . . .

We acknowledge . . . the inherent dangers of undertaking to regulate any form of expression. State statutes designed to regulate obscene materials must be carefully limited. . . .

As a result, we now confine the permissible scope of such regulation to works which depict or describe sexual conduct. That conduct must be specifically defined by the applicable state law as written or authoritatively construed.[17] A state offense must also be limited to works which taken as a whole appeal to the prurient interest in sex, which portray sexual conduct in a patently offensive way, and which, taken as a whole, do not have serious literary, artistic, political or scientific value.

The Supreme Court continued:

The basic guidelines for the trier of the fact must be: (a) whether "the average person, applying contemporary community standards" would find that the work, taken as a whole, appeals to the prurient interest, . . . (b) whether the work depicts or describes in a patently offensive way, sexual conduct specifically defined by the applicable state law, and (c) whether the

---

17. The Court here refers us to a footnote which says:

(See, e.g. Oregon Laws 1971, c 743, Art. 29 Sections 255-262 and Hawaii Penal Code, Title 37, Sections 1210-1216, 1972 Hawaii Session Laws pp. 126-129 Act. 90 II, as examples of state laws directed at depiction of defined physical conduct, as opposed to expression. Other state formulations could be equally valid in this respect. In giving the Oregon and Hawaii statutes as examples, we do not wish to be understood as approving of them in all respects nor as establishing their limits as the extent of the state power. We do not hold as Mr. Justice Brennan intimates, that all States other than Oregon must now enact new obscenity statutes. Other existing state statutes as construed heretofore or hereafter may well be adequate. See U.S. v. 12 200-ft. Reels (n. 7) (1973).

work, taken as a whole, lacks serious literary, artistic, political or scientific value. We do not adopt as a constitutional standard the "utterly without redeeming social value" test of Memoirs . . . ; that concept has never commanded the adherence of more than three justices at one time[18]. . . . If a state law that regulates obscene material is thus limited, as written or construed, the First Amendment values applicable to the States through the Fourteenth Amendment are adequately protected by the ultimate power of appellate courts to conduct an independent review of constitutional claims when necessary.

We emphasize that it is not our function to propose regulatory schemes for the States. That must await their concrete legislative efforts. It is possible, however, to give a few plain examples of what a state statute could define for regulation under the second part (b) of the standard . . . supra:

(a) Patently offensive representations or descriptions of ultimate sexual acts, normal or perverted, actual or simulated.

(b) Patently offensive representations or descriptions of masturbation, excretory functions, and lewd exhibitions of the genitals.

Sex and nudity may not be exploited without limit by films or pictures exhibited or sold in places of public accommodation any more than live sex and nudity can be exhibited or sold without limit in such public places. . . .[19]

Under the holdings announced today, no one will be subject to prosecution for the sale or exposure of obscene materials unless these materials depict or describe patently offensive "hard-core" sexual conduct specifically defined by the regulating state law as written or construed. . . .

2. The Relevant Community

The Court next discusses the meaning of the phrase "contemporary community standards" (41 L. W. 4929):

Under a national constitution, fundamental First Amendment limitations on the powers of the states do not vary from community to community, but

18. Court in footnote also says: "We also reject, as a constitutional standard, the ambiguous concept of 'social importance.' "
19. Court here refers to a footnote to say, "The states have greater power to regulate nonverbal, physical conduct than to suppress depictions or descriptions of the same behavior. . . ."

this does not mean that there are or should or can be fixed uniform national standards of precisely what appeals to the "prurient interest" or is "patently offensive." These are essentially questions of fact and our nation is simply too big and too diverse for this Court to reasonably expect that such standards could be articulated for all 50 states in a simple formulation, even assuming the prerequisite consensus exists. When triers of fact are asked to decide whether "the average person, applying contemporary community standards" would consider certain materials "prurient," it would be unrealistic to require that the answer be based on some abstract formulation. The adversary system, with lay jurors as the usual ultimate factfinders . . . has historically permitted triers-of-fact to draw on the standards of their community, guided always by limiting instructions on the law. To require a state to structure obscenity proceedings around evidence of a <u>national</u> "community standard" would be an exercise in futility. . . .

We conclude that neither the state's alleged failure to offer evidence of "national standards" nor the trial court's charge that the jury consider state community standards were constitutional errors. . . .

It is neither realistic nor constitutionally sound to read the First Amendment as requiring that the people of Maine or Mississippi accept public depiction of conduct found tolerable in Las Vegas or New York City. . . . People in different states vary in their tastes and attitudes and this diversity is not to be strangled by the absolution of imposed uniformity. . . . We hold that the requirement that the jury evaluate the materials with reference to "contemporary standards of the State of California" . . . is constitutionally adequate.

3. Commercial Exploitation of Obscene Material Is Not Commerce in Ideas

The First Amendment protects works which taken as a whole, have serious literary, artistic, political or scientific value regardless of whether the government or a majority of the people approve of the ideas these works represent. . . . "The protection given speech and press was fashioned to assure unfettered interchange of <u>ideas</u> for the bringing about of political and social changes desired by the people." But the public portrayal of hard-core sexual conduct for its own sake and for the ensuing commercial gain is a different matter.[20]

20. In its footnote the Court indicates that:

the petitioner was plainly engaged in the commercial exploitation of the morbid and shameful craving for materials with prurient effect.

The court also continued to recognize

. . . Mr. Justice Brennan finds "it is hard to see how state ordered regimenta-tion of our minds can ever be forestalled. . . ." These doleful anticipations assume that courts cannot distinguish commerce in ideas, protected by the First Amendment, from commercial exploitation of obscene material. . . .

In sum we (a) reaffirm the <u>Roth</u> holding that obscene material is not pro-tected by the First Amendment, (b) hold that such material can be regulated by the states, subject to the specific safeguards enunciated above, without a showing that the material is "<u>utterly</u> without redeeming social value" and (c) hold that obscenity is to be determined by applying "contemporary com-munity standards"; see <u>Kois v. Wisconsin</u> . . . and <u>Roth</u> . . . , not "national standards."

The Judgment of the Appellate Department of the Superior Court, Orange County, California is vacated and the case remanded to that Court for further proceedings not inconsistent with the First Amendment standards established by this opinion. See <u>United States v. 12 200-ft. Reels.</u> U.S. 1973 (P. 7 n. 7).

IX. Commentary on Miller v. California

1. The New Standards

The new standards for determining obscene material are as follows:
(a) It appeals to pruriency.
(b) It contains patently offensive descriptions or depictions of sexual conduct specifically defined by the applicable state law as written or construed.
(c) The work taken as a whole lacks serious literary, artistic, political, or scientific value.

Rejected are the so-called tests of "utterly without redeeming social value" and "utterly without redeeming social importance." While not made part of its standards (or test) for obscenity, the Court states that the ma-terials proscribed are materials that "depict or describe patently offensive 'hard-core' sexual conduct."

It is not clear from the court's decision whether or not it equates the phrase "patently offensive" with "hard-core." It could be so argued, since it did not include that phrase in its standards although enunciating them twice. Conversely, it could also be argued that the use of the word, *hard-core* later

that because of its strong and abiding interest in youth . . . a state may regulate the dissemination to juveniles of, and their access to, material objectionable to them, but which a state clearly could not regulate as to adults.

on in the case on two occasions would be redundant when used after the words *patently offensive,* unless they were words of modification, or unless the quote around "hard-core" serves the function of a bracket, i.e., [hard-core]. Unfortunately, the Court makes no attempt to clear up this ambiguity nor does it define "hard-core."[21]

2. *Appeal to Pruriency*

It is to be noted that the Court reiterated the Roth test relating to pruriency dropping the phrase "dominant theme." It can be assumed that it substituted the phrase "lacks serious literary, artistic, political or scientific value" for the dominant theme concept, since if it has such serious value, Miller will apparently assume that this constitutes a satisfactory substitute for the "dominant theme" concept. This result was in a sense foreshadowed by the Kois v. Wisconsin decision, above. The concept of "average person" is retained as in Roth, but Miller makes it clear that it means judged by the average person and also its "impact on the average person" (41 L. W. 4930). As previously indicated, this is the person with "average sex instincts."[22]

The contemporary community standards are spelled out as something less than national. The Court specifically permits state-wide standards and infers that more local standards would also be acceptable. (Quoting with approval, "Communities throughout the Nation" in Miller v. California.) In Miller the Court refers in a footnote to "local tastes" in reference to defining a community and reminds us of Chief Justice Warren's statement that "community" means "community" and not the nation. Miller has been widely interpreted as permitting local communities to make their own determinations under the new standards. It certainly admits of such interpretation. The local community (where less than state-wide) will probably be at the county level where a state statute is involved and a city, village, or town level where a local ordinance is being tested. The governing factor will probably be the area from which a jury is drawn, where a jury is utilized, or the area of jurisdiction of a municipal court in cases where juries may not be utilized.[23]

21. Three other places in the decision contain the phrase "hard-core": once to modify "sexual conduct" and twice to modify "pornography." These uses are inconclusive to assist us in making the distinctions above. There is a distinct possibility that the court meant that the coalescence of the three standards or tests produces "hard-core" pornography. In other words, the formula is (a) plus (b) plus (c) equals "hard-core pornography." See also footnote 7 in the case of *U.S. v. 12 200-ft. Reels,* infra.

22. Footnote 9, supra.

23. See Jones v. City of Birmingham, 224 So. 2d 922 (ct. App. ALA, 1969). See also Justice Warren's complete statement in Jacobellis v. Ohio, 378 U.S. 184 (1964) where he said (p. 201), "It is said that such a community approach may well result in material being proscribed as obscene in one community, but not in another, and in all probability, this is true. But, communities throughout the nation are diverse. . . ."

3. Patently Offensive Descriptions or Depictions

We have discussed above the possible coalescence of the terms "patently offensive" and "hard-core." We now propose to indicate the definition of patent offensiveness and attempt to fathom the concept of the phrase "sexual conduct specifically defined by the applicable state law as written or construed."

"Patent offensiveness" seems to be taken bodily from the opinion of Harlan and Stewart in Manual Enterprises v. Day:

These magazines cannot be deemed so offensive on their face as to affront current standards of decency—a quality that we shall hereafter refer to as "patent offensiveness" or "indecency". . . . Obscenity . . . requires proof of two distinct elements:

(1) "patent offensiveness" and
(2) "prurient interest" appeal

Both must conjoin before challenged material can be found obscene. . . . In most obscenity cases . . . the two elements tend to coalesce, for that which is patently offensive will usually carry the requisite prurient interest appeal.[24]

Patent offensiveness could easily be equated with the test approved in the Roth case of going "substantially beyond the limits of candor in description or representation." The California statute in Miller used this phrase, and yet the Supreme Court remanded for reconsideration, indicating that the California statute could be construed to meet the new guidelines.

The Court next suggests that the particular descriptions and depictions of sexual conduct must be defined by applicable state law as written or construed and it gives us some examples of types of sexual conduct which might be so specifically defined by state law.[25]

It also directs us to the Oregon and Hawaii statutes as examples of "state laws directed at depiction of defined physical conduct as opposed to expression." Pertinent parts of the Oregon and Hawaii statutes are set forth below.[26] It would appear that many of the descriptions used in the Oregon

---

24. 370 U.S. 478, 8 L. Ed. 2d 639 (1962)
25. See Discussion, supra, under VIII (1).
26. Oregon Laws of 1971, Chap. 743 reads in pertinent part as follows:

(9) "Sado-masochistic abuse" means flagellation or torture by or upon a person who is nude or clad in undergarments or in revealing or bizarre costume, or the condition of being fettered, bound or otherwise physically restrained on the part of one so clothed.

(10) "Sexual conduct" means human masturbation, sexual intercourse, or any touching

and Hawaii statutes could be used in addition to the examples given by the Court. A close question will be the extent to which nudity will be tolerated. The court has, in the past, indicated that nudity per se is not obscene but in the Miller case it goes out of its way to indicate that "nudity may not be exploited without limit by films or pictures exhibited or sold in places of public accommodation."

While to this point we have avoided quoting lower court cases and even though we perhaps will not know the meaning of "hard-core" in "close" nudity questions until the Supreme Court rules, it may perhaps be helpful to set forth below cases interpreting this phrase in relation to specified conduct.[27]

It seems clear that Miller will permit state courts to construe existing statutes in accordance with the new standards without amendment. Where a state has not built into its statute "social value" or "social importance" or

of the genitals, pubic areas or buttocks of the human male or female, or the breasts of the female, whether alone or between members of the same or opposite sex or between humans and animals in an act of apparent sexual stimulation or gratification.

Hawaii Act 9, Part II reads in pertinent part as follows:

(7) "Sexual conduct" means acts of masturbation, homosexuality, lesbianism, bestiality, sexual intercourse or physical contact with a person's clothed or unclothed genitals, pubic area, buttocks, or the breast or breasts of a female for the purpose of sexual stimulation, gratification, or perversion.

27. *People v. Stabile,* 296 N.Y.S. 2d 815, 821, 823 (N.Y. City Cr. Ct. 1969); *People v. Kaplan,* 252 N.Y.S. 2d 927, 930 (N.Y. City Cir. Ct. 1964); *Donnenberg v. State,* 232 A. 2d 264 (Md. Court of Spec. Aps. 1967); *State v. Lebewitz,* 202 N.W. 2d 648, 650 (Sup. Ct. Minn. 1972); *State v. Carlson,* 202, N.W. 2d 640, 646 (Sup. Ct. Minn. 1972); *Lancaster v. State,* 256 A. 2d 716, 720 (Ct. of Spec. Aps. Mod. 1969); *U.S. v. Wild,* 422 F. 2d 34, 35 (C.A. 2d Cir. 1970); *U.S. v. Koehler,* 353, F. Supp. 476 (U.S. Dist. Ct. N.D.-Iowa 1973). It is to be noted that in a long line of *Redrup* decisions (386 U.S. 767-1967), the Supreme Court refused to let convictions stand on graphic "girlie" magazines. The *Redrup* approach was specifically abandoned in *Miller.* However, on the accession of Justices Powell and Rehnquist to the Supreme Court on January 10, 1972, the *Redrup* approach had in effect been abandoned and in two cases of "girlie" magazines convictions for obscenity were upheld 6-3 over the objection of the minority that *Redrup* counselled otherwise. These cases were *Monger v. Florida* 249 So. 2d 433 (Sup. Ct. of Florida 1971) *Cert. Denied* U.S. Sup. Ct. 405 U.S. 958, 31 L. Ed. 2d 239 (2/28/72); and *McKinney v. Alabama,* 254 So. 2d 714, (Sup. Ct. Ala. 1971) (*Cert. Denied*) 405 U.S. 1073, 31 L. Ed. 2d 809 (4/17/72). The McKinney case is particularly important because it shows a type of nude exposure which the Supreme Court indicates may be constitutionally suppressed. The lower Court citation contains a description that may spell out the dividing line for the education of those who are deciding post *Miller* cases or preparing legislation to conform to *Miller.*

has eliminated it, there would appear to be no great difficulty. Where such phrases exist (as in California) and as in New York, Miller implies that a proper construction may be rendered. Miller tells us that Roth "presumes" that material which appeals to the prurient interest and goes beyond customary limits of candor (is patently offensive) is utterly without redeeming social value or social importance. It would appear, therefore, that "social value" or "social importance" even if erroneously built into a statute may be ignored if the other criteria are met since lack of such quality will conclusively be presumed.[28]

Those states that amend their statutes to incorporate a "laundry list" of patently offensive sexual acts to comply with Miller will no doubt insert a "saving clause" to the effect that if particular described sexual conduct is held to be lawful, such decision shall not vitiate the statute as to other described patently offensive sexual conduct.

It would also appear important that in amending a state statute, flexibility be provided for the court to "authoritatively construe" the statute so as to add to the "laundry list" additional "sexual conduct" which may not be presently anticipated by the legislator and which may be legalized by failure to include. For example, if a state statute simply proscribed "obscene works" and it contained in addition the "basic guidelines for the trier of the fact" as outlined above, and also under those guidelines indicated the guideline (b) would be "whether the work depicts or describes in a patently offensive way, sexual conduct specifically defined herein or "authoritatively construed" to be included under the phrase "an obscene work" then the state court would have sufficient flexibility to construe the phrase "an obscene work" to include other "patently offensive sexual conduct" not specifically described in the state law. If, however, the "laundry list" is exclusive and there is nothing to construe, then the state will be left only with the "sexual conduct" outlined in its "laundry list." See U.S. v. Thevis, 42 LW 2182 (5th Cir. 1973) in this regard.

4. Lack of Serious Literary, Artistic, Political, or Scientific Value

Here is the concept that will create the greatest difficulty in interpretation and application of the standards. To put it bluntly, the exception carves a hole big enough to drive a truck through and creates an incompleteness in

---

28. Since the decision in Miller, most of the state courts that have considered the matter have "authoritatively construed" their existing statutes as valid in the light of Miller. See State v. J.R. Distributors, Inc., 512 P. 2d 1049 (Wash. Sup. Ct. 1973); Commonwealth v. California, 298 N.E. 2d 888 (Mass. App. Ct. 1973); State ex rel Sensenbremer v. Adult Bookstore, 301 N.E. 2d 695 (Ohio Sup. Ct. 1973); People v. Enskat, 109 Cal. Rptr. 433 (Cal. Ct. Apps. 1973); see also U.S. v. Thevis 42 LW 2182 (5th Cir. 1973); and U.S. v. 1 Reel of Film, 481 F. 2d 206, (1st Cir. 1973).

the proposed statutory scheme which, unless remedied by future modifications, may make the whole scheme unworkable.

The serious value requirement, as previously indicated, appears to be an attempt to find a substitute for the "dominant theme" approach used in Roth. Miller has dropped this part of the Roth formulation. However, under Roth even if a work had serious value, that value was to be weighed against the erotica to determine its "dominant" theme. As Justice White said in Fanny Hill:

The character of the book is fixed by its predominant theme and is not altered by the presence of minor themes of a different nature. . . . "Social importance" . . . is relevant only to determine the predominant prurient interest of the material.

Now in the 1972 Kois v. Wisconsin decision, frequently cited in Miller, the Supreme Court said attempts at serious art:

must be considered in assessing whether the dominant theme of the material is to prurient interest.

If we have abandoned the "dominant theme" concept set out in Roth and Kois, cannot the dominant theme be prurient and sexually explicit and the subservient theme be artistic or political or literary and still be not obscene? Or, must we say that because the dominant theme is erotic and the work is prurient, then even though a subservient theme has some serious value, the work *taken as a whole* lacks serious value? In other words, does the phrase "taken as a whole" mean that the whole work must be of serious value and not just a minor theme? Will a minor theme or a portion thereof of the work that is artistic, political, or scientific supply the third ingredient? It is just not clear.[29] Literally any serious value, of the nature specified, in the work "taken as a whole" appears to launder the dirt. We wonder if the Court really meant it. Let us try to apply the concept not abstractly but in the concrete.

Literally, the quality of lack of serious value which obscenity must have means that even where you have pruriency (appeal to lust) and patently offensive "hard-core" sexual conduct specifically defined, it is legal to publish it or present it if the work has serious literary or artistic value. Let us now apply this concept to a form of media, for example television (in color). Does not the Supreme Court opinion say that you can present explicit hard-core sex or bestiality on TV if the "play" or "film" or "live performance" has literary or artistic value? It would appear that most

29. See Reference to S 1400, infra.

Americans obviously would not tolerate this. While they might tolerate these distinctions in books, magazines, or even motion pictures, they would not tolerate the concept that they must switch the dial to avoid such performances on TV or radio or that they must be concerned that their minor children may be exposed to the same.

From this exposition, it is quite obvious that different standards must be applied to TV, radio, and perhaps motion pictures. Television and radio communications certainly partake of the nature of a public access thoroughfare (albeit an electromagnetic one), and what may be prohibited on the public street should be equally prohibited on TV and radio. This includes undoubtedly all soft-core or hard-core sexual, explicit conduct as well as nudity. These programs come into the home, and under the doctrine of Breard v. Alexandria, 341 U.S. 622 (1951) the usual broad play afforded free speech may be curtailed.[30] This may be done by passage of a statute by the federal government (and where intra-state, by state governments) prohibiting offensive presentations on television and radio. It would not be necessary to prove such productions of explicit sex or nudity obscene in the abstract, just as it is not necessary to prove obscenity to prohibit nudity or seminudity in public. The new definition of obscenity cannot be practically or feasibly extended to TV or radio in its present form.

What is the quality in public nudity that permits the law to inhibit it without proof of obscenity? The same rationale would extend and does extend to an artistic, political, scientific, or literary production attempted to be played on the public street.

We suggest that the quality involved is "Intrusiveness" (as in Breard). Where this quality is present, obscenity *vel non* need not be proved. Just as a citizen is entitled to walk down the public street without the necessity of having to avert his eyes to avoid a public nude performance, so too he is entitled to "flip the dial" without viewing intrusive nudity or explicit hard-core sex. Is he supposed to review the program for 30 minutes or one hour to determine if the work "taken as a whole" has artistic, literary, political, or scientific value"? Most probably the Supreme Court did not intend this result[31] and is awaiting the opportunity to correct this deficiency as soon as a proper case in this area presents itself for adjudication. In the meantime, we are left with the anomaly.

X. Other June Obscenity Decisions of the U. S. Supreme Court

Since our main object has been to attempt to define obscenity from a

---

30. See also Stanley v. Georgia, 394 U.S. 557 (1969).

31. See Chief Justice Burger's concurring opinion in Rabe v. Washington, cited in Miller, 405 U.S. 313, 317.

legal standpoint, we shall only summarize the other important obscenity decisions announced in June of 1973.

1. *Paris Adult Theater I v. Slaton* [32]

This case stands for the following:

1. "*Expert*" testimony is not necessary in obscenity prosecutions.
2. There is no immunity from stated obscenity laws because obscene films are patronized only by "*consenting adults.*"
3. The state has an interest in the enforcement of obscenity laws even for "consenting adults." This includes the interest of the public in the quality of life and the total community environment, the tone of commerce in the great city centers and possibly, the public safety itself. The Hill-Link Minority Report of the Commission on Obscenity and Pornography indicates that there is at least an arguable correlation between obscene materials and crime. [33]
4. States have the right to prohibit obscenity for adults first because it is not free speech and secondly because the state has the power to prohibit public exhibition or commerce in obscenity based on its judgment that such material has a tendency to injure the community, to endanger public safety or jeopardize the State's "right" to maintain a decent society.

2. *U.S. v. Orito* [34]

This case rejects the attempt to extend the Stanley v. Georgia decision (referred to later in this writing) which permits an individual to peruse obscenity in the privacy of his home, to a "right" to have the obscenity transported in interstate commerce.

3. *Kaplan v. California* [35]

This stands for the proposition that obscene material in book form is not protected merely because it has no pictorial content. The Court again quotes

---

32. Case #71-1051, 41 L. W. 4935, U.S. Sup. Ct. (1973)

33. In *Miller* and related cases, the U.S. Supreme Court cites the Pornography Commission's Hill-Link Report on four occasions. The legal and philosophical premises of the Hill-Link Report have been adopted, and the Pornography Commission's Majority Report, which urged legalization of obscenity for adults had been rejected. This means that the "majority report" has been rejected by the U.S. Senate 60-5, by the President of the United States, and now by the Supreme Court.

34. Case No. 70-69, 41 L. W. 4956 (6/21/73) U.S. Sup. Ct.

35. Case No. 71-1422, 41 L. W. 4958 (6/21/73) U.S. Sup. Ct.

the Hill-Link Minority Report to show the tendency of such material to reach the impressionable young.

4. U.S. v. 12 200-ft. Reels[36]

(1) Importation of obscene matter may be proscribed by Congress even if importation is for private, personal use of importer. Stanley v. Georgia, confined to its facts.

(2) The U.S. Supreme Court *construes* U.S. obscenity statute as incorporating standards of Miller and to include the examples of specific hard-core sexual conduct as given in Miller, leaving to Congress to define other types of prohibited hard-core conduct.

5. Heller v. New York[37]

It is not necessary to have a prior adversary hearing before a motion picture may be seized as obscene pursuant to a warrant issued after a judge had viewed the film and authorized the warrant, provided the defendant is permitted to copy the film if desired, pending conclusion of trial of the issue.[38]

XI. Pending Bills in U.S. Congress Defining Obscenity

S-1 and S-1400 are Criminal Code Revisions pending in Congress. S-1 incorporates the Roth formulation without the Fanny Hill accretion and S-1400 appears to anticipate the Miller decision in setting forth specific hard-core activities as part of the definition.[39]

The main objection to S-1400 is that it would permit hard-core sex on TV and radio if the Bill is enacted in its present form. S-1400 obviously needs amendment to prohibit "offensive intrusiveness" on TV and radio. If it is necessary, it may be defined as a separate crime. See our remarks above in this regard.

XII. Summary and Conclusion

The 1973 Supreme Court decisions will inhibit hard-core pornography. It is a new ball game. Its new formulation of the definition of obscenity is unsuitable for application to TV and radio and will, no doubt, be modified in this respect.

---

36. Case No. 70-2, 41 L.W. 4961 (6/21/73) U.S. Sup. Ct.
37. Case No. 71-1043 41 L. W. 5067 (6/26/73) U.S. Sup. Ct.
38. Roaden v. Kentucky, decided same day (no prior judicial review) 41 L. W. 5020
39. See Section 1851 of proposed S-1400—additional descriptions of acts described in *Miller* will no doubt be added thereto before final passage by Congress.

Perhaps the most important contribution of Miller and its sister cases is the reaffirmation of the state's right to protect and promote public morality in relation to its adult population as well as to its nonadult members and to use this concept as the philosophical underpinning of its obscenity legislation.

The sum of experience including that of the past two decades affords an ample basis for legislatures to conclude that a sensitive, key relationship of human existence, central to family life, community welfare, and the development of human personality can be debased and distorted by crass commercial exploitation of sex (Paris Adult Theatre I v. Slaton).

Comments and Conclusions

The gist of these chapters suggests that the law is a living body, capable of growing and changing, and the outcomes in the courts and in the legislatures are always a result of a continuing struggle between opposing ideologies. But somehow in a remarkable way the will of the majority is eventually expressed.

One remarkable fact emerges, though it is hardly ever discussed. It has to do with the fact that while we have a considerable history of legal controls in the area of obscenity common to nearly all civilized countries, controls have never existed in the area of media violence. However, cockfights, bullfights, and similar exhibitions involving cruelty to animals are prohibited, probably as much out of concern for the animals as for the debasement created in the human spectators. Yet in the area of filmed human violence, where there is so much evidence suggesting harm to some viewers, almost no thought has been given for legally controlling or restraining this kind of public material.

If the law is a reflection of our values and cultural idiosyncrasies, this anomaly may reflect a curious double standard. Explicit over-the-counter sex or sexual imagery is "bad," but aggression with violent imagery is "good" (e.g., stimulating, recreational, diverting) and as "American as apple pie."

What this all suggests, in sum, is that the law is what we want it to be. Society shapes its laws more than the law or our constitution shapes society. And thus we can permit as much freedom of expression and dramatic license as we wish. There is, however, probably somewhere a cost-benefit ratio. If "speech" becomes too disruptive and society suffers too much, in our self interest we say "no"; we draw a line; we refuse to tolerate it. However, it takes some kind of sizable consensus of our citizenry to draw the line. When a minority has attempted to assume this role, historically they have nearly always been rebuffed.

VIOLENCE IN THE MEDIA

. . . We but teach
Bloody instructions, which, being
  taught, return
to plague the inventor.
                    William Shakespeare

Introduction

Probably of all issues in the social sciences that have been of concern to our society, none has been so well researched and studied as the effect on behavior of violence in the media, particularly in motion pictures and on TV.

In the opening chapter of this book, with remarkable succinctness and clarity of style, Liebert, Davidson, and Neale give us an overview of the TV violence issue. While they make use of scores of studies from the recent Surgeon General's Report on TV violence, they are actually giving us the best of what we know from several decades of work in this area. Their focus is on the sophisticated and experimentally well-controlled study, using powerful statistical procedures to tease out the most valid possible findings.

In her chapter, Alberta Siegel gives us a fascinating mixture of social science theory in explaining the etiology of violent behavior, along with a number of behavioral research studies which support these theoretical notions.

The chapter by Cline, Croft, and Courrier, is an example from beginning to end of a typical kind of empirical research study where, in the laboratory, children's reactions to filmed violence are carefully assessed through the use of elaborate gear of the psychophysiologist and carefully drawn comparison groups (e.g., children who have had high or low exposure to TV violence in their earlier lives).

Our purpose in this section is to acquaint the reader with the state of the art with regard to research on media violence and its behavioral effects and to assess what the accumulated wisdom of our cultural experience as well as multitudes of research studies have to say about this issue.

Fredric Wertham, a practicing psychiatrist and author of the fourth chapter, has used clinical case studies of individuals as the data base in his research on media violence and its effects on behavior. Wertham has for several decades evaluated, studied, and treated individuals engaged in acts of

111

extreme violence—a good share of these being juveniles. Each case is seen as unique even though there are often similar causal threads or elements weaving through cases studied. The correlation coefficient and carefully drawn control group are of little interest to Wertham, but the individual in his particular setting and his unique history are. Wertham uses with great skill and logic the experience of our culture, along with rational argument, in presenting his evidence.

Concluding this section is the succinct and unequivocal statement of the Surgeon General on the subject of televised violence.

Aggression in Childhood: The Impact of Television

Robert M. Liebert, Emily S. Davidson,
and John M. Neale

How does watching violent television programs affect children? This question has been posed continually since the advent of television sets as a common fixture in American and European homes almost two decades ago. Answers to it, based both on simple opinion and on research which reflects varying degrees of sophistication, have ranged from confident statements that television's influence is uniformly pernicious to equally glib assertions that merely watching entertainment fare can do little to shape children's social behavior.

Although literally hundreds of studies have been focused directly or indirectly on television and its effects upon youngsters, the series of investigations commissioned by the Television and Social Behavior Program of the United States National Institute of Mental Health constituted one of the first systematic and purposefully coordinated attempts to employ the efforts of a large group of researchers with relevant expertise and diverse viewpoints. As psychologists specializing in children's development—both normal and abnormal—each of us contributed to the Television and Social Behavior inquiry. This involvement gave us an opportunity, over the past few years, to read and study all of the technical documents, research reports, and summaries as they were prepared and to evaluate them in the light of past and other recent research.

For concerned citizens the task of keeping informed of this work has been

Robert M. Liebert, a professor of psychology at the State University of New York at Stony Brook, received his undergraduate training at the University of London and Tulane University. He received his Ph.D. degree at Stanford in 1966, later teaching at Vanderbilt, Antioch, and the University of Minnesota. For a year he was a senior investigator at the Fels Research Institute. He is currently a consulting editor for the *Journal of Abnormal Psychology* and is author-creator of some seventy books, films, and articles. His interests unfortunately complicated by the fact that the Television and Social Behavior Program generated almost 5,000 pages of technical material; the official summary (Cisin et al., 1972), while considerably shorter, is clouded by the participation of five network representatives who persistently minimized the effects of television and confused the significant issues (cf., Boffey and Walsh, 1970; Morgenstern, 1972; Paisley, 1972). A full account of the Program's work and related evidence has been presented elsewhere (Liebert, Neale, and Davidson, 1973). The purpose of this paper is to summarize briefly the state of our present knowledge as it has grown out of these and later investigations and to reflect on some possibilities for the future.

Observational learning and TV aggression

The scientific issue most fundamentally related to the particular question of the effects of television revolves around the nature of *observational learning,* the way in which the behavior of children and adults changes as a function of exposure to the behavior of others. Regardless of their other theoretical views, social scientists have virtually all acknowledged that a child's values and behavior are shaped, at least in part, by observational learning. Research has shown that the simple observation of others can be very potent in changing such widely varied aspects of social behavior as a child's willingness to aid others, his ability to display self-control, and his learning of language. Young children's observation of others on film has been shown to increase sharing and to markedly reduce fear reactions—if, of course, the content is designed to teach these lessons.

This list represents only a few examples from the impressive body of evidence which suggests that learning by observation is a critical aspect of the social learning processes through which the child is informed about the world around him and molded into an adult member of his society. It is in this context that social scientists asked whether viewing violent television entertainment has a significant impact on the young. In answering, they had to consider four points: How much violence is shown on television? How

have focused on such things as behavior therapy, modeling, children and TV violence, interpersonal negotiation, and test anxiety.

Emily S. Davidson, with a B.A. from Southern Methodist University, is currently receiving her Ph.D. at Stony Brook, where she works with Liebert and Neale. Her interests have similarly focused on TV violence, imitative learning, and research methods in the behavioral sciences. Thus far she has eight publications to her credit.

John M. Neale, with a Ph.D. in 1969 from Vanderbilt University, is an associate professor at Stony Brook. A Canadian citizen who did his undergraduate work at the University of Toronto, he has a score or so of publications which focus on the area of research methodology, TV violence and child aggression, schizophrenia, socially disadvantaged children, and children who are high-risk for psychiatric breakdown.

much violent entertainment is actually seen by children? What do they learn from this exposure? And, finally: Does such learning lead to changes in real-life behavior?

How much violence is shown on entertainment television?

Although violence has always been part of American entertainment in television, its frequency has increased steadily over the past twenty years. In 1954, for example, violence-saturated action and adventure programming accounted for only 17% of prime time network offerings; by 1961 the figure was 60% (Greenberg, 1969). Translating such figures into concrete terms, during one week of television in 1960 there were 144 murders, 13 kidnappings, 7 torture scenes, 4 lynchings, and a few more miscellaneous acts of violence, all occurring before 9:00 p.m. By 1968 the National Association for Better Broadcasting estimated that the average child would watch the violent destruction of more than 13,400 persons on television between the ages of five and fifteen (Sabin, 1972).

The most accurate estimate of current levels of violence on television during prime time and Saturday morning has been provided by Gerbner et al. (1972a; 1972b), who define violence as:

The overt expression of physical force against others or self, or the compelling of action against one's will on pain of being hurt or killed (1972a:34).

In Gerbner's work, carefully trained observers watched a full week of network entertainment programs on all of the major networks, with striking results. In 1969 about eight in ten shows contained violence, and the frequency of violent episodes, as defined above, was almost eight per hour. Further, the most violent programs of all were those designed exclusively for children—cartoons.

The average cartoon hour in 1967 contained more than three times as many violent episodes as the average dramatic hour. The trend toward shorter plays sandwiched between frequent commercials on fast moving cartoon programs further increased the saturation. In 1969, with a violent episode at least every two minutes on all Saturday morning cartoon programming (including the least violent and including commercial time), . . . the average cartoon hour had nearly six times the violence rate of the average adult television drama hour, and nearly twelve times the rate of the average movie hour (1972a:36).

Gerbner has continued his analysis of network television dramas, and the data for 1970 and 1971 have recently been made available. He summarizes the new findings: ". . . New programs in 1971 spearheaded the trend toward more lethal killers by depicting record high proportions of screen killers" (1972b:3).

The level of violent programming over the five-year period studied by Gerbner can be seen in Figure 1, which shows the percentage of programs containing violence, and the number of violent incidents per program hour.

FIGURE 1

Percentage of Network Programs Containing Violence (a)
and Average Number of Violent Episodes per Program
Hour (b) over the Period 1967-71

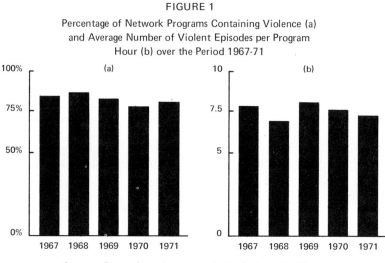

Source: Drawn from data appearing in Gerbner, 1972b

Clearly, violence on television is not decreasing at any appreciable rate. Prime time drama was still, in the 1971-72 season, overwhelmingly violent. The new figures are of special interest since they reflect a long history of unfulfilled network promises. In the mid 1960s network officials had promised a sharp decrease in TV violence and then claimed that the promise had been met. Gerbner's 1967 and 1968 data showed that it had not. The promise was reissued, but, again, the appearance of Gerbner's 1969 data (published in 1972 because considerable time is required for sophisticated data processing) showed little change. It was then claimed that substantial changes had certainly occurred during the 1970 to 1971 seasons. Now, again, the facts have answered with unfortunate monotony: little change.

How much TV violence do children see?

Portrayals of violence on television cannot produce an effect unless they are seen. Therefore, we must ask about the frequency with which children actually view such shows. Lyle and Hoffman (1972) conducted an extensive survey of media use among more than one thousand children from widely varied backgrounds. They concluded that "television saturation was almost total; only 2% of the students stated that there was not a working TV set in their home." The data also showed that more than one-third of the first-graders are still watching television at 8:30 p.m. on weeknights, and more than one-half of the sixthgraders are doing so. Likewise, Stein and Friedrich (1972) reported that in a sample of about 100 preschool children, television viewing was among the most frequently reported waking activities. Indeed, exposure to television is, for children, so pervasive that Lesser (1970) contends that a child born today will, by the age of 18, have spent more of his life watching television than in any other single activity but sleep.

The impact of television can be seen even more clearly by moving from percentage figures to absolute numbers. McIntyre and Teevan (1972), citing the Violence Commission staff reports of 1969, remind us that "on one Monday during the period covered, over five million children under the age of 12 . . . were still watching between 10:30 and 11:00 p.m. . . ." They also point to the Commission's observations that "there is a great deal of violent content available, at all times of the day, for all manner of intended audience."

Moreover, cartoons, the most violent of all types of TV entertainment, are among those most often watched by young children. In the Lyle and Hoffman reports, for example, 24% of the first grade children said that cartoons were their favorite type of program. A similar pattern was found in Stein and Friedrich's study of preschoolers, whose parents reported that they watched cartoons an average of more than seven hours per week; even adult violent programs were watched more than a full hour per week by these three-to-five-year-old children.

It is important to note, though, that high exposure to violence is more a result of saturation by broadcasters than a strong preference for this type of programming by youngsters. Among first graders, for example, the two most popular programs are situation comedies ("My Favorite Martian" and "I Love Lucy"); preschoolers prefer "Sesame Street" to violent cartoons (Lyle and Hoffman, 1972a; 1972b).

What do children learn from TV violence?

There is little doubt that children can learn novel forms of behavior—both words and actions—from simply watching others. It is, however, only through systematic research that we are able to see the degree to which this form of learning is effectively mediated by television and televisionlike formats.

Studies by Bandura (summarized in Bandura, 1973), designed to show that brief exposure to novel *aggressive* behaviors can lead to their acquisition by quite young children, have uniformly shown that this influence is potent indeed. In one study, for example, 88% of the children (three-to-five-year-old boys and girls) who saw an aggressive television program displayed imitative aggression in a play situation even though they had not been asked to do so and were free to play with attractive, nonaggressive toys such as a tea set, crayons, cars and trucks, plastic farm animals, and the like.

Further, there is evidence that behavior acquired in this way may be recalled for long periods of time. Hicks (1965) found that children shown a simulated television program similar to those used by Bandura and his associates learned many new aggressive behaviors after a single viewing and could still produce them when tested again, without further exposure, six months later. So there is no doubt that children learn, with the level of repeated exposure which takes place, a good deal of the aggressive repertoire that they see in televised violence.

Beyond teaching specific ways of perpetrating aggression and mayhem, contemporary TV entertainment conveys a more general lesson: violence succeeds. In an early investigation (Larsen, Gray, and Fortis, 1963), for example, eighteen programs were studied, six in each of three categories: adult programs, "kidult" programs (programs where the child or teenage audience comprises at least 30% of the total audience), and children's programs—usually cartoons. In all three program types, violent methods were the ones most frequently used in goal attainment. And, when goal achievement methods were further analyzed for degree of success, it became clear that the most successful methods were *not* those in the socially approved category. Simply, then, television programming—aimed both at children and at adults—is presenting an antisocial system of values.

Network officials, though, have sometimes justified television violence because the "bad guy" is usually punished for his misdeeds. The argument deserves a closer look. The usual sequence involves aggression or other antisocial behavior by the villain, through which he achieves his immediate objectives (the plans for the latest missile or the crown jewels of England). Next, the hero catches up with and vanquishes the villain—by virtue of exemplary performance in the final brawl or shoot-out. The hero's reward is a raise, a blonde, or a bottle of champagne; if he is lucky, he may get all three plus a vacation in the sun. The lesson is thus that aggression, while reprehensible in criminals, is acceptable for those who have right on their side. But all of us, children and adults, rich and poor, on any side of any legal statute, feel we have right on *our* side. "Every man," William Saroyan wrote many years ago, "is a good man in a bad world—as he himself knows."

Does exposure to TV violence shape children's real-life behavior?

There are now numerous documented instances of direct imitation of TV violence by children which have been truly unfortunate, such as the case of a lad who was stabbed while he and his friends reenacted scenes from the movie *Rebel Without a Cause* which they had seen as a television rerun or the youngster who laced the family dinner with ground glass after observing this tactic used successfully on a television crime show (cf. Liebert, Neale, and Davidson, 1973). A more general influence upon children of televised aggression can be seen from experimental studies.

An example

To illustrate the logic that underlies some of this research, let us examine a study conducted independently of the Television and Social Behavior Program. This study by Steuer, Applefield, and Smith (1971) was designed to show the absolute degree of control which television violence can have on naturally occurring aggressive behavior and involved children enrolled in the preschool of the University of North Carolina's Child Development Center. The youngsters, boys and girls, knew each other before the study began. First, they were matched into pairs on the basis of the amount of time they spent watching television at home. Next, to establish the degree to which aggressive behavior occurred among these youngsters *before* any modification of their television "diets," each was carefully observed for ten sessions in play with other children, and the frequency of aggressive responses were recorded.

Steuer and her associates used a demanding measure of physical interpersonal aggression including: (a) hitting or pushing another child, (b) kicking another child, (c) assaultive contact with another child, such as squeezing or choking him, and (d) throwing an object at another child from a distance of at least one foot. Only these severe acts of physical aggression were recorded. The initial measure, or baseline, established a remarkable degree of consistency within each pair prior to the modification of their television diet. No one could say, then, that the children differed from one another in aggression before the controlled television experience began.

Next, Steuer and her associates asked about the effects of television. One child in each pair observed, on eleven different days, a single aggressive television program taken directly from Saturday morning program offerings, while the other member of the pair observed a nonaggressive television program. Subsequent observations of the children at play provided continuous measures of interpersonal physical aggression by each child. Changes from the original measures, if any, would have to be caused by television's effects since the children were entirely alike before the television treatment began.

By the end of the eleven sessions, the two groups had departed significantly from one another in terms of the frequency of interpersonal aggression. In fact, for every pair, the child who had observed aggressive television programming became more aggressive than his mate, who had watched neutral fare. In several of the cases, these changes were truly striking, with youngsters showing increases of 200%-300% in aggressiveness. These results are not new or unique.

More than fifty studies have been conducted, involving more than 10,000 children from every type of social background. With remarkable consistency, these studies regularly lead to one conclusion: *there is a clear and reliable relationship between the amount of violence which a child sees on entertainment television and the degree to which he is aggressive in his attitudes and behavior.*

Converging evidence for the conclusion comes, for example, from correlational field studies which relate viewing of violence on television to various measures of aggressive behavior. Working with adolescent subjects, McIntyre and Teevan (1972) reported to the United States government that they had found a consistent relationship between objective ratings of the amount of violence on programs which youngsters reported watching and many kinds of deviant behavior. Moreover, these investigators found a positive relationship between the violence rating of the child's favorite programs and the degree to which he expressed approval of violence by others. For example, they said "those adolescents whose favorite programs are more violent more frequently approve of a teenage boy punching or knifing another teenage boy."

In another study, involving 434 nine-to-eleven-year-old boys, exposure to television violence was related to the boys' approval of and willingness to use violence themselves (Dominick and Greenberg, 1972). Measures were also obtained of the degree to which the boys perceived violence as effective and the degree to which they suggested violent solutions to conflict situations when presented with open-ended questions. Again, exposure to aggressive television was significantly related to the boys' stated willingness to use violence and to their perceptions of its effectiveness when used. The investigators then used the same methods to relate television violence viewing and aggressive attitudes for girls. The results closely paralleled those for boys, with exposure to such aggressive fare making a "consistent, independent contribution to the child's notions about violence. The greater the level of exposure to television violence, the more the child was willing to use violence, to suggest it as a solution to conflict, and to perceive it as effective" (1972:329).

In yet another study conducted for the Television and Social Behavior Program the relationship between viewing televised violence and a variety of measures of aggressive behavior were obtained in two relatively large samples of older adolescents. The investigators reached the following conclusions:

Our research shows that among both boys and girls at two grade levels [junior high and senior high] the more the child watches violent television fare, the more aggressive he is likely to be. . . . Adolescents viewing high levels of violent content on television tend to have high levels of aggressive behavior, regardless of television viewing time, socioeconomic status, or school performance (McLeod, Atkin, and Chaffee, 1972a:187-91).

120

Another correlational study in the Program was longitudinal, designed to determine whether the amount of television violence watched by children at age nine influenced the degree to which they were aggressive ten years later at age nineteen. The findings indicated clearly that, for boys, such a relationship did exist. The investigators reported to the United States government that on the basis of their research ". . . the most plausible single causal hypothesis would appear to be that watching violent television in the third grade leads to the building of aggressive habits" and ". . . that a substantial component of aggression at age nineteen can be predicted better by the amount of television violence the child watched in the third grade [age nine] than by any other causal variable measured . . ." (Lefkowitz, Eron, Walder, and Huesmann, 1972:51-6).

Finally, consider a uniquely important investigation conducted by Stein and Friedrich (1972). They employed the experimental method in a relatively naturalistic situation in order to examine directly some of the effects of observing television upon quite young children. Participants were fifty-two boys and forty-five girls between 3½ and 5½ years of age, who were systematically exposed to television programs of differing content while attending a summer nursery school.

This carefully designed experiment involved an initial measurement period in which the free play of children in the nursery school was observed and rated according to a variety of categories; a four-week experimental period in which children were systematically exposed either to aggressive cartoons ("Batman" and "Superman"), neutral television programming (children working on a farm and the like), or prosocial programming (episodes from the program "Misterogers' Neighborhood"); and a two-week postviewing period in which effects could be observed and assessed.

The children were exposed to the programs for approximately twenty minutes per day, three times a week during a four-week period. During this time, and during the two-week postviewing period, the children's behavior was again systematically observed in the naturalistic preschool situation. Behavior ratings included measures of aggression, interpersonal prosocial behavior, and self-control. They were checked carefully for reliability and collected by raters who were "blind" to the children's treatment.

Stein and Friedrich found that children who were initially in the upper half of the sample in interpersonal aggression subsequently showed greater interpersonal aggression if they were exposed to the aggressive programming than if they were exposed to either the neutral or prosocial programming. The investigators emphasize that:

These effects occurred in naturalistic behavior that was removed both in time and in environmental setting from the viewing experience. They occurred with a small amount of exposure, particularly in relation to the amount the children received at home, and they endured during the postviewing period (p. 247).

Social scientists are carefully trained to avoid statements of certainty. In fact, even in the physical and biological sciences, professional and scientific reports are always couched in terms of probabilities rather than absolutes. Notwithstanding this tradition, it seems to us that it has been clearly demonstrated that watching television violence, sometimes for periods of only a few hours, and in some studies even for a few minutes, can and often does instigate aggressive behavior that would not otherwise occur.

Social significance and implications: Some recurring questions

If TV violence can instigate aggressive behavior—and the data leave little doubt that it can—then we are left with two questions: How socially significant or *important* are the findings? What action, if any, should be taken and by whom? Each of these broad questions can be answered only by considering more specific ones regarding both the data themselves and larger political and social considerations.

How important are the findings?

Let us address this question in several ways that may shed light on the major issues.

For what types of children has an effect actually been shown?

The "official" report of the Surgeon General's Scientific Advisory Committee on Television and Social Behavior states that TV violence might affect ". . . a small portion or a substantial proportion of the total population of young television viewers. We cannot estimate the size of the fraction, however, since the available evidence does not come from cross-section samples of the entire American population" (p. 12).

It is easy to misunderstand this statement, and many commentators have been confused by it. In point of fact, the studies of the Television and Social Behavior Program involved children and adolescents from every type of background. White, black, and Asian American youngsters all participated. They came from both urban and rural homes; from families in which the breadwinners were physicians, lawyers, plumbers and laborers—as well as from families where there was no breadwinner at all. Large samples participated from Maryland, Wisconsin, California, and New York, while other studies were done in Tennessee, Louisiana, and Ohio. No region, ethnic group, or type of economic circumstance is unrepresented in the data collected to date. One team described its results as revealing that "for relatively average children from average home environments, continued exposure to violence is positively related to acceptance of aggression as a mode of behavior" (Dominick and Greenberg, 1972, pp. 331-32). Most of the other researchers could—and did—describe their findings in the same way.

Is the effect limited only to children who are "aggressively predisposed?"

The official report implied repeatedly that the effect of TV violence occurs only among children who are predisposed to it. The suggestion has led to much confusion.

At times, for a variety of reasons, each of us is somewhat more or less predisposed to work hard, eat a steak, or go to a football game; similarly, since not every child will become more aggressive after watching a particular sequence of television violence, we might say that some children are more "predisposed" to show the effect at a particular time than are others. It is presumably in this vein that we should take the committee's observation that the causal sequence is very likely applicable only to those who are predisposed to it. But if we so view the remark, then we must be careful to understand what has been said. As Dr. Steven Chaffee, who made substantial contributions to the research and overviewed the correlational studies, astutely noted:

The "predisposition to aggression" limitation is to some extent a near universal or tautological proposition, in that most children almost surely have at least some latent aggressive tendencies and are thus "predisposed" to aggression if so stimulated. At the other extreme, it could be taken as a statement that only "a few bad kids" (presumably not yours or mine) can be influenced by media violence . . ." (1972, p. 12).

Going on to discuss other evidence, Chaffee concludes: "Perhaps a more defensible conclusion would be that there is a small subgroup of habitually passive and unaggressive children who will *not* be stimulated to perform aggressively regardless of what they see on television." The research clearly favors Chaffee's analysis; the effects are not limited to a small number of peculiarly predisposed children.

Equally important, we must remember that aggressive actions are by their nature social phenomena; continually watching television violence is not the only way an average, normal child can be harmed. Suppose, for example, that a particular youngster either never watches aggressive television shows or is for some reason unaffected by them. He may still be influenced profoundly as the *target* of aggression: one or more of his playmates who has become more aggressive as a result of television violence may select him as a victim. For this reason, there is an important sense in which we can say with confidence that any and every child can be affected adversely by the present TV violence offerings.

How much contribution to the violence in our society is made by extensive television violence viewing by our youth?

The question was first posed by Senator John Pastore in his original charge to initiate the Program. The answer appears, to us, to be that such viewing makes a significant contribution. It is not, of course, the only contributing factor to aggression. Cigarette smoking is by no means the only (or even the most influential) factor contributing to heart disease; moderate exercise is not the only factor contributing to good health. No one would doubt the role of the family, the school, and the entire social milieu in contributing to whether or not a child will act aggressively. But would anyone say that it is any of these other factors, alone, which causes aggression? All are important; and concern for one should never deflect societal attention from the others—but neither should the complexity of aggressive behavior mask the social significance of television's demonstrably great impact on children from widely varied backgrounds.

What should be done?

Some might conclude that television itself is bad for children. We do not. It has been shown, quite unambiguously, that violence on television has an adverse effect. But something else has come from the accumulated research, a finding which is much more fundamental:

Any steady diet of television, regardless of its content,
can exert a powerful influence on children.

Television, we have now discovered, functions for the young as their earliest window on the world, through which they learn, from the repeated examples shown on the screen, how to cope with many aspects of life. *What* they learn depends, quite simply, on what we show them through this window. *How* they learn is a process which we now understand quite well.

Television rests technologically on a complex of twentieth-century electronic inventions, but psychologically its effects are not based on any new or mysterious processes. Television influences children through the inevitable, natural consequences of observing the behavior of others. Purposely or inadvertently, television is foremost a teacher, and its potential can be harnessed to shape our society in directions we deem more desirable. Indeed, evidence for this enormous potential has already begun to emerge. The Stein and Friedrich (1972) study, mentioned earlier, showed how selective viewing can have positive effects on a wide range of behavior in normal preschool children. Recall that each group watched television for approximately twenty minutes, three times a week for four weeks. The first group watched aggressive programs, the second watched so-called neutral programs, and the third watched programs that showed prosocial behavior. It is the last group which is of interest now. The children who had watched the positive programs now showed more self-control, in a variety of ways, than did the children who watched either the aggressive programs or the neutral ones. These significant changes were achieved after only four weeks—and even though children in all three groups continued to watch regular television at home.

In our own work we have begun to redirect our efforts toward investigating the potential of television for the teaching of positive lessons, focusing on three related tasks. The first is the development of a code defining prosocial behavior, now proceeding in our laboratory. Several complex issues surround the undertaking, the most important being the nature of *prosocial behavior* as a construct. "Prosocial behavior" does not permit an inclusive, yet specific definition; it is, instead, a class which must be divided further into categories so that each can be defined more precisely. Our code presently includes seven such behavior categories, shown in Table 1, and is being tested and refined with network programs.

TABLE 1
Types of prosocial behavior that can be shown on television and a definition of each

Terms	Definitions
1. Providing aid or assistance to another	Spontaneous gift or loan of one's possessions to another; giving aid (instructions, physical assistance) to another. Includes two or more people helping each other to achieve either a mutual goal or independent goals.
2. Control of aggressive impulses	Demonstrations or suggestions of alternatives to aggression in frustrating situations.
3. Making up for bad behavior	Verbal apology, including admission of mistake, or some other behavior (e.g., sharing) which is clearly intended as reparation.
4. Delay of gratification	Putting off or foregoing completely some smaller reward for the sake of a larger reward later. Will usually involve some verbalization of this intent. Includes taking time on tasks so that product will be better, and task persistence.
5. Explaining feelings of others	Teaching, explaining why someone acts the way he does, what other people think and feel.
6. Sympathy	Verbalizing concern for others and their problems. Distinct from friendliness.

| | May also include a specific nonverbal behavior. |
| 7. Resistance to temptation | Resisting opportunity to engage in prohibited behavior that would be of some benefit to the individual. |

With the code, we will be able to assess the whole spectrum of network dramatic offerings, including information such as that collected by Gerbner about violence: who is involved, as actor and recipient, under what circumstances, and with what results? What types of programs contain the most prosocial actions? What is the ratio between aggression and prosocial behavior in any particular program or series?

The second task is more extensive exploration of the *effects* of prosocial programming. Except for successful "therapeutic" uses of television with specialized programs and audiences (e.g., O'Connor, 1969), this job is just recently begun. Our own effort is two-pronged, involving both the identification of existing commercial programs which have positive effects and—more importantly—the creation of new programs which teach a variety of such lessons.

For networks to change their programming policy, they must be assured that new shows with prosocial themes woven in will have high ratings; the commercial structure of American television dictates that prosocial programs must be able to earn their share of the TV audience. Learning more about preferences and reactions to programs is our third task. In our laboratory we are now conducting studies in which, while a child watches television, a camera watches and records his behavior. Subsequently, the video tape of the child's facial reactions can be coded along dimensions such as interest and enjoyment. This information has already assisted us greatly in the initial design of new programs which can have beneficial effects *and* be commercially viable.

References

Bandura, A.
    1973   Aggression: A Social Learning Analysis. Englewood Cliffs, New Jersey: Prentice-Hall.

Boffey, P. M., and J. Walsh
    1970   Study of TV violence, Seven top researchers blackballed from panel. Science, May 22, pp. 949-52.

Chaffee, S. H.
    1972   Television and growing up: Interpreting the Surgeon General's report. Paper presented to Pacific chapter, American Association for Public Opinion Research, Asilomar, California, March.

Cisin, J. H., T. E. Coffin, I. L. Janis, J. T. Klapper, H. Mendelsohn, E. Omwake, C. A. Pinderhughes, I. de Sola Pool, A. E. Siegel, A. F. C. Wallace, A. S. Watson, and G. D. Wiebe
1972 Television and growing up: The Impact of Televised Violence. Washington, D.C.: U.S. Government Printing Office.

Dominick, J. R., and B. S. Greenberg
1972 Attitudes toward violence: The interaction of television exposure, family attitudes, and social class. In G. A. Comstock and E. A. Rubinstein, eds., Television and Social Behavior. Vol. III: Television and Adolescent Aggressiveness. Washington, D. C.: U.S. Government Printing Office, pp. 314-35.

Gerbner, G.
1972a Violence in television drama: Trends and symbolic functions. In G. A. Comstock and E. A. Rubinstein, eds., Television and Social Behavior. Vol. I; Media Content and Control. Washington, D.C.: U.S. Government Printing Office, pp. 28-187.

1972b The violence profile: Some indicators of the trends in and the symbolic structure of network television drama 1967-1971. Unpublished manuscript, The Annenberg School of Communications, University of Pennsylvania.

Greenberg, B. S.
1969 The content and context of violence in the mass media. In R. K. Baker and S. J. Ball, eds., Violence and the Media. Washington, D.C.: U.S. Government Printing Office, pp. 423-52.

Hicks, D. J.
1965 Imitation and retention of film-mediated aggressive peer and adult models. Journal of Personality and Social Psychology 2:97-100.

Larsen, O. N., L. N. Gray, and J. G. Fortis
1963 Goals and goal-achievement methods in television content: Models for anomie? Sociological Inquiry 8:180-96.

Lefkowitz, M. M., L. D. Eron, L. O. Walder, and L. R. Huesmann
1972 Television violence and child aggression: A followup study. In G. A. Comstock and E. A. Rubinstein, eds., Television and Social Behavior. Vol. III: Television and Adolescent Aggressiveness. Washington, D.C.: U.S. Government Printing Office, pp. 35-135.

Lesser, G. S.
1970 Designing a program for broadcast television. In F. F. Korten, S. W. Cook, and G. L. Lacey, eds., Psychology and the Problems of Society. Washington: American Psychological Association, 208-14.

Liebert, R. M., J. M. Neale, and E. S. Davidson
1973 The Early Window: Effects of Television on Children and Youth. New York: Pergamon Press.

Lyle, J., and H. R. Hoffman

1972a   Children's use of television and other media. In E. A. Rubinstein, G. A. Comstock, and J. P. Murray, eds., Television and Social Behavior. Vol. IV: Television in Day-to-day Life: Patterns of Use. Washington, D.C.: U.S. Government Printing Office, pp. 129-256.

1972b   Explorations in patterns of television viewing by preschool-age children. Ibid., pp. 257-73.

McIntyre, J. J., and J. J. Teevan, Jr.

1972   Television violence and deviant behavior. In G. A. Comstock and E. A. Rubinstein, eds., Television and Social Behavior. Vol. III: Television and Adolescent Aggressiveness. Washington, D.C.: U.S. Government Printing Office, pp. 383-435.

McLeod. J. M., C. K. Atkin, and S. H. Chaffee

1972a   Adolescents, parents, and television use: Adolescent self-report measures from Maryland and Wisconsin samples. In G. A. Comstock and E. A. Rubinstein, eds., Television and Social Behavior. Vol. III: Television and Adolescent Aggressiveness. Washington, D.C.: U.S. Government Printing Office, pp. 173-238.

1972b   Adolescents, parents, and television use: Self-report and other report measures from the Wisconsin sample. Ibid., pp. 239-313.

Morgenstern, J.

1972   The new violence. Newsweek, February 14.

O'Connor, R. D.

1969   Modification of social withdrawal through symbolic modeling. Journal of Applied Behavior Analysis 2:15-22.

Paisley, M. B.

1972   Social Policy Research and the Realities of the System: Violence Done to TV Research. Institute for Communication Research: Stanford University.

Sabin, L.

1972   Why I threw out my TV set. Today's Health, February.

Stein, A. H., and L. K. Friedrich

1972   Television content and young children's behavior. In J. P. Murray, E. A. Rubinstein, and G. A. Comstock, eds., Television and Social Behavior. Vol. II: Television and Social Learning. Washington, D.C.: U.S. Government Printing Office, pp. 202-317.

Steuer, F. B., J. M. Applefield, and R. Smith

1971   Televised aggression and the interpersonal aggression of preschool children. Journal of Experimental Child Psychology, 11:442-47.

The Effects of Media Violence on Social Learning*

Alberta Siegel

Is social behavior affected by the media? Do children who have grown up on a steady diet of television behave differently than they would if it did not exist?

These questions lie at the heart of our current concern about the media and violence. Serious and disinterested observers differ as to how to frame the best answer on the basis of our present knowledge. Observers with a stake in the media capitalize on our ignorance to reassure one another that the status quo will hold.

Behavior is guided by belief. People act in a context of convictions about the meaning of their acts, what acts are appropriate in particular settings, and what responses may be expected from others. Action emerges from beliefs about the world and how one should respond to it.

Human social behavior is learned. Much of this process occurs through trial and error, especially in the earliest years of life. It does not seem likely

*This chapter is excerpted from Violence and the Media: A Staff Report to the National Commission on the Causes and Prevention of Violence, Vol. XI. Washington, D.C.: U.S. Government Printing Office (1969).

Alberta Siegel, a widow, is professor of psychology in the Department of Psychiatry at Stanford Medical School. She received her doctorate in developmental and social psychology at Stanford in 1954. After receiving her degree she taught child development at Pennsylvania State University, following which she spent two years as a Fellow at the Center for Advanced Study in the Behavioral Sciences at Palo Alto. From there she moved into the Department of Psychiatry as a research associate and ultimately as a full professor at Stanford. In 1971 she was appointed associate dean of undergraduate studies at Stanford.

She is the joint author of one book and author of scores of scientific articles and book chapters. She has had a long-time interest in children and especially in studying the causes that television, motion pictures, and other noninteractive media play a role in such learning since they cannot provide differentiated "feedback" to an individual. Whether an infant is crying or quiet, awake or asleep, hungry or full, walking or sitting, behaving well or mischievously, the television drones on and on, uninfluenced by the infant's behavior. Such an unresponsive communications system does not enter into trial and error learning.

A great deal of human social life, and behavior, is also learned through observation and imitation. As the years pass, children acquire the ability to model their behavior after certain others, and this ability seems to be independent of rewards and punishments. To explain a child's behavior, we inquire about the observational learning opportunities which have been available to him—"Where in this world did he learn to do *that?*" We know that children watch television. Do they also imitate what they observe there? The inherent authenticity of television and movies makes it easy to believe that they do. Children understand such presentations as authentic and credible and assume that the world is really the way it appears there. It is natural for them to take the behavior they observe on television as a model for their own. An illustration of this comes from Britain:

> *Presenting a resolution urging the Government to consider a code of conduct to guide people responsible for selecting television programs, Fred Armstrong (a member of the Rural District Councils Association, speaking at its annual conference) said that during one half-hour program the word bloody had been used 30 to 40 times.*
>
> *Was it surprising, he asked, when a 6-year-old boy told a woman in a shop that she was a "bloody silly old moo" because his favorite candy was sold out?*[1]

Although Americans might differ with this Briton as to the seriousness of the behavior he described, most would agree with him that the child's use of the proscribed word "bloody" probably resulted from his watching shows in which it was used by the characters he subsequently imitated. At the other extreme is another account of imitative behavior in Britain, this time about a

of aggression in youth. She has also focused on such problems as the effects upon children of working mothers and changing schools, future employment for college women, and war-separated children.

Dr. Siegel served as a member of the U.S. Surgeon General's Scientific Advisory Committee on Television and Social Behavior as well as on committees of the National Institute of Mental Health and the National Institute of Child Health and Human Development. She edited a quarterly journal, *Child Development*, in the sixties as well as serving in a variety of capacities in the American Psychological Association.

1. "Children in Britain, 13 to 14, called Rulers of the TV Set," *New York Times,* July 17, 1967, p. 12.

twelve-year-old boy who was found dead at his home in Leicester, in the English Midlands.

Television chiefs issued a warning to millions of youngsters today after an inquest on a boy who died while imitating his masked and cloaked hero, "Batman." . . . His father . . . told the inquest yesterday he thought his son, hanged while wearing a homemade Batman-style outfit, had been leaping from a cabinet in the garden shed when his neck caught in a nylon loop hanging from the roof. The inquest verdict was misadventure. After the inquest [the father] said that he hoped the Batman show would be taken off British television. "It is far too dramatic and hair-raising," he said. "It encourages children to attempt the impossible." A television spokesman said:

"We regret that the death of Charles Lee should be attributed to his viewing of Batman. Young viewers are cautioned that they should make no attempt to imitate Batman's activities.

"Before each episode young viewers are reminded that Batman does not in fact fly and that all of his exploits are accomplished by means of his secret equipment."[2]

What are we to think of this event? In what sense is television "responsible" for this child's violent death? Is this twelve-year-old's imitative behavior in the same category as the six-year-old's remarks about a "bloody silly old moo?"

Adult behavior, as well as children's, may be imitative. On December 13, 1966, the National Broadcasting Company presented a filmed drama entitled "The Doomsday Flight."

The plot of the film centered on the placement of a bomb on a transcontinental airliner. . . . The plane emerged safely because it landed at an altitude above that at which the bomb was triggered to go off. The supposed suspense lay in tracing the deranged man who kept teasing officials with information on his deadly act.[3]

While the film was still on the air, a bomb threat (which turned out to be a hoax) was telephoned to one U.S. airline. Within twenty-four hours of the show, four more had been phoned in. Within the week following the show, eight such hoax calls in all were received by various U.S. airlines, including American, TWA, Eastern, PanAmerican, and Northwest.[4] These eight bomb threats in one week equaled the number of such calls that had been received

2. "Young Britons Told Not to Copy Batman," *New York Times*, 25 August 1966, p. 42.

3. Jack Gould, "The Doomsday Flight," *New York Times*, 15 December 1966.

4. Jack Gould, "A Bomb Backfires," *New York Times*, 16 December 1966.

the entire previous month, according to the Federal Aviation Agency.[5]

Before the film was shown, the Air Lines Pilots Association had urged NBC to keep the program off the air in the interest of air safety. They advised NBC that experience had shown that "the mentally unstable are highly responsive to, and easily provoked by, suggestions."[6] The pilots indicated that they feared the program could cause an irrational person to commit an act of sabotage. Telegrams were sent by the president of the pilots' association, to the author of the script, to an NBC vice-president, to the West Coast publicity director for NBC, and to the producer of the film at a Hollywood studio.[7] When no response was received, another representative of the pilots' association telephoned another NBC vice-president in a further attempt to convince the network to call off the program.

These efforts proved unsuccessful. The film was shown, and the feared rash of bomb hoaxes did ensue. Fortunately, there is no record that a bomb was in fact placed on any plane. Unfortunately, we have no information on the identities of the individuals who translated screen behavior into acts in their own lives. We do not know their ages, their social histories, or whether they were "disturbed," "unstable," or "impulsive." Probably some of them were. Many such individuals do exist in our society, and in our concern for the effects of television, we must consider them as well as the "balanced," "stable," and "restrained" persons for whom such a ready translation from drama to reality may be unthinkable.

For many years, black citizens have objected to the stereotyped representation of Negroes in the mass media. They have resented the fact that blacks were almost always portrayed in subordinate and menial roles, such as servants, shoeshine boys, fieldhands, and ne'er-do-wells. They have felt that these condescending and two-dimensional portrayals would influence the way Americans felt about black people, even the way black Americans would feel about themselves. This argument rests on the assumption that people "accept" and "believe" the fictional representations in the media. The depth of the objections of black citizens lends seriousness to this assumption. It has not been sufficient to reply, "but it's only a story" or, "that's only fantasy." Even the media men themselves have finally accepted the validity of this argument, and serious efforts are now being made to portray blacks in dignified and admirable roles, to represent in the media the true variety of the human condition among black as well as white Americans. They have taken seriously the notion that for some Americans the media

5. "TV Show Blamed by FAA for Rise in Bomb Hoax Calls," *New York Times,* 21 December 1966, p. 69.

6. "Air Bomb Threats Follow TV Drama," *New York Times,* 15 December 1966, pp. 35-56.

7. Ibid.

constitute their only acquaintance with blacks and that therefore it is important for the media portrayals to be fair and realistic. Should we take seriously the notion that for some Americans the media constitute their principal acquaintance with violence and aggression, and that they learn about these phenomena and how to deal with them solely through the media?

Several research studies have addressed this question. One examined the influence of violence in the mass media upon children's role expectations (Siegel, 1958). An effort was made to study young children's impressions of a taxi driver—a role chosen because taxi drivers are not widely stereotyped in our society. One group of second graders heard a series of radio dramas about taxi drivers. In each "thrilling episode," the taxi driver got into trouble with another person and extricated himself by being violently aggressive against the other person. A second group of children in the same grade heard a series which differed from the other only in the endings. In this series, the endings were not violent; instead, the taxi driver found a constructive way to resolve the problem.

To determine whether the children's reality conceptions had been influenced by these fictional presentations, the researcher gave each child a newspaper test. The child was shown a copy of the local newspaper and was asked to explain what a newspaper is. Only those who understood that a newspaper reports reality were in the final analysis. The individual who showed the newspaper to the child had not been involved in the earlier playing of the dramas on radio, nor did she acknowledge an acquaintance with them. She asked the child to tell her how certain newspaper stories ended. The first stories presented to the child concerned current local news—the current weather, the fact that Lincoln's Birthday was approaching and that it would be a school holiday. Then the child was read stories about local taxi drivers and asked to finish each story. One of these stories related an episode very similar to one the children had heard enacted on the radio. The children who had heard the violent endings to the radio drama gave very different responses to this newspaper story than did those who had heard the nonviolent series. The responses were categorized according to whether the child attributed high, intermediate, or low aggression to the taxi driver in completing the newspaper account. In this Pennsylvania community, taxi drivers are helpful and friendly, so it is not surprising that the children who had heard the nonviolent radio dramas tended to finish the news story in a way that attributed no aggression (two-thirds of the cases) or only intermediate aggression (in the other one-third) to the taxi driver. The children who had heard the violent series, on the other hand, apparently thought that taxi drivers in their own town would behave the same way as the fictional ones, for half of them finished the news account in a way that attributed "high" aggression to the local taxi driver, and only one-third attributed no aggression.

This small study would need to be duplicated with various children, roles, and media before we could generalize from its findings. In the meantime, it warns us that the distinction between reality and fantasy may be blurred for normal young children.

A striking series of studies by Professor Albert Bandura and his colleagues at Stanford University has demonstrated that children learn aggressive behavior from television and that they enact this behavior in their play under suitable circumstances. In earlier studies, Bandura had already shown that children will imitate the specifics of aggressive behavior they observe in an adult (Bandura and Huston, 1961; Bandura, Ross, and Ross, 1961). He and his colleagues then conducted a study to determine whether children will imitate agression they observe in a film as readily as they will imitate aggression they observe performed by live adults (Bandura, Ross, and Ross, 1963a).

The study included ninety-six nursery school children, ranging in age from less than three to nearly six, with an average age of 4½. He assigned the children arbitrarily to four categories. A child in the first category, the "Real-Life Aggressive condition," was brought to a room and given some materials to play with at a small table. After the child settled down to play, an adult in another part of the room began playing with several toys, including a mallet and a five-foot inflated plastic Bobo doll. The adult was aggressive toward the Bobo doll in highly novel and distinctive ways, and performed each of these aggressive acts—like pummeling the Bobo on its head with a mallet—several times in the course of the session. The child, of course, observed this aggressive adult behavior occurring in his presence. A child in the second category was brought to the same playroom, set to playing with the same toys, and then shown a color film in which the same adult model displayed the same sequence of novel aggressive behaviors to a Bobo doll. This was called the "Human Film-Aggressive condition." A child in the third category was shown a cartoon film showing an adult costumed as a cat, playing against a fantasyland backdrop of brightly colored trees and butterflies. On this film, the cat was similarly aggressive towards the Bobo doll. Finally, children in the fourth category were reserved as a comparison group, with no exposure to aggressive models in the course of the study.

Immediately after the experience described above, the child was taken to an anteroom containing a variety of highly attractive toys. The experimenter told him he might play with them, but once he had begun, the experimenter purposely frustrated the child by saying she had decided to reserve the toys for some other children. She indicated that instead he could play with some toys in another room. They went to that room, where the adult busied herself with paperwork at a desk, while the child played with the toys. These included toys typically used in aggressive play and others associated with unaggressive activities. Among them was a Bobo doll and a mallet. The child played for twenty minutes, while his behavior was observed and scored by judges watching through a one-way mirror from an adjoining room.

The main finding of this study was that children who had observed adult aggression prior to being frustrated were more aggressive in their subsequent play than those who had been frustrated, but had *not* observed any adult aggression. The average total aggression score for the control child was 54, while the average was 83 for children in the "Real-Life Aggressive" category, 92 for those in the "Human Film-Aggressive" category, and 99 for those in the "Cartoon Film-Aggressive" category.

The second finding was that the aggression of the children who had observed adult models would be imitative. The child's behavior during the play session was rated as imitative, partially imitative, or nonimitative. An imitative act was one which directly copied the adult behavior the child had seen earlier, with the child exhibiting the very acts he had observed or speaking the very words the adult had spoken. In the "Real-Life" and "Human Film" categories, 88% of the children exhibited varying degrees of imitative aggression, and in the "Cartoon Film" condition, 79% did so. Not only were these children more aggressive as a whole, but, more significantly, the character of their aggressive behavior was closely modeled on the behavior they had observed in adults, whether live or on film. Scores for imitative aggression were significantly higher for the children who had observed models than for the control children, and the same was true for scores of partially imitative aggression. On the other hand, aggressive gunplay was displayed equally by the various groups. This is an example of aggressive behavior which had not been modeled by the adults in the experiment.

This study holds special interest not only because it demonstrates that children mimic the aggressive behavior of adults, whether they observe this behavior in the flesh or on film, but also because it demonstrates that the kind of film seen does not seem to affect the mimicking process significantly. The fantasy-reality distinction in which adults believe seems to have little significance for the bright middle-class preschool children Bandura and his colleagues studied.

One reason that Bandura's work is so widely respected by other psychologists is that his conclusions do not rest on a single study. He has conducted a series of investigations over the years, using different children and different films. Each study adds to the strength of the conclusions we can draw.

A second study meriting close consideration here used nursery school children whose ages ranged from three to five years, with an average of just over four years (Bandura, Ross, and Ross, 1963b). They were assigned at random to different categories. A child in the first category was taken to the playroom where the adult experimenter worked at a desk while the child watched a five-minute film projected on a TV console. This film concerns two adult men, Rocky and Johnny. At the beginning, Johnny is playing with his highly attractive collection of toys. Rocky asks to play with some, and Johnny refuses. Rocky then behaves aggressively toward Johnny and his possessions, enacting a series of highly unusual and distinctive aggressive behaviors while making hostile remarks. (These unusual and distinctive acts of aggression were employed in this series of studies to enable observers to distinguish imitative acts of aggression in the child's subsequent play from other stereotyped acts common to the play of many children.) Rocky is the victor as the result of his aggressive behavior, and the "final scene shows Johnny seated dejectedly in the corner while Rocky is playing with the toys, serving himself generous helpings of 7-Up and cookies and riding a large bouncing hobby horse with gusto. As the scene closes, Rocky packs the playthings in a sack and sings a merry tune" (Bandura, Ross and Ross, 1963b:602). A commentator announces that Rocky is the victor.

Another film was used which also involved aggression between Rocky and Johnny, but was rearranged in sequence so that the aggressive behavior shown by Rocky results in his being severely punished. "Rocky is thoroughly thrashed by Johnny. As soon as he succeeds in freeing himself, Rocky flees to a corner of the room where he sits cowering, while Johnny places his toys in a sack and walks away. The announcer comments on Rocky's punishment" (Bandura, Ross, and Ross, 1963b:602).

After viewing one of these films, the child was taken to a room for a twenty-minute play session which was observed and scored by judges behind a one-way vision screen. This room contained some toys similar to those in the film, and others as well—the latter being present to avoid loading the dice. The child's imitative aggressive acts and his nonimitative aggressive acts were recorded.

The total aggressive scores of the children in the "Aggressive Model-Rewarded" category were 75.2, which is significantly higher than the total for children in the "Aggressive Model-Punished" category (53.5). In contrast, children who had seen neither film but who simply were brought to the playroom for a twenty-minute play session had total aggression scores that were intermediate (61.8). Most of the aggression was not sufficiently close to that exhibited by Rocky and Johnny to be called imitative, but the imitative aggression that was observed occurred more commonly among the Model-Rewarded children than among the Model-Punished children and both showed more imitative aggression than the controls, who had never observed the distinctive adult behaviors.

After the play session was over, a child was asked to evaluate the behavior exhibited by Rocky and Johnny and to select the character he preferred to emulate. Among the children who had seen Rocky emerge the victor because of his aggressiveness, 60% preferred him, 5% preferred Johnny, and 35% voiced no preference. Among those who had seen Johnny triumph despite Rocky's aggressiveness, 20% preferred Johnny, 20% preferred Rocky, and 60% had no preference.

Almost without exception the children who said they preferred Rocky as a model were nonetheless critical of his behavior. They preferred him despite his infamy, siding with the sinner: "Rocky is harsh, I be harsh like he was, 'Rough and bossy,' 'mean' . . . Rocky beat Johnny and chase him and get all the good toys.' 'He come and snatched Johnny's toys.' 'Get a lot of toys' . . . 'He was a fighter. He got all good toys' " (Bandura, Ross, and Ross, 1963b:605). Bandura's comment on the meaning of this finding deserves to be quoted:

> *The finding that successful villainy may outweigh the viewers' value systems has important implications for the possible impact of televised stimulation on children's attitudes and social behavior. The present experiment involves only a single episode of aggression that was rewarded or punished. In most televised programs, the "bad guy" gains control over important resources and amasses considerable social and material reward through a series of aggressive maneuvers, whereas his punishment is generally delayed until just before the last commercial. Thus children have opportunities to observe many episodes in which antisocially aggressive behavior has paid off abundantly and, considering that immediate rewards are much more influential than delayed punishment in regulating behavior, the terminal punishment of the villain may have a relatively weak inhibitory effect on the viewer (Bandura, Ross, and Ross, 1963b:605-6).*

These two studies demonstrate that young children imitate the specific acts of aggression they have observed in the behavior of adults on film or television. This imitation occurs whether the dramatic presentation is realistic or fantasylike. Imitation is enhanced if the aggression brings rewards to the adult who is observed and minimized if the aggression brings punishment.

A third, more recent, study by Bandura again confirms the finding on imitation. However, it is somewhat more ominous in its implications, for it shows that children acquire from watching television the capability of performing imitatively many more acts of aggression than they spontaneously exhibit—that children learn more from television than their spontaneous behavior reveals.

The sixty-six children who participated in this third study were again of nursery school age, averaging just over four years of age (Bandura, 1965). They were assigned at random to three categories, "Model Rewarded," "Model Punished," and "No Consequences." A child in the first category began his participation by watching a five-minute television show in which an adult exhibited physical and verbal aggression toward a Bobo doll. In the closing scene of the "Model Rewarded" film, a second adult appeared bearing an abundant supply of candies and soft drinks, informed that model that he was a "strong champion," and that his superb performance of aggression clearly deserved a treat. He then gave the model various desirable foods, and while the model consumed these, he continued to describe and praise the model feats.

A child in the "Model Punished" category saw a performance which was identical to the above in its initial sequences, but concluded with a second adult's reproving rather than praising the model:

"Hey there, you big bully, you quit picking on that clown. I won't tolerate it." As the model drew back he tripped and fell, and the other adult sat on the model and spanked him with a rolled-up magazine while reminding him of his aggressive behavior. As the model ran off cowering, the agent forewarned him, "If I catch you doing that again, you big bully, I'll give you a hard spanking. You quit acting that way" (Bandura, 1965:591).

Finally, a child in the "No Consequences" category saw a performance involving only the initial section of the above film, the part showing the adult's aggression toward the Bobo doll.

Each child was then observed in a ten-minute play session while alone in a room containing a variety of toys, among which were some similar to those used by the adult model on the film. Judges observed through a one-way screen and recorded the occurrence of imitative aggressive responses. Then the experimenter returned to the playroom, bringing an assortment of fruit juices and booklets of sticker pictures to be presented to the child as rewards. She then asked, "Show me what Rocky did in the TV program," and "Tell me what he said," promising to reward the child for each imitation performed.

The findings of this study have to do with how much imitative aggression each child performed spontaneously in the ten-minute session as compared with how much imitative aggression he showed himself capable of performing when offered an incentive.

As might be expected from the earlier studies, the children in the "Model Rewarded" and the "No Consequences" categories mimicked the adult model in their own free play, doing so more frequently than those in the "Model Punished" category. Again we have a demonstration that children imitate aggression they observe on television and again the finding that punishment of the adult in the television show serves to inhibit the children's tendency to imitate spontaneously.

When requested to imitate the adult's behavior and offered an incentive, each group of children performed more imitative acts of aggression than had been performed spontaneously in free play. This demonstrated that the children were capable of more imitative aggression than they had initially shown. Further, those in the "Model Punished" category could imitate aggressive acts just as efficiently as those in the "Model Rewarded" and "No Consequences" categories. Remarkably, the girls in this study (as had the girls in the other two) exhibited less imitative behavior in their own free play than the boys, but when offered an incentive for imitating aggression, they mimicked essentially as many aggressive acts as the boys.

Thus, this third study of Bandura's reinforces the theory that children learn some of the behavior they observe. Some sequences of their learning are exhibited spontaneously in their play, and others can be elicited if the setting is right. This is equally true whether the observed behavior was condemned and had painful consequences, was rewarded and had positive consequences, or was neither rewarded nor punished and had no known consequences. The study suggests that the observed consequences of behavior have some influence on the spontaneous mimicking of that behavior but none of the retention of the capability to imitate the behavior when offered an incentive for doing so.

A related study deserves brief mention. The participants were seventy-two children, ages six to eight, from a lower-middle-class neighborhood (Bandura, Grusec, and Menlove, 1966). Every child saw the same four-minute color film showing an adult performing a series of novel acts with various toys. For example, when he first came on stage the adult had his right hand cupped over his eyes. Later, he tossed bean bags at a target, but instead of standing erect, he bent over with his back to the target and threw bean bags through his legs.

Children were assigned at random to three categories. Some simply observed the film. Others were instructed to verbalize every action of the model as they watched the actions unfold on the TV screen. Those in the third category engaged in competing symbolization, counting aloud while they watched the TV film: "1 and a 2 and a 3 and a 4. . . . "

Each child was then taken to a room containing the toys the adult had used in the film. The experimenter asked him to demonstrate every one of the model's actions he could recall. She praised and rewarded each correct response. She also prompted the child with a standard set of cues, asking him to show the way the adult behaved in the opening scene, to demonstrate what the adult had done with the dart gun, the Bobo doll, and the bean bags, and to portray the adult's behavior in the closing scene.

The children did very well in mimicking the adult they had just observed. Those who had simply watched the four-minute television show were able to reproduce an average of fourteen sequences of behavior. Not surprisingly those children who had verbalized the sequences as they watched the same film could reproduce even more—an average of seventeen. As expected, competing verbal activity interfered with the child's retention of the film content—the children who had counted aloud during the film could reproduce only nine of the sequences afterward.

Again we have a demonstration of the child's powers of observation and retention. Such demonstrations have interested other psychologists, and a number of them have conducted studies providing independent confirmations of this phenomenon (cf., Rosenkrans and Hartup, 1967; Kuhn, Madsen and Becker, 1967). What is especially significant about these studies is their concern with the child's behavior. Many questionnaire and interview studies report what people say they think and what they say they might do or not do, but these report what the subjects actually do.

Conclusions

Every civilization is only twenty years away from barbarism. For twenty years is all we have to accomplish the task of civilizing the infants who are born into our midst each year. These savages know nothing of our language, our culture, our religion, our values, or our customs of interpersonal relations. The infant knows nothing about communism, fascism, democracy, civil liberties, the rights of the minority as contrasted with the prerogatives of the majority, respect, decency, ethics, morality, conventions, and customs. The barbarian must be tamed if civilization is to survive. Over the centuries, man has evolved various methods of accomplishing this.

Our methods of "socializing" the barbarian hordes who invade our community every year rely on their remarkable learning abilities. The infant learns by trial and error, and man has capitalized on this ability by rewarding infants for acceptable behavior and punishing them for unacceptable behavior. The infant develops a close attachment to one or two persons who care for him and meet his needs, and because of this he desires to conform to their wishes and expectations. Man has capitalized on the infant's propensity to make attachments by assigning special educative responsibilities to mothers and fathers. The young child learns through observation and imitation, and throughout the ages man has provided opportunities for young people to learn from their elders in apprentice relations—the girl learning housewifery by watching her mother, the boy learning farming skills by working alongside his father, the youngsters learning hunting skills by observing the experienced hunters. The young child learns through oral instruction, and man makes use of this opportunity by talking to children about the social group and its values and ideals, by relating legends, telling tales, gossiping, sermonizing, lecturing, conversing, explaining, scolding, and moralizing. The young child learns from graphic representations, and for many years parents have created pictorial representations of the culture, its religious symbols, its heroes, and its workers. All of these age-old techniques of socialization have enabled man to teach most of the young barbarians how to behave as members of the group if civilization is to flourish.

In the modern era, these techniques continue to be very important, but they have been joined by others whose impact is less well understood. At first, the new methods of teaching were available only to a privileged few. Thus, the method of teaching through written instruction reached only to a privileged few. Thus, the method of teaching through written instruction reached only those who had been taught to read and who could gain possession of rare scripts. As the technology of printing and distribution of printed materials advanced, more and more individuals had access to the printed word, and more and more were taught the literacy skills needed to gain meaning from print. Thus the printed word became important in socializing the young. Any educated person is impressed with the extent of this importance, and perhaps it is worthwhile to remind the reader that the ability to read is acquired late in a child's life, long after his basic social learning has been accomplished, and the ability to read efficiently comes even later. The child is well advanced before he is so skillful in reading that the printed page can modify his behavior or alter his beliefs.

The newer forms of communication circumvent this difficulty. As we have discussed, they are meaningful to the illiterate as well as to the tutored. The most powerful of these new forms, movies and television, communicate with the individual both audibly and visually. The most powerful medium of all, television, accomplishes this feat in the individual's own home, bringing into that arena instantaneous reports of events in the world around him, not only in his neighborhood and city, but in his nation and other nations.

The fact that we do not think of the new media as being instructors for our young does not affect their teaching ability. Although it is not governed by a board of education, TV does teach. We think of radio, movies, and TV as "entertainment," but in fact children learn efficiently from them. Our media-saturated college students, born eighteen or twenty years ago, just as television was coming into prominence, get their kicks from playing "Trivia," a campy game of inconsequential questions and answers about radio, TV, movies, comic books, and popular songs in which the effectiveness of these media as teachers is demonstrated by the young people's ability to answer questions like "Who won the Super Bowl three years ago?" "What was the consolation prize on 'The $64,000 Question'?" and "Who was the singer who popularized a well-known 'hit' song?" A Trivia Contest was held at Columbia University in 1967, with teams from Princeton, Yale, Pennsylvania, Barnard, and other elite schools battling it out and with the winner receiving a trophy while a chorus sang the Mr. Trivia song—"There he goes, think of all the crap he knows." The proud winner declared, "You have to get your basic training from the time you are six until perhaps twelve or thirteen," and credited his success to "my garbage-filled mind."[8]

The new media speak directly to the child's two best developed senses, conveying a reality which is not very different from the other realities he experiences. A child who has seen the president of the United States on television would recognize him instantly if he should encounter him; a child who has only read about the president or heard his name spoken would not recognize him on sight but instead would need to be told, "That's our president." It is precisely the direct correspondence between reality and the television representation of reality—with no need for reliance on verbal labels for encoding and decoding—that makes television so powerful.

8. "Triviaddiction," *Time,* 10 March 1967, pp. 69-70.

American children spend many hours a week watching television. They begin watching at a very young age and are faithful to the set on weekdays and weekends, throughout the summer, and during the school year, with the result that at age sixteen the average American child has spent as many hours watching television as he has spent in school. Is it a fair bet that the two sources of information have affected his social learning equally?

Perhaps, but one might lean toward television. The child turned to "the tube" at a younger and more impressionable age, and he attended the television school on his own initiative and volition, not because of the combination of social pressures, parental expectations, and truancy laws which enforce school attendance. One hears a great deal about school dropouts, but very little about those who do not watch television. The ability of television to hold its audience better than our schools can hold their students may tell us something about its superior effectiveness as a communicator and thus as a teacher.

What is this electronic mechanism teaching the child? The *Christian Science Monitor* completed a survey of TV programming six weeks after the assassination of Senator Kennedy. In eighty-five half hours of programming in prime evening hours and on Saturday mornings, eighty-four killings were observed. Both acts of violence and threats of violence were recorded.

The survey found that the most violent evening hours were between 7:30 and 9:00, when, according to official network estimates, 26.7 million children between the ages of 2 and 17 are watching television.

"In those early evening hours, violent incidents occurred on an average of once every 16.3 minutes. After 9:00 p.m., violence tapered off quickly, with incidents occurring once every 35 minutes," the paper said.

"In the early evening, there was a murder or killing once every 31 minutes," the survey reported. "Later, once every two hours." [9]

Everything that social scientists know about human learning and remembering tells us that this carnage is being observed and remembered by the audience. If children can remember and reproduce fourteen or fifteen sequences of behavior from one of Bandura's amateurish five-minute films, how much do they remember from hour after hour of professionally produced TV?

The fact that a student can recall the 1946 singing commercial, "Use Ajax, boom, boom, the foaming cleanser" when playing Trivia does not mean that

9. "84 Killings Shown in 85 ½ TV Hours on the 3 Networks," *New York Times,* 26 July 1968, p. 29.

he *will* use that foaming cleanser when he grows up and has to scour his toilet bowl. Similarly, the fact that children watch TV "pictures of mayhem, mugging, and murder"[10] does not mean that they *will* perform comparable acts of violence in their own lives. This is obvious from our crime statistics, which show that children are among the least violent of our citizens and that violence is most characteristic of the adolescent and young adult male.

However, television time is sold to sponsors on the conviction that although the Ajax ad will not guarantee that the viewer will buy the product, it raises the probability that he will. Social scientists would simply make the same claim for filmed or televised violence, whether fictitious or real. Viewing the carnage does not guarantee that the viewer will "go forth and do likewise," but it raises the probability that he will.

Media spokesmen make much of the fact that as yet social scientists have no convincing proof for this hypothesis.[11] They minimize the fact that the evidence for it is accumulating year by year and at an accelerating rate. They also ignore the fact that there is no convincing scientific evidence for or against most of our social practices and policies.

To the media spokesman one is tempted to reply "Media man speaks with forked tongue." The television industry exists and reaps its profits from the conviction that television viewing does affect behavior—buying behavior.

Is it fanciful to imagine that there may be a relation between the Trivia game at Columbia in 1967 and the violence at Columbia in 1968? Where did the students learn the attitudes and the aggressive behaviors that they vented against the police? Where did they learn the implicit values that seemed to justify their expressing what may be entirely legitimate grievances in such profoundly antisocial ways. They acknowledge that their minds are "garbage filled" by the media, and we may wonder whether they are "aggression stuffed" by the same sources.

The evidence that we do have indicates that films and television are profoundly educative for their viewers, teaching them that the world is a violent and untrustworthy place, and demonstrating for them a variety of violent techniques for coping with this hostile environment. Whether this message is beamed as fact or fiction, it is accepted by young children. They incorporate in their own behavior patterns all the sequences of adult behavior they observe on television.

Whether they will ever employ these aggressive behaviors in their inter-

---

10. Morris Ernst, quoted by George Gent in "Human Life Seen as Devalued by Violence in the Mass Media," *New York Times,* 17 September 1968, p. 78.

11. Joseph A. Loftus, "CBS Man Doubts Violence Theory: Tells Panel Studies Fail to Establish Links to TV," *New York Times,* 17 October 1968, p. 87. This is an account of the testimony of Joseph T. Klapper before the National Commission on the Causes and Prevention of Violence.

personal relations depends on many complex factors. Every individual is capable of more different behaviors than he has occasion to display. Many of us remember our high school French, and although years pass without presenting us with any occasion to speak it, we continue to retain some capability of doing so when the occasion does arise. The analogy to television violence is not exact, for television as a school for violence enrolls adult viewers as well as high school students and has them in class for many more hours than any French teacher ever did. When the occasion arises that calls for violence, one does not have to cast his mind to his high school classroom, but only to last night's or last week's "thrilling episode."

What else will he remember from that episode? There was a murder every half hour during prime viewing time on network television. How many instances are there of constructive interventions to end disagreement? What other methods of resolving conflict are shown? How many instances of tact and decency could an avid televiewer chronicle during the same hours? How often is reconciliation dramatized? How many adult acts of generosity are provided to children for modeling? What strategies for ameliorating hate are displayed? How many times does the child viewer see adults behaving in loving and helpful ways? What examples of mutual respect does he view? What can he learn about law and order? How many episodes of police kindness does he see? How frequently does the glow of compassion illuminate the screen?

Addendum

Editor's Note: Dr. Siegel, as a member of the Surgeon General's Scientific Advisory Committee on Television and Social Behavior, was invited to testify before the Subcommittee on Communications of the U.S. Senate Committee on Commerce in March, 1972. She reviewed the scientific report summarizing many studies with the following words:

The substance of our report, based on a careful review of the twenty-three studies commissioned by our program and also of previous research, was that there is now evidence for a causal link between watching TV violence and subsequent aggressive behavior by the viewer. Such a causal link has long been suspected or presumed by well-informed social scientists, by concerned parents, and by many other thoughtful observers. The evidence for it comes both from experimental studies in social scientific laboratories and from field surveys in natural situations.

There is no reason to believe that TV watching is the principal cause of violent behavior by adolescents and adults. The causes of aggression are many, and they include both biological and cultural sources. In childhood, perhaps the single most important source of later aggressiveness is gross parental neglect and abuse. The child of a harshly punitive parent is very likely to become a punitive adult himself in later life, and the victim of child neglect is likely to become a neglectful and abusive parent. In adolescence and young adulthood, incarceration in our prisons is undoubtedly one of the major sources of later aggressiveness; our jails and prisons as they presently operate are schools for crime. Those who seek the single most effective steps that might be taken in our society to reduce violence must be advised to consider strenuous interventions to aid abused children and sweeping reform of our local, state, and federal systems of incarceration of charged and convicted criminals.

Commercial television makes its own contribution to the set of factors that underlie aggressiveness in our society. It does so in entertainment through ceaseless repetition of the message that conflict may be resolved by aggression, that violence is a way of solving problems. In TV entertainment, children may observe countless acts of murder and mayhem, may learn through observation how to perform these acts, and may learn that such acts are admired by other people. Thus commercial television is itself a school for violence. And American children are attending this school as many hours a year as they attend the schools sponsored by their local school boards.

Research has shown that not all children are equally vulnerable to the negative influences of television watching. Indeed, it is a minority of all children who display these influences in their later behavior. My own guess is that TV violence has negative effects on all child viewers, but that countervailing forces overcome these effects in the majority. In the minority, the positive influences in their lives are not sufficient to counteract the baneful effects of hours of watching aggressive modes of conflict resolution. The result is that the children adopt these aggressive modes in their own lives. When we talk about a minority of American children, it is important to remember that we are talking about millions of children. It is important also to remember that most negative influences in our society have overt effects on only a minority. For example, only a minority of young adults use heroin, yet no one doubts that it is a very serious social problem. Only a tiny minority of American children ever contracted polio, yet our society strove energetically to eliminate that disease. The "minority" of American children who display the effects of too much violence on TV is surely a much larger group numerically than either the heroin users or the polio victims; they need our concern.

Who are the children who are most affected by watching TV violence? They are the very children who have been predisposed to be aggressive by other influences in their lives. In other words, they are the least capable of interpreting and resisting the antisocial influence of TV violence, because they have the poorest defenses against it. The fact that they are already predisposed to be aggressive should make us especially cautious about any additional negative influences in their lives and should hardly make us complacent that it is their "predisposition" which enables vicarious violence to becloud these children's lives further.

145

References

Bandura, A.
1965   "Influence of models' reinforcement contingent on the acquisition of imitative responses." Journal of Personality and Social Psychology, vol. 1, pp. 589-95.

Bandura, A., J. Grusec, and F. L. Menlove
1966   "Observational learning as a function of symbolization and incentive." Child Development, vol. 37, pp. 499-506.

Bandura, A., and A. Huston
1961   "Identification as a process of incidental learning." Journal of Abnormal and Social Psychology, vol. 63, pp. 311-18.

Bandura, A., D. Ross, and S. A. Ross
1961   "Transmission of aggression through imitation of aggressive models." Journal of Abnormal and Social Psychology, vol. 63, pp. 575-82.
1963a   "Imitation of film-mediated aggressive models." Ibid., vol. 66, pp. 3-11.
1963b   "Vicarious reinforcement and imitative learning." Ibid., vol. 67, pp. 601-7.

Kuhn, D. Z., C. H. Madsen, and W. C. Becker
1967   "Effects of exposure to an aggressive model and 'frustration' on children's aggressive behavior." Child Development, vol. 38, pp. 739-45.

Rosenkrans, M. A., and W. W. Hartup
1967   "Imitative influence of consistent and inconsistent response consequences to a model on aggressive behavior in children." Journal of Personality and Social Psychology, vol. 7, pp. 429-34.

Seigel, A. E.
1958   "The influence of violence in the mass media upon children's role expectations." Child Development, vol. 29, pp. 35-36.

The Desensitization of Children to TV Violence

Victor B. Cline, Roger G. Croft,
and Steven Courrier

A number of hypotheses have been advanced trying to explain or understand the phenomena of uninvolvement of citizenry when their fellows have been assaulted or attacked within range of their helping. The most publicized recent event dealt with Kitty Genovese, a Brooklyn girl who was assaulted, raped, and murdered in a New York apartment complex over a period of time in excess of a half an hour. A later investigation revealed that more than forty people were aware of her distress and need for help but no one came to her aid directly or indirectly (such as anonymously calling for police help by phone). The My Lai incident wherein American soldiers killed a number of Vietnamese civilians represents only the most publicized event of this kind which apparently occurred on a more minor scale on other occasions during the Vietnam war. Trial transcripts suggest a lack of concern by many of the American soldiers involved in these killings of unarmed civilians which included children.

The work in systematic desensitization by such investigators as Wolpe, Bandura, and Eysenck suggests the hypothesis that where people have been exposed to a great deal of prior violence, either directly or vicariously as in newspapers, movies, TV programming, and other media, there may, in time, occur a kind of psychological blunting, a "turning off" or "tuning out" of the normal emotional responses to these types of events. This might repre-

Victor B. Cline is a professor of psychology at the University of Utah. Prior to receiving his Ph.D. from the University of California at Berkeley in 1953, he worked for a year there as a graduate research psychologist at the Institute of Personality Assessment and Research. Later he became a research scientist at George Washington University's Human Resources Research Office. His interests have included interpersonal perception, psychodiagnostics, psychotherapy, effects of media violence and pornography, successful marriage, delinquency, values, and personal and scientific competence. For many years he

sent, possibly, a gross type of desensitization or deconditioning to violence stimuli.

The work of Bandura (1969) and his associates, Hanratty (1970), and others in a social learning field would suggest that through the process of modeling and imitative learning people and their behavior can be influenced by violence witnessed on the TV or movie screen. The more recent work of Liebert and Baron (1971), Stein, Friedrich, and Vondracek (1971), in a series of studies financed by the Surgeon General's Office, presents stronger evidence suggesting a causal link between witnessed violence and an observer's subsequent aggressive behavior.

If one combines the effects of desensitization (which could potentially have the result of reducing the effects of "conscience and concern") with the effects of modeling, which provides (through our media entertainments) the explicit cognitive formulations and mechanics for committing violence, it may not be too surprising to see not only major increases in our society of acts of personal aggression but also a growing attitude of indifference and nonconcern for the victims by the aggressor. It next might be noted that 96% of all American homes contain at least one TV set (1970 Census) and that it has been fairly well documented that children become "purposeful TV viewers" by the age of three, meaning that they have established patterns of favorite programs and viewing times (Murray, 1971). Various surveys have shown that most children watch television from fourteen to forty-nine hours a week, depending on age and socioeconomic level (National Commission on the Causes and Prevention of Violence, 1969). This means that children spend more time in front of a TV set than in front of a teacher during a year's time, suggesting its pervasiveness as a socializing and teaching agent. In the preschool years alone the average child spends more time watching TV than he would in the classroom during four years of college (Looney, 1971). Looney also notes that by the age of fourteen the average child has witnessed more than 11,000 murders on TV. The research of Gerbner, Eleey, and Tedesco (1970) indicates an increasing incidence of violence in TV prime time shows. In sum, these various researches suggest that the more TV children are exposed to, the more violence they see modeled.

has been the program director of a traveling community mental health clinic. He has authored some fifty publications.

Roger Croft is completing his work for a doctoral degree in educational psychology at the University of Utah. He is the author of seven publications focusing on such areas as attitude change, classroom instructional techniques, learning theory, and others. He has taught university courses in social psychology and adolescence.

Steve Courrier is a student at Westminister College, completing work for his bachelor's degree. He was involved heavily in working out the instrumentation procedures in the research discussed in this article, wherein autonomic nervous system responses were measured by the six-channel physiograph.

In this research we addressed ourselves to the question, "What physiological effects are brought about within the child who is constantly exposed to violence on TV?" That is, is there a measurable physiological difference in emotional response (e.g., of the autonomic nervous system) to filmed violence between children who are high exposure TV viewers (and hence see more violence) and children who are low exposure TV viewers? In other words, do children become desensitized, to some degree, to violence? The research of Lazarus (1962) and associates is relevant here. They exposed their subjects to films of a primitive tribal ritual involving painful and bloody genital mutilations. They found that viewers became increasingly less emotionally responsive with repeated observations of this type of scene, suggesting a progressive desensitization to a specific type of filmed violence. Zuckerman (1971) in reviewing a number of studies correlating galvanic skin response, pupillary (eye) response and other physiological responses to witnessing erotic photos and movies has noted a "habituation" or desensitization effect after repeated exposure to this type of stimulus.

It was the hypothesis of the authors that prolonged exposure to violence as depicted in TV and movies would also produce desensitization in children (using standard psychophysiological instruments to measure emotional arousal and a violence film as a standard stimulus).

Eighty male children between the ages of five and twelve were divided into two groups on the basis of *(a)* having witnessed TV four or fewer hours per week for the preceding two years, and *(b)* having witnessed TV twenty-five hours a week or more for the previous two years. Viewing time was verified by interviews with parents and children plus an "after the study" intensive telephone interview check. These two groups were referred to as the "High TV exposure group" and the "Low TV exposure group." The children were recruited by advertisements in the local daily newspapers, forty for each group. The researchers encountered no difficulty in locating children for either category. Each was paid $5.00 for participating. The mean weekly TV exposure time of the "high" group was 42.0 hours. The mean weekly TV exposure time of the "low" group was 3.8 hours.

In an effort to determine if our high and low TV exposure children came from different backgrounds or social climates, samples of high and low TV watchers were compared on social-class level (using the fathers' occupation and educational level [years of education completed] as indirect measures of this).

Significant differences were found between the two groups on both measures. The low TV watchers came from family backgrounds where the father had more education and higher occupational status. This was consistent with the findings of the National Commission on the Causes and Prevention of Violence in *Violence and the Media* (1969) which indicated that, "Generally speaking those in the lower socioeconomic categories are more likely to be heavy users of the pictorial media, particularly television."

The major question this raises is whether children who come from somewhat different socioeconomic (though overlapping) backgrounds could be presumed to respond on the GSR and plythesmograph (autonomic/emotional) measures in some systematically different ways. We have reviewed the literature and can find no data to suggest this. Another way of approaching the problem was to compare the base levels on the various autonomic response measures of the two groups prior to exposing them to the experimental violence film. This was done, and no significant differences were found. Thus, though the two samples differ to some degree on the socioeconomic dimension, there is no evidence to suggest that this should effect in some systematic way their autonomic/emotional arousal to a violence film.

A Narco Physiograph Six and related amplifiers and equipment were used to measure autonomic/emotional arousal. A film fourteen minutes in length in 16mm black and white was shown, consisting of three segments: (*a*) a two-minute, nonviolent ski film narrated by Bill Stern, (*b*) a four-minute chase sequence from the W. C. Fields film, *The Bank Dick*, and finally (*c*) an eight-minute sequence from the Kirk Douglas film, *The Champion*, depicting a brutal boxing match. The boxing film contained an equal amount of active violent content and nonviolent material (the nonviolent material between rounds). This made it possible to study each child's response to both violent and nonviolent elements in the film. At the same time, the physiograph made a continuous recording throughout the entire film of each subject's autonomic/emotional responses.

Only one child was tested at a time. Each was seated in a large comfortable armchair and connected by wires to the physiograph which was hidden. A continuous measure of physiological responses was recorded for each youngster starting before the showing of the three films and continuing until the end. This physiological record was "time hacked" automatically every five seconds. This allowed the researchers to identify frame for frame what was being projected in the film with what the subject was seeing and producing autonomically or what was being recorded on the physiogram.

Five violent segments from *The Champion* and five nonviolent segments from the same film were identified. These averaged eleven to thirty-four seconds in length. It was during these specific segments that precise measurements were made, for every subject, of the plythesmograph (blood volume) responses.

Blood volume pulse amplitude, one type of heart response data, was measured by attaching a photoelectric cell to the index fingertip inside a small cuff. Changes in blood volume pulse amplitude were analyzed by taking measurements of needle tracings from the diastolic trough to the systolic peak at the indicated points on the record. Thus, changes in blood volume were measured during the ten different segments in the film. The blood volume *changes,* then, measures of peripheral vaso-constriction (in percentage of change), were taken from the active violent and nonviolent segments of the film. This was the primary "arousal" or comparison index (a percent change figure) used to assess differences between the two experimental groups.

Next, forty-one male children between the ages of seven and fourteen, divided into a group of twenty high TV exposure subjects and twenty-one low TV exposure subjects, were recruited and experimented with in a manner similar to the earlier described research, except that two children were tested simultaneously, one from the high and the other from the low TV exposure groups.

In addition to blood volume pulse amplitude, skin conductance (GSR) was also measured with a Narco Physiograph Six in the following manner:

Two 16-mm surface skin electrodes were attached to the palm of the subject's hand with a 4-cm separation between the electrodes to measure skin conductance (GSR). The tracings from the physiograph were scored both before and after the ski sequence and for both nonviolent movie sequences and active violent segments of the boxing match. Scores were secured for the number of responses (GSR: the actual count of individual "bumps") to individual films during the ten measured segments of time as described in the first experiment.

In Tables 1 and 3, where GSR and blood volume responses of high and low TV exposure boys are compared, it will be noted that there are no significant differences in the "before the film" and "after the neutral ski film" conditions. Both groups respond essentially similarly with regard to their GSR and blood volume tracings. However, when both groups are exposed to filmed violence, we do obtain significant statistical differences in their responses. The low TV exposure boys are significantly more aroused emotionally (according to GSR and blood volume pulse amplitude as indices of emotional arousal). We note with GSR (Table 1) that even during the *nonviolent* segments of the boxing match, the low exposure boys tend to be somewhat more aroused (though not significantly) than the high exposure boys. Since the violent and nonviolent segments of the film separated each other by mere seconds, it would suggest that the low TV exposure boys were not able to "recover" as quickly from the emotional arousal of the violence witnessed. Thus this research suggests that a desensitization effect or possibly a habituation-to-violence effect has set in for the high exposure boys. Also of significance is the fact that in the urban area where the research was conducted, the film *The Champion* had not screened commercially or on TV in the two years prior to the present research, which would suggest a possible "generalizing" effect of violence viewing on TV. If children get desensitized or habituated to violence in a general sense, this would be somewhat different and have more serious implications than mere desensitization to a particular violence segment in a particular film.

TABLE 1
Differences in Number of Galvanic Skin Responses (GSR) of High and Low
Television Exposure Boys While Watching Filmed Violence[1]
Mann-Whitney U Analysis

Experimental Condition	Subjects	No. of Subjects[2]	Mean No. Galvanic Skin Responses	U	Significance Level
Before film begins	High TV exposure boys[3]	19	2.26		N.S.
	Low TV exposure boys	21	2.29	198.5	
At conclusion of "neutral" ski film but before violent film	High TV exposure boys	19	1.89		N.S.
	Low TV exposure boys	19	2.58	141.0	
During selected nonviolent segments of boxing film[4]	High TV exposure boys	17	6.76		N.S.
	Low TV exposure boys	15	11.67	85.5	
During selected violent segments of boxing film	High TV exposure boys	17	13.88		
	Low TV exposure boys	15	21.13	22.5	$p < .05$

1. The film was an eight-minute boxing sequence from *The Champion* with actor Kirk Douglas.

2. The number of subjects varies slightly in the various comparisons because the physiograph recording stylus "went off the recording paper" during several recordings, rendering the particular protocol unsuitable for scoring in the *portion used.*

3. "High exposure boys" refers to an average viewing of TV for 42.0 hours per week for the previous two years. "Low exposure boys" refers to an average 3.8 hours weekly viewing of TV for the previous two years.

4. A series of GSR readings were taken during the moments in the film where there was no actual physical violence being depicted, such as between rounds, where there was a cutaway to a sportscaster commenting on the action, etc. These segments lasted only a few seconds.

In Table 2 the results of two studies using the other index of autonomic/ emotional arousal are presented. In this case we compare high and low TV exposure boys to filmed violence, using a measure of blood volume pulse amplitude (via a plythesmographic recording). The results are essentially identical to Table 1, with the high TV exposure boys in both studies showing significantly less autonomic arousal, which might be interpreted as some degree of desensitization to the filmed violence.

The results of these several studies using two different measures of autonomic response corroborate each other and suggest that some children who are heavy TV watchers (and see more violence) may become, to some

TABLE 2

Differences in Blood Volume Pulse Amplitude of High and Low
Television Exposure Boys While Watching Filmed Violence[1]
Mann-Whitney $\underline{U}$ Analysis

	Experimental Condition	Subjects	No. of Subjects[2]	Mean % Change[3]	$\underline{U}$	Significance Level
Study I	Nonviolent vs. violent stimulus elements of boxing film	High TV exposure boys	36	8.8%	58	$p<.01$
		Low TV exposure boys	31	17.1%		
Study II	Nonviolent vs. violent stimulus elements of boxing film	High TV exposure boys	14	22.3%	60	$p<.05$
		Low TV exposure boys	15	28.2%		

1. The film was an eight-minute boxing sequence from *The Champion* with actor Kirk Douglas.

2. There was some attrition and variation in number of subjects from those originally recruited due to such miscellaneous reasons as equipment malfunction, and other things. Experiment I had 40 boys in each category, and Experiment II had 20 and 21 in each category.

3. The boxing film had a mixture of violent segments (where the boxers are hitting each other) and nonviolent segments (as between rounds or cutaway shots to a sports-caster commenting on the fight). A series of measures were taken (for each boy-participant) of blood volume pulse amplitude during the violent segments and compared with the same thing during the nonviolent segments. The percent change in amplitude was the measure of "arousal."

TABLE 3
A Comparison of Base Levels in Blood Volume Pulse Amplitude of High and
Low Television Exposure Boys Prior to Viewing Filmed Violence
Mann-Whitney U Analysis

Experimental Condition	Subjects	No. of Subjects	Mean Blood Volume Level	U	Significance Level
Prior to showing of any films	High TV exposure boys	16	7.61	121.0	N.S.
	Low TV exposure boys	18	6.90		
After viewing two neutral films but just prior to seeing violence film	High TV exposure boys	17	7.75	125.5	N.S.
	Low TV exposure boys	19	6.42		

degree, habituated, or "desensitized" to violence generally. This raises the possibility of a blunting of "conscience and concern" when children are exposed to a great amount of filmed violence. If our children may be regarded as an important national resource, and if, as Liebert and others have suggested, we are just one generation from potential savagery, then these findings suggest some concern that we teach our children wisely. The kinds of fantasies we expose them to may make a great deal of difference as to what kind of adults they become and whether we will survive as a society.

References

Baker, R., and S. Ball
    1969   A staff report to the National Commission on the causes for prevention of violence. Violence and the Media. Washington, D.C.: U.S. Government Printing Office.

Bandura, A.
    1969a   Influence of model's reinforcement contingencies on the acquisition of imitative responses. Journal of Personality and Social Psychology 1:589-95.
    1969b   Principles of Behavior Modification. New York: Holt, Rinehart & Winston.

Berkowitz, L.
1969   Roots of aggression. New York: Atherton.

Eysenck, H. J.
1963   Behavior therapy, extinction, and relapses in neurosis. British Journal of Psychiatry 109:12-18.

Gerbner, G., M. F. Eleey, and N. Tedesco
1970   Violence in television: A study of trends and symbolic functions. Report to the National Institute of Mental Health, Rockville, Md.

Hanratty, M. A., E. O'Neal, and J. L. Sulzer
1971   The effect of frustration upon imitation of aggression. Paper presented at the meeting of the Western Psychological Association, San Francisco, April.

Lazarus, R., J. Speisman, A. Mordkoff, and L. Davison
1962   A laboratory study of psychological stress produced by a motion picture film. Psychological Monographs 76(34).

Leibert, R. M., and R. A. Baron
1971   Short term effects of televised aggression on children's aggressive behavior. Paper presented at meeting of the American Psychological Association, Washington, D.C., September.

Looney, G.
1971   Television and the child: What can be done? Paper presented at meeting of American Academy of Pediatrics, Chicago, October.

Murray, J.
1971   Television in inner city homes: Viewing behavior of young boys. Report to National Institute of Mental Health, Rockville, Md.

Stein, A. H., L. K. Friedrich, and F. Vondracek
1971   Television content and young children's behavior. Report to the National Institute of Mental Health, Rockville, Md.

Wolpe, J., and A. A. Lazarus
1966   Behavior Therapy Techniques. Oxford: Pergamon Press.

Zuckerman, M.
1971   Physiological responses and exposure to erotica. Paper presented at meetings of American Psychological Association, Washington, D.C., September.

School for Violence, Mayhem in the Mass Media

Fredric Wertham

If somebody had said a generation ago that a school to teach the art and uses of violence would be established, no one would have believed him. He would have been told that those whose mandate is the mental welfare of children, the parents and the professionals, would prevent it. And yet this education for violence is precisely what has happened and is still happening; we teach violence to young people to an extent that has never been known before in history.

This has become possible through two circumstances. One, of course, consists in tremendous technological advances. The other is the fact that the effects of mass media on the young were not sufficiently recognized. It was a new dimension of the environmental influence on the child. That some ingredients might, do, and have done harm was as little suspected as it was with cigarette smoking until it was studied clinically.

Solution by violence is a great temptation; control of violence is a difficult task. That is why promotion of violence in all its forms and disguises is a threat to progress. For thousands of years mankind has striven to get away from it. All the wise men who have ever written and spoken about it, as

Fredric Wertham, a psychiatrist, received his medical training in Germany and England and did postgraduate studies in France, England, and Austria. He has been chief resident psychiatrist at Johns Hopkins, senior psychiatrist at Bellevue Hospital in New York, and director of psychiatric services at Queen's General Hospital. He is now consulting psychiatrist at Queen's and also maintains a private practice for both children and adults.

Wertham has taught psychiatry at Johns Hopkins and New York Universities. He founded the first psychiatric clinic in Harlem (the Lefargue clinic) and directed the first psychiatric clinic in a major U.S. court in which all convicted felons were examined. He was the first psychiatrist admitted to a federal court as an expert for the defense in a

Schopenhauer pointed out, have said more or less the same thing. But what happens is that we, at the height of power and prosperity, fill the minds of children with an endless stream of images of violence, often glamorous, always exciting. The youngest children are stimulated and encouraged to a primitive response of "hitting out." That, in the School for Violence, is the elementary lesson. Preschool children learn it. The advanced course is the pursuit of happiness by violence.

That there is an inordinate amount of violence in the mass media is an indisputable fact. No other ingredient plays such a predominant role. If one wanted to list all possible varieties and methods of killing, torturing, or injuring people, no more complete source would be available than the mass media. Textbooks of forensic psychiatry and criminology are left far behind.

The modern child is exposed to a variety of mass media: radio, movies, television, comic books, magazines.

Television represents one of the greatest technological advances and is an entirely new, potent method of communication. Unfortunately, as it is presently used, it does have something in common with crime books: the devotion to violence. In the School for Violence, television represents the classical course. Many of the movies being shown increasingly on the TV screen also have a lot of violence in them and so merge with the overall picture.

We must make clear to ourselves what mass audience means in terms of television. Suppose a murder is shown on the stage in a theater in a large metropolitan city and is shown on the TV screen. In order to reach an audience as big as television provides in one single evening, the play would have to run in the theater to full houses for half a century. (This is one answer to people who excuse violence on television by saying that good drama may have violence too.) The quantity of violence on the screen is staggering. In one week, mostly in children's viewing time, one station showed 334 completed or attempted killings. Promotion spots showed over and over again eight murders within sixty-second periods (sometimes it was only thirty seconds and four murders). The future historians of our civilization cannot afford to ignore such items. The different channels in one large city showed in one week 7,887 acts of violence and 1,087 threats of violence (such as "I'll break your legs!"). Not counting war pictures, there were in

book banning case and has since appeared for the defense in similar cases. Not only was he the sole psychiatric consultant to the Kefauver Senate Subcommittee for the Study of Organized Crime but he was also the first psychiatrist to investigate the effects of school segregation by clinical psychiatric methods. His investigations were part of the case which led to the U.S. Supreme Court's decision abolishing school segregation.

He is the author of many articles in professional journals as well as in the popular press. He has also authored six books, *Seduction of the Innocent, A Sign for Cain, The Show of Violence, The Brain as an Organ, Dark Legend: A Study in Murder,* and *The Circle of Guilt.*

one week 895 completed or attempted homicides. One single episode of a well-known Western series showed to millions of children on Christmas night twenty-one violent acts. Thirteen of them were killings, five were fights, and three were assaults. Programs featuring violence constitute more than half of prime viewing time in the evening on two major networks. An average American youth may, between the ages of five and fourteen, see on the screen the violent destruction of more than 12,000 people. In half an hour on the screen a child may witness more violence than the average adult now experiences in a lifetime. According to the official British Report of the Committee on Broadcasting, scenes of physical violence are an almost invariable ingredient of all American importations (other than comedy and musical shows).

Apart from the number, it is equally necessary to look at this in the round and consider how the violence is committed. The portrayal is always vivid. All varieties of injury or killing occur: the deliberately cruel, the gruesome, the mad, the fanatic, the sneaky, the passionate, the sadistic, the clearly sexual, and so on. Most prevalent is the casual, matter-of-fact, kill-as-you-go violence. It is all made very simple for the young and not-so-young minds. The man is in the way, he disagrees with you, he is of the opposite faction, you want his property, he has wronged you—so of course you kill him. What alternatives are there? A new program is announced with this slogan: "Sometimes Killing Is the Only Answer."

Violence on the screen is depicted as a method of life. Few arguments or conflicts on TV are settled without a fight. Never, literally never, is it taught in this School for Violence that violence in itself is something reprehensible. There is no such course. Most Westerns live entirely on violence. The patriotic, historic, or geographic disguise makes it appear that murder in this setting is different. But homicide on horseback is the same as homicide on foot, in a car, or in a spaceship. The alleged historical authenticity of some Westerns is merely a smoke screen. The stories are not of violence for history's sake, but of history for violence's sake.

Whenever possible, vivid violence is introduced. Shakespeare only suggests the terror that follows Macbeth's ascent to the throne. In the screen version, you see men hanged from trees. In the show about historical Jesse James, you see him as he begins to shoot down twenty-six young, unarmed prisoners. Ever-new motives for violence are dug up: a beautiful young girl in one of the usually good TV series has the desire to see men killed over her and satisfies that desire until she is finally killed herself. In one of the medical series, the psychiatrist as "therapy" punches a man in the jaw.

Nobody can understand the violence in the world of today if he does not know what we put and permit on the airwaves. We are hypocritically surprised when young people in slums fight the police. On the screen, the sport of killing policemen flourishes. Television too has the scene (shown Saturday afternoon, for example) of the policeman asking for a license and being promptly shot and killed. A policeman is shot twice in the back, and you are shown his blood in close-up. Police brutality is also graphically displayed.

Children appear on the screen as instigators of violence as well as killers and victims of killers. The little boy reproaches the old sheriff for not shooting an outlaw: "Isn't there anything you can do?" he asks, "even if you aren't young?" So the ex-sheriff thus exhorted does shoot the man. A little girl is shown being lured and killed by a "monster" in human form. Race and national prejudice is common and is even used as a prop for plots. In a historical film often shown, the particular cruelty of a man is explained at the end by the fact that he had "Indian blood" in him—a lesson not in history, but in prejudice.

Sometimes the brutality is extreme. People are kicked in the face; a man is beaten and thrown alive into a garbage can to die; a man is suspended by his hands with his feet over a fire ("I'll kill you my way, slow-like," says his tormentor); in one episode of a well-known series, a lawyer's tongue is cut out, then the knife is brandished in a pretty girl's face with the threat that the same thing will happen to her and nobody will kiss her any more. This is followed by a singing commercial about a brand of milk: "Today's brand milk pours like cream." Whatever the qualities the milk may have, it was certainly not the milk of human kindness.

Scenes of what may be called sneering sadism are typical, in which the torturer or murderer expresses cynical contempt for his victim while hurting him. For example, while one man lies on the ground with an arrow in his chest, a second man says, "Don't worry, it won't hurt much longer," and pushes the arrow deeper into his chest and kills him. I have heard children call such remarks "cute." The "School" has evidently not taught them that violence is never cute.

The "eye motif" is also prevalent on the screen. During a fight, a man throws mud in another man's face, aiming for his eyes; a lighted match is thrown into a man's face; a man is blinded by acid thrown into his face; molten lead is thrown into a man's eyes and face—he screams out in pain and falls down; "Do exactly what I tell you," the strong-arm man says to the man he is beating. "The chances are you won't lose more than an eye"; and so on ad nauseam. One device consists in using a bullwhip to injure an eye. In one show a prisoner's eye is put out with such a whip; in another an observer comments on a man wielding such a whip, "He can pick a man's eye out with that whip as easy as picking a grape!"

While injury to the eyes is blatantly represented, an injury to genitals is only suggested—but it is not forgotten. A man heats the rowel of a spur over a flame and runs it over the middle of another man's body from the neck down, to the accompaniment of shrieks and groans from the tortured victim.

Monster shows, sometimes in a pseudoscientific setting of outer space, are frequent screen fare. The monsters serve as a convenient disguise for violence. They have been given a moral carte blanche to get away with all sorts of black deeds that ordinary humans might not so easily be permitted. The monster programs combine the cult of violence with the cult of ugliness which we foist on children. Some of these horror shows might be better named cruelty shows. The moral confusion that is presented to youth is shown by the behavior of censors and producers. A scene where an animal approached another animal with mating intent was cut out by the censors, while scenes where a human being was tortured and killed by another human being were given a clean bill of heath. And a producer of horror films said with pride, "Our pictures are absolutely clean. The monster might abduct the young bride, but only to kill her." "Only" is the significant word here.

A good example of the mass media's presentation of violence to the young is the screen history of Jack the Ripper. It is a sign of the times that from all the crimes in the world these most sadistic ones were selected. Five young women are stabbed and killed in the film. There are close-ups of the knife blade and faces of the victims. When this sex-murder film was shown in some movie houses, the younger set was regaled in addition with a cartoon show. The program was announced over the radio and in newspapers like this:

COME ALL KIDDIES!! CARTOON SHOW
FOLLOWED BY JACK THE RIPPER

Recently, Jack the Ripper was shown on television eight times in one week, at times particularly available to children and young people. On Saturday it was shown at noon, immediately after a program specifically addressed to children. On Sunday it was shown twice in the time between 11:30 a.m. and 3:30 p.m. The different showings were followed by a promotion spot showing the killing of four police officers. This is the intensive course.

What are the effects of all this mass-media mayhem? The harmful effects are still doubted or denied by some. Among writers on the subject, we must distinguish two psychological types of experts. The fundamental driving power of some of them is centered in the living human being, the child. The basic interest of others, consciously or unconsciously, is influenced by a leaning toward the mass-media industry. We may call the first group of writers child directed (CD) and the second group, industry directed (ID).

The economic specific gravity of the mass-media industries in our society is so great that investigators and writers are influenced, whether they realize it or not, to veer toward apologetic views. As a result, much research, or rather, pseudoresearch, by ID experts has misled the public. Even UNESCO has fallen into this trap. In its pamphlet on the "Effects of Television on Children and Adolescents," we find all the old cliché alibis minimizing the harm done by mass-media violence. The pamphlet claims to present an inclusive survey of research results but departs from scientific custom by completely omitting contrary findings in American and European scientific journals.

Three methods have been used to study mass-media effects: the questionnaire method, the experimental method, and the clinical method. The first two, the questionnaire and the experimental methods, give only partial and often highly misleading results. They disregard the clinical examination of actual cases, thus leaving out what is truly human in the child. From their results, the real, concrete child as he exists in our society does not emerge. Within narrow limits, both the experimental and questionnaire methods can provide useful hints, but they cannot provide the backbone of valid conclusions in this field. The third method, the clinical one, is the only one that can give valid, lifelike results.

In the questionnaire method, children are given a list of questions to answer. Their answers are then compared with those of a control group and statistically evaluated. This method sounds objective and is, in fact, regarded by many as an objective, sociological approach. In reality, however, it is very subjective, rigid, and based on arbitrary presuppositions. The questionnaire-answer method is sometimes disguised by such euphemistic terms as "semi-structured interview." Even if they mean to, children cannot tell you whether or how much they have been influenced. These children are not examined. It is assumed that what is not in the questions is irrelevant. Subjecting a child to such a set of form questions is very different from—in fact, almost the opposite of—a clinical examination. The whole child is not considered, his spontaneity is not taken into account, his concrete life situation is neglected. No statistical refinement can overcome the errors and ambiguities contained in the original data. Strictly comparable control groups do not exist in this intricate field because there are too many variable factors. The statistical-control-group method of the physical sciences has been inappropriately applied to emotional and mental phenomena. Nobody has proved statistically with control groups, for instance, what the effects are of coveting your neighbor's wife.

In the experimental method, a film with violent scenes is exposed and the reactions of the subjects are tested by various devices and recorded. At best, the results of this technique for measuring "aggressive" attitudes are fragmentary and superficial. These artifically set-up experiments are similar to animal experiments, but they are not adequate because children are not rats. Moreover, the immediate effects after seeing a show are relatively unimportant compared with the significant long-range consequences. We neglect the difference between animals and men if we underestimate the fact that children have imagination. The experimental situation is unlifelike and does not mirror or reproduce real life. The many human potentialities cannot be reduced to simple experimental terms. The human part gets lost. What we want to study is the meeting of the two settings: the world of make believe of the mass media and the world of the child's real environment. That is not a mechanical encounter. Between the images of television and the effects on a child in the audience is the profound personal reaction of that particular child.

The only method that permits us to arrive at carefully developed, valid results is the clinical method, which permits us to study the whole child and not just one facet. Nothing can replace concrete clinical analyses of actual significant cases. Clinical study means thorough examination and observation, follow-up studies over a considerable period, analysis of early conditioning, study of physique and of social situation. Playroom observations are helpful with young children, group sessions with adolescents and teenagers. Psychological tests are an important adjunct, such as the Mosaic test, which shows ego organization, or the Duess test, which in young children is valuable for analysis of the family and social relationships. The clinical approach is not content with a cross section through a subject's life at a given moment. It aims at a longitudinal view of his life and an understanding of psychological processes. You cannot question or interview a child as if he were a job applicant. You must gain his confidence and show him that you are really interested.

Most important is an open-mindedness for the finding of any harmful factors, however inconspicuous. Wrong psychological presuppositions prevent us from seeing things in their proper perspective. False theories lead not only to wrong conclusions but to wrong observations. For example, in publications from the Gesell Institute at Yale University are these statements: "Many perfectly normal children at some ages of childhood, particularly around seven to eight years of age, experience a spontaneous and apparently uninduced love for blood, murder and torture." And: "Normal school-age children often have an addiction to violence which . . . surpasses anything they will see in print." And again, in another place: "Relish for death and destruction appears to be just plain natural for many children." In considering theories like this, we go far beyond the narrow problem of mass-media effects. We face a widespread attitude which regards such curses of mankind as violence and torture as natural.

By clinical analysis, we can disentangle the various elements that enter into a person's thinking and behavior. We can trace the connections between different events, thoughts, and actions and follow the subtle conditioning that molds minds. While adults are by no means immune, it is the immature minds of children and adolescents that are most vulnerable to all kinds of untoward influences. This is most clearly known from brain pathology. The disease, epidemic encephalitis, attacks both adults and children, but it is mostly in children that it causes definite psychological symptoms.

It was with the clinical method that I discovered and demonstrated for the first time that excessive radiation of children's minds with violent images by the mass media is a definite harmful influence. It meant taking seriously what seemed to be a triviality. But it was a new dimension in physical pathology.

The profusion of mass-media violence has potentially an adverse effect on children's lives. It is lamentable that one first has to prove that. My conclusions are based specifically on the clinical study of three hundred cases in large mental-hygiene clinics and in private practice. The cases included both poorer and well-to-do youths. Many of them were not patients, but relatives (sons, daughters, brothers, sisters) of patients. The younger the child, the more he is exposed; but no age group is invulnerable. Children with emotional, intellectual, or social handicaps are more apt to be affected in certain directions. But there is no clinical evidence that the healthy, well-adjusted, and lovingly brought-up child is immune. On the contrary, according to the principle *corrupto optimi pessima*—the corruption of the best is the worst— the influence on the character development of some of these children and adolescents is especially deplorable. Overlooking the mass-media factor is as unscientific as overstressing it. For example, through the neglect of mass-media influences, many false diagnoses of childhood schizophrenia have been made, especially in underprivileged and culturally deprived children. Mass-media violence does not produce psychological effects simply or mechanically. Like other environmental factors, it impinges on a living human being in whom pliable and controlling forces contend. Many a child well adjusted to the social values inculcated by comic books and television has been called maladjusted.

Children have absorbed and are absorbing from the mass media the idealization of violence. Not the association of violence with hate and hostility, but the association of violence with that which is good and just—that is the most harmful ingredient. We present to children a model figure to emulate and model method to follow. The model figure is the victorious man of violence. The model method is the employment of violent means. The hero's reasoning is usually only a gimmick; his violent action is very real. The child who sits down to view one of his ubiquitous Westerns or similar stories can be sure of two things: there will be foul play somewhere, and it will be solved by violence. The ideal is not the pursuit of happiness, but the happiness of pursuit. That is their introduction to life. It is an entirely false and dangerous conception. This stock of images fastens itself on the subconscious of children's minds and is used by them almost automatically to interpret situations in real life. No wonder so many come to stumble over it later in one form or another! They have learned to think in terms of violence. That is not easy to undo with reeducation or psychotherapy.

The idealization works in two areas: the glamour of the violent act and the glorification of the man of ready violence. Hero worship and the glorification, which is a natural phenomenon, become violence worship. Typical is the reply of a twelve-year-old boy who was asked what he liked best in the adventure and Western stories. His reply: "The shooting and the beating. The heroes!" That is the lesson, and it has been learned. Identification with a heroic figure is one of the great means of education, but when the hero is one who overcomes all obstacles through sheer brutal strength, it becomes miseducation.

The influence of mass-media violence varies with different age groups, personality types, and social circumstances. But the most important underlying effect, distilled from my examinations and observations, can be summed up concisely: the blunting of sensitivity. Many young people have become hardened. That is a clinical fact. We are bringing up, and have brought up a generation not of ugly Americans but of hard Americans. If we want that—and it may be that there are some who do—we are doing an excellent job. As Dostoevski wrote: "The best man in the world can become insensitive from habit." Our children have been conditioned to an acceptance of violence as no civilized nation has ever been before. How? That is very simple. You crowd the minds of the young with violent images continuously, relentlessly, in every context and costume. It begins in the nursery when we arm children physically and disarm them morally. We teach them that violence is fun. We have silently passed an amendment to the Sixth Commandment: "Thou shalt not kill, but it is perfectly all right for you to enjoy watching other people do it."

The desensitization manifests itself on different levels. Children have an inborn capacity for sympathy. But that sympathy has to be cultivated. This is one of the most delicate points in the education process. And it is this point that the mass media trample on. Even before the natural feelings of compassion have a chance to develop, the fascination of overpowering and hurting others is displayed in endless profusion. Before the soil is prepared for sympathy, the seeds of sadism are planted. The clinical result is that feeling for others is interfered with. These youngsters show a coarsening of responses and an unfeeling attitude. Their indifference to acts of brutality on the screen and in life is not a simple, elementary quality consisting merely in an absence of emotion. I have studied children who were profoundly blasé about death and human suffering, yet showed spontaneously the most generous and altruistic impulses. While some adults winced, seven-year-old children watched the murder of Lee Harvey Oswald by Jack Ruby with unruffled equanimity. They had seen quick, remorseless killings so often! Hurting other people is the natural thing. They had learned in the school for violence that the victim is not an individual but a "bad guy," a criminal, an outcast, an enemy, a radically inferior person. He is not a person but a target. Children have been conditioned to identify not with the victim but with the one who lands the blow.

In older children, teenagers, and young adults, the blunting of sensitivity can lead to a false image of human relationships. They develop what may be called an I-don't-want-to-be-involved attitude, a social indifference. Instead of the principle of "creative cooperation" that H. B. Wells used to talk about, they think in terms of destructive competition, of winning and losing instead of right and wrong. They are guided by the power instinct and by feeling that cruelty is all right if it is successful. Once they have become so unfeeling by habit, these young people miss a lot of the minor excitements that come from ordinary human relationships. This emotional emptiness may drive them to extravagant acts, especially to violent ones. All this is, of course, not caused or furthered by mass media alone. However, that fact that there are so many other influences working in a similar vein does not make the mass-media factor less potent but more so. Whatever the seeds of sadism may be, we certainly fertilize the ground for them to grow in.

I know of few methods for hurting, torturing, or killing people that have not been displayed to young people in the mass media. For many years, men have been trying to abolish physical torture as a legal method for obtaining confessions. Montaigne's writing and the French Revolution were milestones in this endeavor. Now young people have been conditioned by the mass media to believe that beating and torturing are legitimate to make people tell the whereabouts of the opponent or to reveal where the loot is. They consider it a sophisticated and manly method for getting at the truth. This psychological effect is a combination of the idealization of violence and blunting of sensitivity. In one study, 78% of schoolchildren felt that it is "O.K. to beat up outlaws to make them confess." These are our future citizens, our law-enforcement officers, voters, and soldiers.

In addition to the methods, almost all the motives—especially the baser ones—that may lead to violence are represented in the mass media. Every form of hate is espoused as a vehicle for a plot and as an excuse for revenge. In the phrase of Francis Bacon, in his essay "Of Revenge," we have tried "to weed it out" by law. In the mass media it is a stock motive. Many young people have learned to take hate and revenge for granted. They have absorbed the idea that individual revenge is natural, necessary, and heroic. An elaborate TV show in a well-known series has the title "The Sweet Taste of Vengeance." This describes well the spirit of innumerable television stories.

In a number of instances recently, victims have been robbed, beaten, stabbed, raped, or killed while bystanders and witnesses watched without attempting to help or to call the police. A lot has been written about such cases, and many reasons have been adduced for this callous behavior. One important factor has not been pointed out. These noninterventionists had seen in the mass media so many vivid portrayals of revenge that their behavior was affected by it: if a man is discharged from jail, of course he forthwith devotes all his energy to killing or injuring a judge, a witness, or anybody else whom he holds responsible for his arrest. If you help the law, the lawbreaker will get you. So don't get involved. That is the lesson. We should not be so surprised at the predictable behavior of the graduates.

The mass media mediate lessons and impulses. Most of the impulses remain latent and do not lead to overt actions. What are induced are dispositions and tendencies. Sometimes clinical study permits us to predict the danger of future violent acts. But so many combinations of psychological and social factors may enter into violent acts, both in juveniles and in adults, that often we cannot—

> Look into the seeds of time
> and say which grain will grow and which will not.

Midway between dispositions and fantasies on the one hand and real violent acts on the other is children's play. When children play sex, we are alarmed: when they play killing, we are not. In fact, we provide them with weapons. If a visitor from Mars were to inspect our crime and Western television shows he would conclude that on earth intercourse is forbidden and killing is taught. In the last decade-and-a-half, children's play has become more violent. From the nature of the play it is demonstrable that this is partly due to the influence of the mass media. What used to be playful fighting now is apt to be hitting and choking for real. Boys used to play "fresh" with girls in a bantering manner. Now not infrequently they play roughly, "tie them up," and really hurt them. Many children act out TV stories in playroom observation and therapy. For example, a nine-year-old boy played the criminal and "gunned down" the other children, calling some of them enemies, others policemen. Finally he said, "Now, here comes the good guy, like on television—they always have one. He kills the criminal. This is the end of the story."

The effect on mental attitudes is the most important, even if a less dramatic, consequence of mass-media violence on individual and social health. In addition, the saturation with violent stories is a contributing causal factor to some overt violent acts. Two sets of facts are indisputable. First, in real life, more violent acts are committed by younger people, an increase not explained by the growth of population. Second, there is an inordinate amount of violence and cruelty in the mass media to which millions of young people are exposed. To assume that these two sets of facts have nothing to do with each other and that they are purely coincidental is both frivolous and unscientific. The connection is never mechanical. We have to decide in the individual case by clinical judgment whether and to what extent the mass media plays a role. Sometimes it is the whole atmosphere of violence exuded by the media which conditions immature minds to react with violence. In a department store a little boy approached Santa Claus and gave him a vicious kick in the shins saying, "Here, that's for last year!" That particular scene wasn't one the boy had seen on the screen, but he had seen enough beating and kicking of every variety. Other boys in my case material push little kids out of a swing, which they also have not seen in mass media; it is their translation of more mature forms of brutality they *have* seen there.

The idea of violence may attach itself to feelings of kindness. A gentle boy of twelve was devoted to his dog and took very good care of him. One day the dog was inadvertently run over. The boy walked up to the driver and said very seriously, "If that dog dies, I'll kill you." Like many other children, he had seen so much supposedly justified killing on the screen that a threat like that occurred to him naturally, like a reflex.

Even children who are naturally sensitive and fundamentally nonhostile may become indurated to callousness by the overexposure to what Morris Ernst has called the "gospel of violence." They have become used to images of injury and violent death. They have learned from the media that to take pity on somebody is a sign of weakness. The stereotyped world of brutal force has become their frame of reference. That has limited their horizon and given them a distorted perspective. On the one hand, mass media have a specific appeal to the conscious thinking of people. On the other, they provide a climate, a social opinion, a norm. They have already established a tradition of violence.

Violent acts, both mild and serious, may be the result of very different psychological processes. In an equally great variety of ways, the mass-media factor may be connected with these processes. At one extreme it may merely tip the scales at the last moment. Only a slight impetus may be needed to translate ideas into actions. At the other extreme it may be a prime incitement and incentive.

Usually the effect lies between: crime and violence shows arouse an appetite for violence, reinforce it when it is present, show a method to carry it out, teach the best way to get away with it, stimulate the connection between cruelty and sex (sadism), blur the child's awareness of its wrongness. That is the curriculum of the School for Violence.

Why is there so much violence in the mass media? That is a question not to be shirked. Is it merely accidental? Can we dismiss it as merely a symptom of the times?

There are three main reasons. First, violence is exciting; it is an effective attention-getting device. You know the story of the man who said he could persuade a mule to do anything by first whacking him over the head to get his attention. We have become somewhat like that mule. Violence onstage is an easy way to arouse interest and to win an audience and hold it. To keep the interest up, more and more violence is needed. In the words of a film critic, the appeal of violence "is calculated as coldly as if it were money—which indeed it is."

Second, the mass media violence is a reflection of a part of our social reality. There are people who half-conscientiously believe that violence is a good method for solving problems. They may not intend it explicitly in the individual case, but they tolerate it because they think the violent are the strong and will win. The imagination of some statesmen does not seem to reach much further. They want to send the Marines as quickly as Superman flies out the window.

Third, the excessive display of violence exists against the background of a whole system of defense arguments, alibis, and rationalizations. The same story's reasons are repeated over and over again with the resounding voice of conviction. One or the other continually crops up in newspapers, magazines, books or scientific papers, publicity releases, radio and TV discussions, PTA meetings, practically all the books on mass-media effects, government brochures, articles about juvenile delinquency, mental-hygiene pamphlets, and so on.

What makes these arguments and others like them so important is that they not only amount to an acceptance of violence in advance but are applied to other social evils, such as poverty, slums, racism, alcoholism, and so on. They are comforting assumptions and evasions which tend to relieve us of responsibility. It is necessary to take a good look at them.

It is variously claimed:

1. That the emotionally healthy and well-adjusted child from a harmonious family is not harmed—as if we could be sure of such a blanket of immunity against the suggestive and seductive influences to which millions of children are exposed. The healthiest child from the most harmonious family may have some weak points that are not readily apparent. Every child is immature and therefore susceptible to harmful influences.

2. That it is all up to the family to shield the child—as if we were still living on farms and in the preelectronic age. It is fashionable to blame parents, especially mothers, for any kind of maladjustment of their offspring. In this way, all the outside influences are disregarded—those which come to the child over the parents' heads and over which the family has little control. Parents have been so brainwashed into a belief in their own guilt that it is hard to reverse it. To put all the emphasis on the family means to bypass the community, the society which conditions the family.

3. That the mass media merely give the public, and the children, what they want. If you tie a goat to a post, he will eat the grass that he can reach. That does not mean he prefers it. Clinical child psychiatry cannot agree with Dr. Spock when he writes in his book on baby and child care: "The people who write and draw [comic books] are only turning out what they have found that children want most," and "When children show a universal craving for something, whether it's comics or candy or jazz, we have got to assume that it has a positive constructive value for them." Children did not call for crime and horror TV and comic books, for murder, blood and torture. It was foisted upon them. When will we learn what Goethe's mother knew so long ago, that we don't need blood in the nursery? A network executive, as quoted in the magazine *Television Age*, has explained very clearly how you can make an appetite for special programs: "You make it just as you make an appetite for violence by selling violence."

How misleading this children-want-violence argument is can be seen from a comparison of present research results with investigations carried out earlier. More than thirty years ago Dr. Edgar Dale reported the answers given by children from nine to thirteen to the question: What do you dislike most in motion pictures? The following replies are typical:

"I don't like to see people killed. Killing makes you too excited."

"Bloody pictures make me sick—show you how to kill."

"Killing makes you have bad habits."

"Shooting and killing bad. Hate to see people suffer."

"It looks awful to see people killed."

Evidently children did not always "want most" to see people killed. We have instilled in them the habits of violence and insensibility.

Those who claim that the adult public merely gets the brutality and violence that it wants can point to a real expert as their witness. Hitler said: "Why should one talk a lot about brutality and violence and get indignant about tortures? The masses want this. They want something that makes them shudder with horror."

4. That violence is part of human life and that you have to teach children to cope with reality. We can teach a child that—unfortunately—there is still violence in the world without overloading his imagination with violent images. You can tell a child where babies come from without showing him.

The blood and brutality in the mass media are not realism but pseudo-realism. It leaves out the continuity of experience, both individual and social.

5. That seeing a lot of murder and torture in the mass media will prevent junior in real life from hitting his little brother or from resenting his mother's urging to do his homework. This is called "getting rid of pent up aggressions vicariously." If I were asked to give an example of brainwashing successfully carried out on a great number of educated people, I would cite the prevalence of this theory. It has become the magic formula to explain and excuse violence by the "catharsis theory."

This formula appears in many forms and variations: violent stories provide children with a natural, harmless outlet for their innate aggressiveness; the screen gives normal children relief from their pent-up aggressions which cannot be discharged in real life; children get a vicarious outlet for their latent hostility by looking at violent pictures; watching violent shows helps children get rid of their frustrations; guilt-free expression of their hostile emotions is afforded; children's hostility can be siphoned off by looking at violent programs; watching violent shows gives children an outlet in fantasy for aggression which otherwise might express itself in reality; an abundance of gunplay relieves the child's latent hostility; the mass media provide a safety valve for children's aggressiveness; and so on and on. All these are formulations taken from professional and lay publications. This is a monotonous cult of the cliché.

This outlet theory is not only overdone; it is false. It is pseudoscientific dogma. There is no shred of clinical evidence for it. In reality the programs do not provide a catharsis for children's feelings. On the contrary, the children are overexcited without being given adequate release. Delinquent behavior is not prevented but promoted. Far from providing an outlet, the brutal and sadistic stories of the mass media stimulate, overstimulate, and lead natural drives into unhealthy channels. For example, the brutal mishandling of girls can lead to sadistic masturbatory daydreams.

170

Mass-media producers and toy-gun and war-toy manufacturers have made ample use of this fallacious defense argument. For instance, one toy manufacturer has made a statement as false as it is frightening to parents, namely, that denying children war toys "can turn young boys without outlets for their aggressiveness and destructive urges into homosexuals." Thus can the old theory be distorted and put to good commercial use—at the expense of the well-being of the children.

For this healthy outlet—getting-rid-of-aggression theory, Aristotle and Freud are sometimes invoked. There is no justification in either case. Aristotle in his *Poetics* wrote about purification (katharsis) through pity (eleos) and fear (phobos) in tragedies presented in the Greek theater. According to Goethe, Aristotle was referring not to the spectator but to the characters in the play. However that may be, the quality of the classical tragedies was very different from the violence hackwork of the mass media. And Greek children did not go to the theater for several hours every day. What's more, violence was never shown onstage in the Greek theater, and Aristotle actually advocated that children should be excluded by law from many plays.

Present-day overstimulation of children with violent stories did not exist in Freud's time. He would have been horrified at the current mass-media violence being declared harmless—or even good!—for children. He advocated relieving repressed emotions through analysis of their causes and understanding of the circumstances through which they arose.

The stereotyped getting-rid-of-aggression theory is not only bad for children; it has dangerous political consequences. In 1940 a well-known American psychoanalyst, Dr. Gregory Zilboorg, stated: "We should do nothing about the Nazis, because they have to live out their aggressions."

6. *That there is no proved relationship between pictures and the printed word on the one hand and human behavior on the other.* Nothing contradicts this except the history of mankind. There are very few human relationships which are better established, although it may be difficult to prove statistically.

7. *That critique of mass-media violence may lead to censorship and interfere with civil liberties.* Social control for the protection of children has nothing to do with censorship for adults. Children have the right to grow up healthy and uncorrupted. The battle for civil liberties should not be fought on the backs of children. Those who fight for freedom of expression would be in a stronger position if they conceded that out-spoken sadism should be withheld from children.

The argument that control of what is advertised and exposed to children would interfere with civil liberties has no historical foundation. Civil liberties are not guaranteed but are vilified if under their protection children are harmed. It has never happened in the history of the world that regulations to protect children—be they with regard to child labor, food, drink, arms, sex, publications, entertainment, or plastic toys—have played any role whatsoever in the abridgment of political or civil liberties for adults. Where freedom has fallen, it has come about in a totally different way.

8. That only the predisposed, maladjusted, emotionally disturbed, abnormal, insecure, immature, unstable, already aggressive, or neurotic child is affected. Such a preclassification into rigid categories, vulnerable and invulnerable, is not possible. Sometimes this theory is put like this: violence will not hurt the child if the child is psychologically healthy. My clinical researches do not bear this out. It is not only the abnormal and maladjusted child who can learn—and be seduced. Every sex offender knows that. Healthy and well-adjusted children are not inaccessible. They learn, they are sympathetic and interested, they can be taught bad as well as good. The School for Violence is an integrated school. It teaches all children.

To say that only the allegedly "predisposed" child is affected is a lame excuse. What this predisposition consists in is left entirely undefined. These children are never concretely, clinically described. All children are impressionable. It is a kind of intellectual violence, and entirely inhuman, to divide children—without examining them—into two groups: the predisposed who are assumed to be vulnerable, and the well-adjusted, who are assumed to be immune. The real child and his problems get lost.

The dogma that harm can come only to the predisposed child leads to a contradictory and irresponsible attitude on the part of the adults. The argument goes like this: constructive programs on TV are praised for giving children constructive ideas; at the same time it is denied that destructive scenes give children destructive ideas. Healthy, normal children are not supposed to be affected by the screen fare. And for unhealthy, abnormal children it is not supposed to matter, because if they were not influenced by the screen, they would be influenced by something else. An extreme version of this view, often expressed, is that a child must have some mental disorder before he can be adversely affected by mass media. We are certainly deceiving ourselves if we think that our social conditions, our education, and our entertainments are so good that only emotionally disturbed children can get into trouble!

9. That violence is also in classical literature and in fairy tales. This means confusing violence for plot's sake with plots for violence's sake. There is a great difference. In good literature, violence is characterized as a calamity, a tragic error, an aberration. Often it is no more than an exclamation after a stirring exposition of dramatic, emotional, and moral conflicts. Death in itself is depicted movingly. In many mass-media stories, violence is a device of common living and a routine commonplace.

Fairy tales are on a totally different psychological and aesthetic level. No child expects a pumpkin to turn into a getaway car. For years crime and comic books had advertisements for guns and switchblade knives, but Grimm's fairy tales never carried advertisements for crossbows. Fairy tales do not exist in such numbers as the endless mass-media violence stories. And, of course, children spend incomparably less time with them.

"In the movies," an eleven-year-old boy told me, "they hit the girl on the face. On TV they shoot her. In horror shows they choke her."

"What about fairy tales?" I asked him.

"Oh, in the fairy tales they don't get killed. They live happily ever after. I don't read fairy tales because I like to look at the hopped-up stuff."

The fact that so many responsible people equate crime and horror stories in mass media with fairy tales is a sign of confusion and complacency about violence in both and is like saying the institutions of marriage and of brothels are the same because in both there is sexual intercourse. Fairy tales are not arbitrarily concocted but often embody some popular folk wisdom. They are unreal on a narrative level but real on a constructive, ethical level. In fairy tales the people play a role in social life. They are fishermen or farmers or millers or parents or children or grandparents. Of course, there are also horrors in some fairy tales, and they are certainly not suitable for young children. Rousseau called these "leçons d'inhumanité." But even they do not stimulate imitation in the everyday world so different from fairyland. The moral of many fairy tales is an integral part of the story. In the mass-media story, if there is a moral, it gets completely lost in the general effect of the action. What remains are images, and it is with these that we have saturated children's minds.

10. That children are so resilient that they can take it. Why should they have to? The child's psyche is not resilient but plastic and pliable. Any long-continued influence on a child is either educational or miseducational, never neutral.

11. That good always triumphs in the end and that therefore the effect can be only salutary. The deep impression made on children (and many adults) by individual exciting scenes is not blotted out by the end. How many adults remember the end and resolution of *Macbeth, Hamlet, War and Peace, Faust, Native Son,* or *Swan Lake*? In most mass-media stories, if the killer is conquered at the end, it is merely the violent continuation of a violent plot. The ending violence makes the criminal a hero because he has been fighting against hopeless odds and dies in glory for his convictions. The sadistic suggestion is retained; the lip service at the very end is forgotten. Younger children do not comprehend the moral; older ones sense its insincerity.

What generally happens psychologically is this: the sadistic stories arouse strong emotions, which in their turn lead to half-automatic reactions. The purely intellectual moral ending cannot prevail against these strong emotions and their effects. The endless repetition of these emotional-sadistic stories finally completely nullifies any possible effect of moral-rational endings. The question is not what "moral" the mass-media editor or producer claims is drawn, but what the child picks up from the story. You cannot teach morals in a context of violence. The nonviolent moral is lost in the violent detail.

Here is an eleven-year-old girl's typical description of a TV program:

"They threaten to kill, to betray. A good man knocks down an old man, they kidnap a girl, the men have guns. Two men are tied, there's a lady captive. They bring money as ransom, but they threaten to kill them anyhow. Two men kick one man with their heels. The criminals shoot each other. A bad Indian captures the lady and uses her as a shield—holds a knife on her. One man is shot. The sergeant kills the Indian by breaking his neck and choking him with an underarm grip."

Such descriptions indicate that children do not learn from these shows that "good guys win over bad guys"; rather, they learn that violence is exciting—and, since we allow so much of it to be shown to them, that it is probably a pretty good thing. (A child accustomed to such a rich diet of murders and other violence on the screen may have trouble understanding why his minor transgressions, such as slugging his little sister, call for any punishment.)

What some children do absorb from screen violence is that all life is a fight, that gentle persuasion is never successful—and is sissy anyhow. In spy stories and shows, the ingenuous and intrepid spy appears to youths often as more attractive than the representative of the law. A little boy, when asked what he wanted to be when he grew up, answered, "I want to be a security risk!"

In many mass-media stories, the "good guys" are not so different from the "bad guys." The dignity of the individual is violated by both. The winning heroes are often vigilante types. It is generally accepted that in the end, good triumphs over evil. That is how we allow ourselves to be lulled into unconcern. Content analysis shows that in some of the most exciting stories, just the opposite happens. One TV story: A man kills his wife by hitting her over the head with an iron poker. He makes an ingenious defense and goes completely free. At the story's end, he is happily tending the roses in his garden, glad to be rid of his nagging wife, who did not like roses. This is a real school lesson both in method and in morals.

12. That any trouble does not come from the media but is determined by what the child brings to them. As the man said when his dog killed a rabbit, it was the rabbit that had started the fight. We cannot rigidly separate what is in the environment. There is a subtle interaction between them. Physicists studying a bridge know that because of the interaction of the "free vibrations" (from the structure of the bridge) and the "forced vibrations" (induced from outside), even a relatively small load may be dangerous under certain circumstances.

13. That only contact with significant real persons in the child's life influences him, while pictures and printed words do not. The great success of the many printed advertisements and television commercials directed at children would indicate that they have considerable effect. This is well known to the "significant real persons" who have to pay for the advertised products.

14. That children are not affected by mass-media violence because they know it is only make-believe and not really true. Suppose you showed on television a bed and a man and a woman doing something they should not be doing on TV. Would you let your small child watch that and say, "Oh, she knows that is just make-believe?" In sex we realize this is suggestive and exciting. But when it comes to violence we are blinded.

Quite apart from the fact that it is not always easy for children to distinguish between what is fantasy and what is reality, this argument comes from a misunderstanding of how propaganda works, for children as well as adults. Propaganda is based not on reason and truth but on emotion.

15. That the character of a child has "jelled" at the age of seven (others say at five or three) and that later influences are therefore negligible. This, like some of the other arguments, is misunderstood and misapplied Freud. As Alexander Pope wrote: "So by false learning is good sense defaced." Of course, early infantile experiences play a role. But they do not determine the future course of a person mechanically and fatalistically. To say, as often has been said, that mass media cannot do harm unless the parent-child relationships have been disturbed in the first place in unscientific, both for practical purposes and in theory. What Freud said about outside influences was that up to the age of seventeen, children were "still in the formative period . . . and ought not to be exposed to perverse influences." And in one of his last writings, he stated about the causes of disturbed behavior that in addition to early childhood experiences, "we must not forget to include the influences of civilization."

16. That to see a relationship between mass media and behavior means using mass media as a scapegoat for social problems. The modern mass media in their present state are a social problem.

Statement of the Surgeon General Concerning Television and Violence*

Jesse L. Steinfeld

When I appeared before the Subcommittee on Communications of the Senate Commerce Committee, September 28, 1971, the Chairman said: "I would hope that the Surgeon General in due time will come before this Committee, not with a lot of ifs and buts but will tell us in simple language whether or not the broadcasters ought to be put on notice and be very, very careful in this area because it might have an effect on certain people."

After review of the Scientific Advisory Committee's report and the five volumes of original research undertaken at the request of the Senate Subcommittee, as well as a review of the previous literature on the subject, my professional response is that the broadcasters should be put on notice. The overwhelming consensus and the unanimous Scientific Advisory Committee's report indicate that televised violence, indeed, does have an adverse effect on certain members of our society.

While the Committee report is carefully phrased and qualified in language

*An edited version of remarks presented at *Hearings,* March, 1972, by the U.S. Public Health Service's Surgeon General before Subcommittee on Communications of Committee on Commerce, U.S. Senate on the Surgeon General's Report by the Scientific Advisory Committee on Television and Social Behavior, U.S. Government Printing Office, 1972.

Dr. Jesse L. Steinfeld, who held the post of Surgeon General of the U.S. Public Health Department when this chapter was composed, was born in West Alequippa, Pennsylvania, in 1927. He is married and has three children. He secured his M.D. degree from Western Reserve and later taught medicine at the University of California at San Francisco, George Washington University, and the University of Southern California. His several score publications have tended to focus on the area of cancer research, especially on the role of chemotherapy and plasma proteins. He was on the National Cancer Institute Committee that reviewed the controversial Krebiozen several years ago.

acceptable to social scientists, it is clear to me that the causal relationship between televised violence and antisocial behavior is sufficient to warrant appropriate and immediate remedial action. The data on social phenomena such as television and violence and/or aggressive behavior will never be clear enough for all social scientists to agree on the formulation of a succinct statement of causality. But there comes a time when the data are sufficient to justify action. That time has come.

I would also emphasize that no action in this social area is a form of action: It is an acquiescence in the continuation of the present level of televised violence entering American homes.

In stating this causal relationship, it is important to keep in mind that antisocial behavior existed in our society long before television appeared. We must be careful not to make television programming the whipping boy for all of society's ills. Yet we must take whatever actions we can when we do identify factors contributing to antisocial behavior in our society.

While the Department of Health, Education, and Welfare has no regulatory responsibility in the field of communications, it does, however, have a responsibility for both the mental health and the education of our citizens. The Department stands ready to assist those federal and other governmental or voluntary agencies concerned with television programming by providing scientific information and advice as appropriate.

I am certain that members of the Federal Communications Commission, members of the academic community, other legislators, and members of the broadcasting industry will have suggestions both as to how to achieve a reduction of televised violence in programming, as well as suggestions for television content designed to induce prosocial behavior. I believe that the Subcommittee on Communications of the Senate Commerce Committee, in requesting the formation of this Scientific Advisory Committee, and the Committee members have provided a valuable service to our society. I believe that this report represents a significant step forward. These conclusions are based on solid scientific data and not on the opinion of one or another scientist.

I believe further that the research reported in these five volumes, the Scientific Advisory Committee's deliberations, this Subcommittee's deliberations, and this Subcommittee's hearings will provide a stimulus to other social scientists to build on the solid foundation which has now been erected in this important field of communication.

Comments and Conclusions

Concerning probably no other issue in the social sciences has the evidence been so overwhelming or convincing as that regarding the influence of media violence on values and behavior. The evidences suggest many significant reasons for concern. Television and motion pictures are powerful teachers of values, behavior, and social conduct. Their influence can be for good or for evil and can be a potent force in shaping societal norms toward almost any end. Printed matter in the form of books, newspapers, and magazines probably exerts a lesser, though still potent, influence.

One might justifiably ask if there is any evidence or data suggesting other conclusions. In his chapter in this volume, James Q. Wilson notes some of the limitations of the earlier research on media violence and makes mention of the work by Seymour Feschback who is about the only investigator in the literature to come up with "no harm" findings. His research, as with most other studies, has been subject to critical review. His findings have also been unable to be replicated by other scientists. In fairness, individual studies can always be nitpicked; however, the overwhelming consensus of the research still suggests that media violence does affect us, and potentially adversely. How and to what degree will be determined by a host of other factors, predispositions, family and peer influences, chance happenings in the environment, and others. But this in no way lessens the significant role of the media in suggesting, teaching, and even triggering increased aggressive behavior toward our fellow man.

THE WORLD OF PORNOGRAPHY AND EROTICA

We had fed the heart on fantasies,
The heart's grown brutal from the
*   fare.*

                    William Butler Yeats

Introduction

As in the media violence issue, we will attempt to assess the state of the art with regard to our scientific knowledge about pornography's effects.

Since by far the most impressive, ambitious, and well-financed adventure in this area was the recent Presidential Commission's Report on Obscenity and Pornography, with several million in funding, we will present in the first chapter of this section synopses as well as verbatim summaries of their findings. Two chapters by Victor Cline, following the Commission Report, critique the report and present a body of new data, along with older data overlooked by some of the Commission Report writers, all of which suggest revised conclusions about pornography's effects. In addition, the reader is taken "back stage" to see the inner workings of the Commission and the way in which the ideologies and backgrounds of some of the commissioners and their staff probably affected their perceptions and their use of scientific data.

The fourth chapter in this section is an essay by psychoanalyst Ernest van den Haag who approaches the pornography effects issue from the viewpoint of a literate, broadly educated clinician.

This section, then, addresses itself to the issue of the extent to which exposure to varieties of erotica affect behavior. Is there any good evidence that it ever really harmed anyone, or is it something that moralists get concerned about because it primarily offends their sense of decency or their notions of what proper sexual conduct should be? When the president of the United States and the Senate overwhelmingly denounced and rejected the conclusions of the Pornography Commission Report, were they merely playing politics and the game of expediency, or did they strongly suspect that all the facts had not yet been revealed?

And in the section's final chapter, Cline cross-examines psychiatrist Blaine McLaughlin, who has appeared as expert witness in scores of obscenity trials.

We see what his motivations are, what it's like to be on the firing line and to be cross-examined for hours, what his strategies are, and what his rationale is for the positions he takes on the subject of obscenity.

Summary of the Report of the National Commission on Obscenity and Pornography [1]

On September 30, 1970, the Commission on Obscenity and Pornography issued a final report summarizing its findings. This consisted of four panel reports, a set of recommendations suggesting repeal of most pornography laws (assented to by twelve of the eighteen Commissioners), and eight "dissenting" reports which mildly or strongly qualified the views of individual commissioners concerning the text of the main body of the report.

The four panel reports dealt with (1) traffic in and distribution of pornography, (2) effects of pornography, (3) positive approaches to erotica and sexuality, and (4) law and law enforcement.

The Commission had been previously established under Public Law 90-100 in October, 1967, because Congress had found traffic in obscenity to be "a matter of national concern." Many congressmen were being besieged by a greater number of letters from their constituents about pornography being sent unsolicited through the mails to their homes than about the war in Vietnam. For Congress, setting up such commissions as this had become an increasingly popular method of giving the appearance of doing something about nettlesome national problems.

The Commission was assigned four tasks by Congress: (1) to analyze pornography control laws and evaluate and recommend definitions of obscenity, (2) to assess traffic, methods of distribution, and volume of pornography, (3) to study the effects of pornography on the public, especially minors, and its relationship to crime and other antisocial behavior, and (4) to recommend such legislation and administrative or other advisable and appropriate actions as the Commission might deem necessary to regulate

---

1. On occasion this has also been called the President's Commission on Obscenity and Pornography.

effectively the flow of such traffic without interfering with Constitutional rights.

The eighteen-member Commission was chosen and appointed by President Lyndon Johnson with William B. Lockhart, a law dean from the University of Minnesota, elected chairman.

The remainder of the Commission consisted of two more attorneys, three clergymen, two psychiatrists, two sociologists, a librarian, an English teacher, a graduate student-teacher in broadcast journalism, a book publisher, a magazine and book distributor, a judge, a state's attorney general, and a CBS research director.

Since the commissioners lived and worked in various parts of the country and continued in their full-time local employments, they met together only at erratic intervals a day or two at a time and hired a full-time support staff to do the actual day-to-day work of contracting out research, writing report summaries, and other routine work.

In this chapter we will present brief summaries of two of the panel reports (Traffic and Positive Approaches) plus the verbatim summaries of the Effects and Legal panels.

A. Summary of the Traffic Panel Report

The first panel studying traffic in obscenity found a 60- to 70-million-dollar annual business in sexploitation films; a 70- to 90-million-dollar annual sale of pornographic magazines and books, and a 12- to 14-million dollar yearly market in mail-order sexually oriented materials. They also found that the majority (70-85%) of both adolescent and adult males and females had been exposed to some pornography at one time or another. Over the decade they found a significant increase in the amount and explicitness of erotic material in the cinema and in over-the-counter magazines and books. While the first experience with erotica occurs usually in adolescence, young people below the age of twenty-one rarely purchase sexually explicit books, magazines, and pictures; they obtain these materials from "friends." The adult bookstores and cinema appear to be patronized by predominantly white, middle-class, middle-aged, married males.

B. Summary of the Positive Approaches Panel Report

Three aspects of the positive approaches problem were identified. The first focused on sex education. It was felt that if adolescents had access to adequate information about sex through appropriate sex education, their interest in pornography would be reduced. So the panel recommended that sex education programs be established in the schools because "the existing alternatives were found to be inadequate or undesirable."

The second area of focus was on citizen action groups. The panel felt that such groups could demonstrate and seek support for an "enduring set of values," and provide a legitimate forum for discussion of these issues; however, on the negative side, they might also illegally harrass bookstores and theaters and seriously interfere with the availability of legitimate materials in the community (e.g., books, films, art works). The panel felt that the important factor determining whether these groups might be helpful would be whether the group was representative of the total community and "not whether pornography is perceived as a problem in the community."

The third issue was "industry self-regulation." Here they noted that the comic book industry as well as radio and television have long maintained codes as guidelines and standards in programming. For example, they noted that in radio and television, "profanity, obscenity, sexual material and vulgarity" are forbidden. These codes also stress that programming should foster and promote the commonly accepted "moral, social and ethical standards and ideals characteristic of American life." With regards to motion pictures the only attempt at self-regulation has been the rating of commercial cinema as G, PG, R and X, which at least allows the patron to have some advance notion about the explicitness of the sex depicted, its suitability for children, and other characteristics. They noted that the weakest element in this rating procedure is the local enforcement of age restrictions for admission. This panel concludes its review of industry self-regulation by commenting, "It is very possible that self-regulation, often reinforced by pressures from a vigilant minority, not only sets up rules and internal procedures for deleting or blunting material deemed offensive, but also inhibits experimentation with new ideas, dampens response to social change and limits the sources of cultural variety." Thus, they felt that industry self-regulation had some negative consequences which had to be weighed against any possible advantages.

C. Summary of the Effects Panel Report[2]

The Effects Panel of the Commission undertook to develop a program of research designed to provide information on the kinds of effects which result from exposure to sexually explicit materials and the conditions under which these effects occur. The research program embraced both inquiries into public and professional belief regarding the effects of such materials, and empirical research bearing on the actual occurrence and condition of the effects. The areas of potential effect to which the research was addressed included sexual arousal, emotions, attitudes, overt sexual behavior, moral character, and criminal and other antisocial behavior related to sex.

2. The Report of the Effects Panel of the Commission provides a more thorough discussion and documentation of this overview.

Research procedures included (1) surveys employing national probability samples of adults and young persons; (2) quasi-experimental studies of selected populations; (3) controlled experimental studies; and (4) studies of rates and incidence of sex offenses and illegitimacy at the national level. A major study, which is cited frequently in these pages, was a national survey of American adults and youth which involved face-to-face interviews with a random probability sample of 2,486 adults and 769 young persons between the ages of fifteen and twenty in the continental United States.[3]

The strengths and weaknesses of the various research methods utilized are discussed in Section A of the Report of the Effects Panel of the Commission.[4] That report is based upon the many technical studies which generated the data from which the panel's conclusions were derived.

1. Opinion Concerning Effects of Sexual Materials

There is no consensus among Americans regarding what they consider to be the effects of viewing or reading explicit sexual materials. A diverse and perhaps inconsistent set of beliefs concerning the effects of sexual materials is held by large and necessarily overlapping portions of American men and women. Between 40% and 60% believe that sexual materials provide information about sex, provide entertainment, lead to moral breakdown, improve sexual relationships of married couples, lead people to commit rape, produce boredom with sexual materials, encourage innovation in marital sexual technique, and lead people to lose respect for women. Some of these presumed effects are obviously socially undesirable while other may be regarded as socially neutral or desirable. When questioned about effects, persons were most likely to report having personally experienced desirable rather than undesirable ones. Among those who believed undesirable effects had occurred, a greater number of them attributed their occurrences to others rather than to self. Mostly the undesirable effects were believed to have happened without reference to self or personal acquaintances.

Surveys of psychiatrists, psychologists, sex educators, social workers, counselors, and similar professional workers reveal that large majorities of such groups believe that sexual materials do not have harmful effects on either adults or adolescents. On the other hand, a survey of police chiefs found that 58% believed that "obscene" books played a significant role in causing juvenile delinquency.

---

3. The study was conducted by Response Analysis Corporation of Princeton, New Jersey, and the Institute of Survey Research of Temple University, Philadelphia, Pennsylvania.

4. See also the preface of the Commission's Report.

2. Empirical Evidence Concerning Effects

A number of empirical studies conducted recently by psychiatrists, psychologists, and sociologists attempted to assess the effects of exposure to explicit sexual materials. This body of research includes several study designs, a wide range of subjects and respondents, and a variety of effect indicators. Some questions in this area are not answered by the existing research, some are answered more fully than others, and many questions have yet to be asked. Continued research efforts which embrace both replicative studies and inquiries into areas not yet investigated are needed to extend and clarify existing findings and to specify more concretely the conditions under which specific effects occur. The findings of available research are summarized below.

Experimental and survey studies show that exposure to erotic stimuli produces sexual arousal in substantial numbers of both males and females. Arousal is dependent on both characteristics of the stimulus and characteristics of the viewer or user.

Recent research casts doubt on the common belief that women are vastly less aroused by erotic stimuli than are men. The supposed lack of female response may well be due to social and cultural inhibitions against reporting such arousal and to the fact that erotic material is generally oriented to a male audience. When viewing erotic stimuli, more women report the physiological sensations that are associated with sexual arousal than directly report being sexually aroused.

Research also shows that young persons are more likely to be aroused by erotica ·than are older persons. Persons who are college educated, religiously inactive, and sexually experienced are more likely to report arousal than persons who are less educated, religiously active, and sexually inexperienced.

Several studies show that depictions of conventional sexual behavior are generally regarded as more stimulating than depictions of less conventional activity. Heterosexual themes elicit more frequent and stronger arousal responses than depictions of homosexual activity; petting and coitus themes elicit greater arousal than oral sexuality, which in turn elicits more than sadomasochistic themes.

3. Satiation

The only experimental study on the subject to date found that continued or repeated exposure to erotic stimuli over fifteen days resulted in satiation (marked diminution) of sexual arousal and interest in such material. In this experiment, the introduction of novel sex stimuli partially rejuvenated satiated interest, but only briefly. There was also partial recovery of interest after two months of nonexposure.

4. *Effects Upon Sexual Behavior*

When people are exposed to erotic materials, some persons increase masturbatory or coital behavior, a smaller proportion decrease it, but the majority of persons report no change in these behaviors. Increases in either of these behaviors are short lived and generally disappear within forty-eight hours. When masturbation follows exposure, it tends to occur among individuals with established masturbatory patterns or among persons with established but unavailable sexual partners. When coital frequencies increase following exposure to sex stimuli, such activation generally occurs among sexually experienced persons with established and available sexual partners. In one study, middle-aged married couples reported increases in both the frequency and variety of coital performance during the twenty-four hours after the couples viewed erotic films.

In general, established patterns of sexual behavior were found to be very stable and not altered substantially by exposure to erotica. When sexual activity occurred following the viewing or reading of these materials, it constituted a temporary activation of individuals' preexisting patterns of sexual behavior.

Other common consequences of exposure to erotic stimuli are increased frequencies of erotic dreams, sexual fantasy, and conversation about sexual matters. These responses occur among both males and females. Sexual dreaming and fantasy occur as a result of exposure more often among unmarried than married persons, but conversation about sex occurs among both married and unmarried persons. Two studies found that a substantial number of married couples reported more agreeable and enhanced marital communication and an increased willingness to discuss sexual matters with each other after exposure to erotic stimuli.

5. *Attitudinal Responses*

Exposure to erotic stimuli appears to have little or no effect on already established attitudinal commitments regarding either sexuality or sexual morality. A series of four studies employing a large array of indicators found practically no significant differences in such attitudes before and after single or repeated exposures to erotica. One study did find that after exposure persons became more tolerant in reference to other persons' sexual activities although their own sexual standards did not change. One study reported that some persons' attitudes toward premarital intercourse became more liberal after exposure, while other persons' attitudes became more conservative, but another study found no changes in this regard. The overall picture is almost completely a tableau of no significant change.

Several surveys suggest that there is a correlation between experience with erotic materials and general attitudes about sex: Those who have more tolerant or liberal sexual attitudes tend also to have greater experience with sexual materials. Taken together, experimental and survey studies suggest that persons who are more sexually tolerant are also less rejecting of sexual material. Several studies show that after experience with erotic material, persons become less fearful of possible detrimental effects of exposure.

6. Emotional and Judgmental Responses

Several studies show that persons who are unfamiliar with erotic materials may experience strong and conflicting emotional reactions when first exposed to sexual stimuli. Multiple responses, such as attraction and repulsion to an unfamiliar object, are commonly observed in the research literature on psychosensory stimulation from a variety of nonsexual as well as sexual stimuli. These emotional responses are short-lived and, as with psychosexual stimulation, do not persist long after removal of the stimulus.

Extremely varied responses to erotic stimuli occur in the judgmental realm, as, for example, in the labeling of material as obscene or pornographic. Characteristics of both the viewer and the stimulus influence the response: For any given stimulus, some persons are more likely to judge it "obscene" than are others; and for persons of a given psychological or social type, some erotic themes are more likely to be judged "obscene" than are others. In general, persons who are older, less educated, religiously active, less experienced with erotic materials, or feel sexually guilty are most likely to judge a given erotic stimulus "obscene." There is some indication that stimuli may have to evoke both positive responses (interesting or stimulating), and negative responses (offensive or unpleasant) before they are judged obscene or pornographic.

7. Criminal and Delinquent Behavior

Delinquent and nondelinquent youth report generally similar experiences with explicit sexual materials. Exposure to sexual materials is widespread among both groups. The age of first exposure, the kinds of materials to which they are exposed, the amount of their exposure, the circumstances of exposure, and their reactions to erotic stimuli are essentially the same, particularly when family and neighborhood backgrounds are held constant. There is some evidence that peer group pressure accounts for both sexual experience and exposure to erotic materials among youth. A study of a heterogeneous group of young people found that exposure to erotica had no impact upon moral character over and above that of a generally deviant background.

Statistical studies of the relationship between availability of erotic materials and the rates of sex crimes in Denmark indicate that the increased availability of explicit sexual materials has been accompanied by a decrease in the incidence of sexual crime. Analysis of police records of the same types of sex crimes in Copenhagen during the past twelve years revealed that a dramatic decrease in reported sex crimes occurred during this period and that the decrease coincided with changes in Danish law which permitted wider availability of explicit sexual materials. Other research showed that the decrease in reported sexual offenses cannot be attributed to concurrent changes in the social and legal definitions of sex crimes or in public attitudes toward reporting such crimes to the police, or in police reporting procedures.

Statistical studies of the relationship between the availability of erotic material and the rates of sex crimes in the United States present a more complex picture. During the period in which there has been a marked increase in the availability of erotic materials, some specific rates of arrest for sex crimes have increased (e.g., forcible rape) and others have declined (e.g., overall junvenile rates). For juveniles, the overall rate of arrests for sex crimes decreased even though arrests for nonsexual crimes increased by more than 100%. For adults, arrests for sex offenses increased slightly more than did arrests for nonsex offenses. The conclusion is that, for America, the relationship between the availability of erotica and changes in sex crime rates neither proves nor disproves the possibility that availability of erotica leads to crime, but the massive overall increases in sex crimes that have been alleged do not seem to have occurred.

Available research indicates that sex offenders have had less adolescent experience with erotica than other adults. They do not differ significantly from other adults in relation to adult experience with erotica, in relation to reported arousal, or in relation to the likelihood of engaging in sexual behavior during or following exposure. Available evidence suggests that sex offenders' early inexperience with erotic material is a reflection of their more generally deprived sexual environment. The relative absence of experience appears to constitute another indicator of atypical and inadequate sexual socialization.

In sum, empirical research designed to clarify the question has found no evidence to date that exposure to explicit sexual materials plays a significant role in the causation of delinquent or criminal behavior among youth or adults.[5] The Commission cannot conclude that exposure to erotic materials is a factor in the causation of sex crime or sex delinquency.

5. Commissioners G. William Jones, Joseph T. Klapper, and Morris A. Lipton believe that

in the interest of precision a distinction should be made between two types of statements which occur in this report. One type, to which we subscribe, is that research to date does not indicate that a causal relationship exists between exposure to erotica and the various social ills to which the research has been addressed. There are, however, also statements to the effect that "no evidence" exists, and we believe these should more accurately read

D. Summary of Legal Panel Report[6]

1. Existing Obscenity Legislation and Cost of Enforcement[7]

Federal Statutes. There are presently five federal laws which prohibit distribution of "obscene" materials in the United States. One prohibits any mailing of such material (18 U.S.C. section 1461); another prohibits the importation of obscene materials into the United States (19 U.S.C. section 1305); another prohibits the broadcast of obscenity (18 U.S.C. section 1464); and two laws prohibit the interstate transportation of obscene materials or the use of common carriers to transport such materials (18 U.S.C. sections 1462 and 1465).[8] In addition, the 1968 federal Anti-Pandering Act (39 U.S.C. section 3008)[9] authorizes postal patrons to request no further mailings of unsolicited advertisements from mailers who have previously sent them advertisements which they deem sexually offensive in their sole judgment, and it further prohibits mailers from ignoring such requests. There is no present federal statute specifically regulating the distribution of sexual materials to young persons.

Five federal agencies are responsible for the enforcement of the foregoing statutes. The Post Office Department, the Customs Bureau, and the Federal Communications Commission investigate violations within their jurisdictions. The FBI investigates violations of the statutes dealing with transportation and common carriers. The Department of Justice is responsible for prosecution of other judicial enforcement.

The cost to the federal government of enforcing the five federal statutes generally prohibiting the distribution of obscene materials appears to be at

"no reliable evidence." Occasional aberrant findings, some of very doubtful validity, are noted and discussed in the report of the Effects Panel. In our opinion, none of these, either individually or in sum, are of sufficient merit to constitute reliable evidence or to alter the summary conclusion that the research to date does not indicate a causal relationship (p. 32).

6. The Report of the Legal Panel of the Commission provides a more thorough discussion and documentation of this overview.

7. A description of the history of obscenity prohibitions is set forth in the Legal Panel Report.

8. Two other statutes impose supplementary regulations. First, 39 U.S.C. section 3006 (numbered 39 U.S.C. section 4006 prior to the 1970 Postal Reorganization Act) authorizes the Postmaster General to block incoming mail to persons using the mails to solicit remittances for obscene matter; second, 47 U.S.C. section 503(b)(E) imposes civil penalties upon prohibited broadcasts of obscene matter.

9. This Act was numbered 39 U.S.C. section 4009 prior to the 1970 Postal Reorganization Act.

least $3 to $5 million per year. Enforcement of the Anti-Pandering Act has cost the Post Office about an additional $1 million per year.[10]

State Statutes. Forty-eight of the states have statutes which generally prohibit the distribution[11] of "obscene" materials. In addition, the statutes of forty-one states contain some type of special prohibition regarding the distribution of sexual materials to minors. The cost of enforcing these statutes cannot be determined with any precision. The total of all state and local enforcement activity, however, far exceeds federal enforcement in terms of number of arrests and prosecutions, so that the aggregate cost of state law enforcement for all jurisdictions is, conservatively, $5 to $10 million per year. More than 90% of all state and local prosecutions recently have involved distribution to adults rather than enforcement of juvenile statutes.

Federal and State Statutory Definitions of "Obscenity." None of the federal statutes generally prohibiting the distribution of "obscene" material defines that term. State statutes generally prohibiting the distribution of obscene material either do not define the term or verbally incorporate the constitutional standard established by the Supreme Court and discussed below. State juvenile statutes frequently incorporate relatively specific descriptive definitions of material prohibited for minors, qualified by subjective standards adapted from the constitutional standard for adults.

2. The Constitutional Basis for Prohibitions upon the Dissemination of Explicit Sexual Materials

For many years the Supreme Court assumed, without deciding, that laws generally prohibiting dissemination of obscenity were consistent with the free speech guarantees of the Constitution. In 1957, in the case of Roth v.

---

10. The cost to the Post Office Department in fiscal 1968 is estimated by that department as approximately $1 million—$.75 million allocated to the Postal Inspection Service, which attempts to detect violations, and $.25 million allocated to the General Counsel's Office. The cost to the Customs Bureau in fiscal 1968 is estimated by that Bureau at approximately $1 million. Neither the FBI nor the Justice Department supplied cost figures to the Commission. Other data supplied by the Justice Department indicate significant enforcement activity on the part of the FBI, the Justice Department, and several United States Attorneys' offices throughout the country of the statutes within their jurisdictions. The Commission believes that these costs would aggregate at least $1 million per year. To the foregoing total of about $3 million must be added the costs to federal courts and the cost to the Federal Communications Commission. In addition, obscenity enforcement activities on the part of at least two of the departments—Post Office and Justice—have increased substantially since fiscal 1968.

11. Several of these statutes contain narrowly drawn exemption provisions such as exemptions for persons distributing materials in the course of scientific or artistic pursuits.

United States, the Court held that such laws were constitutional, but it required that they utilize a narrowly restrictive standard of what is obscene.

In upholding the constitutionality of obscenity prohibitions, the Roth decision did not rely upon findings or conclusions regarding the effect of sexual materials upon persons who are exposed to them. Rather, the fundamental premise of Roth was that "obscene" materials are not entitled to the protections accorded to "speech" by the First and Fourteenth Amendments to the Constitution. The Court based this conclusion upon its findings (1) that the framers of the Bill of Rights did not intend the free speech guarantee of the First Amendment to apply to all utterances and writings, (2) that obscene speech—like libel, profanity, and blasphemy—was not intended to be protected by the Amendment, and (3) that a universal consensus had existed for many years that the distribution of obscenity should be legally prohibited.

In 1969, in Stanley v. Georgia, the Supreme Court modified the premise of the Roth decision to some extent by holding that the constitutional guarantee of free speech protects the right of the individual to read or view concededly obscene material in his own home. Some lower federal courts have held that the Stanley decision gives constitutional protection to some distributions of obscenity, as well as to its private possession. Specifically, courts have held unconstitutional the federal importation prohibition as applied to the importation of obscene material for private use, the federal mail prohibition as applied to the mailing of obscene material to persons who request it, and a state prohibition applied to films exhibited to adults at theaters to which minors were not admitted. These courts have held that the constitutional right to possess obscene materials established in Stanley implies a correlative right for adults to acquire such materials for their own use or to view them without forcing them upon others. Other lower federal courts have not applied the Stanley decision to these situations. The Supreme Court has not yet explicitly passed upon these questions, but has set for argument in the 1970 term three cases raising these issues.

3. Constitutional Limitations upon the Definition of "Obscene"

Adult Obscenity Statutes. Although upholding the constitutionality of broad prohibitions upon the dissemination of obscene materials, the Roth decision imposed a narrow standard for defining what is obscene under such prohibitions. Subsequent decisions have narrowed the permissible test even further.

The prevailing view today in the Supreme Court of the United States, the lower federal courts and the courts of the states is that three criteria must all be met before the distribution of material may be generally prohibited for all persons, including adults, on the ground that it is obscene. These criteria are: (1) the dominant theme of the material, taken as a whole, must appeal to a "prurient" interest in sex; (2) the material must be "patently offensive" because it affronts "contemporary community standards" regarding the depiction of sexual matters; and (3) the material must lack "redeeming social value." All three criteria must coalesce before material may be deemed obscene for adults.[12]

The requirement that the material appeal to a "prurient" interest in sex is not clear in meaning but appears to refer primarily to material which is sexually arousing in dominant part. Material must appeal to the prurient interest of the "average" person, unless it is designed for and distributed to a particular group, in which case it is the interests of the members of that group which are relevant. The Supreme Court has never settled the question whether the community by whose standards offensiveness is to be determined is a national community or whether it is the state or locality where the distribution occurs. Whatever the relevant community, a substantial consensus that particular material is offensive is apparently required to violate the community's standard. There is some disagreement in the Supreme Court over the precise role played by the "social value" criterion. All the Justices have agreed that social value is relevant to obscenity determinations. A plurality (not a majority) has held that unless material is *utterly* without redeeming social value it may not be held to be obscene; a minority of Justices would permit a small degree of social value to be outweighed by prurience and offensiveness. Nor has the Court authoritatively defined what values are "redeeming social" values, although it has suggested that these may include entertainment values as well as the more firmly established scientific, literary, artistic, and educational values. Finally, the Court permits the manner of distribution of material to be taken into account in determining the application of the three criteria, at least where the material itself is close to the line of legality.

The application of these three Roth criteria to specific materials requires a great deal of subjective judgment because the criteria refer to emotional, aesthetic, and intellectual responses to the material rather than to descriptions of its content. As noted above, the precise meaning of the criteria is also unclear. This subjectivity and vagueness produces enormous uncertainty about what is obscene among law enforcement officials, courts, juries, and the general public. It is impossible for a publisher, a distributor, a retailer, or an exhibitor to know in advance whether he will be charged with a criminal offense for distributing a particular work since his understanding of the three tests and their application to his work may differ from that of the police, prosecutor, court, or jury. This uncertainty and consequent fear of prosecution may strongly influence persons not to distribute new works which are

12. The Supreme Court, after this was written, updated its views on obscenity in its historic June 1973 "Miller" decision. This is discussed in McGeady's chapter in this volume.

entitled to constitutional protection and may thus have a damaging effect upon free speech. These definitional problems are also cited by law enforcement officials at all levels as their chief difficulty in enforcing existing obscenity laws. There is, therefore, almost universal dissatisfaction with present law.

A series of decisions of the Supreme Court, generally rendered without opinion, has given an exceedingly narrow scope of actual application to the constitutionally required three-part standard for adult legislation. These decisions leave it questionable whether any verbal or textual materials may presently be deemed obscene for adults under the constitutional standard and suggest that only the most graphic pictorial depictions of actual sexual activity may fall within it. Present law for adults is therefore largely ineffective.

The results of empirical research regarding the application of the three constitutional criteria confirm the difficulties of application as well as their exceedingly narrow scope. Several studies have found that "arousingness' and "offensiveness" are independent dimensions when applied to sexual materials; that is, material that is offensive may or may not be arousing, and material that is arousing may or may not be offensive. Only a very restricted range of materials seems to be capable of meeting both of these criteria for most people. Further, there is very little consensus among people regarding either the arousingness or the offensiveness of a given sexual depiction. A wide distribution of judgments in these two areas occurs, for example, for depictions of female nudity with genitals exposed, for explicit depictions of heterosexual sexual intercourse, and for graphic depictions of oral-genital intercourse. In addition, judgments differ among different groups: Males as a group differ from females as a group in their judgments of both "offensiveness" and "arousingness"; the young differ from the old; the college-educated differ from those with only a high school education; frequent church attenders differ from less frequent church attenders.

An additional and very significant limiting factor is introduced by the criterion of social value. In the national survey of American public opinion sponsored by the Commission, substantial portions of the population reported effects which might be deemed socially valuable from even the most explicit sexual materials. For example, about 60% of a representative sample of adult American men felt that looking at or reading such materials would provide information about sex and about 40% of the sample reported that such an effect had occurred for himself or someone he personally knew. About 60% of these men felt that looking at or reading explicit sexual materials provided entertainment and almost 50% reported this effect upon himself or someone he personally knew. Half of these men felt that looking at or reading explicit sexual materials can improve sexual relations of some married couples, and about a quarter of the sample reported such an effect on themselves or on someone they knew personally. Fewer women reported such effects; but 35%, 24%, and 21% reported, respectively, information, entertainment, and improved sexual relations in themselves or someone they personally knew as a result of looking at or reading very explicit sexual materials. As previously indicated, two experimental studies found that a substantial number of married couples reported more agreeable and enhanced marital communication and an increased willingness to discuss sexual matters with each other after exposure to erotic stimuli.

In pursuit of its mandate from Congress to recommend definitions of obscenity which are consistent with constitutional rights, the Commission considered drafting a more satisfactory definition of obscene for inclusion in adult obscenity prohibitions, should such prohibitions appear to be socially warranted. To be satisfactory from the point of view of its enforcement and application, such a definition would have to describe the material to be proscribed with a high degree of objectivity and specificity, so that those subject to the law could know in advance what materials were prohibited and so that judicial decisions would not be based upon the subjective reactions of particular judges or jurors. In light of the empirical data, described above, showing both the lack of consensus among adults as to what is both arousing and offensive and the values attributed by substantial numbers of adults to even the most explicit sexual materials, the construction of such a definition for adults within constitutional limits would be extremely difficult. In any event, the Commission, as developed in its legislative recommendations set forth later in this report, does not believe that a sufficient social justification exists for the retention or enactment of broad legislation prohibiting the consensual distribution of sexual materials to adults. We, therefore, do not recommend any definition of what is obscene for adults.

Specific Obscenity Statutes. The extreme definitional problems which occur for adult obscenity under the Roth case do not apply to statutes which do not seek to interfere with the right of adults to read or see material of their own choice. In 1967, in Redrup v. New York, the Supreme Court noted that, in contrast with general obscenity laws prohibiting sale to adults, legislatures have much wider latitude when formulating prohibitions which restrict themselves to impeding only certain types of distributional conduct—such as distribution of explicit sexual materials to unwilling recipients through unsolicited mail and public display. Definitions in these areas need only be rationally related to the problem which the legislation seeks to address and no particular definitional formulation is constitutionally required.

Specific prohibitions incorporating broader definitions than are permissible in adult legislation must be restricted in their application to the specific area of their concern. Thus, statutes designed to protect minors from exposure to material which may not be deemed obscene for adults may only prohibit distributions to minors; prohibitions may not be placed upon all adults in order to protect minors. Public display and unsolicited mail prohibitions which restrict material which may not constitutionally be deemed obscene for adults must also be carefully drafted to avoid interference with consensual adult distribution or exhibition.

The areas of latitude for greater control overlap the areas of greatest public concern. Prosecuting attorneys who reported a serious community concern about obscenity to the Commission attributed this concern primarily to the thrusting of offensive materials upon unwilling recipients and to the fear that materials would be distributed to minors. It is in these areas that effective legislative prohibitions may be formulated and enforced.

Although greater latitude is allowed constitutionally in restricting explicit sexual materials in the areas of public display, unsolicited mailings, and direct disseminations to minors, satisfactory definitions again require the use of explicit objective provisions specifically describing the material to be restricted. Concern about rigidly codifying in law definitions which may soon be outmoded by changing social custom can be alleviated by building into laws a periodic review of their content.

4. Public Opinion Concerning Restrictions on the Availability of Explicit Sexual Materials

A national survey of American public opinion sponsored by the Commission shows that a majority of American adults believe that adults should be allowed to read or see any sexual materials they wish. On the other hand, a substantial consensus of American adults favors prohibiting young persons access to some sexual materials. Almost half the population believes that laws against sexual materials are impossible to enforce. Americans also seem to have an inaccurate view of the opinions of others in their communities; the tendency is to believe that others in the community are more restrictive in outlook than they actually are.

Public opinion regarding restrictions on the availability of explicit sexual materials is, however, quite divided in several ways. Principally this split of opinion is related to the characteristics of the person expressing the attitude and the issue of potential harmfulness of the material.

Characteristics of Persons Expressing the Attitude. Advocacy of restrictions on the availability of explicit sexual materials is more likely to be found accompanying an orientation against freedom of expression generally. In addition, females tend to be more restrictive than males, older people more restrictive than younger people, those with a grade school education more restrictive than the high school educated, who in turn tend to be more restrictive than the college educated, and people who attend church regularly tend to be more restrictive than those who attend less often.

The Potentiality of Harmful Effects. When questioned as to whether they favored access of adults or young persons to sexually explicit materials, about 40% of all the respondents on the national survey made their responses contingent on the issue of whether or not such materials cause harm.

About two-thirds of the persons who favor no legal restrictions said their views would be changed if it were clearly demonstrated that certain materials have harmful effects. On the other hand, about one-third of the persons who favor some restrictions or extensive restrictions would change their views if it were clearly demonstrated that sexual materials have no harmful effects.

5. *Obscenity Laws in Other Countries*

Countries other than the United States differ widely in the terms of and extent of their legal restrictions regarding the distribution of explicit sexual materials. A summary of existing legal provisions in fifteen other countries is contained in the report of the Legal Panel of the Commission.

A trend has appeared in recent years toward substantial reevaluation and revision of obscenity laws, often through the use of commissions similar to this Commission. Such an official commission report in Denmark has resulted in the repeal of that country's adult obscenity legislation (with juvenile and nonconsensual exposure restrictions being retained). A similar recommendation has been made in Sweden, and final enactment of the repeal of adult legislation in that country will apparently take place in the fall of 1970. Advisory commissions in Israel and the United Kingdom have also recently recommended elimination of prohibitions upon distribution of sexual materials to consenting adults. The constitutional court of West Germany presently has under consideration the question of the constitutionality of that country's adult legislation in view of free speech guarantees. Advisory commissions in countries other than the United States have, like this Commission, all concluded that consensual exposure of adults to explicit sexual materials causes no demonstrable damaging individual or social effects.

Following the presentation of the overviews, or summaries, of each of the four Commission panel reports, a series of recommendations were issued. These were then followed by the full and lengthy complete Panel Reports. For anyone wishing to read them, they are available in a U.S. Government Printing Office version as well as in Bantam Books.

The Commission's nonlegislative recommendations were that the country (1) initiate a massive sex-education program; (2) continue open discussion on the issues regarding obscenity and pornography, making use of the factual information uncovered by the Commission's research; and (3) conduct additional research and collect additional information about the issues of pornography and that (4) citizens organize themselves at local, regional, and national levels to aid in the implementation of the foregoing recommendations. With regard to their legislative recommendations, the Commission urged that all "Federal, state, and local legislation prohibiting the sale, exhibition, or distribution of sexual materials to consenting adults should be repealed" because the Commission (or more accurately, the Effects Panel) had "found no evidence to date that exposure to explicit sexual materials plays a significant role in the causation of delinquent or criminal behavior among youth or adults." About a third of the commissioners failed to concur in this recommendation.

The Commission also recommended that *public displays* of sexually explicit pictorial materials be prohibited as well as unsolicited pornography ads sent through the mails to persons not wanting them. With regard to protecting juveniles, they recommended that sales of pictorial pornography (not textual) be prohibited.

Another View: Pornography Effects, the State of the Art

Victor B. Cline

The Presidential Commission Report on Obscenity and Pornography (1970) is the last major published overview[1] of the issue of pornography's effects. After carefully reviewing all the Commission's original research as well as the data in the open literature, it is my judgment that the Commission's final report was marked by certain ideological biases which, in Hans Eysenck's words, ". . . implied a slide from scientific discussion to propaganda." It is to this issue, as well as to a consideration of the current state of the art concerning effects of pornography that I address this review. You may wish to read and critique some or all of the original Commission-financed research reports (which are now published and available through the

The credentials and professional background of Victor B. Cline have been previously reviewed. However, since the following two chapters by him not only deal with the issue of pornography's effects but also reveal the facts behind the establishment and operation of the Presidential Commission on Obscenity and Pornography (showing how they arrived at their surprising "no harm" conclusions and their recommendations to abolish most existing obscenity legislation), it is appropriate and necessary to mention in this prefatory section Cline's relationship to the Commission.

In the early 60s Cline became involved in several seminars and symposia at professional psychological meetings dealing with the issue of pornography and its possible effects on behavior. This stimulated in him an interest in building, over the years, an intensive literature file on that subject. His expertise created the demand for him to make public appearances to discuss the issues. Such a demand, in turn, motivated him to keep abreast of the scientific literature on the subject.

In October, 1967, following the establishment of the Commission on Obscenity and Pornography by the Congress, it became increasingly apparent from a flood of news

1. Goldstein et al. briefly also reviewed some of this literature in their 1973 book, *Pornography and Sexual Deviance.*

U. S. Government Printing Office) to determine for yourself the answers to some of the questions raised by this chapter.

Since May, 1970, because of my experience with the Commission's research and report, I have repeatedly recommended and suggested the appropriateness of the reevaluation by an independent panel of scientists of the work done by the Commission. This recommendation has not been acted upon. Perhaps an occasional scientist will dig into the data and come up with a few isolated facts at variance with the Commission's report, but probably not much more will be done.

It is my judgment that the pornography commission's evaluation of some of their scientific data was flawed because, apparently, of some of the very human biases and social-political views held by some of their members. Also, as indicated by their own writings, some were concerned by the behaviors and the views of the antipornographers whom they saw as censors or dangerous authoritarians who, in ominous and repressive ways, might threaten our most basic freedoms—who would attempt to enact and enforce laws which might eventually jeopardize our freedom of speech and expression.

Or, in the words of Cody Wilson, Director of the Research for the Commission (1971, pp. 116-7), "Why then should we worry about pornography: We should worry about pornography because there is a segment of our society for whom facts (that pornography is harmless) are not relevant and who cling, for some reason or other, to fears: . . . moral crusades and political repression often go hand-in-hand."

Since the eighteen Commission members came from extremely diverse backgrounds and life settings, nearly all with impeccable reputations, how would it be possible for any man's particular bias or point of view to prevail? How would it be possible for anything but an honest document to emerge

releases that the Commission was sharply divided, apparently along ideological lines. There were frequent charges of coverup, a runaway commission, and skullduggery, all of which raised questions about bias and misuse or misinterpretation of scientific data.

In May, 1970, when the Commission held open hearings in Los Angeles and Washington, D.C., Cline took this opportunity to testify before the Commission about some of the issues, the methodological problems, and the review of the scientific literature on the subject of pornography as he saw it. Several months following this presentation Commissioner Morton Hill invited Cline to review all of the Commission-financed behavioral research reports as well as drafts of the final report being prepared by the Commission majority. Because of crucial flaws in this final report, omissions in the reporting of negative effects data, and other discrepancies, Cline agreed to write a chapter critiquing the Effects Panel's conclusions for the Hill-Link Minority Report. This led to a number of later opportunities for Cline to interview some members of the Commission as well as the professional staff, to review their later writings on their experiences, and ultimately to write these two chapters.

from their joint deliberations? The next two chapters suggest how and what appears to have happened.

The basic crucial "fact" which led twelve of the eighteen commissioners to vote for a repeal of all pornography control laws (except for pictorial pornography for children,[2] open public displays, and unsolicited mail pornography) was their finding that:

Empirical research designed to clarify the question has found no evidence to date that exposure to explicit sexual materials plays a significant role in the causation of delinquent or criminal behavior among youth or adults" (p. 32)[3], or causes "social or individual harms such as crime, delinquency, sexual or nonsexual deviancy or severe emotional disturbance" (p. 58).

With almost monotonous regularity, variations of this statement appear again and again in the report of the Commission and in public and professional journal articles authored by those who worked on the report. It is also showing up in encyclopedias and psychiatric texts as established fact (e.g., *World Book, Americana, Handbook of Psychiatry*).

Commission members Morris Lipton and Edward Greenwood (both psychiatrists) felt so certain about the "no harm" findings that they wrote an additional separate statement appended to the majority report which emphasized their views even more strongly:

We would have welcomed evidence relating exposure to erotica to delinquency, crime and antisocial behavior, for if such evidence existed we might have a simple solution to some of our most urgent problems. However, the work of the commission has failed to uncover such evidence. They [the research studies] *fail to establish a meaningful causal[4] relationship or even significant correlation* [emphasis added] *between exposure to erotica and immediate or delayed antisocial behavior among adults. To assert the contrary from available evidence is not only to deny the facts, but also delude the public . . . (p. 452).*

Joe Klapper (sociologist and CBS Social Research Director), a member of the Effects Panel of the Commission, also endorses the above proposition:

2. The Commission's recommendation of prohibition of commercial sale of pornography to children did not apply to written or textual erotica, only pictorial, and this only if it constituted a dominant part of a work and was not of artistic or anthropological significance. It also recommended that TV and radio be exempt from any pornography control legislation (leaving it up to the FCC to deal with such matters).

3. When merely page numbers are given throughout this chapter, they refer to the Bantam Book edition of the Report of the Commission on Obscenity and Pornography.

4. See Addendum A at the end of this chapter for clarification of the differences between a correlational and cause-effect relationship between two variables.

The personal statement of Commissioner Morris A. Lipton and Commissioner Edward D. Greenwood so closely approximates my own position, and is in my opinion so soundly stated that I would like to assert my general agreement with it (p. 443).

Thus Lipton, Greenwood, and Klapper (all scientists) say that not only are there no causal linkages between exposure to pornography and harm but neither are there significant relationships or correlations of any kind between the two. This statement is contradicted by the senior author of the all-important Effects Panel Report, Weldon Johnson, who notes in a later Duquesne *Law Review* article (1971:203): "The Commission . . . reported many statistical relationships concerning exposure to erotic materials and sexual behavior which might be regarded as undesirable." Johnson cites several examples and points out that these are real statistical relationships, but of course by themselves cannot prove causation. The Commission's own studies as well as research by investigators in the outside literature give evidence of many examples of relationships (some causal) between exposure to pornography and undesirable consequences (to be discussed later). These, with several exceptions, are never mentioned by the Commission report writers.

Two other members of the Effects Panel (both sociologists), Otto Larson and Marvin Wolfgang, also issued a separate clarifying statement about their identical positions. They called for repeal of *all* pornography laws, including those controlling pornography advertisements sent through the mail into people's homes, unsolicited and unwanted; obscene public display ads; and pictorial pornography for children (in the face of no clinical or experimental youth data). The rest of the Commission refused, however, to go along with this position. Larson, who was the chairman of the all-important Effects Panel, and Wolfgang made the following claim:

There is no substantial evidence that exposure [of pornography] *to juveniles is necessarily harmful. There may even be beneficial effects. . . . Moreover, there is no significant association between what society has declared is criminal or delinquent, in general, and exposure to erotic stimuli (p. 447).*

Thus, Larson and Wolfgang deny (as do Lipton, Greenwood, and Klapper) not only causal linkages but also correlational associations between exposure to erotica and antisocial behavior.

The fifth, and final, member of the Effects Panel, G. William Jones, was a graduate student working on his doctorate in instructional communications at Syracuse University at the time he was called to be a Commission member. He had been teaching previously at Southern Methodist University in broadcast film art and had been a Methodist minister.

In Jones's brief separate statement he declared that he believed the work of the Commission to be a "milestone in the history of human communications":

. . . as one who follows a Leader who said, "They shall know the Truth and the Truth shall set them free," I believe that the search for truth is liberating and thus a holy quest and that science has often proven itself to be God's handmaiden in this quest. Although many religious persons may be distressed by the findings of our research, they must certainly rejoice that misconceptions and prejudices are being replaced by knowledge. . . .

Jones, then, endorsed the position of the rest of the Effects Panel without question.

The general theme that "pornography has been judged and found guiltless" (or at least that no evidence exists that it causes harm) was spread abroad in the land not only in the report of the Commission but also in countless public addresses, court appearances, and scientific publications by some of the Commission members and researchers (e.g., Bender, 1973; Johnson, 1971; Lipton, 1971; Lipton and Greenwood, 1971; Wilson, 1971).

In some of these papers, disapproving comments were made about the moralists for whom "scientific facts are irrelevant" (Wilson, 1971:116), who are not members of the scientific community and who, if they had been, might thereby understand science and not become so concerned about pornography. Thus, those who opposed the majority report were seen as antiscientific, rejecting of empirical facts, and moralizing, in dangerous ways, perhaps, engaging in political repression. The Commission majority, on the other hand, were seen as the scientists, who say, "Give me the facts" and on the basis of empirical data arrive at accurate judgments about tough social issues. So we might appropriately ask (to the extent that it is possible to determine the answer in the social sciences), "What are the facts?"

1. Evidence from the Modeling and "Imitative Learning" Literature

In the Cairns et al. review of the literature on pornography's effects in the Commission's Technical Reports (unavailable to the public for several years) they report the following effects:

A related issue concerns behavior changes which are induced by the viewing of obscene materials. To what extent will a modeling effect occur in that the viewer or reader imitates the behaviors that are depicted? Only two studies of the modeling of sexual behaviors of another person have appeared and both have yielded positive results (Kobasigawa, 1966; Walters, Bowen, and Parke, 1964). Children and adults did imitate "sexual" behaviors if they watched another person perform such activities . . . the empirical phenomena of observation learning (or elicitation) cannot be disputed (1971:17).

The reviewers correctly note that these studies occurred in the laboratory, and one has to be cautious about extrapolating them to real life. But they are cause-effect studies and are most germaine to the harm issue. Neither the Effects Panel nor the Commission mention the above study, even though they contracted for and financed this literature review and had it at their disposal while writing their reports. If children and adults are influenced to imitate the "sexual" behaviors modeled for them, as the above research suggests, why would they not also be influenced by pornographic materials to imitate or engage in antisocial, criminal, or deviant sexual behavior? Are the laws of learning somehow repealed or inoperative here but not in the rest of life?

2. Sexual Deviations Created and Treated in Laboratory Using Erotica

In reviewing the evidence on the origins of sexual deviance, Bandura (1969:511) sums up a great deal of evidence suggesting that it is learned. This includes such things as homosexuality, transvestism, and sexual sadism.

Rachman, at the Institute of Psychiatry, Maudsley Hospital, London (1966, 1968) has demonstrated repeatedly that sexual deviations can be created in the laboratory using pornographic, erotic pictures. He exposed male subjects to colored photographic slides of nude females in sexually arousing positions along with a picture of female boots. Eventually through simple conditioning the male subjects were sexually aroused at merely seeing only the picture of the female boot. In other words, he created in normal men a form of sexual deviation, using pornographic stimuli.

Ethical considerations would constrain Rachman or any other researcher from creating sexual deviations of a more socially harmful nature in the laboratory. But it is not difficult to imagine a situation where a young man sees a series of pornographic movies or pictures depicting the explicit rape of females; he is sexually aroused at the same time that he sees aggressive acts performed against females. Through simple conditioning it would be possible for him to associate rape and inflicting pain on the female (or a variety of other antisocial acts) with sexual arousal. This association could then recur in fantasy and later, possibly, in behavior. A number of studies suggest that deviant sexual fantasies are related to later acted-out deviant sexual behavior (cf., Bandura, 1968:520; Davison, 1968:84; Evans, 1967:17; Jackson, 1969:133; McGuire et al., 1965:185).

Or consider some explicit sexual materials which in words and pictures show middle-aged or mature men having great varieties of explicit sex with minors (a type of erotica widely available in adult bookstores in America). Again, the viewer-reader is sexually stimulated and associations are made with minor girls or boys. It appears entirely possible that one could create a "child molester" in the scientific laboratory, or by "accident" in the laboratory of real life. As Rachman puts it, "There seems little question, therefore, that sexual arousal can be conditioned to previously neutral stimuli" (1966:295). Thus it is easily conceivable from available scientific evidence that a healthy heterosexual male could, under proper circumstances, be conditioned into sexual deviancy. Whether he would act out these deviant tendencies would depend on a number of countervailing factors which would vary from individual to individual.

All of this evidence, of course, is of the causal type and powerfully suggests possible damaging consequences of exposure to pornography for some people under certain circumstances. These kinds of studies, reported in the open literature, are reviewed and discussed in two separate literature reviews printed in the first volume of the Commission's Technical Reports by Jay Mann (p. 23) and Cairns, Paul, and Wishner (p. 5) but are not mentioned, considered, or reviewed by the Effects Panel in their final report to the rest of the Commission and to the Congress.

3. Using Erotica to Change Sexual Orientation

Barlow and Agras (1971) have demonstrated that it is possible to directly alter sexual arousal to heterosexual stimuli with a subject who is homosexual. They used a technique whereby they gradually and systematically *increased* the brightness of a slide of a female nude projected on a screen (a slide which had elicited no prior sexual arousal in their homosexual) while simultaneously *decreasing* the brightness of a superimposed slide of a male nude (which had greatly aroused the young man, as measured by penile volume change). They used an experimental design where the fading (of lightness to darkness of the various slides) was introduced, reversed, and reintroduced while associated changes in sexual arousal were measured. Not only did they demonstrate arousal responses to the female slide used, but the response generalized to other female nude pictures, and during the first fading-in phase, the young man reported sexual attraction to females in his daily routine. This is a remarkable demonstration of the power of erotica to help shift sexual orientation in a controlled laboratory setting.

There is an additional vast literature (reviewed by such people as Bandura, 1969; Feldman, 1966, 1968; Rachman and Teasdale, 1969) which suggests that sexual orientation can successfully be changed in many individuals (e.g., homosexual to heterosexual) via the use of erotic stimuli and aversive conditioning techniques. Essentially what occurs is to show the homosexuals, for example, erotic photographs of other persons of the same sex nude, so as to sexually arouse them. When aroused they are given an electric shock or a chemical-like apomorphine (which causes nausea). The subjects of such techniques are "turned off" to what was previously sexually exciting to them. At the moment the shock is stopped and the erotic homosexual picture flashed off the screen, they are immediately shown a picture of a sexually attractive female. Thus relief from shock and the accompanying good feeling are associated with the female. This is all done in carefully controlled laboratory or clinical settings. A number of successes in changing sexual orientation have been demonstrated[5] (Blakemore et al., 1963:29; Feldman and MacCulloch, 1964:167; Glynn and Harper, 1961:619; Rachman, 1961:235; Raymond and O'Keefe, 1965:579). This literature suggests that erotic materials have great potential power to assist in the shift of sexual orientation when used under certain prescribed conditions. The possibility of deliberate or accidental real-life conditionings in the reverse direction has to be given due consideration here. For example, predatory homosexuals who specialize in the seduction of adolescent boys often use pornography as an initial step in the seduction procedure. The boy is exposed to this material and sexually aroused, and this is followed by more explicit seductive behaviors, frequently leading to sexual relations. For an adolescent boy whose sexual orientation is not fixed or who has minor homosexual tendencies, such an occurrence could have a traumatic or crippling effect on his future heterosexual adjustment.

4. The Role of Pornography and Fantasy in the Formation of Sexual Deviations

Another group of studies (not funded by the Commission but in the open literature) has demonstrated that sexual deviations can apparently arise from exposure to witnessed real-life sexual acts (or pornography) which may now or later stimulate the victim sexually. He thereafter masturbates to the fantasy of that deviant sexual activity.

Aberrant sexual fantasies (after being introduced into the mind) are selectively reinforced by masturbating to them, and, as Bandura puts it, "They eventually become able to provoke corresponding homosexual, exhibitionistic, and voyeuristic behavior" (1969:520).

McGuire and his colleagues (1965:165) refer to this as "masturbatory conditioning." They note that the sexual experience is not sufficient by itself to immediately establish a deviant preference—but it stimulates a fantasy for later masturbation. As the person repeatedly masturbates to the fantasy (such as having sex with children or animals or raping a female) as his exclusive sexual outlet, the pleasurable experiences endow the deviant fantasy with increasing erotic value. The orgasm experienced then provides the critical reinforcing event for the conditioning of the fantasy preceding or accompanying the act. Other related studies by Evans (1968:16) and Jackson (1969:133) support this thesis. They find that deviant masturbatory

5. I would caution against the view that we have an instant panacea for treating all sexual disorders. The treatment procedures mentioned are far more complicated than suggested above; therapists and researchers obtain widely differing "cure rates" for reasons that are not entirely understood.

fantasy very significantly affects the habit strength of a subject's sexual deviation (making more difficult the cure of those with strong deviant fantasies). McGuire indicates that any type of sexual deviation can be acquired in this way, that it may include several unrelated deviations in one individual and cannot be eliminated even by massive feelings of guilt (1965:187). The study cites many case histories to illustrate this type of conditioning. Many carefully detailed psychoanalytic histories of masturbatory fantasies provide excellent illustrations of how sexually deviant behavior may have been learned through such a conditioning process. Examples of such histories may be found in Berest's (1970) report on a case of sadism; Friedemann's (1966) description of two cases of male transvestism; McCawley's (1965) paper on cases of exhibitionism; Shenken's (1964) account of bestiality cases; Yalom's (1960) study of cases of voyeurism; Gorman's (1964) report on fetishism in identical twins; and Annon's (1971) various case histories and excellent presentation of the whole issue.

This would suggest that motion pictures depicting explicit sex, especially modeling deviant and antisocial activities, could provide the fantasies for the susceptible viewer to later masturbate to and then convert into behavior. Subsequent masturbation to the memory of the deviancy would "maintain" it during the periods between the overt acts—which would explain why deviant sexuality is so resistant to extinction and difficult to treat with regular psychotherapy.

This kind of evidence runs directly counter to the notion that a lot of exposure to pornography will keep rapists off the street—the so-called "catharsis hypothesis." This hypothesis has been generally discredited in the violence area, where apologists for TV violence for awhile claimed that media violence might be healthy for children in that it "drained off their hostile feelings and impulses." A great deal of research suggests just the opposite.

Probably what occurs in the areas of both violence and sex is that materials depicting these kinds of behaviors (a) stimulate and arouse, (b) show or instruct in detail how to do the act, and (c) when seen frequently enough (in fantasy, on the screen, or in real life) desensitize so as to reduce feelings of conscience, guilt, or controls in participating in a deviant act. Also the act is in a sense legitimized by its repetitious exposure.

As a clinical psychologist and psychotherapist, I have recently treated a young married male with a sexual deviation of voyeurism. He prefers to stimulate himself sexually by watching erotic movies or reading pornographic novels, then to masturbate while so engaged rather than have sexual relations with his wife, for whom he claims affection. His sexual impulses have been to some extent rechanneled away from normal heterosexual relations. This has been having a serious impact on the marriage. His wife, who is very attractive, feels massively rejected; a woman cannot understand why her husband prefers a two-dimensional female on the screen or in a book for sexual stimulation and release to her, who represents a real-life, three-dimensional human being who has affection and commitment for him.

Another case involves a middle-aged man who prefers female minors for his sexual outlet. Even though he has had satisfactory relations with his wife in the past, his sexual deviation is creating major problems in their marital adjustment. His history reveals some exposure during adolescence to very young females as well as to pornography (written textual materials) depicting pedophilia (child molestation). The two of these together have provided him with rich deviant sexual fantasies which he masturbates to and occasionally acts out in real life. While deeply religious and guilt-ridden about his behavior, he appears to have only erratic and limited control over what he does. He finds that he is able to curb his antisocial sexual behavior for awhile, but under stress or depression his controls break down. Then he acts out the fantasies that in the past he only masturbated to. There is no doubt that his early life experience and pornography jointly contributed to and helped maintain this deviation.

A Los Angeles firm is currently marketing an 8mm motion picture film which depicts two Girl Scouts in their uniforms selling cookies from door to door. At one residence they are invited in by a mature, sexually aggressive male, who proceeds to seduce them and subject them to a number of unusual and extremely explicit sexual acts, all shown in greatest detail. This film is what is usually termed hard-core pornography. If the research of Rachman, McGuire, and others has any meaning at all, it would suggest that such a film could be dangerous and could potentially condition some male viewers to fantasies and later behavior involving seductive sexual experiences with female minors. These types of deviant pornographic films are of fairly recent origin, unknown to the older sex offender. One might, with some confidence, predict an increase on the national scene of aberrant sex offenses. In any event, with the scientific knowledge we have now, it would take a very courageous (or, a better word, foolish) father to knowingly expose his minor daughter to individuals who have seen much of this kind of pornography.

5. Violence Plus Sex

The recent Surgeon General's report on TV violence (1972) has suggested that there has now been found a causal relationship between children's exposure to TV/movie violence and participation in more aggressive behavior. It would be hard to believe that exposure to pornography depicting deviant sexual activities wouldn't similarly effect the behavior of the viewer, especially if the pornography were to model, for example, sado-masochistic sexual activities (sexual and violent acts combined).

Meyer (1972) notes that, "While sexual behavior and aggressive behavior may appear at first glance to be distinctly different types of behavior, comparisons of physiological characteristics of the organism in both states of arousal show a great deal of similarity." Kinsey (1953) made note of this occurrence when he observed that of the fourteen basic physiological changes taking place during sexual and aggressive arousal, only four differ between the two states. In his studies in *Human Aggression,* Anthony Storr (1970:18) notes that it is not uncommon for one response to suddenly change into the other.

In five of the Commission's studies plus one other (Tannenbaum, 1970; Mosher, 1970; Mosher and Katz, 1970; Byrne and Lamberth, 1970; Schmidt and Sigusch, 1970; Davis and Braucht, 1970), all of them found evidence of aggressive arousal in subjects who were first aroused by erotic sexual stimuli. In follow-up research by Meyer (1972, p. 324), he finds that observing sexually arousing films can also lead to increases in aggressive behavior and concludes: ". . . The results of this experiment suggest that public concern and fears of the harmful effects of television and film violence should also be extended to closely allied effects of sexually arousing content." In other words, this research suggests that sexual arousal in males is linked to associated aggressive arousal. Thus, it is probably no accident that some of the four-letter terms for sexual intercourse are frequently used in a hostile, derogatory sense, or that intercourse itself, as in rape or near rape, is sometimes dynamically a hostile aggressive act performed *against* a female.

While the Meyer study wasn't available at the time the Commission report writers put together their report, all of the other studies linking sex with aggression were, plus the findings of the earlier violence commission.

In another Commission-sponsored research by Mosher and Katz (1970), studying male verbal aggression against women in a laboratory setting, they concluded (p. 373) that "the data clearly support the proposition that aggression against women increases when that aggression is instrumental to securing sexual stimulation [through seeing pornography]." This finding was particularly true for men with severe conscience systems as well as for those feeling guilt about being aggressive. This suggests that the need for sexual stimulation (via pornography) can overrule conscience and guilt in "permitting" aggressive behavior towards women. And while this is a laboratory demonstration, with limited generalizability, it still constitutes another "negative effects" type of evidence to which no attention was paid or of which no mention was made by the writers of the Commission report.

In still another series of experiments, Tannenbaum (1971) exposed his male subjects to three types of films: neutral, erotic, and aggressive in content, then had them play a question-answer game with a confederate. If their partner gave a wrong answer, they were to shock (punish) them by pushing one of ten buttons, each giving an increasingly higher (more painful) level of shock. They were free to choose at what level they would shock or punish the confederate. Tannenbaum found that the erotic film elicited the highest level of aggressive response in shocking others, with the aggressive film coming in second and the neutral film lowest. When *both* the aggressive and erotic films were shown to the subjects, an even higher level of aggressive response was elicited. While this is a controlled laboratory study where no real injury was permitted to be inflicted on the subjects, it still is a powerful type of cause-effect study linking exposure to erotica to aggressive behavior. This was financed by the Commission, but no mention is ever made of these results (Tech Report Volume 8, pp. 334, 340).

6. Studies of Pornography and Group Sex Behavior

Other kinds of studies bearing on pornography's effects would include those which reach into what might be regarded as sexually deviant groups practicing mate swapping and group sex. These studies are not scientifically rigorous, but still, on the basis of intensive interviews with participants, yield some enlightening data. Gilbert Bartell in a two-year study of group sex among 350 mid-Americans (1970:113) found that, "In an attempt to 'turn themselves on' the males push their women into having sexual relations with another girl. Most of them got the idea from either books or pornographic movies. Again, the male experiences disaster. Why? Sixty-five percent of the female respondents admit to enjoying their homosexual relationships with other females and liking it to the point where they would rather 'turn on' to the female than to the males." This again suggests the power of deviant modeling in films or books to suggest sexual activities destructive to the self-interest of the viewer. And while not every participant in such activities will necessarily be "burned," the risks are real, and negative outcomes do in fact occur with some individuals.

7. The Davis and Braucht Research

Davis and Braucht (1971), in a sophisticated and well-done Commission-financed study of seven different populations of subjects comprising 365 people, assessed the relationship between exposure to pornography and moral character, deviance in the home and neighborhood, and sex behavior. Samples of city jail inmates, Mexican-American college students, black college students, white fraternity men, conservative protestant students, and Catholic seminarians were studied intensively. In addition, each had one female friend fill out a character scale about his behavior.

In their study, which was impressive in its rigorous methodology and statistical treatment, they conclude, "One finds exposure to pornography is the strongest predictor of sexual deviance among the early age of exposure subjects" (p. 206). Later they note, "In general, then, exposure to pornography in the 'early age of exposure' subgroup is *not* related to having deviant peers [bad associations and companions] and similar variables; it would be difficult to blame the sexual promiscuity and deviancy of these subjects on other influences such as being influenced by friends [rather than pornography] into these kinds of antisocial activities."

Also, "Heavy exposure to pornography is apparently more strongly related to solitary sexual activity [masturbation] and to homosexual experience, whereas peer pressures are more strongly related to precocious and extensive heterosexual experience" (p. 207).

Also, "At the very least this argues for a pattern in which exposure to pornography is part of a strongly deviant life style, including in some cases strongly homosexual patterns and including in other cases a high level of heterosexual experience with little regard for the quality and duration of the relationship . . ." (p. 211).

Also, "In the case of sexual deviance, we have found a positive relationship between deviance and exposure to pornography at all ages of exposure levels" (p. 213).

And, "In the early age of exposure [to pornography] subgroup, the amount of exposure was significantly correlated with a willingness to engage in group sexual relations, frequency of homosexual intercourse, and "serious" sexual deviance; and there were trends for the number both of high school heterosexual partners and total homosexual partners to be positively related to [pornographic] exposure" (p. 206).

Correlation alone never demonstrates a causal relationship; however, it does permit a reasonable hypothesis. And in this study where, in part, the researchers have assessed and partialled out other significant variables (such as peer influences), the possibility of causation is highly suggested.

Let us keep in mind that this research was contracted and financed by the Commission, that it was in the hands of the Commission's staff for many months, that it is referred to many times in their report (i.e., "moral character" is unaffected by pornography); but no mention is made in their report of these negative finds. However, the September 3, 1970, issue of the *New York Daily News* and an earlier edition of the *Washington Post* carried stories on this research, linking exposure to pornography with sex deviancy—a critical finding suggesting real danger in exposing children and young adolescents to heavy quantities of pornography.

Obviously more research must be done here, but just as in the early studies linking smoking with lung cancer, it seems irresponsible not to report such findings—especially in the Commission's Effects Panel Report—since so few people have either access to the original research or the scientific expertise to understand and evaluate the elaborate and highly complex statistical analyses.

Keith Davis, the senior author of the Davis-Braucht research, was later to comment (1971), "As a contributor to some of the research on which the *Report of the Commission on Obscenity and Pornography* was based, I have been discouraged by the lack of serious debate of the commission's report. . . . The key issue is that of moral corruption and the debasement of human sexuality. It is hard to imagine that what a society tolerates in its mass media as a portrayal of sexual reality will not come to be the kind of sexual reality that society's next generation lives."

As I encountered a series of evidences and data from the Commission's own technical reports like the Davis-Braucht research, I was haunted by the refrain repeated so often in the Commission Report (p. 58), "Extensive empirical investigation, both by the Commission and by others, provides no evidence that exposure to or use of explicitly sexual materials play[s] a significant role in the causation of social or individual harms such as crime, delinquency, sexual or nonsexual deviancy or severe emotional disturbances"—and by the reassurance of Lipton and Greenwood to all their fellow psychiatrists in the *Psychiatric News* (1971): "The many varied studies . . . are remarkably uniform in the direction to which they point. This direction fails to establish a meaningful significant causal relationship *or even significant correlation* [italics added] between exposure to erotica and immediate or delayed antisocial behavior. . . ."

8. The Goldstein-Kant-Hartman Study

In a retrospective study of sex offenders, homosexuals, trans-sexuals, pornography users, blacks, and controls, the Goldstein et al. study concludes, "The research reported in this work clearly tends to support the view that pornography does not incite criminal or antisocial acts. Indeed some of the data suggests the reverse may be true . . ." (1973:161).[6]

The Goldstein research represents a major effort to shed light on the "pornography effects" problem. It is in many ways thoughtful, well written, sophisticated, erudite, and frequently enlightening, though it does suffer from some limitations, as will be noted below.

This study also represents, in an almost classic way, an example of the way in which individual investigators can arrive at differing conclusions after examining the same body of data.

Goldstein bases his "no harm" conclusion (to oversimplify a little) on interview data suggesting that the sex offenders have been exposed to less pornography than their "normal controls," that they felt more guilty about what they saw, and, in the case of the rapists, "were least likely (of the various comparison groups) to attempt imitation of the desired erotic activity" (e.g., that had been modeled by the pornography witnessed) (1973:82). The book concludes with a theory suggesting that rapists have self-generated sexual fantasies or day dreams which are distasteful and uncontrollable that

6. An earlier version of this research was published by the National Pornography Commission (1971). A serious reviewer of their work should have both versions since each has some unique data as well as much that is overlapping.

stimulate them to antisocial behavior. Pornography is seen as a means or an aid for these individuals to ward off anxiety, disgust, and guilt about these disturbing daydreams.

This discussion of the role of fantasy in the use of erotica for rapists has been previously critiqued (Cline, 1971)[7] and the suggestion made, in sum, that they have no crucial tests of the hypotheses underlying their theory and that the data used to arrive at their conjectures is based in part on comparisons of noncomparable groups, using differing interview sets which make crucial data comparisons unmeaningful. Their theory may still be valid and correct, but their supporting data are not definitive or in any way conclusive.

In this study, as in some of the other Commission studies, there is the suggestion that sex offenders have come from sexually deprived backgrounds and have been exposed to less erotica than normal controls (Appendix E, this chapter, deals with this issue more extensively). While this may represent a true and valid finding, some artifacts of sampling may also exist that may make this finding more apparent than real. Studies such as those by Berger (1971), Abelson et al. (1971), and others suggest that those individuals having highest exposure to pornography generally tend to be the young, the middle-upper classes, and the better educated. Goldstein's control sample is significantly younger, better educated, and of higher socio-economic status than any of his three sex-offender groups. Thus only 21% of his normal controls versus 36% of the rapists, 50% of the child molesters with male targets, and 70% of the child molesters with female targets are thirty years of age or older. Fifty percent of the control group versus 26% of the rapists, 30% of the child molesters with male targets, and 5% of the child molesters with female targets have been to college. In addition, on the Edwards's Occupational Scale of Socioeconomic Status, 30% of the control group versus 11% of the rapists, 15% of the child molesters with male targets and 15% of the child molesters with female targets are in "present occupations" rated clerical and above. Striking differences in marital status occur, also, among the samples. While Goldstein and Kant correctly caution the reader that the matching of their various groups was only "fair," and one should be cautious about interpreting conclusions where group comparisons are made, they later tend to disregard this earlier caution in their conclusions—some of which are unsupported or contradicted by their own data.

In any event, at this date we do not know for sure whether or not differences exist in sex offenders' and normals' early exposure to erotica which might not be accounted for by social class and educational difference.

---

7. Though he did not publish this material in book form until 1973, John Hartman, the author, graciously allowed Cline to have an advance copy of the material, which was presented as part of a symposium at meetings of the American Psychological Association (1971) and critiqued in a paper by Cline.

Even if the sex offenders received more exposure to erotica at an earlier age—this does not prove it harmed them. Other research would be needed to answer this question.

In Goldstein's interviews, he asked his subjects if they had ever "tried out" the sexual behavior depicted during a peak adolescent exposure to pornography. Fifty-seven percent of his rapists replied yes (1973:76, Table 9). Yet in his chapter summary, Goldstein curiously comments, "While [the rapists] noting an intense desire to imitate the [sexual] activities shown [by the pornography], only rarely did they satisfy it (1973:79). The use of the term "rarely" to describe the 57% of the rapists who acted out or imitated the pornography modeled for them, then, is inaccurate. Their data show that 77% of the child molesters with male targets and 87% of the child molesters with female targets reported trying out or imitating the sexual behavior modeled by the pornography seen during this peak adolescent experience. But even more interesting, in some ways, is the fact that 85% of the normal controls also indicated they had imitated behavior modeled by the pornography. All groups, then, were potentially stimulated and affected by the pornography—if we can believe their verbal self-report. Apparently if you are "normal" you tend to choose safer outlets. If you are a rapist, you occasionally engage in antisocial, aggressive, sexual acts. If you are a child molester, you molest children. Data with similar trends are presented for peak adult experiences with erotica. Goldstein found that both his homosexuals and users of pornography tended to have less exposure to erotica in their growing up years as compared to the normal controls. Their sex behavior, also, was more conservative and delayed in adolescence. Then, later, a crossing over occurred for both homosexual and pornography users, resulting in a high obsession for, an interest in, and a use of pornography—associated with a high incidence of deviant sex (in the case of the homosexuals) and the "broadest range of sexual practices" for the pornography users. This included the highest rates of extramarital sex, anal sex, and oral sex among the nine comparison groups. This, at the very least, suggests a possible facilitating and modeling role for pornography in both of these groups. All of this would imply that pornography can affect behavior—sometimes adversely. It would also suggest concerns about exposing young people—in particular, those whose sexual identities are not entirely fixed—to erotica modeling deviant or antisocial sexual behavior.

Probably certain other conditions (X, Y, and Z) would have to coexist in the child to make him vulnerable to pornography's influence (such conditions as having low impulse control, a defective or traumatic family environment, and a delinquent peer culture).

However, if the careful reviewer will look at the Goldstein et al. data in both their 1971 and 1973 publications (not always at what they say, particularly), he would find considerable evidence suggesting possible cause-effect harm for some viewers of pornography—if we can accept retrospective self-report data as valid.

The reader is invited to look at this data. Tables 9 and 10 in their 1970 publication and tables 6, 8, 9, and 10 in their 1973 work are particularly enlightening.

9. The Propper Study

If we review the research of Propper, found in the Commission-sponsored study of 476 reformatory inmates (see Table 1), we note again and again a relationship between high exposure to pornography and sexually promiscuous and deviant behavior at very early ages, as well as an affiliation with groups high in criminal activity and sex deviancy. While correlation alone never demonstrates a causal relationship, it does permit a reasonable hypothesis, and in an area involving health and welfare, it can suggest reasonable concerns. This study was financed and contracted by the Commission, and while the research refers to Propper's study often, no mention is made of any of these specific negative results in the Commission Report. This study was for many months in the hands of the Effects Panel committee that assembled and wrote the report. It was also available for the inspection of any of the Commission members who wished to read it (but to no one else). In this study are striking statistical (though not proven causal) relationships between heavy use of pornography and various kinds of sexual acting out, deviancy, and an affiliation with high criminality groups.

10. The Opinions of Professional Workers about Pornography

In its summary section the Commission's report states, "Professional workers in the area of human conduct generally believe that sexual materials do not have harmful effects." While this appears to be true, these conclusions are based primarily on a mail-back survey by Lipkin and Carns (1970), in which less than a third of their sample responded. They also neglect to state that in this study 254 psychiatrists and psychologists reported cases in which they had found a direct causal linkage between involvement with pornography and a sex crime. Another 324 professionals reported cases where such a relationship was suspected. This is by actual count, then, 578 professionals. While these therapists represent in percentage a minority group, their reports should not be ignored. What if 800 of 1,000 physicians indicated that they had observed no relationship between cancer of the cervix and use of the coil contraceptive, but the other 200 physicians indicated that in their practice they had come across cases where there was a suspected or definite relationship, do we discount the experience of the minority because they are outvoted where a possible health hazard is involved?

Additionally, the Commission members did not report (although they were aware of its existence) a survey conducted in 1967 by another group,

TABLE 1

Exposure to Sexually Oriented Materials Among Young Male Prison Offenders

by Martin Propper

Sample: 476 male reformatory inmates, ages 16-21

Activity Engaged In	Subjects Having Lo Exposure to Pornography	Subjects Having Hi Exposure to Pornography
1. Age of first intercourse 11 or under (Table 30)	37%	53%
2. Having intercourse with 4 or more partners (Table 27)	59%	76%
3. Intercourse with more than 1 person at a time (p. 348)	35%	59%
4. Belongs to a high sex deviant peer group[1] (Table 35)	44%	77%
5. Belongs to high antisocial crime group[2] (Table 36)	55%	82%

6. Table 26 in the Propper study shows the relationship between viewing textual depictions of homosexual activity and participating in it:

	Never	10 or more times
Participation in homosexual activity after seeing textual depictions of same	12%	40%

7. Table 31 in the Propper study also reveals among the younger boys a very high relationship between (a) the age at which they saw a picture of sexual intercourse, and (b) the age at which they first engaged personally in sexual intercourse. This means that if a boy saw pictures of intercourse at a very early age, he engaged in intercourse at a very early age. If he saw intercourse pictures later, he engaged in intercourse later. While the data do not provide evidence of causal linkage, they certainly raise the possibility. They also remind one of Bandura's work in imitative learning, where children learn by imitating what they've seen.

1. The sexual behaviors which constituted this measure included: (a) sexual intercourse, (b) group sexual intercourse, (c) going to a prostitute, (d) getting a girl pregnant, (e) participating in orgies.

2. The activities which constituted this measure included: (a) friend's suggestions to violate the law, (b) friends in jail or reform school, (c) friends in trouble with the law, (d) purchase of stolen goods by friends, and (e) friends who were members of gangs.

the Archdiocese of New Jersey, wherein psychiatrists saw a relationship between involvement with pornography and obscenity, and antisocial or delinquent behavior. The majority (84%) of therapists in this study reported noting such a relationship at some time during their practice. This study is also flawed because of a low return of mail-backs by the professionals. Such omission of contrary evidence is difficult to justify.

11. No Experimental Research on Pornography-related Crime and Delinquency

While the Effects Panel report writers claim finding no evidence that pornography *causes* delinquent or criminal behavior, they fail to mention that *not a single one of the fourteen Commission-sponsored experimental studies (where subjects were actually exposed to pornography and their behavior noted and where cause and effect might potentially be determined) actually investigated crime, delinquency, or antisocial behaviors.*[8] Thus, it is understandable that the Commission report writers could report no causal evidence linking pornography with antisocial, criminal, or delinquent behavior. They simply did not study the issue. The data in other studies of sex offenders was all retrospective, verbal self-report and of the type which could only suggest associations but could not prove cause and effect. However, many of these associations did suggest potential harms; and they went unmentioned.

12. Sex Crimes in Denmark and Pornography

The popular press has repeatedly reported that the rate of sex crimes in Denmark has declined since the liberalization and repeal of pornography laws there. This is interpreted as an example or proof from a living laboratory that pornography's influence is essentially benign and harmless.[9] The researchers who wrote the Pornography Commission's Effects Panel Report declare essentially the same thing (pp. 272-74):

These figures show that the number of reported sex crimes (in Copenhagen) declined during the period even though pornography became increasingly

8. The closest anyone came was the Mann, Sidman, and Starr study of Palo Alto middle-class married couples who were asked to check on a sheet of paper if they had engaged in sex with other than their spouses after seeing erotic movies. But such things as rape, child molestation, and all similar illegal behaviors or sex crimes were never assessed.

9. The United States, not Denmark, is actually the country of concern for most Americans. Since erotica has flowered in the United States to about the same degree as in Denmark, sex crime statistics in the United States should have greater interest and relevance to most readers. These are presented elsewhere in this chapter.

available to the general public. The sharpest continuous reduction in sex offenses began in 1967 and has continued through 1969. The onset of this decline occurred when prohibitions regarding dissemination of literary sexual materials were relaxed. Further analysis found that all classes of sex crimes decreased but that some decreased more than others. . . . It was found that changes in the incidences of sex offenses could not be attributed to legislative change, alteration of law enforcement practices, or modified police reporting and data collection procedures. A survey of Copenhagen residents found that neither public attitudes about sex crimes nor willingness to report such crimes had changed sufficiently to account for the substantial decrease in sex offenses between 1959 and 1969.

The average reader as well as most social scientists will never get an opportunity to see the original research report or read what this Danish psychologist, Kutschinsky, actually wrote in his report, which was the source of some of the above conclusions. He, of course, was studying the issue of why, with increasing pornography in Denmark, the rate of some sex crimes had apparently dropped. One of the things Kutschinsky did was to interview intensively a carefully drawn sample of adult men and women in Copenhagen surveying (a) whether they had ever been a victim of a sex crime; (b) whether they ever reported it; (c) whether they would report certain types of sex crimes now or ignore them; (d) whether they had changed their mind over the past few years about the seriousness of certain sex offenses; and (e) whether they felt the same way about these things as they had ten years ago. He found that 26% of the men and 61% of the women of Copenhagen had been victims of some category of sex crime, some minor, some serious. However, only 6% of the males interviewed and 19% of the female victims actually reported these to the police. This is consistent with statements made by the U.S. Department of Justice in its 1970 Uniform Crime Reports. Referring to rape, "This offense is probably one of the most unreported crimes due primarily to fear and/or embarrassment on the part of the victim." This means, of course, that overall sex crime statistics are unreliable and have to be viewed with caution. Kutschinsky, hired by the Commission, concluded after a careful and extended analysis of his data: "The decrease in [sexual] exhibitionism registered by the police during the last ten years may be fully explained by a change in people's attitudes toward this crime and towards reporting it to the police" (1971:285). His conclusion is similar with regard to the sex crime of "indecency toward women" which can involve anything short of a direct rape attempt on a female.

Next, Kutschinsky reported a 69% decrease in "offenses against girls" (child molest) which his analysis cannot justify by a reluctance of people to report or of police to record. His studies appear to reflect a genuine drop over a ten-year period. Further research and experimental studies will have to investigate the causes for this decrease, with pornography's role certainly a legitimate item for study here. Peeping crimes have dropped about 80% over the decade, and Kutschinsky reports that no firm conclusion can be reached but that at least part of the decrease may be attributed to "an unofficial change in the handling of this type of crime by the police."

Thus, the Denmark data suggest in summary that the reported statistical drop in exhibitionism and indecency toward women probably do *not* reflect real drops in the occurrence of these crimes at all but can be explained almost in whole by the reduced number of victims reporting these crimes as well as by relaxed police attitudes in recording them; whereas the evidence on peepers is inconclusive; and regarding offenses against minor females, their reduction is the only one which appears real, but we don't know why.

There is no reduction at all in the numbers reported of violent sex crimes and rapes, both in Copenhagen and in Denmark (see Tables 2 and 3); *and the possibility exists that, in actual numbers, they may have increased, but victims are reporting them less often.*

Additionally, the Commission's presentation of the report of Denmark's sex crimes omits certain types of data such as that regarding incest, venereal disease, illegitimacy, prostitution, and divorce—all of which could be relevant here.

In summary, then, the Effects Panel writers have in some instances misinformed the people about the statistics of the Denmark sex crimes, presenting some conclusions that are a complete reversal of that reported by their own authorized and funded research.

Among reputable scientists, a serious attempt is always made in reporting research to suggest limitations, cautions, and to acknowledge contradictory data or other points of view, especially where there are health and welfare considerations. In scientific journals the main consumers are fellow scientists of the same profession who can respond and rebut shallow presentations and inaccuracies. The audience, however, to which the Commission addressed its report, was primarily nonscientific and included legislators, judges, juries, the public at large, physicians, marriage counselors and sex educators. Therefore, the inaccuracies, omissions, and misrepresentations of the Commission became a serious matter in light of their position of public trust.

13. Pornography and Sex Crimes in the United States

Some have argued that, because sex crimes have apparently declined in Denmark while the volume of pornography has increased, we need not be concerned about the potential effect of this kind of material in our country. However, two considerations must be noted. First, we are a different country and culture, and second, we are actually at about the same stage as Denmark in the distribution and sale of pornography (Sampson, 1970:207). The United States, not Denmark, is the country of concern with regards to pornography's alleged effects. Written pornography can be purchased anywhere in the United States now. Hard-core still-pictures and movies can now be purchased over the counter in most cities. Anything can be purchased through the mails. And in many cities people can attend hard-core pornographic movies. A few cities have live sex shows. However, most relevant are sex crime statistics in this country, not in Denmark. Since pornography began to be sold openly in the United States in about 1960, relevant data should probably be examined from this time on. One cannot impute cause

Table 2
Violent Sex Crimes in Denmark

Year	No. of Crimes
1960	269
1962	189
1964	259
1965	Pornography freely available from this date on
1966	215
1968	217
1969	236
1970	215

Source: *Danish Statistical Yearbook,* 1970.

TABLE 3
Incidence of Rape (Copenhagen only)

Year	
1959	32
1960	21
1961	25
1962	29
1963	22
1964	20
1965	24—Pornography freely available from this date on.
1966	34
1967	23
1968	28
1969	27
1970	31

Source: Danish police records and Berl Kutschinsky in "The effect of easy availability of pornography on the incidence of sex crime: The Danish experience." Journal of Social Issues (in press, 1973).

and effect here, though the Commission infers it (in the opposite direction) from the Denmark sex crime data.

Reported Rapes (Verified)

(absolute increase)	Up 116% 1960-69	Up 146% 1960-71
(controlled for population growth)	Up 93% 1960-69	Up 106% 1960-71

Rape Arrests

(all ages)	Up 57% 1960-69	Up 63% 1960-71
(males under age 18)	Up 86% 1960-69	Up 98% 1960-71

By way of comparison, arrests for all crimes were up 34% for the period of 1960-71 (Source: Uniform Crime Report, U.S. Dept. of Justice, 1970, 1972). Data to 1969 as well as to 1971 are included here to indicate what information was available to the Pornography Commission when they wrote their reports as well as what the situation was later.

Prostitution and Commercialized Vice Arrests: Females

(all ages)	Up 80% 1960-69	Up 87% 1960-71
(girls under 18)	Up 120% 1960-69	Up 196% 1960-71

(Source: Uniform Crime Report, U.S. Dept. of Justice, 1970, 1972).

Sex Offenses (except forcible rape and prostitution)

Down 17% 1960-69   Down 21% 1960-71

Note: The Justice Department indicates that this is a spurious, misleading statistic. It is due to changes in law enforcement policy, primarily involving homosexual acts between consenting adults—now rarely prosecuted, although early in the decade they were (Source: Uniform Crime Report, U.S. Dept. of Justice, 1970, 1972).

Venereal Disease: Primary and Secondary Syphilis

Up 27%   1960-71

Venereal Disease: Gonorrhea

Up 228% 1960-71

(Source: V.D. Fact Sheet 1972, Public Health Service, U.S. Dept. of Health, Education and Welfare [DHEW Publ. No. (HSM) 73-8195], pp. 14-15).

Illegitimate Births

Up 41% 1960-68   In actual numbers: 224,300 to 339,200 (while population increased 13%)

Up 124% 1950-68   In actual numbers: 141,600 to 339,200 (while population increased 31%)

Note: The bulk of this increase is found in females below age 20, who presumably would be less sophisticated and knowledgeable about birth control procedures. (Source: 1970 *New York Times Encyclopediac Almanac,* p. 421 and *1970 Natality Statistics,* U.S. Public Health Dept., p. 31).

Divorce Statistics

Up 70% 1960-69   Up 96% 1960-71
(from 393,000 to 660,000)   (from 393,000 to 768,000)
Up 50% 1960-69   Up 68% 1960-71
(2.2 per 1,000 to 3.3 per 1,000)   (from 2.2 rate to 3.7)

Note: The lower data controls for population increases. (Source: *1973 The World Almanac,* p. 952, and National Center for Health Statistics, HEW).

The above data indicate major increases in nearly every type of social and sexual pathology in the United States. While this is associated with an increase in volume and sales of all types of erotic-pornographic and explicit sexual materials, no conclusion as to a causal relationship can be drawn. These data are presented for comparison with those presented by the Effects Panel. Thus, it would be difficult to argue that there has been a decrease in sex crimes in America as the volume of erotica has increased. Just the opposite, of course, has occurred. And the possibility exists that there may be a cause-effect relationship—though appropriate and suitable research would be needed to conclusively prove this.

14. Sex Offenders Report Pornography as a Contributor to Their Crimes

In another Commission-sponsored study by Walker (1970), seven groups of adult males (sex offenders, mental hospital patients, university students, and others) were tested and interviewed for information concerning exposure to pornography and personal background data. In their analysis of the data, they found that the sex offenders significantly more often than their controls (nonsex offenders whom they were compared with) increased their sexual activity after viewing pornography. A significant minority (39%) of the sex offenders indicated that "pornography had something to do with their committing the sex offense they were convicted of." The researchers also found that their offenders significantly more often claimed they had been influenced by pornography to commit a sexual crime.

The writers of the Commission report note this evidence and rightly raise the possibility that these sex offenders may be "scapegoating" here (blaming something or somebody else for their problem). This possibility is certainly a reasonable one. The alternate possibility, that they might indeed be telling the truth, however, is also reasonable. And until this issue is settled, it would seem injudicious and unscientific to claim that pornography had "no effect."

15. The Howard Study

The Commission financed a study by Howard et al. at the University of North Carolina which proved possibly the most controversial of all the Commission's research (1971:109-10,123). A group of college males were subjected to extremely heavy amounts of pornography for a period of three months. Elaborate psychophysical instrumentation was attached to various parts of their bodies to measure their responses to this erotic material. Various before and after tests were given to determine if pornography might effect them in some way. Two scales showed statistically significant changes. Scores measuring both promiscuity and sociopathic tendencies were significantly higher after the subjects had seen pornographic materials. They also found that those men with high measures of psychopathic tendencies (MMPI Pd scale) tended not to satiate or tire of pornography as much or as quickly as did the normals. Additionally, the high-psychopath men indicated having significantly more sexual frustration and less sexual control; they also showed a significant decrease in measures of personal autonomy. Since the Howard study represents that research in the literature wherein subjects received by far the greatest exposure to pornographic materials ever reported, and since it was a controlled laboratory experiment, these results cannot be lightly dismissed. The Effects Panel never mentions the above findings which represent possibly another type of negative evidence concerning pornography's effects.

16. Additional Significant Limitations in Commission's Research

No Longitudinal Studies

No longitudinal studies[10] were considered or contracted by the Commission in an attempt to determine the long-range effects of exposure to pornography and its effect on sexual activities, sex offenses, and changes in moral values. Most of the studies the Commission cited had run a course of

10. This was not the fault of the Commission. They were working under considerable time pressures. But this in no way lessens the need for this type of study to adequately assess one aspect of the "harm" issue.

only a few days or weeks (and in many cases only an hour or two). The longitudinal study properly done would have given the most powerful evidence concerning pornography's effects. There were none here.

No Clinical Studies

There were no in-depth clinical studies of total individuals and their life circumstances to assess the impact of pornography on attitudes, sex offenses, character, antisocial behavior, marital adjustment, infidelity, and other areas in question.

Omission of Studies on Porno-Violence

No attention was paid to the problem of porno-violence or sadomasochism, wherein pornography and violence are linked together in fiction and increasingly in motion pictures. This omission is particularly surprising in view of the findings in the Final Report of the National Commission on the Causes and Prevention of Violence (1969) and the later Surgeon General's Report (1972)[11] which link visual presentations of violence to increased aggressive violent behavior by the viewer. These findings would have very important implications in situations such as sadomasochism, sexual abuse, and infliction of physical injury. Perplexingly, in its preface (p. 3) to the Report, the Commission indicates its concern with sadomasochistic materials but never again mentions studying its effects.

Omission of Studies and Evidence in Imitative Learning Area

The Commission members discuss (in a limited manner) studies in the area of imitative and social learning, or modeling, by such investigators as Albert Bandura and his associates at Stanford University. Since this body of research suggests that a significant amount of learning occurs through watching and imitating the behavior of others, this concept would have great relevance to pornography effects studies. If Bandura's work (as well as others in this area) have any validity, certain types of pornography involving whole sequences of behaviors probably would affect some, perhaps many, individuals if they saw them consistently modeled on the screen or in fiction. This is certainly powerfully indicated by the findings of the violence literature. In view of the type of evidence and findings presented by the Bandura "school," it would seem that the Commission staff would indicate some cautions or concerns. These are lacking.

---

11. This latter report was not available to the Commission writers, of course, but it repeats essentially the findings of the earlier 1969 Violence Commission of which Otto Larson and Marvin Wolfgang of the Effects Panel were both members.

Absence of Youth Studies

Although in their Final Report the Commission state "... (there) is no evidence[12] that exposure to or use of explicit sexual materials plays a significant role in the causation of social or individual deviancy, or severe emotional disturbances ... or plays a significant role in the causation of delinquent or criminal behavior among youth or adults" (pp. 58, 59), they do not mention that there was not a single experimental study, longitudinal study, or clinical case study involving youth. The only direct useful information they have is data from a questionnaire given to teenagers by Berger et al.[13] (1971), which is subject to the usual problems of willingness to be truthful (especially about sex data), memory, and misinterpretation of questions. The Commission's "no harm" conclusions about youth are incautious in view of not only the extreme paucity of significant youth data, but also the presence of retrospective studies with adults (Propper, Davis and Braucht, Berger, Goldstein, and others) which suggest opposite conclusions.

For all practical purposes, significant data or research dealing directly with the impact of erotica on youth is a void in the Commission's work. It simply doesn't exist. Drawing definitive conclusions about youth and pornography, then, becomes hazardous in the face of such a lack of evidence. The Commission's researchers did make a valiant effort to find data on youth which might have a bearing on the problem, such as noting the number of youth-perpetrated sex crimes over the decade, checking data on illegitimacy, and surveying the opinions of professional workers; but in all of these data the use of erotica was never directly and systematically related to crime, delinquency, and sexual deviance.

Possible Bias in Using Only Volunteers Who Would Submit to Pornography Exposure

All studies which probed sexual histories or exposed individuals to pornography were to some degree biased by using only those people who would submit to such exposure or questioning. This was especially true for female subjects.

Varying Definitions, Types, and Amounts of Erotic Material Used

While some studies used similar pornographic slides or movies, generally a great variation existed in the type of pornography used (sometimes pictures, sometimes movies, sometimes written material). These media varied greatly

---

12. In a footnote on page 32, Jones, Klapper, and Lipton qualify the term "no evidence" to mean "no reliable evidence."

13. A study of pregnant teenagers vs. college girls by Schiller (1970) was so badly flawed as to yield no meaningful results and is not considered here.

also in their erotic and "offensive" qualities. In the "retrospective reports," wherein either people were interviewed or they filled out questionnaires, the researchers often had to rely on their subject's own definition or unique interpretation of what constituted pornography: sexual intercourse on the screen could be seen as something bland or explicitly offensive—as tender and loving or violent and brutal.

In one study (Amoroso, 1970) subjects saw twenty-seven slides projected on a screen for 2½ seconds each; only twenty of these could be regarded as "pornographic"—a total viewing time of fifty seconds for the erotic material. To conclude that pornography affects or does not affect behavior on the basis of such limited exposure and with no control group is incautious.

Summary and Conclusions

A. The majority report of the Commission on Obscenity and Pornography has recommended major changes in laws and social policy in an area of controversy and public concern—also in an area having health and welfare implications for adults and minors (the removal of nearly all controls on pornography for adults and children—except, in the latter case, pictorial materials).

The basis for recommending these changes is that the Commission found no empirical scientific evidence showing a casual relationship between exposure to pornography and any kind of harm to minors or adults. Four of the five members of the Effects Panel even deny the presence of correlational associations in all of the research reviewed.

B. It should be made clear, however, that conclusively proving causal relationships among social-science variables is extremely difficult. Among adults whose life histories have included much exposure to pornography, it is nearly impossible to disentangle the literally hundreds of causal threads or chains that contributed to their adjustment or maladjustment. And the issue isn't restricted to the question, "Does pornography cause or contribute to sex crimes?" The issue has to do with the way in which pornography, over a period of many years, affects or influences—in a cumulative way—the individual (the child and the adult) in his total relationship to members of the same as well as the opposite sex.

The "burden of proof" or demonstration of no harm in a situation such as this is ordinarily considered to be on the shoulders of one who wishes to introduce change or innovation. It might be noted that in areas where health and welfare are at issue, most government agencies take extremely conservative measures in their efforts to protect the public. Monosodium glutamate, for example, recently removed from all baby food by government order, had but weak evidence against it in animal studies. However, because even the remotest possibility of harm existed, measures were immediately taken to protect children from it.

In the area of pornography, very powerful cause-effect data come out of the conditioning laboratories of investigators, such as Rachman, who demonstrate that, with the use of erotica, sexual deviations can be created in individuals. Additionally, the work of McGuire suggests that exposure to special sexual experiences (which could include witnessing certain types of pornography) plus masturbating to the fantasy of this exposure can sometimes lead to participation in deviant sexual acts. The massive literature on therapy for sex deviates suggests that their sexual orientation can be changed with the use of erotica. If these data are valid, then one also has to allow for the possibility that deliberate or accidental exposure to erotica can facilitate antisocial sexual behaviors and conditioning of sexual aberrations. In considering all of this, we are not in any way suggesting that pathological experiences in the family or elsewhere in the environment also may not be significant contributors to sexual deviations, crime, delinquency, or other assorted social ills. But pornography should be considered as one of these causal instigators.

One might plausibly argue that these accidental kinds of conditionings of persons into deviant sexuality through exposure to pornography might be infrequent. However, if pornography were to seduce only one adolescent or adult each year into having disturbed sexual feelings, changed sexual orientation, or some manner of sexual deviancy, and if this person yearly influenced only one other individual, who in turn affected only one other, in twenty years 1,048,575 sexually or otherwise disturbed people would be the result—a major consequence. In 1952 only the very small proportion of 0.024% per 100,000 of U.S. citizens died in auto accidents. Applied to the whole population of the United States, this meant that 37,794 people lost their lives, a significantly smaller number than might be affected by pornography.

C. In the Commission's presentation of the scientific evidence, errors and inaccuracies occur in their reporting of research as well as in the basic studies themselves. Frequently, conclusions which are not warranted are drawn from data. Notable are frequent failures to distinguish or discriminate between badly flawed, weak studies and those of exceptional merit. But most serious of all is the Commission's failure to report data from a number of studies showing statistical linkages between high exposure to pornography and promiscuity, deviancy, and affiliation with high criminality groups.

In critiquing the Commission's majority report, Professor Hans Eysenck, distinguished British psychologist and social scientist, comments,

It should be borne in mind that the Commissioners were concerned to 'make a case,' and that in doing so they may not always have been entirely scrupulous about weighing the evidence impartially.... The writers of the majority report do not enter the necessary caveats in discussing these researches; they tend to generalize too freely, from one group to other groups dissimilar in age and character, and from short, often single exposures, to lengthy and multiple exposures. Such generalizations are not permissible, and though one may recognize the ethical difficulties involved in presenting such material to children, say, or of going beyond the limits of single or at most very limited presentations [of pornography], *nevertheless these limitations should be recognized and emphasized. Failure to do so implies a slide from scientific discussion to propaganda. Worse, the majority report suppresses information that goes against its recommendation" (1972:98).*

Addendum A
Causation versus Correlation

For the average reader uninitiated in the complexities of behavioral sciences and research methodology, mention should be made of an extremely important issue which has to do with whether two things you are studying are related (correlated with each other) and, additionally, if one causes or helps cause the other to happen. You can have the first without the second, and many people, even scientists, come to grief over this issue. As Levitt (1969:247) has so cogently noted:

Correlation alone never demonstrates a causal relationship. A miriad of co-fluxuations in this world are the consequence of an independent cause. The flowers bloom and the grass turns green at the same time each year but one does not influence the other. The price of Cuban rum and the salaries of Presbyterian ministers in New England vary together (are correlated) over the years, but one could hardly hypothesize that either is cause and the other effect. We can allow that the establishment of a correlation permits a reasonable <u>hypothesis</u> concerning cause and effect but no more.

In the early days of the smoking/lung-cancer controversy, a high relationship (or correlation) was noted between the number of packs of cigarettes one smoked a day and the chances of his having lung cancer. Scientists of the cigarette industry loudly and frequently pointed out that even though this was true, it didn't necessarily mean that the one (smoking) caused the other (lung cancer). Later tissue studies in the laboratory finally established beyond doubt that there was indeed a causal relationship between the two.

More recently, researchers at the Boston University Medical Center found a relationship between the amount of coffee consumed and the chances of having a heart attack: Persons who drank one to five cups of coffee a day had a 60% greater chance of heart attack than noncoffee drinkers. Those drinking six or more cups a day incur a 120% greater risk of this type of heart disease.

The Coffee Information Institute quickly pointed out that even though these relationships exist, this does not conclusively prove that coffee drinking causes heart attacks. However, as Dr. Hershel Jick, head of the medical research pointed out, "The *possibility* that coffee contributes to the risk [of heart attacks] cannot be ignored" (Leary, 1973). Thus, when one does find a repeated relationship of this kind between two events, these occurrences can suggest the possibility of a causal relationship. Logic, inference, and a study of the circumstances surrounding these relationships can increase our suspicions and our level of confidence that a causal relationship exists. Often, on simple inspection, certain types of relationships can be seen as not causally related. Elaborate experimentation is unnecessary in these cases.

The sun comes up each morning at about the same time my rooster crows, but this doesn't mean that the rooster causes the sun to rise; and it doesn't take elaborate experimentation to arrive at this conclusion.

A number of studies of pornography suggest a relationship between high early exposure to erotic materials and later sexual promiscuity and deviancy. Pornography could be one cause of the promiscuity. Affiliation with delinquent companions could be a factor contributing to an interest in pornography as well as to a participation in later promiscuous sexual activities. Or promiscuity and pornography could be reciprocally and causally related. That is, each might facilitate the other's occurrence. The pornography helps suggest antisocial acts (e.g., gang rapes) to both the subject and his companions, and it facilitates their acting out possible delinquent behaviors. As in juvenile delinquency generally, however, many contributing causes exist for ultimate delinquent acts or a psychopathic life-style.

Sometimes behavioral science methodology cannot disentangle all of these influences and precisely measure their individual unique contributions. But that we can't adequately measure them does not mean that they do not occur or that they have no effect. So frequently good judgment, correct inference, and sound logic have to be used—along with proper scientific data analysis—in order to arrive at significant conclusions.

In the meantime, people have to make decisions now, without final knowledge, as they have had to do for thousands of years: whether or not to continue smoking, whether to take job A instead of job B, whether or not to marry Helen, whether or not to purchase a certain stock or piece of property, whether or not to take some weight off, ad infinitum. And legislatures regularly decide on issues involving probable harm even though final evidence may never be available.

Thus, when the FDA banned monosodium glutamate from all baby foods, it was on the basis of inconclusive data gathered from rat studies. When rats were fed massive amounts of this substance, a few of them developed cancers. Only a relationship was found, not a cause-effect in any final sense; and this occurred in rats, not in babies, and only when massive amounts of the substance were administered in proportions that infants or adults would never be exposed to. Nevertheless, on the basis of a suspicion, a decision was made to ban this substance in baby food. And even though the decision was based on a remote possibility, in the end it might prove to be sound social and medical policy.

Much pornography depicts and suggests antisocial sexual activities such as rape, sado-masochistic acts, and child molestation. Some people feel that final, absolutely certain, scientific evidence is not entirely necessary before restricting this kind of material. Pornography might be considered to affect the moral climate of the community or to be offensive, requiring censure in the same way that houses of prostitution, exhibitionism, public nudity, and similar events and scenes are limited and controlled. Ultimately these issues will be decided through democratic processes by the elective bodies of individual communities. They will reflect a societal consensus. Not everyone will be pleased, and certain inevitable tensions will occur. And with time community standards may change. But, of course, this reflects the true nature of a democracy.

Addendum B
Do People Become Satiated through Overexposure to Pornography?

In the Commission's single study involving twenty-three college males and investigating satiation of sexual arousal and interest in pornography (after fifteen days of heavy exposure), they have pretty well demonstrated the obvious (e.g., that people under conditions of massive exposure temporarily can get weary of it). But it is also true that the sex appetite, while quickly satisfied, also returns quickly. Voltaire's *Candide* also found this to be true. Clinical experience indicates that a man may be stimulated by his partner's body for many years, even though there may be temporary periods of satiation. The periodicity of the sex drive suggests continued cycles of interest and satiation continuing throughout life. The Commission's conclusion implies that if people get all the pornography they want, they'll soon get tired of it and not want more. This is certainly one popular theory advanced by some students of the issue. But the evidence here suggests only that if college males are given a great glut of pornography in a laboratory setting, they will temporarily satiate. Essentially the same may be said of having sexual intercourse, eating and drinking. Considering the limited time this experiment ran, then, no proof can be given of permanent satiety. Another limitation of the Commission's study was that it did not approximate a real-life situation or the use of pornography in a subject's own social milieux. It involved a deliberate forced "over feeding" of pornography for pay. It also meant removing all their clothing and placing electrodes and other instruments on the body (under a loose robe), measuring sexual and autonomic system arousal, observing them through a one-way window, and keeping them in an isolation booth for 1½ hours a day for fifteen days.

According to other Commission studies (such as those by Charles Winick, 1970) of consumers of explicit sexual materials "out in real life" such as patrons of adult movies and bookstores, 52% are regular customers and are "regular or heavy users" of erotica. In other words there is no evidence that people satiate in real life. The consumption of pornography is regulated to the tastes of the individual consumer. In Nawy's (1970) study of the "San Francisco Marketplace," 70% of the patrons of erotica he surveyed attend sex movies once a month or more. He also found that 49% of these people were currently having sex with two or more partners in and out of their households, and 25% had been having sex with six or more partners in the past year. Frequency of intercourse rates were very high for Nawy's sample, suggesting that erotica may have had a "booster or accelerating" effect on sexual activity. In any event the data outside the laboratory where people are studied in their own environment suggest that those interested in erotica or pornography consume it regularly and for sexual reasons.

In his survey of 473 working class adolescents, Berger (1970) concludes, "It would appear that even high levels of exposure to sexually explicit materials did not bore the young people who participated in this study." None of this is mentioned in the Commission's discussions of satiation, even though all of these data come from Commission studies.

Addendum C
Limitations in Commission's Experimental Effects Studies

The Commission Report states in its conclusions (p. 28), "When people are exposed to erotic materials some persons increase masturbatory or coital behavior, a smaller proportion decrease it, but the majority of persons report no change in these behaviors. In general, established patterns of sexual behavior were found to be very stable and not altered substantially by exposure to erotica." These conclusions need to be qualified by the following considerations: (a) in a number of the sixteen studies focusing on this problem, behavior was studied for *only* the 24 hours before and after exposure to the pornography; (b) in another study (Amaroso, 1970) the total exposure time to erotica for all subjects was only fifty seconds, while in yet another study (Byrne and Lamberth, 1970) total exposure was 6½ minutes (hardly sufficient to conclude that exposure to erotica has or has not an effect); but probably the major methodological problem is the fact that (c) thirteen of the sixteen groups who were deliberately exposed to pornography were limited to young college students; a fourteenth group were middle-aged couples almost all college educated, and the final two groups were "sex offenders." Since a great deal of evidence from the Commission studies indicates that young college-educated persons (especially males) are those who already have high exposure to pornography (compared to conservative, older, lower-class subjects), this means that most of their subjects had *already been repeatedly exposed to pornography.* If it were to have a "corrupting" effect, this effect would probably have already started to occur. This also would mean that one wouldn't expect, experimentally, great changes in sexual behavior before and after a brief exposure to erotic materials even if in fact pornography were indeed to have a "viciously depraving influence." Failure to control for this factor of previous exposure in all of their studies makes the conclusions of the Commission on "no effects" even more questionable. And (d) it is highly unlikely that any subject in such an experimental study under such close scrutiny would engage in any antisocial sex behavior, or even if he did, that he would admit to it. *In every experimental study reported, interestingly, they fail to even ask this type of question!* Another consideration is that (e) all samples were restricted to only those volunteers who chose to be exposed to pornography, a fact that introduces an unknown degree of systematic bias. And (f) finally, as Davis and Braucht point out, these samples (mainly the young and college educated) are not the people of "popular concern" (e.g., the unstable, the more vulnerable, those from defective environments). That scientists confidently conclude on the basis of these kinds of data that there are essentially no significant sex-behavior changes or an increase in antisocial sexual activity does not reflect sufficient regard for the necessary caveats, cautions, modesty, and impartiality usually associated with scientific inquiries.

Addendum D
The Purchasers versus Consumers of Erotica

The Commission Report (p. 25) suggests that the primary purchasers of erotica appear to be well-educated, middle-class males in their thirties and forties. It should be noted that this conclusion is based on studies made mostly in downtown urban areas where a surveyor guessed at the age and the socioeconomic level of a buyer he saw in an adult bookstore or a theater. When interviews were conducted, they consisted of the interviewer's approaching men as they emerged from an adult movie and having an "informal conversation over coffee" with them (no notes were taken until later). And of 270 people approached in the Winick (1970) study, only 37% agreed to "have coffee," creating sampling problems. When they tried to get people to fill out questionnaires, as in the Nawy (1970) study of the "San Francisco Marketplace," only 29 out of 150 bookshop customers cooperated, and only 190 out of 800 movie patrons so obliged. This small percentage of respondents makes generalizing about these data extremely risky. In his analysis of the Denver area, Massy (1970) concluded that the type of customer for pornography is related to the location of the store and the time of day the erotica is purchased.

Probably the major issue is discovering not who buys erotica but who consumes and uses it. Because for every purchaser of hard-core materials there may be 10 to 100 viewers or users of the merchandise. In the Abelson National Survey (1970) of Youth and Adults we find that mostly girls fifteen to twenty and young men fifteen to twenty-nine get the heaviest doses of pornography. Abelson found that more boys than adult men have seen visual pornography (87% vs. 80%), and more girls have seen it than adult females (80% vs. 53%). In other words, the heavy users and those most highly exposed to pornography are adolescent females and adolescent and young-adult males.

Addendum E
The Issue of Whether or Not
Sex Offenders Come from Sexually Deprived Backgrounds

In its Effects Panel Report and elsewhere the Commission cites data to show that sex offenders come from conservative, repressed, sexually deprived backgrounds. Quotations from chapter five of the Effects Panel Report capture the essence of their conclusions: "Sex offenders generally report sexually repressive family backgrounds, immature and inadequate sexual histories and rigid and conservative attitudes concerning sexuality" (p. 286). And: "The early social environment of sex offenders may be characterized as sexually repressive and deprived. Sex offenders frequently report family circumstances in which, for example, there is a low tolerance for nudity, an absence of sexual conversation, punitive or indifferent parental responses to children's sexual curiosity and interest. Sex offenders' histories reveal a succession of immature and impersonal sociosexual relationships, rigid sexual attitudes, and severely conservative behavior" (p. 285).

Or still another quote: ". . . Sex offenders' inexperience with erotic material is a reflection of their more generally deprived sexual environment. The relative absence of such experience probably constitutes another indicator of atypical and inadequate sexual socialization" (pp. 31-32).

A number of things limit or suggest caution in accepting these conclusions. In some of the studies where they compare sex offenders and nonoffenders, for example, they lump all different types of offenders together "into one bag" (e.g., Cook and Fosen, 1970; Johnson et al., 1970). The problem here, as the Kinsey Institute studies well demonstrate, is that there are at least twenty-one categories of sex offenders showing striking differences in personality characteristics, family, sexual, and psychosocial backgrounds. To draw general conclusions about such a diverse group would be akin to doing a study on what "religious people" are like, including in the group Catholics, Unitarians, Buddhists, and Black Panthers, treating them as a single type. For example, aggressive rapists are very impulsive, revealing not only extremely high levels of sexual activity from an early age but also high degrees of criminality. They are dangerous. The "peeper," on the other hand, has a low rate of sexual experience, tends not to marry, and is poorly socialized.

Additionally, these samples of sex offenders are taken from only those who have been convicted and jailed, a fact that introduces a lower social class bias. Wealthier, upper-class sex offenders (as in all other types of crime) are less often convicted and more often paroled.

Another weakness in the Commission's report is the frequent use of inadequate control groups or none at all. To illustrate how this might cause serious problems, consider the following conclusion and the way in which it was reached. "Protestants are a more criminally inclined group of citizens than atheists." We study a group of protestants at the state prison and compare them with atheists taken from the general population, and sure enough our conclusion is correct. However the experimental and control groups are not suitably matched. Or another (again made purposely absurd to illustrate the point: "It is reputed that men who drink carrot juice will experience increased mental activity, with resultant higher IQs." Then we compare college professors who drink a quart of carrot juice daily with unskilled laborers who do not and conclude that because the professors score higher on our IQ tests, carrot juice causes, or contributes to, higher intellectual functioning. The test, of course, has demonstrated no such thing. If we report this conclusion, however, and fail to mention that we did not have a comparable control or comparison group and that the comparison groups were from differing socioeconomic levels, we have made a second serious error.

One of the studies that the Commission cites as providing evidence that sex offenders come from sexually deprived backgrounds is that of Thorne and Haupt (1966). Six percent of their college students report TRUE "I have never had a sexual orgasm" against almost 30% for the rapists. While the researchers do not have a matched control group to compare the rapists to, they do have data on murderers and property-crimes offenders who would tend to be more similar in social class, intelligence, and age to the rapists than to the college students. We find that 40% of the murderers and other criminal offenders indicate never having had a sexual orgasm. To what can we attribute this remarkable claim?

By the very nature of the rapists' offense, it would be difficult to believe that 30% of them had never experienced orgasm; nor is it any easier to believe that 40% of the other prison group had not. And in view of the Kinsey findings that very nearly all of the rapists they studied engaged in premarital intercourse and nearly 80% engaged in extramarital sex after they married, these findings are even more difficult to believe. However, if one is aware of the fact that most rapists, murderers, and property-crimes felons *who are convicted* come from lower socioeconomic backgrounds and have less education and more limited vocabulary than the average citizen, one arrives at an obvious conclusion: a significant number of these men probably didn't understand what the term *sexual orgasm* meant. As a result, incorrect inferences may have been drawn from the data involving these subjects.

Matched control groups, therefore, are of extreme importance. If we use the murderers and property-crimes felons as controls for the rapist sampling and investigate the ways in which this typical sex-offender group compares with their control group on sexual repression and deprivation, we find that the rapists do tend to feel more guilty about their sexual behavior (probably because they are in jail for a sex crime), but there are no other real differences in the two groups. However, if we compare the sex offenders or total prison population with the college students on attitudes, we find the prison group a little more prudish in what they say but *not, apparently, in what they do.* This probably reflects the differences between the middle- and lower-class cultures out of which they emerge. Undoubtedly, sex offenders have disturbed psychosexual histories, but each class or type of offender has to be studied as a unique entity. Lumping dissimilar subjects together distorts and destroys any meaningful understanding of their psychopathology.

Goldstein and associates (1970) attempted to obtain an adequate control sample with which to compare their sex offenders, but they were not successful. Their controls were significantly younger and better educated than the sex-offender groups. (Example: nearly 80% of the control group were under thirty; whereas only 25% of one of the child molester groups was under thirty.) When discrepancies of this nature occur in comparison groups, conclusions drawn from studies made of them may be invalid. Remember the carrot juice example and its relation to intelligence? Goldstein correctly cautions his readers about some of his control sample problems. The Effects Panel writers fail to do this.

The evidence from many studies would indeed suggest that certain types of sex offenders are sexually immature and regressed, but other types are sexually aggressive, highly criminal, very promiscuous, and potentially dangerous from very early ages. Making these kinds of distinctions is most important in an evaluation of the research literature.

References

Abelson, H., et al.
    1971   "National survey of public attitudes toward and experience with erotic materials." Technical Report of the Commission on Obscenity and Pornography, Vol. VI, Washington, D.C.: U.S. Government Printing Office.

Annon, J. S.
    1971   The therapeutic use of masturbation in the treatment of sexual disorders. Paper presented at the Fifth Annual Meeting of the Association for the Advancement of Behavior Therapy, Washington, D.C., September.

Athanasiou, R., and P. Shauer
    1971   "Correlates of heterosexuals' reactions to pornography." Journal of Sex Research 7(4)(November):298.

Bandura, A.
    1969   Principles of Behavior Modification. New York: Holt, Rinehart and Winston.

Barlow, D. G., and W. S. Agras
    1971   An experimental analysis of "fading" to increase heterosexual responsiveness in homosexuality. Paper presented at the 17th annual meeting of the Southeastern Psychological Association, Miami Beach, Florida, April.

Bartell, G.
    1970   "Group sex among mid-Americans." Journal of Sex Research 6(2)(May):113.

Bender, P.
1973   "The obscenity muddle." Harpers, February.

Ben-Veniste, R.
1971   Pornography and sex crime: The Danish experience. Technical Report of
          Commission on Obscenity and Pornography, Vol. III. Washington, D.C.:
          U.S. Government Printing Office.

Berest, J. J.
1970   "Report on a case of sadism." Journal of Sex Research 6:210-19.

Berger, A., et al.
1971a   Pornography: High school and college years. Technical Report of
          Commission on Obscenity and Pornography, Vol. IX. Washington, D.C.:
          U.S. Government Printing Office.
1971b   Urban working-class adolescents and sexually explicit media. Ibid.

Berkowitz, L.
1971   "Sex and violence: We can't have it both ways." Psychology Today,
          December.

Byrne, D., and J. Lamberth
1971   The effect of erotic stimuli on sex arousal, evaluative responses, and sub-
          sequent behavior. Technical Report of Commission on Obscenity and
          Pornography, Vol. VIII. Washington, D.C.: U.S. Government Printing
          Office.

Cairns, R. B., et al.
1971   Psychological assumptions in sex censorship: An evaluative review of
          recent research (1961-1968). Technical Report of Commission on
          Obscenity and Pornography, Vol. I. Washington, D.C.: U.S. Government
          Printing Office.

Cline, V. B.
1970   Critique of Commission behavioral research. Chapter 3 in *Hill-Link
          Minority Report* in the Report of the Commission on Obscenity and Por-
          nography. Washington, D.C.: U.S. Government Printing Office.

Cline, V. B.
1971   A critique of methodology strategies in erotica research. Paper presented
          at meetings of American Psychological Association, Washington, D.C.,
          September.

Cook, R. F., and R. H. Fosen
1971   Pornography and the sex offender: Patterns of exposure and immediate
          arousal effects of pornographic stimuli. Technical Report of Commission
          on Obscenity and Pornography, Vol. VII. Washington, D.C.: U.S.
          Government Printing Office.

Davis, K. E.
1971   Pornography and censorship, New York Times, April 25, p. 21.

Davis, K., and G. N. Braucht

1971a   Exposure to pornography, character and sexual deviance: A retrospective survey. Technical Report of Commission on Obscenity and Pornography, Vol. VII. Washington, D.C.: U.S. Government Printing Office.

1971b   Reactions to viewing films of erotically realistic heterosexual behavior. Technical Report of Commission on Obscenity and Pornography, Vol. VIII. Washington, D.C.: U.S. Government Printing Office.

Dean, S. J., R. B. Martin, and D. L. Streiner

1968   "The use of sexually arousing slides as unconditioned stimuli for the GSR in a discrimination paradigm." Psychonomic Science 13:99.

Evans, D. R.

1968   "Masturbatory fantasy and sexual deviation." Behavioral Research and Therapy 6:17.

Eysenck, H. J.

1972   "Obscenity—officially speaking." Penthouse, July.

Feldman, M. P., and M. J. MacCulloch

1971   Homosexual Behavior: Therapy and Assessment. New York: Pergamon Press.

Friedman, M. W.

1966   "Reflections on two cases of male transvestism." American Journal of Psychotherapy 20:270-83

Gebhard, P. H., et al.

1965   Sex Offenders. New York: Harper and Row.

Goldstein, M. J., et al.

1971   Exposure to pornography and sexual behavior in deviant and normal groups. Technical Report of Commission on Obscenity and Pornography, Vol. VII. Washington, D.C.: U.S. Government Printing Office.

Goldstein, M. J., and H. S. Kant

1973   Pornography and Sexual Deviance. Berkeley: University of California Press.

Gorman, G. F.

1964   "Fetishism occurring in identical twins." British Journal of Psychiatry 110:255-56.

Hayes, P. J.

1967   "Correlation between modern communication media and social behavior. ' Bloomfield, N. J., Archdiocese of Newark.

Hearings Before the Sub-Committee on Communications of the Committee on Commerce.

1972   U.S. Senate, March 21-24, on the Surgeon General's Report by the Scientific Advisory Committee on Television and Social Behavior. Washington, D.C.: U.S. Government Printing Office.

Howard, J. L., et al.
1971   Effects of exposure to pornography. Technical Report of Commission on Obscenity and Pornography, Vol. VIII. Washington, D.C.: U.S. Government Printing Office.

Jackson, B.T.
1969   "A case of voyeurism treated by counter-conditioning." Behavioral Research and Therapy 7:133.

Johnson, W. T.
1971   The pornography report: "Epistemology, methodology and ideology." Duquesne Law Review 10:190.

Jones, G. Wm.
1967   Sunday Night at the Movies. Richmond, Va.: John Knox Press.
1971   "The relationship of screen mediated violence to anti-social behavior." Ph.D. thesis, Syracuse University.

Kutschinsky, B.
1971   Towards an explanation of the decrease in registered sex crimes in Copenhagen. Technical Report of the Commission on Obscenity and Pornography, Vol. VII. Washington, D.C.: U.S. Government Printing Office.

Leary, W. E.
1973   "Tests link coffee, heart ills." Associated Press Dispatch, Salt Lake Tribune, 14 July.

Levitt, E. E.
1969   Pornography: Some new perspectives on an old problem. Journal of Sex Research 5(4)(November):247.

Lipkin, M., and D. E. Carns
1970   Poll of mental health professionals. Cited in University of Chicago Division of Biological Sciences and the Pritzker School of Medicine Reports. Chicago, Winter, 20(1).

Mann, J.
1971   Experimental induction of human sexual arousal. Technical Report of Commission on Obscenity and Pornography, Vol. I. Washington, D.C.: U.S. Government Printing Office.

Mann, J., et al.
1971   Effects of erotic films on the sexual behavior of married couples. Technical Report of Commission on Obscenity and Pornography, Vol. VII. Washington, D.C.: U.S. Government Printing Office.

McCawley, A.
1965   "Exhibitionism and acting out." Comprehensive Psychiatry 6:396-409.

McGuire, R. J., J. M. Carlisle, and B. G. Young
1965   "Sexual deviations as conditioned behavior: A hypothesis." Behavior Research Therapy 2:185.

242

Meyer, T. P.
"The effects of sexually arousing and violent films on aggressive behavior."
Journal of Sex Research 8(4):324.

Mosher, D.
1971   Sex callousness toward women. Technical Report of Commission on Obscenity and Pornography, Vol. VII. Washington, D.C.: U.S. Government Printing Office.

Mosher, D.L., and H. Katz
1971   Pornographic films, male verbal aggression against women, and guilt. Technical Report of Commission on Obscenity and Pornography, Vol. VII. Washington, D.C.: U.S. Government Printing Office.

Nawy, H.
1971   The San Francisco erotic market place. Technical Report of Commission on Obscenity and Pornography, Vol. IV. Washington, D.C.: U.S. Government Printing Office.

Rachman, S.
1966   "Sexual fetishism: An experimental analogue." Psychological Record 16:293.

Rachman, S., and R. J. Hodgson
1968   "Experimentally-induced 'sexual fetishism': Replication and development." Psychological Record 18:25.

Rachman, S., and J. Teasdale
1969   Aversion Therapy and Behavior Disorders: An Analysis. Coral Gables: University of Miami Press.

Report of the Commission on Obscenity and Pornography, The
1970   New York: Bantam Books.

Sampson, J. J.
1971   Commercial traffic in sexually oriented materials. Technical Report of Commission on Obscenity and Pornography, Vol. III. Washington, D.C.: U.S. Government Printing Office.

Schiller, P.
1971   Effects of mass media on the sexual behavior of adolescent females. Technical Report of Commission on Obscenity and Pornography, Vol. I. Washington, D.C.: U.S. Government Printing Office.

Schmidt, G., and V. Sigusch
1970   Psychosexual stimulation by films and slides: A further report on sex differences. Cited in The Report of the Commission on Obscenity and Pornography. New York: Bantam Books.

Shenken, L. E.
1964   "Some clinical and psychological aspects of bestiality." Journal of Nervous and Mental Disease 139:137-42.

243

Stephens, W. N.
1971   A cross-cultural study of modesty and obscenity. Technical Reports of Commission on Obscenity and Pornography, Vol. IX. Washington, D.C.: U.S. Government Printing Office.

Storr, A.
1970   Human Aggression. New York: Bantam Books.

Tannenbaum, P. H.
1971   Emotional arousal as a mediator of erotic communication effects. Technical Report of Commission on Obscenity and Pornography, Vol. VIII. Washington, D.C.: U.S. Government Printing Office.

Walker, E. C.
1971   Erotic stimuli and the aggressive sexual offender. Technical Report of Commission on Obscenity and Pornography, Vol. VII. Washington, D.C.: U.S. Government Printing Office.

Wilson, W. C.
1971   "Facts vs. fears: Why should we worry about pornography?" American Academy of Political and Social Science Annals, September, p. 105.

Yalom, I. D.
1960   "Aggression and forbiddenness in voyeurism." Archives of General Psychiatry 3:305-19.

Zurcher, L. A., and R. G. Cushing
1971   Collective dynamics of ad hoc antipornography organizations. Technical Commission on Obscenity and Pornography, Vol. V. Washington, D.C.: U.S. Government Printing Office.

Zurcher, L. A., and R. G. Kirkpatrick
1971   Collective dynamics of ad hoc antipornography organizations. Technical Report of Commission on Obscenity and Pornography, Vol. V. Washington, D.C.: U.S. Government Printing Office.

The Pornography Commission: A Case Study of Scientists and Social Policy Decision Making

Victor B. Cline

After a group of investigators have reached a decision on a controversial issue, concerned bystanders are usually eager to obtain and sift the facts surrounding that decision. Here, then, for interested or concerned bystanders, are some of the facts concerning the origins of the report of the 1970 National Obscenity and Pornography Commission.

Members of the Commission

The first relevant fact concerning the Commission is that its members were chosen from a variety of backgrounds, promising a balanced representation. But as it turned out, the "balanced representation" led to a polarization of viewpoints with considerable resultant dissension.

Heading the team was William B. Lockhart, dean of the College of Law at the University of Minnesota. A decade earlier he (with Robert C. McClure) had written several important law review articles on the issue of obscenity, which the Supreme Court cited in the landmark Roth and later decisions. These articles suggest erudition, thoughtfulness, and a balanced fairness in the approach to obscenity control. Respect for the First Amendment and freedom of speech is readily apparent; yet a thoughtful regard for the possibility of social harm from exposure to hardcore pornography is also suggested.

The other seventeen members of the Commission included three sociologists, three men of the cloth (a priest, a rabbi, and a minister), a librarian, a judge, a state's attorney general, a book publisher, a magazine and newspaper distributor, two psychiatrists, a college English teacher, two lawyers, and a graduate student working for his Ph.D. in instructional communications. One of the attorneys, Barbara Scott, represented motion picture interests, while one of the sociologists, Joe Klapper, was employed by the broadcast media (CBS).

The Commission's Four Panels

Another important fact concerning the Commission is that it was divided into four separate panels to study the subissues which were of concern to the Congress. The significance of this division, as shown later, is that it made overall, collective decision making very difficult.

These four study groups were (1) a Legal Panel, (2) a Traffic Panel (studying the traffic in and distribution of pornography), (3) a Positive Approaches Panel (for fostering healthy attitudes toward sex), and (4) an Effects (of pornography) Panel. Through a process of self-selection and negotiation, the seventeen Commission members became assigned to one or the other of the four panels. Chairman Lockhart was an ex-officio member of all panels, but, as a lawyer, had as his main investment the Legal Panel.

Since all of the Commission members were fully employed at scattered locations around the United States, they found it impossible to do all the leg work which their job required: contracting out of research grants, collecting data, reviewing literature, writing reports, and all of the other tasks associated with the day-to-day operation of such a commission. Therefore they recruited a full-time, small, professional staff to do the bulk of the chore work. In all, twelve professionals and ten clerical-secretarial support staff were hired with Cody Wilson, a social psychologist, appointed as Executive Director and Director of Research.

The Congress gave the Commission the following mandate:

(1) With the aid of leading Constitutional law authorities, to analyze the laws pertaining to the control of pornography and obscenity and to evaluate and recommend definitions of obscenity and pornography.

(2) To ascertain the methods employed in the distribution of obscene and pornographic materials and to explore the nature and volume of traffic in such materials.

(3) To study the effects of obscenity and pornography upon the public (particularly upon minors) and its relationship to crime and other antisocial behavior.

(4) To recommend such legislative, administrative, or other advisable and appropriate action as the Commission deems necessary to regulate effectively the flow of such traffic, without in any way interfering with Constitutional rights.

From the time of the creation of the Commission in October, 1967, until April, 1969, eighteen months later—the Commission, including its subpanels, held only twelve meetings. However, between May, 1969, and September, 1970, when the final report was released, meetings increased in frequency. At the very last, commissioners flew into the Washington headquarters office several times a month, the meetings sometimes lasting several days.

Each panel operated fairly independently with its own chairman, budget, and agenda—in general conducting its particular business and finally making its own recommendations in its separate panel report. To a considerable extent this meant that the members of one panel did not have access to the research and data of another panel unless they made a special point of requesting it. Only at the very last, in several hectic days, did the Commission as a whole sit together and review all four panel reports. The setting was one where members of one panel, not having been involved in all the months of review of data or discussions or another panel, found it difficult to question or knowledgeably challenge particular conclusions of another panel. Since everyone was overloaded with work on his own panel, and a good share of this had been put on the backs of the full-time support staff, a commissioner had little opportunity or time to review carefully or read in detail through the thousands of pages of technical data of the other panels. This was especially true in the case of the Effects Panel, which had the major share of the budget and produced the bulk of the highly technical research reports (many with complicated statistical analyses) which, in most cases, only someone trained as a behavioral scientist could adequately evaluate and interpret. Additionally, as might be expected, all of the commissioners who might be regarded as behavioral scientists (with psychiatrist Greenwood as the possible exception) ended up on the all-important Effects Panel, with the nonscientists distributed among the other three panels.

Beginnings of Dissension

Another fact about the Commission, brought out in personal interviews with some of its members, is that dissension began soon after its inception. This led to considerable acrimony at times and a polarization between the so-called majority and minority members.

Morton Hill, Jesuit priest and national head of Morality in Media, an antipornography organization, became concerned when the White House made Lockhart unofficial head of the Commission (contrary to the terms of the enabling legislation which established the Commission). Hill's concern was triggered by the fact that Lockhart was a member of the American Civil Liberties Union, which had a long history of defending pornographers on free-speech grounds. However, the majority of the Commission endorsed the White House decision and voted confirmation of Lockhart as chairman.

Shortly thereafter, when staff was being recruited, Lockhart sought attorney Paul Bender as chief legal counsel to the Commission. Bender was also an active member of the ACLU. Again, in spite of concern shown by Hill and several other members, the majority of the Commission sustained Bender as legal counsel.

In June, 1969, Kenneth B. Keating, Jr., resigned from the Commission, to be replaced shortly thereafter by a Nixon appointee, Charles H. Keating, Jr. (not related to the first Keating), an attorney and national head of Citizens for Decent Literature. Keating was so concerned by what he perceived to be biases operating on the Commission and by the direction the Commission was taking that he decided to take a nonparticipative stance. Resigned to the fact that his vote would not be sufficient to reverse the tide of majority over minority on any of the substantive issues, he rarely attended meetings and issued occasional press releases denouncing the Commission as a "runaway commission" oriented toward permissiveness. At the end he issued his own dissenting report and concurred with the Hill-Link minority report.

The Crucial Effects Panel

Still another fact concerning the Commission is that the other panels depended to some degree upon the findings of the Effects Panel to give their own panels direction on some of the substantive issues. Whether pornography were to be found either "harmful and deleterious" or "guiltless" would profoundly affect what not only the Legal Panel would recommend (either tougher or more permissive laws) but also what should be done about "traffic in erotica," and "positive approaches." Thus, the Effects Panel became the crucial pivot panel.

In the early discussions of the Commission members, they decided to focus great weight on the problem of effects and invest a major portion of the appropriated money in finding out if pornography adversely influenced the behavior of people, causing sexual crimes and contributing to juvenile delinquency, as well as contributing to other assorted social ills. Several of the Commissioners, especially Morton Hill, objected to this tack. Their point was that the government's interest in regulating pornography had always related primarily to the prevention of moral corruption and not to the prevention of overt criminal acts and conduct or to the protection of persons from being shocked or traumatized. This line of reasoning was rejected by most of the other commissioners, including chairman Lockhart, and the decision was made to put a sizable share of the funds into effects studies. Besides, it was noted, Congress had indicated an interest in the effects question.

Factors Bearing on the Effects Panel "No Harm" Findings

Probably the two most controversial facts or events relating to the Pornography Commission was (1) the finding by the Effects Panel that pornography caused no harm (or at least there was no evidence suggesting harm), and (2) the recommendation stemming from this finding, concurred in by twelve of the eighteen commissioners, that most pornography control laws should be repealed. To understand how these conclusions were arrived at requires a closer look at those individuals comprising the Effects Panel, consisting of five commissioners and two full-time support staff. Three of the commissioners were sociologists: Otto Larson (University of Washington), Marvin

Wolfgang (University of Pennsylvania), and Joe Klapper, director of social research at CBS. Morris Lipton, the fourth commissioner, was a psychiatrist at the University of North Carolina, and the fifth was a graduate student at Syracuse University working on his Ph.D., G. William Jones, who had previously taught in the area of broadcast and film art at Southern Methodist University but had returned to school to get an advanced degree.

The dissenting addendum to the majority pornography report by Effects Panel chairman, Otto Larson, and his colleague, Marvin Wolfgang, suggests something about their social-political philosophies. In their dissent they rejected the majority recommendations to repeal most pornography laws—not because the majority had gone too far but because they hadn't gone far enough. Chairman Larson and Wolfgang recommended repealing *all* laws, even those controlling the exposure of children to pornography. None of the other sixteen Commission members agreed with this recommendation. In fact, two of their psychiatrist colleagues, Lipton and Greenwood, acknowledged that "a significant deficiency in the work of the Commission was the failure to comprehensively study the effects of erotica on children and juveniles whose sexual behavior is not yet fixed" (p. 454), suggesting an absence of significant data which might support such a recommendation. Despite the absence of almost any research bearing on pornography's impact and effect on children, Larson and Wolfgang still recommended total repeal of all such laws, even suggesting that beneficial effects might be found in exposing children to such material (p. 447).

The two of them next called for repeal of all public display ordinances or laws which now prohibit exhibiting pornography or explicit erotic materials in open public places (which would include such things as billboards, signs in front of theaters, TV spots, and others). Such a course of action would, in effect, disregard the rights of possibly a majority of people who might be offended by obscenities in public places or by having their children exposed to erotica in a way they would have little control over.

Third, Larson and Wolfgang recommended repeal of all laws that would prohibit mailing to anyone's home unwanted pornography advertisements, despite the possible objection of that individual to the gross invasion of, or intrusion of such materials upon, his privacy. In defense of their position, Larson and Wolfgang cited a savings of "enormous expenditures by the government" if these laws were done away with. Their position could certainly be regarded as atypical, compared with those held by most Americans, as judged by the Pornography Commission's own national poll (Abelson et al.), as well as those of Gallup and Roper dealing with public attitudes towards pornography.

Interestingly, the two-person, full-time staff recruited to survey literature, do research, write, and contract out studies for the Effects Panel were two students of Larson and Wolfgang: sociologists Weldon Johnson and Lenore Kupperstein. Otto Larson was the professor at the University of Washington supervising Johnson's Ph.D. dissertation and acting as chairman of his doctoral committee at the time Johnson was hired. Wolfgang was a former teacher and employer of Kupperstein. Johnson and Kupperstein were later to write the all-important Effects Panel Report which would be so influential in pointing the direction the Commission as a whole would take. It should be noted, however, that the final draft of this report also had input from most of the Effects Panel commissioners.

Another interesting fact that later emerged concerning the membership and recommendations of the Effects Panel was that at least one member of the Panel was later charged with misrepresenting data submitted by the Surgeon General's Advisory Committee studying the effects of TV violence (1971). Joe Klapper, a CBS TV executive and sociologist, third member of the Effects Panel, became identified as one of the "network five" appointed to the Surgeon General's committee. According to *Newsweek* (14 February 1972, p. 66), this network five "tried to rig the Surgeon General's study in their favor. To a considerable extent they succeeded." And: "They managed to obfuscate and dilute most key findings that were detrimental to television's image." (6 March 1972, p. 55.) In this article *Newsweek* identifies Klapper, from among the five, as the most ardent defender of the TV industry. Senator Pastore's Senate hearings on TV violence (Hearings, p. 149) refer critically to Klapper's role and prejudicial influence. And Albert Bandura, later to become president of the American Psychological Association, commented, "The Surgeon General's report demonstrates that the television industry is sufficiently powerful to control how research bearing on the psychological effects of televised violence is officially evaluated and reported to the general public" (Hearings, p. 19), and "The irate researchers whose findings were irresponsibly distorted in the Surgeon General's report are fully justified in the objections they have raised. In addition to distorting research evidence, some highly pertinent studies [*sic*] demonstrating that violence-viewing causes children to behave aggressively are not even mentioned, [*sic*] a double standard is used in evaluating individual studies depending on how their findings relate to the industry viewpoint . . ." (Hearings, p. 11).

This report summarizing the research on the effects of TV violence was prepared by the Advisory Committee of which Klapper was a member instead of by the scientists who did the research. It was at first interpreted by the press to indicate that "TV violence [is] held unharmful to youth" (11 January 1972, *New York Times*). This misinterpretation, according to Joseph Morgenstern, occurred because "the Advisory Committee misrepresented some of the data, ignored some of it and buried all of it alive in prose that was obviously meant to be unreadable and unread" (*Newsweek*, 14 February 1972).

The fourth member of the Effects Panel was psychiatrist Morris Lipton. In his separate addendum to the Commission majority report (coauthored with

Edward Greenwood and concurred in by Joe Klapper [p. 443]) he writes that the work of the Commission had failed to uncover evidence relating exposure to erotica to delinquency, crimes, and antisocial behavior and not only fails to establish a meaningful causal relationship but claims that *neither is there a significant correlation* between exposure to erotica and immediate or delayed antisocial behavior among adults (p. 452, italics ours). The denial of even correlational associations would appear incautious and is not supported by the data. In addition, Weldon Johnson's later defense of the Commission Report (1971, p. 203) contradicts and denies Lipton's assertion by listing seven instances of correlational associations with "undesirable" behavior. Weldon Johnson, of course, was the senior author of the all-important Effects Panel Report.

A fact, too, is that in 1967 the final member of the Effects Panel, Bill Jones, had published a paperback book, or monograph, entitled, *Sunday Night at the Movies,* which demonstrates the value of films as excellent resources or stimulus material for discussions of values, human sexuality, and interpersonal crises and conflicts—especially for young people. The book is partly a defense of the violence and sex viewed on television and in movies (chapter 8, p. 107). In his book Jones tends to reject the notion of their supposed negative influence and sees movies and television as scapegoats, receiving much of the blame which "rightly lies at the steps of home, parents, and church." Jones saw censorship of sexual films for youth (in commercial cinema) as a "tragedy" in that censorship "protects youth from the truths that they badly need to know" (p. 110). He is, of course, partly right about the responsibility of "home, parents, and church"—but his nearly total exoneration of the media conflicts with much contrary evidence assembled by two national commissions on violence. On the basis of his stated position in a previous publication, then, it would appear that Commissioner Jones's views were promedia and anticensorship.

Thus, briefly reviewing the members of the key pivotal Effects Panel, we have, first, Larson and Wolfgang with their rejection of the majority recommendations for their not having gone far enough to emancipate pornography; second, their two students, Johnson and Kupperstein, as support staff; third, Joe Klapper, later to be accused of misrepresenting data in another key commission report; fourth, Morris Lipton, who denied even correlational associations between pornography and harms (refuted later by Johnson); and finally, Jones, with a pre-Commission point of view amounting to anticensorship for erotica in the media.

It is possible, though this is conjecture, that the scientists on the Effects Panel shared some similar or at least overlapping social-political perceptions about our society, human sexuality, and notions regarding the nature of man which may have contributed to their selective perception of research data leading to their "no harm" conclusions. It is probably naive to argue that scientists do not have values which to some extent intrude into their research and writing as well as into their personal life decisions.

In any event, scientists with special expertise dominated the Effects Panel and, indirectly, the rest of the Commission. No one else on the Commission was equipped to challenge them, much less to understand and adequately evaluate the technical data which supported their "no harm" findings. Commissioners of the other panels were uninvolved in any significant way in what the Effects Panel wrote, and most of these other commissioners read relatively few of the research studies which constituted the scientific base for the decisions the Effects Panel reached.

Commissioner Winfrey Link (on the Traffic Panel) deplored that he not only did not receive many of the research studies on "effects," but that on one occasion shortly before the final report was to be released became acquainted, for the first time, with a key study suggesting negative effects through reading an article in the *Washington Post* one morning at breakfast. Logically, then, the thirteen commissioners on the other three panels had to accept in good faith the findings of the Effects Panel scientists. If they had doubts, they had not the scientific training or technical expertise to challenge the Effects Panel in any significant way. Yet data exists to support strongly such a challenge. And that data comes in part from the Commission's own research.

Let us review briefly, for example, some of the information from the previous chapter in this book. Five commission studies (some causal) linked pornography and sexual arousal with aggression; commission-financed literature reviews told how sexual deviations could be created in the laboratory using erotic pictures; 254 psychotherapists reported cases in their practices where pornography was found to be an instigator or contributor to a sex crime or antisocial act, and another 324 professionals suspected such relationships in cases they had worked with; another study reported 84% of the psychiatrists finding similar harmful effects. Additionally, violence literature linked media violence with aggressive behavior, a fact that would have a major bearing and relevance to pornography as a model for sadomasochistic and sexually violent behavior; a vast relevant literature showed that erotica had been used to change sexual orientation, and literature on fantasy and masturbation revealed their relationship to sexual deviancy. And the modeling and imitative learning research in the area of sex also suggested possible harms.

In addition to these omissions was the omission of nearly 90% of the negative-effects evidence from the Commission's own research as well as most of the evidence from the outside literature. Some of the statistics concerning the Danish and United States sex crimes were reported by the Effects Panel exactly the opposite from those given in the original sources.

In sum, then, a great variety of common errors, omissions, and drawing of incorrect conclusions from flawed research, as well as a manifest systematic bias in marshalling evidence and reporting it existed in the report of the Effects Panel.

The Values Issues versus Pornography

Probably those individuals and organizations which have shown greatest concern about pornography are most deeply committed to the Judeo-Christian tradition. It is thus perhaps not an accident that the rabbi, the priest, and the minister on the President's Commission were among those not agreeing to the lifting of curbs or the repeal of laws controlling obscenity, despite the finding of its apparent harmlessness. The Judeo-Christian sexual ethic has always taken a position that fidelity and responsibility are vitally important. Pornography is generally seen as a direct assault on this position, suggesting a letting down of sexual standards; licentiousness; an abandonment of reason to libidinal impulse; an attack on the family and the bonds of loyalty, love, self-discipline, and restraint which hold it together.

In his analysis of obscenity and sexual practices in ninety-one cultures (for the Commission, 1970:405) William Stephens has noted that modesty, chastity, and sexual restraints are common to all four of the world's great religious denominations: Buddhism, Christianity, Hinduism, and Islam. Stephens finds that the growth of religion and sexual responsibility and restraints are also associated intimately with the increase in cultural complexity and political development. Or in Stephens' words, "Modesty-chastity seem closely tied to cultural complexity and political development. There is a regularized, highly predictable change in culture along a broad front, as social evolution proceeds."

He also finds that obscenity is rampant in primitive societies. The most "immodest" societies tend to be the primitive tribes, especially those where the notion of private property is little developed. These tribes lowest on the scale of cultural evolution have the most sexual license as well as the greatest interest in obscenity. This all suggests that in a nation where the notion of family is strong and sexuality is to some degree controlled and sublimated, a more disciplined, goal-directed individual is produced—an individual whose energies are rationally directed and distributed in more than just sexual channels. Thus it is no accident that the antipornography groups have roots in a religious commitment which energizes their opposition to (as they view it) a hedonistic society. Without the help of scientific studies they intuitively sense in pornography an attack upon their most basic values. The two leading antipornography groups in the United States, Citizens for Decent Literature and Morality in Media, Inc., are deeply, though indirectly, tied to religious institutions for interfaith support.

In two studies of antipornography organizations (1970:83; and 1970:143), Zurcher has repeatedly noted that the religiosity factor is highly related to attitudes about pornography. Those individuals opposing pornography were found to be more religiously affiliated, more active and supportive of the traditional notion of the family. And contrarily, those individuals opposed to attempts to control pornography (hence, probably supportive of it) were found to be much less religiously committed and less supportive of traditional family ideology.

In the study of Wallace et al. of 1,061 Detroit citizens' responses to twenty-one pornographic-erotic pictures, the key dimension determining whether a picture was rated as (1) acceptable or (2) offensive was the degree of religiosity of the observer (1970:27).

Leonard Berkowitz, a professor of psychology at the University of Wisconsin, has commented on the peculiarly different findings of the national Violence Commission as opposed to those of the Pornography Commission. The Violence Commission said that media violence could induce persons to act aggressively, whereas the Pornography Commission said that the portrayal of sexual deviations does not promote similar actions. He raised the question of whether these seemingly different conclusions were not affected, to some extent, by a prevailing liberal ideology that sex is good and violence is bad. Thus, if aggression is bad, then we disparage those things that we think are connected with it. Similarly, if we think that sex is good, we are reluctant to condemn the things associated with it. Berkowitz comments, "It seems to me that the general conclusions drawn in both the Violence and Pornography Commissions, and by the public at large, have been influenced as much by values, ideologies, suppositions, and biases as by the actual findings" (Berkowitz, 1971:14).

If his commentary is true, this raises some very serious problems about the use of the behavioral sciences in resolving major social issues. If the scientists are not objective, if they engage in selective perception, if they consciously or unconsciously rig their studies or reviews to favor their particular social-political philosophy or their personal values, then what can ordinary citizens believe when confronted with a mass of correlation coefficients and analyses of variances which "prove" someone's pet point of view? The answer to this is that if this occurs in a free society such as ours, there will always be objective scientists around who will be able to refute and expose any selective perception. Unfortunately, it sometimes takes years to get the whole story told. And in the meantime, citizens, legislatures, judges, and juries may make faulty decisions on the basis of erroneous data and conclusions. But even though democracies have never been noted for efficiency and speed in dealing with major social issues and often take zigzag courses, indulging in occasional excesses, then over-correcting these later—in most cases, fortunately, the will of the people ultimately is realized.

The irony of what the Effects Panel scientists did was that they represented anticensorship positions, and yet they themselves engaged in a kind of censorship in their treatment and playing down of that scientific data suggesting conclusions they didn't agree with. Most of the other commissioners merely voted, for the most part, as they felt the scientific evidence dictated—accepting the word of the Effects Panel report that pornography's influence was apparently benign. The personal values of the commissioners

254

on the Effects Panel probably played a greater role than any of them realized in their perceptions and interpretations of scientific data. Thus, perhaps, scientists, no less than clergymen, attorneys, or what have you, bring their values to the commissions they serve. And the recommendations of any commission will undoubtedly be flavored by the predominant biases of its members.

A deliberate attempt was made, no doubt, to put "committed" people on the pornography commission—people representing diverse interests: the clergy, heads of national "decency" organizations, representatives of the media, book publishers, and others, in an effort to let every sector be heard. But unfortunately, what happened was that a polarization occurred among the participants which led to a taking of sides and ultimately to an inability of the various factions to communicate effectively or to negotiate with each other. And the will of the side, or orthodoxy with the most members, prevailed.

Can We Learn Something from This Experience?

Possibly. When future commissions are organized, it might be wise to draft individuals who are uncommitted on the issues under study and who have reputations for exceptional fairness and judiciousness. Thus, on a violence commission one wouldn't have commissioners who had affiliations with the TV or entertainment industries, whose livelihood and continued employment might be affected by the postures and positions they took. But similarly, we could exclude researchers and scientists whose studies had committed them to certain strong positions. However, we would invite both groups of individuals, as well as others, to testify, present evidence, and be heard before such a commission. But the ultimate voting and recommendation-making would be as in a jury, by a group of individuals having no immediate vested interest in the outcomes (to the extent that this is possible), who would be free to weigh and evaluate all the evidence with a minimum of bias.

Ultimately, the real issue here is not whether exposure to pornography harms or causes antisocial behavior. The most ardent supporter of freedom for pornography would undoubtedly—in a frank moment—admit that in some cases it might have, or it could have, or it has some negative consequences. Everything in our environment influences us, pornography included, and sometimes negatively. The issue is, are the harms sufficient or serious enough to cause us to want to censor or restrict erotic materials for adults? Most people agree that children probably wouldn't be benefited by some of these materials, and it shouldn't be sold to them; that is not the key issue, of course. However, when adults obtain it, somehow children do also.

A fact also is that most adults as children got a glimpse of erotic material a time or two (or maybe more) without being too badly damaged. So that leads us back to the trade-off problem, or the balancing of different interests. How much harm must exist before we restrict what adults can buy or see on the open market? And by "harm" we mean more than sex crimes. We would also include the more elusive but still very real moral climate of the community. If the harm is negligible, even though some exists, we might decide that we can pay that price in order to have a more free and open society. But unfortunately we usually don't have precise data on this sort of thing. So this means that ordinary citizens and ordinary legislators are going to have to use their common sense and make judgments on the basis of incomplete data as they have been doing for thousands of years. If they err, they'll revise their statutes later. And it is the trade-off between perceived or real harm versus the benefits of greater freedom of expression that is the nub of the issue. Ordinary citizens, not scientists, will ultimately decide this. And it will usually be decided on the basis of shared community values and majoritarian ethical consensus.

Democracy and Pornography

Ernest van den Haag

*The mutual ties have ceased to exist
and a gigantic and senseless dread
is set free. . . . The disappearance of
the emotional ties which hold the
group together [produces] . . . the
cessation of all feelings of consideration
(Freud, Group Psychology and the
Analysis of the Ego, pp. 46 ff.).*

I

In times past censorship[1] was meant to hinder the spread of philosophical and political ideas thought to undermine the social order—the institutions which shape the relations of men to each other. Censorship of ideas continues in communist and, to a lesser degree, in populist, and in old-fashioned authoritarian societies; but in democracies it has been abandoned. There is insufficient agreement on what ideas to protect; more important, there is a widespread impression that one (or more) of the following propositions is correct, and inconsistent with censorship.

1) With a "free marketplace of ideas" the best ideas will win; without, they will not. (I know of no evidence for either proposition.)

2) There is no certain way to separate innocuous from noxious ideas; at least, public authorities are unlikely to seek or find one. (There is some evidence for the last proposition.)

Ernest van den Haag has studied at the Sorbonne, the universities of Florence and Naples, the State University of Iowa, and New York University—where he obtained his Ph.D. degree in sociology. He is presently adjunct professor of social philosophy at New York University and is a lecturer in sociology and psychology at the New School for Social Research. He is a practicing psychoanalyst and a Fellow of the American Sociological Association. In 1967 he was a Guggenheim Fellow and in 1973 a Senior Fellow of the National Endowment for the Humanities.

He has authored books such as *Political Violence and Civil Disobedience, The Jewish Mystique,* and *Passion and Social Constraint,* as well as a vast number of journal articles and chapters in books and has written introductions to such works as Krafft Ebbing's *Psychopathia Sexualis.*

1. The distinction between "censorship" proper—advance governmental licensing of public communications—and the *post facto* prosecution of prohibited (e.g., lewd) publications, although important, is not relevant here. However, censorship must be distin-

3) Individuals have a right to form and communicate any belief; society has no right to hinder them or those who wish to read or see what they produce. (An axiom rather than a proposition and not subject to proof.)

4) It is possible to allow the formation and communication of antisocial ideas and ideals while yet effectively preventing antisocial actions. (There is evidence that this is possible sometimes, and temporarily, but not always or forever.)

5) A shared value or belief system is not necessary for society, or
    a) freedom leads to such a system, or
    b) freedom will not undermine it, or
    c) censorship could not protect it anyway, or
    d) censorship would cause damage in excess of any benefit. (This argument will be considered below.)

While some measure of freedom can be justified on other grounds, these propositions seem wrong to me in different degrees, and for different reasons. Yet, democratic societies have accepted them; censorship has been abolished, with the exception—universal until quite recently—of sexual matters. This exception is puzzling. What is to be achieved by penalizing obscene communications?[2] What are the benefits (and costs)—what would be lost if obscene communications were permitted? It seems odd that, having abandoned the defense of the social and political order against subversive ideas, the censor should make a stand on what appears to be a comparatively trivial and semiprivate cultural matter: sexual mores. Is censorship an historical remnant then, or could it be that obscenity might threaten the social order in a more fundamental or pervasive way than political ideas?[3]

Antiobscenity statutes usually prohibit the sale of materials which appeal dominantly to the "prurient interest" of the purchaser.[4] Thus, the laws seem directed against the sexual stimulation for the sake of which the obscene materials are purchased. Yet it is unlikely that sexual stimulation as an end,

---

guished from inability to publish, owing to rejection, *sua sponte*, by some, or by all individual publishers. Censorship refers primarily to governmental prohibitions, not to inability to publish because of rejections, unless these are centrally, monopolistically and purposefully organized. Secondarily, "censorship" may refer to organized pressures—not dissuasions or abstentions—on publishers to refrain from publishing what they would otherwise publish.

2. For the sake of brevity, all sexual materials, films, communications, pictures, spectacles, and similar materials to be subjected to censorship are referred to as "obscene" or "pornographic." A distinction used to be made between the former (dirty, and always disapproved) and the latter (writing about whores or, more generally, writing invitingly about sex, but not always disapproved). Whatever distinctions are useful require a different vocabulary now.

3. I have to ignore the historical background of obscenity legislation.

4. In the United States the materials must also violate "contemporary standards."

or the sale of the means, can be regarded as wrong. We permit most other demands to be stimulated (and satisfied) by commercial means; and we do not prohibit sexual stimulation when the means are not "obscene." Both sexes are openly invited to arouse their mutual desire by purchasing goods and services to that end and much public entertainment is based on sexual allure, literary or pictorial. Even chemical means of stimulation—drugs promising to increase potency or desire—are quite legal. Why, then, is "obscene" stimulation not? Censorship is not opposed to the sale of psychic sexual stimulants in general. It is addressed to a specific *kind* of sexual incitement, to the means purveyed to produce it, and, possibly, to a distinctive effect obsenity is thought to have.

What kind of sexual stimulation does pornography provide? While dreary and repulsive to one part of the normal personality, pornography is also seductive to another: it severs sex (the Id) from its human context (from Ego and Super Ego) and thus from reality and morality, from restraints, from sublimations, and from all but the most archaic and infantile emotions. Pornography reduces the world to orifices and organs, human action to their combinations. Sex rages in an empty world as people use each other as its anonymous bearers or vessels, bereaved of individual love and hate, thought and feeling, reduced to bare sensations and fantasies of pain and pleasure, existing only in and for incessant copulations without apprehension, conflict, or relationship—without human bonds. By de-individualizing and dehumanizing sexual acts, which thus become impersonal, pornography reduces or removes the empathy and the mutual identification which restrain us from treating each other merely as objects or means. This empathy is an indispensable internal barrier to nonconsensual acts, such as rape, torture, and assaultive crimes in general.[5] Without it we are not humane to each other; and finally, as we become wholly solipsistic, our own humanity is impaired. Pornography thus is antihuman and antisocial. If we do not feel empathy, we all too easily relegate others beyond the pale, to become merely means. By inviting us to reduce others to sources of sensation, pornography invites us to destroy the psychological bonds that bind society. Laws but proclaim, reinforce, and enforce such bonds. But the bonds must be cultivated before they can be legislated.

---

5. Psychologically things are more complicated. Sadistic acts attempt to deny or remove the humanity of the victim but could not yield pleasure without some initial identification with the victim. The sexual sensation seems produced by the process, de-identification, which is endlessly repeated. *Total* de-identification (the result, not the process) permits mistreatment of the victim but the mistreatment would not yield pleasure and therefore would not become an end in itself. Yet from a social viewpoint, these matters can be neglected: any encouragement of de-identification is likely to prompt socially undesirable behavior.

The pornographic reduction of life to varieties of sex invites us to regress to a premoral world by returning to, and spinning out, preadolescent fantasies which reject reality and the burdens of individuation, restraint, tension, conflict, commitment, thought, consideration, and love, of regarding others as more than objects—burdens which become heavier and less avoidable in adolescence. Thus, at least in fantasy, a return to the pure libidinal pleasure principle is achieved. And fantasy, once on its way, pulled by pornography, may regress to ever more infantile fears and wishes: people, altogether dehumanized, are tortured, mutilated, and literally devoured. Such fantasies are acted out whenever authority fails to control or supports the impulses it usually helps to repress or sublimate. When authority permits or encourages the reduction of human beings to mere means, concentration camps become possible. The bond of human solidarity is broken with authoritative sanction; inmates are seen but as obstacles, or means, as sources of pleasure and displeasure, and not as ends. The failure of authority to punish public sale or performance of obscene material is to many minds a public sanction of invitations to dehumanizing fantasies, if not actions.[6]

Pornography desublimates: by regressively disowning empathy and identification, by reducing others to objects, it excludes love, affection, and any individual relationship—indeed, any human relationship—while it makes sadistic acts possible and even inviting. Once gratification by relations in which others are more than means is precluded, rage against these ungratifying others is generated: they must be made to suffer for having allowed themselves to be made into objects, and yet not becoming objects altogether, claiming somehow to be more, claiming to be human. The sadist's rage at his solitude, at his solipsistic isolation, at his own inability to accept the independent existence of others—to relate to or even love them—is discharged against those who precipitate it by presuming, and thereby demanding, what he cannot give. Unprotected by identification, they become both the occasion and the target of revenge.

If sadism were directed against a specific human group such as Jews or Negroes, the libertarian ideologues who now oppose censorship would advocate it. Should we find a little Negro or Jewish girl tortured to death and her agony carefully taped by her murderers known to be saturated with sadistic anti-Semitic or anti-Negro literature, most liberals would want the sale of such literature prohibited.[7] (De-identification is often facilitated by

6. The literary *locus classicus* of the sexual fantasy of de-identification is de Sade, or, more recently, *l'Histoire de O* by the pseudonymous Pauline Réage. Because they are unfocussed, not institutionalized, and not *positively* sanctioned, these invitations lead to fewer and less traceable direct actions than those of Nazis or Communists.

7. Ian Brady and Myra Hindley, who murdered ten-year-old Lesley Ann Downey and taped her long agony professed to be influenced by the sadistic literature found in their home. They were tried in Chester, England (1966).

actual and putative ethnic differences; but they are not indispensable and are easily replaced, for instance, by a feeling of, or wish for, great superiority over the victims.) Why should humanity as such be less protected than the specific groups which constitute it? That the hate articulated, or the de-identification urged, is directed against humanity in general rather than exclusively against Jews or Negroes makes it as dangerous to more people and not less dangerous to any.

One need not be a Christian to realize that a society in which people perceive each other mainly as sources of, or obstacles to, pleasure is not likely to cohere at all. It would lack the identification required for cohesion, and it would exclude love and affection: emotional commitments to persons and not to the impersonal pleasure yielded by them.[8] In their most sublimated form, these commitments are least dependent on impersonal sensations (and on the sources thereof) and most dependent on personal feelings.

Feelings cannot be legislated or manufactured, but they can be cultivated; some cultural climates foster and others impair them. Laws can protect their cultivation and penalize what might destroy them. Pornography, in exalting the instrumental use we can make of each other, depreciates and destroys the emotions that go with devotion to, or consideration for, others as ends. Yet love and affection are precious—and precarious—heritages of our civilization, and their socialized modes, compassion and empathy, are indispensable to it. To be sure, cultivation of these feelings is not indispensable to all civilizations. In some, a shared concern for something other than one's fellow man, such as survival of the tribe, or fame, or salvation, may altogether take the place of compassion and empathy. This might have been the case in antiquity and occasionally in the Middle Ages. But in our culture such a replacement is unlikely without a return to barbarism, be it sponsored by Communists or Nazis or by more inchoate chiliastic movements.

Shouldn't adults be able to control themselves, to read, or see, what they know to be wrong, or, at least, illegal, without enacting it? They should, and some are. But not all. (Incidentally, it is impossible, at least in the American environment, to limit anything to adults; children and adolescents are not supervised enough. And the authority of their supervisors has been too weak for too long.) Too many grownups are far from the self-restrained healthy types envisaged by much libertarian theory. They may easily be given a last or first push by obscene literature.

This is no secret. People know that their "spirit is willing but the flesh is weak." They pray that they may not be led into temptation. If they did not feel tempted, there would be no problem. Censorship laws are, in the first

---

8. This is why Freud regarded barriers to the gratification of the sexual impulse as indispensable to the achievement of love. (See his *The Most Prevalent Form of Degradation in Erotic Life.*)

place, a defense for those who fear temptation: they help restrain impulses of which the actor fears to become the victim before anyone else does. In the second place, they protect third persons who might be victimized. As are many other laws, censorship laws are enacted because we are enticed—in different degrees—by what they prohibit and have decided not to yield and, therefore, want to reduce the temptation. Above all, censorship laws proclaim the scope of the social ethos, the social rejection of pornography—however unavoidable the furtive survival of some of it.

In all known societies, people function by controlling their own impulses, in part consciously or semiconsciously, and in part by means of unconscious repression. The more the last is the case, the more ambivalent they feel about whatever may remobilize what has been repressed. The impulse stirs when stimulated, and so do the defenses. Wherefore, as a matter of psychic economy, people tend to avoid what may upset their equilibrium too much. They want the law to help them avoid it.

Obscene communications, it is feared, may make it hard, even impossible, to control the craving they are meant to arouse; these cravings are felt by many persons as threats to what personality integration and Ego dominance they have achieved. It matters not at all whether the loss of control would actually occur. What matters is the fear of losing control. (It is often projected on others: the fearful person may see them as uncontrolled, himself as victim.) This felt threat arouses enough anxiety in many people to value censorship: censorship functions as the social analogue to individual repression and defense of sublimation. Neither would occur, did it not have necessary functions, which do not become psychologically unnecessary if we demonstrate that they are rationally unneeded. Simply telling a patient what he has repressed and expecting him to deal with it, is, at best, ineffective, at worst, dangerous. The defense, repression, has served a function, and, unless the patient collapses, a defense mechanism will reappear as long as it is needed. So will censorship if we abolish it. But as do defenses, it will reappear in more extreme and sweeping form.

Neither (individual) repression nor (social) censorship are ideal solutions to the problem of anxiety. But we do not live in an ideal world with ideal people. And "solutions" that ignore (or define away) the problems actual people have in the actual world are not helpful. They may make matters worse: the elimination of legal censorship might well provoke arbitrary and damaging nonlegal attempts at repression by private persons and groups—just as stimulation which it cannot handle may bring about sweeping defensive repressions in the individual psyche.

Let me summarize the argument before descending to specifics. Human societies can be analyzed and, up to a point, managed quite rationally, but they are not held together by reason. They are cemented by feelings of human solidarity, compassion, identification and empathy, or, in some cases, by shared objects of worship or goals. Some degree of mutual identification is normally acquired, or at least reinforced, in the process of socialization. It is further intensified, limited, or enlarged by a variety of norms, customs, and institutions cultivated in associations, all of which enjoin some version of the golden rule, or of the categorical imperative. Part of us always rebels against repressions, restraints, and sublimations, and would use others as means for our own impulse gratifications. Pornography tends to encourage such regression and thereby not only to encourage crime but also to weaken human solidarity among those who stay within the law. Further, pornography tends to erode our cultural heritage by inviting us to desublimate and to sever the link forged in our society between love or affection (individual feelings for other individuals) and sex (impersonal appeals to the senses).

II

What specific effects can be expected from pornography? Obviously, human action is influenced by communications. Else the Bible, *Das Kapital, Mein Kampf,* or the *Sorrows of Young Werther* would have had no impact. Our sexual impulses have not changed; our sexual mores have. They were influenced by ideas and attitudes spread, sometimes even created, by books. So are changes in crime. Books influence what we feel, what we love and hate, indulge or restrain, cultivate or repress, and, finally, what actions we take. They influenced Hitler, Martin Luther King, and King's murderer.

Different personalities are influenced in different ways and degrees by the same books. After all, personalities differ inasmuch as their reaction to the same thing differs, owing to different constitutions and experience. However, if objects such as books or pictures were not perceived similarly on some level, and reacted to in similar ways, they would not be recognized as the same objects. The world would be but projection. Beauty (or obscenity) would, indeed, be in the eye of the beholder. Except for ophthalmic peculiarities, I would not be less beautiful than the current Miss Universe or my paintings inferior to Leonardo's.[9] Yet I think there is a relationship other than identity between subject and object; the object has some influence on how it is perceived and even reacted to at least by people in roughly the same culture. Thus, people react similarly: they do not eat books; they read them. And obscene communications tend to be identified, perceived, and reacted to in roughly similar ways by most persons—although, of course, there are individual differences, largely of degree. (Very different personalities might read altogether different books though there is usually some overlapping. But even a person who wholly refrains from reading pornographic books is affected by the attitudes and actions of those who do.)

9. This absurdity is believed because aesthetic qualities are hard to demonstrate and some people think that whatever is not (or cannot be) demonstrated does not exist or is "subjective." But existence, truth, and demonstrability differ as knowledge and its objects do. The subjectivity of knowledge or belief does not lessen the reality of objects.

The extent to which reaction to pornography is affected by prior experience (or age, sex, class) is nearly unknown. But it seems as wrong to say, "He reads what he reads *only* because he is what he is" as it is to say, "He became what he is *only* because of what he read." Reading is a variable which influences dispositions and actions more or less importantly depending on prior and concomitant conditions. It may or may not precipitate, if not cause (or cause, if not precipitate) action—suicide, homicide, divorce, marriage, wife swapping, sex murders, bank robberies, or entry into a monastery.

By and large three reactions to pornography seem likely. Some might be vicariously gratified by pornographic communications and, perhaps, stimulated to masturbation. In the absence of pornography, such persons might find other means of vicarious gratification, or do without. (I do not believe that vicarious gratification can go far: hunger is intensified rather than gratified by reading about or seeing food.) A second group of persons might harmlessly emulate what pornography invites to; or they may harm mainly themselves and consenting partners; or, finally, some may emulate pornography viciously and be inspired by it to the point of criminality.[10] (To deny this probability is to deny that advertising and books can influence fashions and purchasing patterns, thoughts, and actions.[11]) Nothing is known about the size of these two groups, but my impression is that both are fairly small as far as habitués are concerned, although many persons may belong for a short time.

Most persons probably do not emulate pornography directly or use it habitually to stimulate themselves. Yet it exercises a cumulative influence on their lives by affecting public morality and their own attitudes, values, and ambitions. Any model of action attractive to some part of the average person (even if rejected otherwise), when presented often enough, will influence his attitude and make what is modelled—be it anti-Semitic or sadistic or Communist—more acceptable. Extolling of martial or pacific virtues will make them more acceptable. So will the inviting presentation of sexual vices. (Obscenely described, sex becomes a vice.)

Persons who would not be lead into harmful actions by pornography will be deprived of a harmless pastime if it is outlawed. If others are protected

10. It is silly to insist that unless criminal sex acts can be traced directly to consumption of pornography by the criminal, pornography must be harmless. Lack of evidence for harmfulness is not evidence for harmlessness. Moreover, there is no reason to assume that the de-identification supported by pornography will find directly sexual outlets. Finally, the influence of pornography is usually diffuse and often indirect, as is the case of manners or religion.

11. Of course, advertising does not originate these, nor does pornography. However, both can intensify, spread, persuade. Neither would exist if it did not have some influence which occasionally will go all the way to imitation, within or outside the law. Cigarette advertising surely does not cause smoking—but it does give social sanction to it.

from harm thereby, and if society is, censorship is as justifiable as it is to impose a speed limit, or to prohibit the keeping of lions, however tame, in city apartments.

III

If pornography is undesirable, as I believe to have shown, so are many other things which are not outlawed because we might lose, endanger, or impair desirable things. Thus the problem still to be dealt with becomes: is pornography unavoidable with, or necessary to, freedom and art? is it inseparable from either, or both, inasmuch as censorship—owing to intrinsic indivisibilities, or to human frailty—could not but be so arbitrary as to do more damage to freedom or art than is tolerable, or worth suffering, for the sake of outlawing pornography? If not, can censorship reduce the harm that would be done by what it censors enough to offset other costs, and if so, how effective could it be? I think that censorship of pornography need not damage freedom, art, or literature; that it can be effective enough and that the advantages would offset the costs.

In "hard-core" cases it is fairly easy to separate pornography from literature. The material is pornographic if, in the opinion of the deciding body (best, a jury), two of the following three criteria are met: (1) If the pornographic intention is proved by admission, testimony, or circumstances; (2) if the marketing in the main is directed at prurient interest; (3) if the prevalent effect is sexual arousal.[12] (Since effects differ, a jury would consult witnesses and its own reaction.) The difficulties have been greatly exaggerated here. I have yet to meet a person who cannot separate most pornography from most literature.[13]

Consider, then, instances in which one might disagree on intent or effect. Perhaps the effect is prurient, but it cannot be shown that the intent was; or, the prurient effect is much less than universal, or it is combined with apparently valuable elements of style or content. Or the work is obscene yet not arousing, i.e., unsuccessful as a stimulant with most persons, although otherwise retaining the deleterious effects described. Here one must keep in mind the aesthetic functions of art and literature which distinguish both from obscene or prurient works. Pornography has one aim only: to arouse the reader's (viewer's) lust so that, by sharing the fantasy manufactured for him, he may attain the vicarious sexual experience it is intended to produce (which may be, but need not be, harmless). Literature, however, aims at the

---

12. If the arousal is universal, it is by definition impersonal. (These criteria have been updated and somewhat changed by the 1973 *Miller* decision. —Ed.)

13. It is not surprising that lawyers, for the sake of clients, have invented interpretations which obscure and nullify the statutes; it is surprising, however, that the courts have been so inept in clarifying them and in carrying out the obvious and legitimate intent of the legislators.

contemplation of experience, at the revelation of its significance. Art is not an *Ersatz* experience, nor does it invite direct emulation.[14] If "high art" does not, as Santayana said, "cancel lust," it also does not aim at arousing it or at separating it from context.[15] Revelation, too, is an experience—but one which helps illuminate, understand, and enlarge the possibilities and complexities of the human career; whereas pornography narrows and simplifies them until they are reduced to a series of more or less sophisticated but anonymous (therefore monotonous) sensations. Artistic and literary experiences are intellectual and emotional in nature; they are perceived through the senses but experienced as feelings and thoughts.[16]

Since it is impossible to serve pornography pure, the vicarious experience it supplies must occur through some medium, words or pictures, and in a setting that permits the suspension of disbelief. This is as far as the similarity with literature goes. Aesthetic merit would be distracting. Pornography and literature are mutually exclusive. Pornographers no more produce literature than accountants do, or copywriters. Pornographers avoid distraction by using well-worn and inconspicuous cliches and conventions which do not encumber the libidinous action. Thus, in Joyce or Lawrence the reader's arousal, if it occurs at all, is necessarily incidental to the aesthetic experience, as it is in Hubert Selby (*Last Exit to Brooklyn*). To be sure, these authors may be read, whatever their intentions, for the sake of masturbatory fantasy. But the separation from human context and the avoidance of literary experience would not come from them—it would be the reader's doing. Despite his intent to separate them, such a reader might actually benefit by reading what he wants conjoined to what he tries to separate it from.

Although many pretend to be, it is hard to imagine a literary critic actually unable to tell pornography from literature. What could a critic tell us if he cannot tell pornography from literature? If he is as incompetent as he professes to be, why take him seriously? If he feels that, for the sake of freedom, he must pretend he cannot discriminate—just as communists used to be unable to tell democracy from dictatorship whenever such a distinction would interfere with their ideology—why take the pretention seriously?

---

14. Freud, at times, thought of art as a substitute. I have suggested why I think him wrong on this in my "Of Happiness and of Despair We Have No Measure" (Chapt. 19, *Passion and Social Constraint*).

15. V. Jean Genet (*Playboy,* April 1954): "I now think that if my books arouse readers sexually, they are badly written because poetic emotion should be so strong that no reader is moved sexually."

16. Susan Sontag's (*Styles of Radical Will*, 1966) fashionably campy attempt to establish pornography as an art form is unconvincing. Note, however, that her instances of pornographic "art" all are instances of pornographic sadism. When ambitious, pornography usually becomes sadistic without becoming art—however "artistic" the critic's approval.

Nor is distinguishability impaired by contested, or by a few actual border-lline cases. Disagreement among experts does not entail an impossibility to judge. There is, indeed, a twilight zone where light and darkness merge; yet they can be distinguished from each other. And the law can draw a fairly clear line, arbitrary only insofar as most things in reality are continuous but must be separated if we wish to distinguish them. Certainly the line will be drawn differently at different times and in different places. But if dress changes with fashion, we know at any given time what is, or, at least, what is not permissible. So with pornography.

The judgments of the jury thus need not be more arbitrary than other judgments. And censorship is not likely to be costly. Few cases are likely to be brought to court—most censorable material is unlikely to be published. Nothing could be lost, for, if something has aesthetic value, by definition it cannot be pornography. As for effectiveness, laws, of course, never eliminate but, by penalizing it, reduce the frequency of the prohibited action. And pornography laws will reduce the accessibility and public nature of the remaining pornography as well and proclaim public disapproval.

IV

Social cohesion, any social order, rests on shared values, customs, and traditions which identify us in our roles as members of a society. We are disposed accordingly to empathy, cooperation, lawful behavior, and even altruistic acts. We understand each other, for we "speak the same language," that is, we share the same values, perceptions, identifications, ideals, re-actions, and rules of action. A social order is both the effect and the source of shared values and beliefs.

Social cohesion does not extend equally to all persons or require that all hold exactly the same values, nor does it extend equally to all activities of each. There are dissenters and deviants; and they can be useful. But they dissent or deviate from something—the shared values of society. Usually they do so according to shared ideas about dissent and are dealt with according to shared ideas about legitimacy. These shared ideas do change over time and space, but they do so in a fairly continuous manner. Social cohesion requires that the central values of a society be held by its leadership and followed by its majority and transmitted and elaborated by its institutions.

Freedom—the range within which the individual can choose values and actions—may be among the shared values of a society.[17] Within a social

17. Actually freedom is a metavalue: the ability to choose values. It cannot itself lead to, although it permits, any shared values; and to the extent to which it prevails, freedom allows the undermining of any shared values. To contend otherwise is to assume that values stem from "human nature." But at most, human nature limits the range of values pursued; it permits great variety within that range—variety far in excess of what any social order can legitimize. Therefore, a social limitation of the range is required to narrow it to less than the "natural" range, to exclude choices nature permits while society cannot. Freedom can exist only within the socially limited range.

order freedom must be balanced against other values when it is in conflict or in competition with them (e.g., the freedom and security of others; defense; law enforcement; welfare; efficiency). Unlike welfare, freedom can be used against itself: we can use freedom to abrogate or undermine it. Hence, freedom, unlike most other values, must be limited to continue. Unlimited freedom in communication is as inconsistent with any social order as is unlimited freedom in action. For the former leads to the latter and cannot be as easily separated from it as John Stuart Mill thought. Communication need not be limited to the same degree or in the same respects as action must be. Roughly the more remote from action and the less noxious to central values, the less need for communications to be restricted.[18]

The mere fact that they erode social cohesion alone would be sufficient to prohibit pornographic communications since they are by definition bereft of any value which might justify retaining them. Elsewhere, as, perhaps, in India, or Israel, dietary norms are more important than sexual ones. In our society sexual norms seem important enough to justify prohibition of what is outrageously (and invitingly) offensive to and destructive of the shared values—obscenity.

V

The report of the Presidential *Commission on Obscenity and Pornography* (Bantam Books)[19] will be briefly considered here. However, it does not seem to be a serious piece of work—although it is an expensive one—as the following may suggest.

The statistical data seem to be selected misleadingly. Thus, one finds (p. 274, Table 33) that from 1958 to 1969 there was a 37.5% decrease in reported (forcible) rape in Copenhagen. *Encounter Magazine* (London, September 1970, p. 95) published figures from 1960 to 1968 taken by the Reuter's correspondent in Copenhagen from the *Statistical Yearbook*. He found variations but no significant change in reported (forcible) rape (e.g., 189 in 1962; 215 in 1966; 217 in 1968). He notes that the conviction rate actually has decreased. (From this one might conclude that only the more unequivocal rapes are reported now.) How is this discrepancy explained? The Commission presented tabulated rapes reported in Copenhagen only,

18. This is a very rough rule. There are cases in which action should be limited less than communication. Thus prostitution and homosexual acts might be as inconsistent with the ethos of a society as is pornography. However, they may be less criminogenic and less infectious. (They tend to appeal to distinctly limited groups.) Further, penalization would inflict considerable suffering on involuntary victims without being very effective. In contrast, the greater and different damage done by pornography is more easily limited, and censorship inflicts no suffering.

19. At this writing, the specific reports on which the Commission's report is based are not available.

whereas the tabulation in *Encounter* refers to all of Denmark. Further, owing to the small base, a decrease from 11 (in 1958) to 8 (in 1969) alleged by the Commission results in a 37.5% decrease! The selection of one city rather than all of Denmark is unwarranted, and, here, misleading. Finally, only two years are given, the intervening ones all omitted, a fact which is not helpful since there are normally fluctuations from year to year, and no trends can be observed. Nor is there a comparison with nonsexual crime rates, age distribution, and other factors.

All the statistical evidence presented in the report is subject to criticism of this sort. I do not believe the data to be meaningful. Nor are the conclusions. (Suppose, for example, that violent sexual crime had actually decreased. This could be the case for a variety of reasons, and it would be entirely logical to argue that, had pornography not been legalized, it might have decreased even more.)

The actually significant changes I find are in offenses that ceased to be reported as offenses. What could be obtained by committing them is now obtainable legally elsewhere. Certainly this applies to voyeurism or exhibitionism. By, in effect, legalizing these we may reduce or even eliminate not the acts but merely the police records connected with them.

Elsewhere the Commission indicates that people who have committed sex crimes have not, or have no more, been exposed to pornography than people not convicted for this type of crime. This means nothing unless other variables are considered with far more care than is indicated in the Commission's report. The incidence of death in the hospital population is greater than outside. Does it really follow that life outside is healthier? Certainly nobody maintains that pornography is the *only* thing that leads to sex crime, or that its absence prevents sex crime. Yet it may be one thing facilitating some crimes—and the Commission statistics are so organized that they can neither confirm nor disconfirm this possibility.

Those who oppose pornography do so because they feel it will change the quality of our lives—the public and the private *ethos*. Serious inquiry would not have presented isolated statistical and experimental investigations (of doubtful pertinence and reliability). Such an inquiry would have considered the possible influence of pornography (and of censorship of pornography) on the social ethos—on the quality of our lives. Instead, the Commission more or less tacitly assumed that unless crime can be specifically traced to pornography, pornography is legitimate and must be permitted. This seems extremely odd.

Note further that the Commission strongly recommends "sex education" although there is no evidence whatsoever of its effects, good or bad, or even of our capacity to impart it. Incidentally, the recommendation does imply that sexual behavior can be influenced by teaching. This is certainly inconsistent with the Commission's disbelief in the influence of pornography. (It is, moreover, contrary to everything we know about the comparatively low influence of cognitive teaching on impulses, emotions, and attitudes. The record of the schools with respect to attitude formation is certainly disheartening to begin with.) I can see little reason for abolishing the apprenticeship system in sexual learning in favor of classroom teaching, or for adding the latter. Here a case can be made for "learning by doing." But let all this go and grant even that, as the Commission seems to suggest, sex education will lead to more "healthy" sex and, therefore, to less sex crime. (Lest I be misunderstood: in the main it is not sex or any act that is healthy or unhealthy; the personalities engaged in it are and make it so.) Suppose such education also leads to more promiscuity. The Commission does not seem to have given a thought to the desirability, or the undesirability, of changes in the moral outlook which sex education may or may not bring about.

I am forced to conclude that the Commission selectively and prejudicially initiated and presented investigations to bolster conclusions which were determined by its formulation of the problem and not by the evidence which a broader definition would have led to.

The Psychiatrist as Expert Witness in Pornography Prosecutions

Blaine D. McLaughlin, M.D.*

Editor's note: The style of this chapter will be similar to a cross-examination of the expert witness (Dr. McLaughlin in this case). The editor will take the role of cross-examining attorney and devil's advocate—and the questioning will go beyond the fairly narrow limits permitted in a typical court.

Ed.: Dr. McLaughlin, what is your occupation?

Dr. M.: I am a physician and a psychiatrist.

Ed.: Doctor, would you tell us your background as far as your educational qualifications and your studies are concerned?

Dr. M.: Well, I had the usual B.S. degree in "premed" at Carlton College. I had some graduate studies at Harvard and took my medical degree at upstate New York in 1942. I had my internship in the Public Health Service and my residency training in psychiatry at the Friends' Hospital in Philadelphia and at St. Elizabeth's Hospital in Washington, D.C. I received my certification by the Board of Psychiatry and Neurology in 1951. In addition to practicing psychiatry, I have taught most of my professional life in such places as Philadelphia, North Dakota, California, and Texas. I am now in private practice and act as a consultant teacher in Fort Worth. I also have over sixty publications. I am past president of the Academy of Psychosomatic Medicine. I have recently retired as professor and chairman of the Department of Psychiatry at the Medical School of the University of North Dakota, and I am listed in *Who's Who in America* as a teacher and lecturer in the field of psychiatry.

*Biographical information about McLaughlin is an integral part of this chapter.

Ed.: Have you ever testified as an expert witness in a federal or state court?

Dr. M.: Yes, I have. In the past five years I have testified as a prosecution expert witness approximately seventy-five times in all sections of the United States.

Ed.: Have you ever appeared as a witness for the defense in obscenity trials?

Dr. M.: I have never appeared but have been asked several times and felt that the material involved could not be defended. I therefore turned down the opportunity.

Ed.: How did a reputable psychiatrist like yourself ever get involved in testifying as an expert witness in pornography prosecutions?

Dr. M.: Actually, I got into this work rather unexpectedly when, in 1969, the U.S. Postal Service authorities approached me and said they would like me to testify in court as to the obscenity of a number of posters showing the nude male body in provocative poses. Apparently a large number of these posters were being advertised and distributed throughout the northwestern area of the United States and, in crossing state lines, were in violation of federal obscenity statutes. Their mailing lists supposedly included a great many homosexuals who either were known or were supposed to be part of the community.

My first feeling was that this was rather silly, inasmuch as homosexuals in general can be stimulated by various types of erotic material, and I couldn't see initially that trying to suppress these nude photo posters would be of any real consequence.

When the Post Office people told me that this was a million-dollar-a-year enterprise and that it was all handled through a mail drop in Minneapolis, I guess my Scotch blood began to boil at the thought that a million dollars could be so easily extracted from these people, and I finally agreed to testify as to the provocative nature of the photographs.

Unfortunately, my clinical experience then did not fully prepare me for the situation in court; when I got there I found that the defense attorneys were far more experienced in all of the literature concerning sexual aberrations and the minutia of psychological research than I was. The first hearing in Fargo, North Dakota, proved more or less a disaster to me, though the government won the case, as it were, because the jury was convinced that these sexual materials should not be distributed regardless of what the legal or scientific people proposed. The case was immediately appealed to the next level of court, and the decision was reversed on a technicality of written law concerning obscenity.

This humiliating experience convinced me that there was more to the problem, and I began a rather systematic study of the psychiatric literature and the social attitudes about sex. I had conferences with a great number of people (both professional and lay) concerning just what obscenity is and just what social attitudes in various groups seemed to be concerning its use or abuse.

Ed.:   What is the major issue that presents itself in a pornography trial?

Dr. M.:   The major issue in most prosecutions in the past was to determine if a particular book, film, magazine, or whatever met the court's "three-pronged" definition of obscenity. The recent federal law and most state laws were based on defining obscenity in terms of whether or not the material was considered to have prurient interest, whether or not it went beyond the usual community standards in candor, and whether or not it was "utterly without redeeming social value." The new Supreme Court ruling changes this definition somewhat. The new test for obscenity includes the pruriency criterion and adds that the depiction must be "patently offensive" and must lack any serious literary, artistic, scientific, or political value. In most trials the prosecution has the job of proving that material is obscene, and in order to prove it, they have to call experts who are accepted as authorities in the elements which make up the definition of obscenity. Under the new Supreme Court ruling, experts are now not necessarily needed to make such determinations.

Ed.:   Just what in your background qualified you as an expert in these parts of the law concerning obscenity?

Dr. M.:   My work for many years has been involved with studying people who have sexual problems and also in doing research on various community and social problems which involve both sex and violence. As a resident in psychiatry, I was required to review the Kinsey work on sexuality, and my reviews were published at that time. Thus, I became involved in interviewing people with sexual problems. Eventually I headed up a project studying sexual offenders in the Pennsylvania prison system. This was during the time I was teaching psychiatry at the Women's Medical College of Pennsylvania. Ultimately we set up research teams who interviewed people in the prisons who had been convicted of crimes of violence. In addition to that, we worked with the probation board and took as clinical patients many sexual offenders who were on probation. The studies I did there led me to research into violence and sexual aberrations, and after I left the Women's Medical College in 1964, I continued this clinical work at the University of North Dakota. I have also done work of this sort in Texas and California. I have been lecturing around the country for many years; I believe I have lectured in almost every state now, focusing on the subjects of violence and immaturity of a sexual nature. After these lectures I have had a chance to talk with other physicians and scientists as well as groups of students, church organizations, women's societies, and many other groups of people. As a witness for the prosecution in the past four years, I have also had opportunities to talk with lawyers and judges as well as with law enforcement officers in almost every section of the United States. I also acted as a consultant in Los Angeles for a research project which proposed to find out by questioning the citizens of every county in California about their attitudes toward obscenity. I had something to do with setting up the type of questions which were proposed and also with evaluating the material in terms of its psychological significance. While no one can understand all of the attitudes in an elaborate community such as the United States, I have probably had as much experience as any psychiatrist at working with people in different sections of the country. And because my work has been with the clinical patient as well as the private patient, I have been able to see a broader range of the community than most examiners. In addition, as a worker with the courts and with the prison system, I was exposed to a part of the social scene that doesn't normally enter into psychiatric practice.

Ed.: What you have stated seems to suggest that you have had experience not only with what is prurient but also with current community standards. However, there is another prong to the obscenity test as it existed before the Miller ruling in June, 1973, and that is whether or not the material is utterly without social value. How did you qualify on this question?

Dr. M.: This is an almost impossible part of the definition to answer positively because there were so many opinions as to what is utterly without social value. And of course, the new Supreme Court ruling eliminates this as a test of obscenity. Almost anything can be considered to have some redeeming social values, however, and many times the defense of obscenity hearings rests on this point. My attitude is that if material is anti-educational, that is, if material tends to say something which is not true, then it is without social value because it proposes to miseducate people. My experience in studying obscenity problems and in studying the people involved in pornography and violence has led me to the conclusion that much of the material which we call pornographic has miseducated people. There is a tremendous void in the education of the average person concerning the psychology and even the physiology of sexual activity. Because of this there is an avid curiosity about almost any sexual material, no matter how blatantly anti-educational. It is my contention that material which is false and misleading is thus utterly without social value because it is utilized in ways which can be injurious to a person.

Ed.: Do you have any scientific articles based on your work with pornography?

Dr. M.: Yes, I have two articles in print directly concerned with pornography and emotional problems in the individual. I have another article on my experiences in the courts, designed for the use of other psychiatrists and physicians; this article was read in Amsterdam at the World Congress of Psychosomatic Medicine in June, 1973.

Ed.: With all the published material you have, I am surprised that you have so few articles directly on pornography.

Dr. M.: Pornography has not been a topic which in itself has been of much interest to the psychiatric world in the past. It's possible that it will be in the future. Most of my published articles concern the recognition and treatment of various types of emotional disorders, both in youngsters and adults. The studies which I have done concerning sexual offenders and people involved with violent acting-out have been on a broader focus, and the data on pornography has been a small part of what goes into the article. I certainly do not consider myself a psychiatrist interested merely in obscenity or sexuality. These are problems which enter into the recognition and treatment of individuals and groups in the world of psychiatry.

Ed.: On the basis of the material which you have presented here, have you been accepted by federal and state courts around the country as an expert on the three-pronged test?

Dr. M.: Yes; I have never been rejected by any court in qualifying as an expert in these areas.

Ed.: What is your definition of prurient?

Dr. M.: Prurient is a word not used in common parlance, and I will refer to its definition in the dictionaries of the English language as material which is shameful or morbid in its depiction of sex or excrement. I believe that any material which produces a feeling of guilt or shame in the average adult person and has reference to sexual matters or excrement is by definition prurient. I also believe that material of a sexual nature which is pathologic, or sick, is morbid in its basic thrust and is therefore by definition prurient.

Ed.: Isn't it true that almost any material of a sexual nature can produce feelings of shame or guilt in some people?

Dr. M.: This is true, and we have to be careful to define the average person in community terms. The definition I use of the average person is an adult of both sexes and of all faiths and all ethnic backgrounds—who has all types of education, all types of health, and all types of economic status. This avoids the impossible question of what is a normal or an abnormal person. If we adhere to such a definition of the average person, my experience both with disturbed individuals and with those who are reasonably well-adjusted leads me to the conclusion that the average person in most cases is not shamed by sexual material which suggests or even reveals sexual activity as a part of the love relationship of committed individuals. This average person is also not shamed by the suggestion or revelation of abnormal sexual material if it is part of a general thesis educating the average person concerning the problems of sexual aberration and if its major thrust is in terms of education and sympathy for such problems. On the other hand, if material implies or reveals sexual matters that suggest that sex without love or commitment is a desirable aim in itself or in other ways suggest that various sexual aberrations are desirable and satisfying, this average person rejects or is harmed by that material. It is my opinion that the common sense of the average person is our best judge in terms of what is prurient. To paraphrase Justice Black—we all seem to know what pruriency is, but it is hard to define in words that differentiate that which is prurient and that which is not.

Ed.:   What is your experience in the second prong of the test, that is, community attitudes toward candor in sexual material?

Dr. M.:   There is no doubt that standards have changed toward a more permissive approach in the last few years. We can all remember when books such as *Lady Chatterley's Lover* or even *Forever Amber* were considered obscene. Today most of the community accept frankness in the description, both photographic and in words, of sexual material if it is part of the basic theme of the material and the basic theme either supports Judeo-Christian standards of sexual conduct or in some real way points up problems in our current thinking about sex as a part of community and personal life. This, of course, includes the humorous pornography and graffiti which have been a part of civilization from time immemorial. Current community standards, however, reject material which tends to—in its major thrust—glorify sexual release for its own egocentric sake without reference to commitment or love. The community also rejects material which suggests that a sexual aberration such as sadomasochism or homosexuality (despite advocacy by the gay liberationists) is a satisfactory way of life and rejects the implication that satisfaction obtained from such aberrations is acceptable. At the same time, the community common sense recognizes the problems of people involved in the com-

276

pulsions of sexual aberrations and holds out a sympathetic hand to such persons without accepting their standards or wishing to see them furthered through anti-educational methods.

Ed.: Don't you believe that some material which describes sexual abnormalities can be beneficial to certain people?

Dr. M.: Yes I do. Many therapists use sexually oriented material, both written and in the form of photographs or movies, in desensitizing people with various sexual problems to their own compulsions. Under the umbrella of the therapeutic relationship of trust, some of this material can be very useful to the ill person in helping him to grope his way back toward identification with humanity and toward peace with himself. I do not believe that this material should, however, be generally accepted and distributed just because within the narrow range of treating emotionally disturbed individuals it might be useful in certain cases. The prosecution of obscenity aims at the needs of the average person. I feel that teaching untruths about sex and the individual's sexual life is a little bit like putting out a booklet describing how to build a privy. This booklet may use slick paper and have beautiful colored drawings of a well-built privy with all the modern conveniences and comforts. However, if the book suggests that it is all right to have the privy drain into the local water supply, the booklet is anti-educational and utterly without social value. It is teaching something which is basically injurious to human beings. We have long since come through the problem of freedom of action in that particular regard, and there is no doubt in the minds of the population or the courts that such a privy would not be allowed to be built regardless of the property rights of individuals. I feel the same about material which suggests to the average person that a slick, egocentrically satisfying sexual experience, documented with all kinds of physical tricks and antics, is desirable either to the individual or to the community. History and our experiences with many patients with a disturbed sexual life show us that humans just don't operate this way, and any material that says they do is anti-educational and therefore under the law utterly without social value.

Ed.: How can you justify yours or anyone else's setting himself up as an authority on what is right or wrong in sexual matters for the average person?

Dr. M.: I consider the problem of sexual behavior something like the problem of physical hygiene. We have long since learned that what seems to be common sense in terms of eating, exercising, or other body activities can sometimes be injurious. We have learned to depend upon authorities who spend their lives studying the body and its many manifestations to advise us so that our lives may be fuller in the proper utilization of nature's equipment. Sexuality is a part of life. The twentieth-century scientific research has led us to feel that the expression of sexuality is a tremendously important part of the maturization process of the human being. We think now that an individual does not grow to full creative maturity unless he goes through the stages of sexual development and expression which lead to full expression of his heterosexual life as an adult without guilt or egocentric blocks. Experts have spent many years in study and research on this problem. Obviously, we would like to see as many individuals as possible reach sexual maturity and gain as much as possible from their sexual lives. We would like to see individuals relieved from the guilts and misunderstandings about the process of growing sexually and the emotional drives which center in sexual expression. All of us need guidance as we grow and wrestle with the conflictual sexual ideas and feelings which plague us, particularly in youth. I feel, therefore, that experts should advise in the use of sexual material by the community at large and that the courts should set up recognized boards of authority to control and improve the sexual education that is available to the average person in American life. I feel strongly that youngsters should be provided with some understanding of the turbulence of sexual feelings that dominate adolescents. Counsel should be available to our developing adults that will help them to be as creative as possible in their expression of sexuality. As a psychiatrist I am for sex. I feel that it is a driving force which leads us toward maturity. I feel that it is the spur to the development of love and commitment which is the life blood of family life and the security of the newly born and developing child. Perhaps more than any other profession the psychiatrist feels committed to education along sexual lines. I never consider myself a comstock who is trying to suppress any material concerning sex. What I am trying to do is have the community understand that the sexual impulse is a great and powerful tool which can lead to creativity or to destruction. I would like to extend the creative part of sexuality and to counteract and re-educate when the individual has gotten off on a destructive sexual tack. Perhaps the more frank discussion of sexuality which has emerged in the last decade or so will in the long run be helpful; but let's not forget that we are dealing with a highly charged instrument that requires some control and responsibility in its expression.

Ed.:   Doctor, do you speak for all of the psychiatric world or is there a difference of opinion in your profession?

Dr. M.: There is definitely a difference of opinion among psychiatrists as to the usefulness of pornographic material. Some psychiatrists go so far as to say that they feel the more exposure to sexual material the better. I have read in psychiatrists' reports that they even carry on sexual relations with their patients as a therapeutic instrument. It is my opinion that these persons do not represent the mainstream of psychiatric thinking. There is a fringe of the psychiatric world who apparently feel that all of our standards and attitudes of the past should be discarded. This is merely a fringe. The medical profession is traditionally conservative. Most of the psychiatric world follows this traditional feeling that we should carefully study the past and be extremely cautious in advocating new and untried ventures either in the body or in the mind. I feel, therefore, that the stand represented here is the main theme of medical and psychiatric thinking. My reading and studies have confirmed this.

Ed.:   Doctor, when the Presidential Commission on Pornography and Obscenity made its report, the majority opinion suggested that there was no harm in pornographic material. Will you please comment on this?

Dr. M.:   It is true that in the majority report of the presidential commission, its proponents felt that pornographic material did not harm the average person. There was a minority report which suggested that it possibly could, and it made a strong plea for the continuation and careful review of the studies. I favor the minority report. We will remember that there was great pressure to get the report before the public, and, as a scientist, I have strong criticism of the validity of some of the studies which were done and the conclusions which were drawn on a basis of the inclusion of some material and the exclusion of other data suggesting possible harm. I am not at all certain how much the average individual, or for that matter, the abnormal individual, is actually harmed by an experience of viewing a pornographic movie or reading pornographic material on a short-term basis. These are the sort of studies which the majority opinion used as data. There is an entirely different frame of reference which the minority suggested. The wide dispersal of pornographic material, the allowing of material in poor taste to be made a part of the social scene, the suggestion to young people that sexually anything goes, the idea that sex was a commodity to be sold and bought, these ideas and attitudes, in my opinion, are definitely harmful. It would be beyond common sense to say that the average individual, in viewing a picture of a couple engaged in some sexual act, would be harmed by that experience. If, however, the experience was a common day-by-day part of his life, if sex became a "thing," the

	desensitization of the individual and the community would be harmful indeed to our culture, our family standards, our respect for the individual, and ultimately to our way of living together.
Ed.:	You seem to suggest a high standard of sexual life. Isn't it possible that you are asking more of a great many people than they can achieve?
Dr. M.:	It is true that I expect a high standard of sexual life, and I do this because as a psychiatrist I feel that much agony and illness have resulted from a failure to live to high sexual standards. I also feel that misunderstandings have led to the loss of creativity in many individuals through their not having had the opportunity to understand the best in sexuality. It is of course true that all of us will at times slip from the highest standard of sexual attitude and behavior. Let us understand that these are slips and not that they are the opening of a new and wonderful way of life and expression. It is, of course, a battle to mature sexually; it is also a battle to mature physically and intellectually. Let us not suggest that the battle is not worthwhile. There is in psychiatric circles a homily along this line. If a pretty girl walks by, and the wind blows up her skirt, almost every man is going to turn his head and see something more. If one man, however, follows her down the street and pushes her into an alley because of what he saw and felt as the wind lifted her dress, this man is abnormal. The man who looked and felt and turned back to his own world was normal. Let us think that the average person fits in to that part of normality.
Ed.:	Have you any evidence that the "loosening" of sexual standards has caused any increase in violent behavior or other antisocial phenomena?
Dr. M.:	I have no direct evidence, and I think it is far too early to get authoritative data on these questions. This is principally the reason that I reject the reports of both the Commissions on Pornography and Violence. This is such a complex question, and there are so many factors involved in social and individual behavior that hard data is impossible to obtain for at least a generation. Some of the signposts that I feel suggest changes are obvious and might be considered. In comparing, on the MMPI (Minnesota Multiphasic Personality Inventory), the personality structure of the Vietnam veteran with that of the World War II veteran, we see a great deal more "acting-out" and a great deal more depression in the veteran returning from Vietnam. Certainly there was much less suppression of basic drives in the soldiers in this latter group. Does further acting-out lead to more depression? It is certainly a question which should be considered seriously.
Ed.:	You have made a case that the rights of the individual to see the

sort of sexual material that he wishes and which would appear to be his Constitutional rights should be set aside because of the danger that badly presented material might be injurious to the population in general. If this is true, why have the courts and juries so many times acquitted defendants and failed to get convictions for the distribution and sale of pornographic material?

Dr. M.: I feel that there is a problem of educating the community and, to a degree, the courts, in just exactly what is injurious material and what is acceptable. Let us take extreme examples. If we presented a situation in which a man got sexual satisfaction out of knifing a woman to death, this action would obviously be unacceptable to almost any court in any community. We know many people do get sexual satisfaction out of this kind of murder. On the other hand, if we presented material which suggested that some men on occasion desire a sexual experience with an unknown woman of beauty and spirit, most courts and communities would accept this as not obscene but merely as a somewhat healthy diversion. Somewhere between those points, the communities, and therefore ultimately the courts, have got to draw some sort of rough line as to what is acceptable and what is not. When that line is clearly drawn, convictions will be frequent and prosecutions on unwarranted cases will be few.

Ed.: Getting back to the Presidential Commission's Report on Pornography—they of course indicated that there was no evidence, at least cause-effect evidence, that pornography harms adults or children. I take it that you disagree with this conclusion.

Dr. M.: Yes. There indeed is evidence, clinical evidence. Working with and treating individuals in their total life setting results in a different kind of evidence than that obtained by simply having people fill out questionnaires. I have found it very easy for the average person, particularly a young and unsophisticated or uneducated person to be deluded by pornographic material into thinking that sexual aberrations of one sort or another are acceptable and desirable in terms of a way of life. My experience, as well as the experiences of many clinical psychiatrists over the years, has demonstrated effectively that a life embracing sexual aberration is an unhappy, and in many cases, a disastrous way of life. And frequently pornography is used as a partial substitute for what psychiatrists would consider mature sexuality. I define pornography as sexual expression without human commitment. I feel that it is a regression to utilize the sexual impact of photographs, movies, or literature for the purpose of sexual release without the human commitment of affection and relationship. In my consulting for the prosecution of obscene films, photographs, and other literary things, I have run into a good many people who have been involved in the production of pornographic material. These people are badly damaged by these experiences. They are utilized as a commodity, and their humanity is exploited. I am concerned when sex becomes simply a commodity, and the buying public is interested in sensationalism of a voyeuristic type. It is a principle in psychiatry that as people fail in mature sexual adjustment, they tend to slip back to a more immature or infantile type of adjustment. It is not the pretty body or the male vigor that makes for satisfying sexuality; it is the commitment through love of one individual to the other.

Ed.: Yes, but what's wrong with regressing occasionally?

Dr. M.: It is much easier for an individual to regress psychologically and slip back to an infantile level of sexual expression than it is for him to go forward into a more mature adjustment. Maturity comes with great effort; regression is a simple thing. When people are ill and have utterly failed in the job of maturation, when they have developed symptoms which are devastating, the psychiatrist often uses regression as a method of relieving anxiety and resting the patient. Remember that this is a controlled situation, and at the time when the patient is ready for it, he can again be gently prodded into another attempt at maturity.

Ed.: But how does pornography enter in to this regression?

Dr. M.: If we find that the pornographic material is substituting for the reality of a sexual commitment, it is definitely a pathological agent and ultimately regressive, destructive, or harmful to the individual. It has been said that in Hollywood today it would be impossible to make a heroic picture. Not only would actors be unavailable, but the whole mechanism of the movie industry has slipped away from the production of anything which symbolizes human heroism, sacrifice, or emotional maturity in terms of commitment and loyalty to other people. However, life without commitment to others is always and ultimately a life of disillusionment.

Comments and Conclusions

While it is obvious that we don't have as great a body of knowledge about pornography's effects that we have about media violence, sufficient data now suggest that certain kinds of pornography—under the right circumstances—can contribute to a change of sexual orientation (either in the laboratory or by accidental conditioning) or development of sexual deviations and do, in fact, sometimes trigger antisocial sexual behavior.

It would be very difficult to argue any more that there is no empirical scientific evidence that pornography can't adversely affect some people. And while many readers of this volume may have been exposed to significant amounts of erotica and still feel undamaged and unharmed, so is it true that many people drink alcoholic beverages with no apparent ill effects. Yet alcohol is by far our number one drug-abuse problem, with five million homes harboring an alcoholic—a fact bearing a significant impact on the quality of life for these individuals so afflicted as well as for their spouses and children. And similarly, probably only a minority of pornography users will be seen as damaged in obvious ways. But in actual numbers this could still represent a large group of individuals, plus their victims.

And, as with media violence, it would be untrue, unfair, and unscientific to suggest that pornography is the major cause of a number of social ills. But it would be fair, true, and scientific to suggest that it can and undoubtedly does contribute (and in some cases triggers) social pathology, as does media violence. And on occasion, of course, the two are mixed or combined in their presentation.

We are the product of our experiences. We are influenced by what happens to us, and the laws of learning apply just as powerfully in the areas of aggression and sexual conduct (and our feeling about these things) as in any other area of life.

WHERE DO YOU DRAW THE LINE?

Where law ends, tyranny begins.
William Pitt, Sr., 1770

Introduction

Where, then, do you draw the line? In the first chapter in this section, Alberta Siegel points out that self-regulation within the television industry has not worked to stem the tide of violent entertainment on television. She lists five suggestions to alleviate the problem.

In a following chapter, James Wilson reiterates discrepancies in the reports of two presidential commissions on the subjects of violence and obscenity and suggests ultimate criteria for judging whether these forms of entertainment and art are harmful.

In an unequivocal statement, following Wilson's chapter, Reo Christenson declares that stronger pornography legislation is needed—that "sex needs to be treated with some caution" in the interest of the well-being of society.

Harry Clor concludes this section with a chapter devoted to the subject of ethics—what is good for us and what is bad for us—and how ethics relates to the controversy over the free use of obscenity. He calls for a "countervailing ethic" to the ethic of self-expression.

Alternatives to Direct Censorship

Alberta Siegel

Self-regulation within the television industry has not worked. Since the late 1940s there have been calls to the TV industry for self-regulation, from Senate committees, from concerned parents, from mental health professionals, from the National Commission on the Causes and Prevention of Violence. Despite pious promises there has been no action sufficient to cleanse TV of this stain. The incidence of violent actions in entertainment programs has not changed notably in the last five years; it remains at a brutally high level.

What alternatives to self-regulation deserve the consideration of your subcommittee? I have several suggestions.

First, I suggest that *we need an independent monitoring agency to provide regular reports on the level of violence in television entertainment.* This agency could issue periodic "smog bulletins," alerting the public to the level of violent pollution currently being emitted by their TV receivers. I suggest that this agency might be privately financed, by one of the foundations, and that reports should be issued at least monthly. These reports should be broadcast over television and should appear in the newspapers and magazines. They should indicate how much violence is occurring, which networks and stations are broadcasting it, the time it is being broadcast, and how many child viewers are estimated to be watching at those times. They should also indicate who the sponsors are for the violent shows. This suggestion has been advanced by my colleague, Professor Albert Bandura of Stanford Uni-

This excerpt is from Dr. Siegel's presentation to the Communications Subcommittee of the U.S. Senate's Committee on Commerce, March 1972, discussing the Surgeon General's Television and Social Behavior Report. Biographical information on Dr. Siegel may be found in her earlier chapter in this volume.

versity. He believes that it would be helpful if the public and those within the industry were aided in identifying the violence vendors.

Second, *I suggest that consumers convey their disapproval of violence vendors in two ways. We may refuse to purchase their products. And we may refuse to buy stock in their firms.* The purpose of commercial television is to sell products. If consumers boycott products that are advertised on programs glorifying aggression and teaching techniques of mayhem and massacre, perhaps the producers of these products will turn their energies to finding other techniques of attracting customers. Many investors today are guided in their investing by social concerns. Churches, universities, foundations, union pension plans, and others are seeking to invest their funds in ways that benefit society. If these groups know who the violence vendors are, they may withdraw investment funds from their firms and instead invest their funds in those manufacturers who sponsor wholesome entertainment for the next generation.

A third suggestion derives from my observation that TV producers are mimics. When one format succeeds one month, it is being widely imitated by other producers six months later. Thus, we have "fads" in television programming, with doctor shows proliferating one season and private eye shows another. When successful new formats of nonviolent entertainment are devised, they will be copied. *I recommend increased support for public television* because I believe that the craftsmen in public television are likely to turn their energies and talents to creating constructive programs for children. As these attract children to their audience, they will be imitated by other producers and a chain of change will have been forged.

It is the imitative capabilities of TV producers that prompt my fourth suggestion as well. All of us who have traveled abroad have observed that programming for children is more successful in other nations than it is in the United States. Our record is unmatched in the neglect we display to our child audiences. *I recommend that travel fellowships be offered to the writers and producers of children's television programs* so they may observe first-hand how our neighboring nations—Canada, England, the European countries, Israel, and others—have succeeded in attracting child audiences without saturating them with violence. These fellowships might be funded by the television industry itself, and funds might also be available on a matching basis from private foundations for this purpose.

Fifth, I believe the Federal Communications Commission could be more effective in obtaining fair treatment for children and adolescents. *I suggest that a child advocate be appointed to the staff of the FCC.* This individual should have frequent and direct communications with the commissioners, advising them on questions bearing on the welfare of children. He or she should be well acquainted with social scientific research and also in close communication with the professions serving children: education, social service, child psychology, pediatrics, and child psychiatry. In the work of the

FCC the child advocate should be alert to decisions that have implications for the child audience, and should take initiatives in recommending changes in policies and procedures that would benefit children.

Violence, Pornography, and Social Science

James Q. Wilson

To the extent that it has a philosophical basis, the case against censorship—at least in this country—typically rests on a utilitarian argument. Indeed, it is a leading utilitarian—John Stuart Mill—who is often cited in opposition to censorship in any form. Though Mill, in his essay *On Liberty,* wrote chiefly of the censorship of political and religious speaking and writing, his position can easily—I should say, must inevitably—be extended to the arts and amusements. "The only purpose for which power can be rightfully exercised over any member of a civilized community, against his will," Mill wrote, "is to prevent harm to others." This principle applies not only to freedom of expression but to "liberty of tastes and pursuits." In this latter realm Oliver Wendell Holmes gave the utilitarian position its most memorable practical expression: "No woman was ever seduced by a book." Though many people echo this as an article of faith, it is of course an empirical statement. The truth or falsity of such factual, consequential statements is the ultimate basis of the utilitarian argument.

If the question of censorship rests on the appraisal of such consequences, then one might suppose that social science should be an important source of information about what public policies are necessary and defensible. Careful

James Q. Wilson, professor of government at Harvard University, was born in Denver during the depression days. He did his undergraduate work at the University of Redlands and completed his Ph.D. at the University of Chicago in 1959. In the middle sixties he was director of the Joint Center for Urban Studies at MIT and Harvard. He has served as a member of the Science Advisory Committee of the President's Commission on Law Enforcement and the Administration of Justice and has chaired the White House Task Force on Crime. He is author, co-author, or editor of seven books and numerous articles on voting behavior, minority groups, police, crime, law enforcement, political parties, and urban affairs. He lives in Belmont, Massachusetts.

research might, in principle, reveal the effect of the dissemination of certain images or words; if harm is to be the criterion, then a showing of such an effect would be a necessary—but not sufficient—condition for justifying the exercise of some form of legal restraint. (It is an important but little-remarked feature of utilitarianism that it can easily justify the most extreme form of social control as it can justify the most perfect liberty; everything depends on consequences.) Of course, disutility is not the only grounds one can imagine for censorship; but in the United States at least (and perhaps in most Western nations) it is almost invariably the only one employed—or, more accurately, the claim that no positive harm will flow from the free circulation of any visual or written material is the most common argument made *against* censorship.

Such, at least, are the philosophical premises of two presidential commissions, each of which has relied on extensive social science research to support quite different positions on the restraint of free communication. One, the National Commission on the Causes and Prevention of Violence, found that "the preponderance of available research evidence strongly suggests . . . that violence in television programs can and does have adverse effects upon audiences—particularly child audiences." The other, the Commission on Obscenity and Pornography, found that "extensive empirical investigation . . . provides no evidence that exposure to or use of explicit sexual materials plays a significant role in the causation of social or individual harms such as crime, delinquency, sexual or nonsexual deviancy or severe disturbances."

On the basis of these findings, the two commissions naturally made very different policy recommendations. The Violence Commission recommended that television broadcasters abandon "children's cartoons containing serious, noncomic violence," that the time devoted to broadcasting programs containing violent episodes be reduced, that the "basic context in which violence is presented" be altered, that there be more support for educational television, that the "validity" of the motion picture rating system ("G," "X," etc.) be evaluated as it applies to violent films, and that there be "further research." [1] The Obscenity Commission, by contrast, argued that the "spirit and letter of our Constitution tells us that Government should

---

1. Lest one assume that the verbal urgings of the Violence Commission to the television industry bear no taint of censorship, bear in mind that television (unlike the publishing of books, pure or impure) is a governmentally-licensed and regulated industry. Were the Federal Communications Commission to indicate that the renewal of these licenses was dependent on the broadcaster's progress in changing television programs to reduce violence, you can be certain there would be less violence on television. Without new legislation of any kind, the federal government today can exercise, should it act on the views of the Violence Commission, a "chilling effect" on the content of television programs. It already exercises that chilling effect with respect to many other matters—the

not interfere with these rights [for each individual to decide for himself what to see or read] unless a clear threat of harm makes that course imperative." Accordingly, the Commission recommends that "federal, state and local legislation prohibiting the sale, exhibition, or distribution of sexual materials to consenting adults be repealed," but that legislation preventing the "commercial distribution or display for sale" of certain sexual materials to young persons and prohibiting the "public display of sexually explicit pictorial materials" be enacted. Finally, it, too, called for more research.

"Violence" and "Sexuality"

The quite different recommendations of the two commissions—one calling for more restraint (which, if taken seriously by the FCC, can only mean more constraint), the other calling for less—might be the result, not of different empirical findings, but of different judgments about similar findings. One might argue that even a slight chance of people becoming more violent as a result of television warrants restraint, whereas even a significant chance of people becoming more "sexual" as a result of looking at obscene books warrants no restraint. Violence is harmful; sexuality is not; therefore, media that might encourage the former should be regulated whereas media that certainly encourage the latter should not.

But saying that violence is harmful and sexuality is not assumes a clear understanding of what we mean by *violence* and *sexuality.* Neither Commission displayed such clarity on this score. War is violent, but the Violence Commission did not call for abandoning news programs about Vietnam. Football and hockey not only appear violent to the viewer, but they are in fact violent for the participant; in contrast to westerns, people actually get hurt in televised sports programs, and the hurt cannot even be justified by a higher cause (he was a "bad guy" or he "did it for his country"). By some standards (not mine), it is the most shocking form of violence, done merely for sport or fun. Yet the Commission passed it by without censure.

As for sexuality, it cannot be utterly benign, for the Obscenity Commission wants to make it illegal for young persons to purchase pornography. On the one hand, the Commission found "no evidence" that exposure to erotica "adversely affects character or moral attitudes"; on the other hand, the

"fairness doctrine," for example, imposes heavy costs on broadcasters who give over programs to one side of a controversial issue by requiring them to provide equivalent time to the other side. (No magazine, book, or film, by contrast, is under any such obligation to be "fair.") Nor is the FCC the only potential source of constraint. Recently the Foundation to Improve Television brought suit to prevent a Washington TV station from broadcasting "The Wild, Wild West" before 10 P.M. on the grounds that the evidence of the harmful effects of violence means that the program "violates the constitutional rights of child viewers."

Commission recommends legislation that will "aid parents in controlling the access of their children to [sexual] materials during their formative years." (Two Commission members—interestingly, the only two sociologists on it—were at least consistent: they wanted no legal restrictions at all, whether for juveniles or adults.)

Moreover, some erotic materials are violent and some forms of violence are sexual. In these cases, which element is to be decisive? The Violence Commission would presumably discourage the explicit portrayal of a rape in a film because it is violent, while the Obscenity Commission would presumably permit it because it is sexual. And what of "violence" that the recipient finds not only bearable but even enjoyable? Are sado-masochistic acts violent or nonviolent?

From Hypotheses to Conclusions

Clarity on these and other matters was not enhanced by the kind of social science research with which the Commissions supplied themselves or the uses to which they put it. In both cases the central defect was the failure or inability to select an appropriate definition of the kind of effects either violence or erotica in the media might produce.

The great bulk of the research relied upon by the Violence Commission consisted of laboratory studies, usually involving young children or college students, in which *aggression* or *violence* was defined (in the case of young children) as a willingness to engage in harmless play activities involving physical force used on inanimate objects or (in the case of the college students) as a greater willingness to administer ostensible electric shocks to other subjects under circumstances such that the student had no choice *whether* to administer the shocks but only how many or with what severity.

On the basis of these laboratory experiments, plus a few other studies of lesser significance, the Task Force on Mass Media and Violence concluded:

Persons who have been effectively socialized into the norms for violence contained in the television world of violence would behave in the following manner:

a) They would probably resolve conflict by the use of violence.
b) They would probably use violence as a means to obtain desired ends.
c) They would probably passively observe violence between others.
d) They would not be likely to sanction or punish others' use of violence.
e) They would probably use a weapon when engaging in violence.
f) If they were policemen, they would be likely to meet violence with violence, often escalating its level.

To be sure, the Task Force does not say any of this has been proved; these are described as "hypotheses" but as ones which are "clearly consistent with and suggested by established research findings and by the most informed social science thinking about the long-run effects of exposure to mass media portrayals of violence." And as for short-run effects, the Task Force is prepared to assert conclusions, not merely hypotheses:

Audiences who have learned violent behavior from the media are likely to exhibit that learning (i.e., engage in acts of violence) if they encounter a situation similar to the portrayal situation, expect to be rewarded for violent behavior, or do not observe disapproving reactions to the portrayed aggression from another person in the viewing situation.

The Violence Commission as a whole put the matter in simpler language: "Violence in television programs can and does have adverse effects upon audiences—particularly child audiences."

The blunt truth is there is almost no scientific evidence whatsoever[2] to support the conclusions of either the Task Force or the Commission. Neither the Task Force nor the Commission gathered any evidence about whether children learn, in the short run or the long run, "violent behavior"—*unless what one means by "violent behavior" is a willingness to engage in certain forms of harmless play.*

Bobo Dolls and Electric Shocks

Consider what is perhaps the largest single series of experimental studies, those done by Professor Albert Bandura of Stanford University. One experiment is typical. Nursery school children watched an adult, sometimes in person, sometimes on film, hit and kick a large inflated doll (a "Bobo Doll"). Afterwards the children were subjected to mild forms of frustration (e.g., having favored toys taken away from them). Then they were observed at play in a room filled with toys, among them Bobo Dolls. Children who had previously watched the adult hit or kick the doll were more likely to hit and kick their Bobo Dolls.

Now, if it were in the public interest to protect Bobo Dolls from being hit by children encouraged to play with them, and if hitting Bobo Dolls was a regular feature of television, then admonishing the media to refrain from such features might be in order. Of course, this is not what the Commission had in mind. But what evidence is there from the Bandura experiments that aggression against dolls is ever transferred into aggression against people or

---

2. Editor's Note: This article was written before the publication of the Surgeon General's report on TV violence (see Chapter 3) with its multitude of studies suggesting "harm" from viewing television violence. However, some of the cautions by Professor Wilson in interpreting scientific data might also apply to this latter group of studies.

even that the children in the experiments define hitting a doll as "aggression"? In the Bandura experiments, there is no evidence at all on either score. Richard Goranson, a consultant to the Task Force, faced up to this problem in his essay. He noted that the definition of "aggression" is crucial to the meaning of the experiments. For some, aggression means "the intentional inflicting of pain or injury on another person." Clearly the Bandura experiments do not measure aggression thus defined. Indeed, it is not even necessary to have laboratory experiments to induce in children the kind of "aggression" Bandura observed; all that is necessary is to give them a football on a Saturday afternoon in October and they will supply plenty of aggression. Bandura argues that his definition of *aggression*—performing certain kinds of physical acts, such as hitting or kicking—is appropriate even though it is directed at nonhuman objects, but it is hard to imagine why it *should* be appropriate unless one can show that the harmless play activity will later be transferred to interpersonal situations. But this is precisely what has not been shown.

The experiments that do seem to measure aggression in the sense of intentionally harming others are those of Leonard Berkowitz and R. H. Walters, using electric shocks. The experiments vary in their conduct, and the results are not entirely consistent, but one, by Walters, suggests the general idea. Subjects were told they were participating in a study of how learning was affected by punishment. Each was told to give "electric shocks" at whatever level he wished to another subject (in reality, a confederate of the experimenter who only simulated the effects of shock, every time the "learner" made a mistake). Then the subjects were shown either a film of a knife fight (taken from *West Side Story*) or a nonviolent film. The "learning" experiment was then repeated. This time, subjects who had watched the fight scene gave slightly stronger shocks (about half a setting higher) than those who had watched the nonviolent film. Here, one might argue, is a clear case of media-induced "aggression." But there are at least two caveats: It is by no means clear that the subjects defined what they were doing as "violent"; they were told, after all, they were trying to make people learn better by punishing them for wrong answers (a not uncommon pedagogical technique) and that it was legitimate to do so. Furthermore, no subject could decide (unless he wanted to drop out of the experiment) not to give any shocks; he could only decide at what severity to administer them.

Very few studies have attempted to measure the incidence of genuinely aggressive behavior among persons in real-life settings and to estimate the association, if any, with exposure to media violence. The obstacles in the way of such a study are obvious—the lack of an opportunity for constant observation, the inability to control the viewing habits of respondents, and so forth. At least one such study has been done, however. Seymour Feschback at the University of California at Los Angeles found an opportunity to use laboratorylike controls in a real-world situation. Boys attending seven residential schools in California were divided into two groups; one was allowed to watch in their cottages only television programs drawn from a list of those featuring violence (cowboy, spy, detective, police, and war shows) while the other was allowed to watch only programs on a list containing nonviolent programs. They were required to watch a minimum of six to fourteen hours of TV a week for six weeks. The boys were told that the purpose was to get their ratings of the programs. Personality tests were administered before and after. In addition, the teachers and cottage supervisors filled out daily reports on the boys' behavior at play and in class. Boys who had watched a steady diet of "violent" television displayed no more signs of violent or aggressive behavior than those who had watched only nonviolent programs. On only one measure did a difference appear: boys watching nonviolent programs, when asked to make up stories, made up fewer stories in which fighting took place.

Feschback has been identified with the so-called "catharsis" hypothesis, that is, that observing media violence enables a person to discharge or vicariously satisfy such violent tendencies as he may have. Much of the laboratory experimentation and a good deal of critical commentary has been devoted to disproving this hypothesis, and any fair summary of the state of the art would have to conclude that there is as little evidence that media violence exercises a cathartic effect as there is that it exercises an arousal effect. But the criticisms of the catharsis view have tended to neglect the larger finding of the Feschback studies, namely, that the media's power to induce aggression, reasonably defined, is unproved.

Begging the Questions

A short review cannot treat all the issues raised by the Violence Commission's hasty and unsupported acceptance of the most farfetched interpretations of the aggression experiments. Perhaps the most distressing aspect of the entire enterprise is the tone of advocacy that pervades some of the chapters written by social scientists who seem more interested in finding any data, however badly interpreted, that will support their policy conclusions. Critics of these studies are dismissed in one place as "apologists for the media." Interlaced between paragraphs recounting experiments is one of pure polemic in which the substantive arguments are advanced by asking rhetorical questions. For example, an account of a child who hanged himself apparently trying to imitate Batman leaping through the air moves Professor Alberta Siegel of Stanford to ask, "In what sense is television 'responsible' for this child's violent death?" No answer is offered to this rhetorical question, nor is any indication given of what one would do with any conceivable answer (perhaps ban costumed figures, from Peter Pan to Superman, from flying on television?).

Repeatedly the argument is made that television "teaches," and that to ignore this fact is perilous. After all, advertisers do spend millions on soap commercials because they hope viewers will buy more of their soap; broadcasters do spend millions on violent television programs apparently because they think violence also "sells." If viewers "learn" to buy Oxydol, why shouldn't we expect them to "learn" violence?

But rhetorical queries and easy analogies beg all the interesting questions. There can be little doubt that television has a profound influence on our life and that we learn much, for better or for worse, from it. The crucial question is to specify the conditions under which something is learned and that "something" is then acted upon. It is interesting that neither the Violence Commission nor the Kerner Commission before it tried seriously to answer the question of whether TV broadcasts of an urban riot stimulated persons in the same city to join in, and aroused persons in other cities to start one of their own. (Indeed, the Kerner Commission dodged the question even though it was explicitly put to it by the president of the United States.) I do not pretend to know the answer to the question, though a plausible conjecture is that portraying in exciting terms actions by real people who are described as outraged by their grievances is more likely to affect behavior than fictional portrayals of imaginary events or obviously staged games. All the interesting variables—the degree of legitimacy attached to the act, the reward or penalty that might be expected from committing it, the opportunity for becoming a participant, the subjective definition of the act itself— are precisely the ones that most of the laboratory studies leave out of account. They cannot be brought back into account with analogies between selling soap and selling violence.[3]

Erotic Effects

The Commission on Obscenity, in finding that obscenity had no adverse effects on users, did not rely (as did the Violence Commission) on existing research; instead, it contracted for its own—ten volumes worth. These volumes (the "Technical Reports") are not yet available, and thus a review of these studies must depend for now on the summary of them given in the Commission report itself and especially in the report of the Effects Panel to the Commission. Perhaps because the Commission fostered new research, perhaps because the Effects Panel included two respected sociologists, the central question of how one defines and measures "effects" was given more serious and thoughtful attention by the Obscenity Commission than by the Violence Commission. Three kinds of effects of erotica were examined—on the incidence of sex offenses in the nation as a whole, on the difference (if any) between sex offenders and nonoffenders in their consumption of

3. For a comprehensive and dispassionate review of studies of media effects, see the chapter by Professor Walter Weiss in *The Handbook of Social Psychology,* 2nd ed., vol. V.

erotica, and on the attitudes and behavior of persons exposed to erotica in experimental or laboratory situations.

The research methods employed included opinion surveys that asked people to recall their exposure to erotica and to report on their sexual behavior and attitudes; comparisons of sex offenders and "matched" groups of nonoffenders with respect to their use of erotica; and controlled experiments in which volunteers, usually college students or married couples, were asked to peruse erotic books and films for periods ranging from a single hour-long session to daily sessions of ninety minutes for three weeks. There was little use of clinical studies (e.g., the psychoanalysts' reports) or police and probation officer experiences (e.g., the frequency with which erotic materials are found in the possession of persons arrested for sexual or violent offenses). No studies were done of children.

By these methods, the Commission concluded that exposure to erotica does produce sexual arousal in varying degrees among both men and women, especially among younger, college-educated persons who are nonreligious and sexually experienced; that some persons briefly change their sexual behavior after exposure to erotica but that most do not; that attitudes toward sex and morality do not change significantly after experimental exposure to erotica; that delinquent and nondelinquent youth have been exposed about equally to erotica; that reported sex offenses in Copenhagen decreased coincident with the repeal of antiobscenity statutes; and that recent changes in arrests for sex offenses in the United States show no clear pattern; some, as for forcible rape, have gone up, while others have gone down at a time when obscenity has become much more readily available.

The Effects Panel acknowledges that there are limitations to these findings. Three are of special importance: long-term effects could not be investigated by a Commission with only a two-year existence, there were almost no studies of the effects on children, and the behavior of volunteer (i.e., self-selected) subjects in experiments cannot be generalized to any known population. Despite these limitations, however, the Effects Panel felt confident in concluding that if a case against pornography is to be made, "it will have to be made on grounds other than demonstrated effects of a damaging personal or social nature." Taking the findings as a whole, "no dangerous effects have been demonstrated on any of the populations which were studied."

Dissents to these findings were filed by three commission members. Two commissioners wrote a detailed critique questioning the reliability and interpretation of the empirical studies; unfortunately, the issues raised cannot be resolved until the full Technical Reports become publicly available. One dissent, by Charles H. Keating, Jr., the head of Citizens for a Decent Literature, Inc., and the sole appointee of President Nixon to the Commission, is an intemperate, unpleasantly *ad hominem* creed in which interesting and perhaps important objections are frequently obscured by a ranting tone.

An Unsettled Matter

For many persons, the social science findings endorsed by a majority of the Commission's members will settle the matter, especially since any effort to maintain even the much-weakened antiobscenity statutes that now survive requires one to support the proposition, abhorrent to many, that the law may rightly proscribe the distribution of certain kinds of books and pictures. Perhaps it is this that leads some to adopt apparently different standards by which to evaluate the effects of obscenity as opposed to violence. Professor Otto Larsen, for example, served as a member of both the Obscenity Commission and as a consultant to the Media Task Force of the Violence Commission. In his former capacity, he finds no justification for any restriction whatsoever on the sale or display of obscenity to adults or to children, even though the Technical Reports contain almost no experimental or clinical studies of the effects of obscenity on children and despite the fact that most Americans no doubt find the display of obscenity in public places to unwitting parties quite objectionable. In his latter capacity, he submitted a paper to the Violence Commission that concluded that laboratory research "mounts a strong indictment of media performance" with respect to the portrayal of violence and that while the present state of knowledge leaves something to be desired, "enough is known" to be sure that we are running "grave risks" in a policy of the "indiscriminate use of violence." And this despite the largely irrelevant, sometimes trivial findings of research on media violence. The reason for the apparently different standards of judgment may be that to control obscenity, "books" must be "censored," while to control violence it is only necessary that the "media" be "regulated." (Professors publish books; they rarely own TV stations.) Or perhaps the argument is that, while the contemplation of the obscene may produce many effects, they are not particularly harmful, whereas exposure to portrayals of violence may produce a few effects which are very harmful. Stated another way, the expected disutility of even a slight risk of a great harm (watching violence) is more serious than a substantial risk of a trivial harm (reading obscenity).

The question, then, is whether the harm from obscenity is trivial or great. On this question, the findings of the Commission are not nearly so conclusive as they are made out to be—provided one adopts a proper measure of "harm." If by harm one means the probability of committing a rape, then it is not surprising that exposure to erotica does not "cause" the act. Criminal actions generally, as the Effects Panel points out, are the product of many influences—social class, peer group relationships, intelligence, early family experiences, and the like. As for national rates of sex crimes, these vary enormously with the changing propensity to report sexual assaults and provide no reliable measure of an "effect" which can be correlated with the availability of erotica, even assuming that such availability could itself be measured. (The majority of the Commission believe that the study of sex

302

crimes in Copenhagen satisfactorily controlled for the propensity to report, but the minority interprets the same data as showing that certain kinds of crimes did not decrease at all with the legalization of obscenity and that changes in other crime rates can be explained by a decreased willingness to call the police. Not having the Copenhagen study available, I can offer no judgment as to who is correct in this.)

The laboratory experiments provide perhaps the weakest evidence. Though such experiments have on occasion provided revealing insights into human behavior, the rigor with which they are conducted is purchased at the price of unreality. One cannot simulate in the laboratory the existence or nonexistence of a lifelong exposure to or preoccupation with obscenity, any more than one can simulate a lifelong exposure to racist or radical opinions. Imagine what one would think of an experiment in which volunteer college students were exposed, for an hour a day for three weeks, to the *Protocols of the Elders of Zion, Mein Kampf,* and an apology for slavery. No one would suppose that more than small and transient changes in behavior towards Jews and blacks, if any changes at all, would occur. Similarly, we should not be surprised that no enduring changes in sexual behavior and attitudes result from equivalent exposure to erotica, any more than we should have been surprised to learn from Professor Feschback that exposure to television violence for a few weeks caused no important changes in the behavior of young boys.

A more revealing experiment would be to compare the attitudes and behavior of a group of children, reared in a community with easy and frequent access to erotica (or media violence, or whatever) to those of a group, carefully matched in all other respects, reared in a community with no access, or only occasional and furtive access, to the obscene (or the violent). Obviously such an experiment would have to last over many years—perhaps two generations—in order to control for prior parental attitudes; and the subjects would have to be carefully monitored to insure that experimental conditions were not violated by, for example, moving to another town or taking frequent trips to New York City to patronize the bookstores on 42nd Street. Just as obviously, such an experiment is utterly absurd even to contemplate; no one, fortunately, can control human lives to that degree in this society or perhaps in any other.

The nearest approximation to such a study would be a comparison of various cultures, some of which maintain a taboo against written and pictorial erotica and some of which do not, to discover what differences, if any, are thereby produced in the moral capacity, social vitality, and political stability of the societies. But even here inferences would be hard to draw—societies differing in one respect are likely to differ in many others as well, and settling upon some measure of effect (what is "moral capacity" anyway?) would be at best controversial and at worst impossible. It is interesting, however, to note that scholars whose job it is to compare cultures appear more willing than other social scientists to support the prohibition against obscenity (Arnold Toynbee, J. D. Unwin, and Pitirim Sorokin have been cited in this connection).

The Limits of Social Science

In short, social science probably cannot answer the questions put to it by those who wish to rest the case for or against censorship on the proved effects of exposure to obscenity, media violence, scurrilous political literature, or whatever. In a society in which the obscene or the violent is not part of the regular literary diet of the young, the furtive or occasional consumption of such material may have little effect or may be at best "one factor among many." In a society in which the obscene or the violent is everywhere on display, whether any given individual is or is not exposed to, say, a dirty book may be less important than the perceptions of life and morality he draws from a community obsessed with the carnal or bestial. In either case, there is not likely to be a significant correlation between *individual* exposure and *individual* attitudes or behavior. Even where the obscene is commonplace, there are likely to be important differences attributable to social class, intelligence, and family structure in the extent to which individuals display a preoccupation with that which is base or ignoble; and thus a social scientific study of the sources of antisocial behavior would probably conclude that these differences in class or family, being the correlates of behavior, were thus the "causes" of such behavior. It would have been as difficult for a social scientist in Nero's Rome to prove that a person who himself did not read erotic stone tablets was thereby benefited as it would have been for a social scientist in Cromwell's London to prove that a person who did read dirty books was thereby harmed; yet most historians would agree that the different attitudes toward public obscenity in Nero's Rome and Cromwell's London are not irrelevant to understanding these two very different societies.

Social science at its best seeks to show a relationship among two or more variables that cannot be attributed to chance or to intervening variables. Showing such relationships persuasively is easiest when the variables can be unambiguously defined (e.g., voting for a Democrat or Republican for president or earning over $10,000 a year) and the variables believed to have causal power are not highly intercorrelated with other variables (e.g., physical height tends to be independent of intelligence or social class, but education tends to be covariant with income, occupation, and race). When social scientists are asked to measure consequences in terms of a badly conceptualized or hard-to-measure "effect" of one among many highly interrelated "causes," all of which operate (if at all) over long periods of time, they tend to discover that there is no relationship or at best a weak and contingent one. This is one of the reasons, for example, for the controversy over human intelligence; the measures of intelligence are much disputed and the correlates of intelligence (race, class, family status, diet, or whatever) are themselves so intercorrelated as to make it hazardous to guess which one or which few variables, and in what temporal sequence, account for changes in I.Q. Or another example: social science studies of the effects of governmental interventions of a broad and diffuse nature (building "better schools" or running a "community action program" or enrolling students in Project Head Start) on various vague social objectives (improving education or strengthening the sense of community) are usually inconclusive and controversial.

The irony is that social science may be weakest in detecting the broadest and most fundamental changes in social values, precisely because they *are* broad and fundamental. Intuitively, it seems plausible that the media and other forces have contributed powerfully over the last generation to changes in popular attitudes about sexuality, political action, and perhaps even violence. But for lack of a control group it is unlikely that this will ever be proved scientifically. Social science may be better at showing the effects of various forces on relatively small and specially selected populations—for example, the effects of prison or childhood experiences on delinquents or the effects of various stimuli (including the media) on phobic persons.

If by its nature social science can be of little help on policy questions of the broader sort, to what mode of inquiry should a reasonable man turn to decide on the issue of censorship (or "regulation")? Reo Christenson has suggested that if social science cannot settle the matter on the grounds of consequences, the average American cannot be blamed for concluding that the views of the majority should prevail—and the majority clearly wants some form of restriction. A person who interprets the First Amendment solely by applying the "clear and present danger" test would of course find a majoritarian solution unacceptable, but it is by no means obvious that a showing of clear and present danger should be the test for all forms of writing and speech—the test was devised for gauging the reasonableness of limitations on *political* writing and speech.

Even the Obscenity Commission, despite its claim that it rests its recommendation for the abolition of restrictions on the distribution of obscenity to adults on the showing of no adverse effect, is not prepared to accept the full implications of that position. In the section immediately following that concerning effects, the Commission writes:

Regardless of the effects of exposure, there is still a considerable amount of uneasiness about explicit sexual materials and their pervasiveness in our society. . . . [But] it is often overlooked that legal control on the availability of explicit sexual materials is not the only, or necessarily the most effective, method of dealing with these materials.

The Commission goes on to note, in generally approving tones, these other ways of "dealing" with erotica, such as industry self-regulation (among comic book publishers and broadcasters, for example) and the possibility of effective citizen action groups at the community level. But if obscenity is not harmful, on what grounds are such informal—and no doubt effective—controls over what we may read or see to be condoned? If no harm ensues, should not this extra-legal form of censorship be sharply criticized? Clearly, the Commission here—as with the public display of erotica and with its circulation among juveniles—is deferring, not to social science, but to popular feelings.

The Ultimate Criteria

It would be easy to dismiss deference to popular feelings by either proponents or opponents of censorship as an unworthy catering to mere prejudice or shallow opinion. And surely in the area of free speech properly conceived—as it relates to argument and instruction, rather than simply entertainment—no one (especially no professor) would want to take popular feelings at any moment as a decisive guide to what should be permissible. But in the absence of social science evidence that is conclusive, and confining our attention to matters of popular amusement, the deeply held convictions of citizens about the relationship between amusement and morality are by no means irrelevant or trivial. As Professor Harry M. Clor writes in *Obscenity and Public Morality:*

People are influenced by what they think others believe and particularly by what they think are the common standards of the community. There are few individuals among us whose basic beliefs are the result of their own reasoning and whose moral opinions do not require the support of some stable public opinion. The free circulation of obscenity can, in time, lead many to the conclusion that there is nothing wrong with the values implicit in it—since their open promulgation is tolerated by the public. They will come to the conclusion that public standards have changed—or that there are no public standards. Private standards are hard put to withstand the effects of such an opinion.

I do not know whether the consequences for private standards of changed public standards will be as Clor predicts. I do know that I have seen no evidence to disprove his view and that many public policies—such as those against racial or sexual discrimination—are based in part precisely on the presumed educative force of law.

I happen to think (though I cannot prove it) that certain kinds of political speeches and writings do inestimable harm to our society; but I also believe that no one should be trusted with the power to decide which speeches and writings those are and thus which should or should not be allowed. I also think as a parent whose children watch Saturday morning cartoons and

Sunday afternoon football on television that they are not in the slightest harmed by what they see; I cannot prove it, and I may be quite naive, but I cannot conceive of a study on this subject that I would find more persuasive than my own knowledge of my children's attitudes and behavior. I also do not want my children to be exposed to sex by way of easily available materials that portray what should be tender and private as base and brutal. I also confess to being quite uncertain as to what forms of legal restraint, if any, this requires. I know that they will encounter prurient materials furtively and that does not trouble me. Perhaps it should; or perhaps I should be worried that I cannot "prove" my belief that human character is, in the long run, affected not by occasional, furtive experiences but by whether society does or does not state that there is an important difference between the loathsome and the decent. I would, for example, want my government to say that race is not to be used as a basis for granting or denying access to public facilities even if social science could not show that such racial restrictions harm individual Negroes—indeed, even if social science could show that such restrictions *benefit* Negroes. A public commitment to equal opportunity and public opposition to disgusting racial distinctions should be made as a matter of right and propriety, whatever the immediate effects; I would also imagine that, over the long term, such public commitments would play a part in shaping individual attitudes in what I take to be a desirable direction.

The failure of the Violence Commission is that it relied, in the case of its task force on the media, on bad (or badly interpreted) social science; the weakness of the Obscenity Commission is that it relied too exclusively on social science research even though that research, within the limited framework of each study, was on the whole quite unexceptionable. The general circumstances under which public decisions can be made—or should be made—on the basis of social scientific findings is by no means clear. It is not hard to imagine issues on which such research could have depositive if not determinative weight and others on which it should have little or no weight. Regrettably, there has been of late a growing unwillingness to make such distinctions, but this may reflect not so much on excessive enthusiasm with the policy value of social science as a general inability to make distinctions of any kind.

In the cases of violence and obscenity, it is unlikely that social science can either show harmful effects or prove that there are no harmful effects. It is unlikely, in short, that considerations of utility or disutility can be governing. These are moral issues and ultimately all judgments about the acceptability of restrictions on various media will have to rest on political and philosophical considerations.

Without Redeeming Social Value?*

Reo M. Christenson

Tougher censorship laws for America? Speaking as a liberal and long-time member of the American Civil Liberties Union (ACLU), I believe stronger pornography legislation is clearly needed.

To most intellectuals these days, censorship in sexual matters is firmly identified with prim little old ladies, country bumpkins, Bob Jones College, backwater conservatism, cultural yahoos—and Puritans in general. (A Puritan is someone whose views on sex are less permissive than yours.) Historian Barbara Tuchman (*The Guns of August*) has observed that prominent writers who favor some censorship where sex is concerned are afraid to speak out openly. Attorney Richard Kuh documents the point in a book which has received far too little attention—*Foolish Figleaves.* (Kenyon political scientist Harry Clor's *Obscenity and Public Morality* deserves a bow, also.)

The case for stricter censorship of pornography runs as follows. More than three-fourths of the American people want it, according to a Gallup Poll in June, 1969. They are affronted by books, magazines, movies, plays, erotic displays, pictures, and records which vulgarize, desecrate, and cheapen sex, or which encourage or glamorize deviant sexual behavior. The Middle Americans—and many others—have a deep-rooted suspicion that all of this will undermine certain moral restraints believed to be essential to the public weal.

*Original title: "Censorship of Pornography, Yes."

Reo M. Christenson is a professor of political science at Miami University at Oxford, Ohio. He received his Ph.D. at the University of Michigan in 1953. At one time he was an editorial writer for the *Toledo Blade* and has authored or coauthored such books as *Ideologies and Modern Politics, Voice of the People: Readings in Public Opinion and Propaganda, Challenge and Decision: Political Issues of our Time,* and *The Brannan Plan: A Study in Farm Politics.* In addition he has produced a score or so of articles in popular and professional journals.

There is no way to proving whether this suspicion is or is not well-founded. But the public's fears about excessive sexual permissiveness are supported more than they are challenged by such inadequate empirical evidence that we have. In *The Sexual Wilderness,* Vance Packard summarizes the findings of those academicians who have given the most attention to the relation between sexual permissiveness and the progress of society as a whole. He cites *Sex and Culture* by former Oxford Professor J. D. Unwin, whose massive studies of eighty primitive and civilized societies reveal a distinct correlation between increasing sexual freedom and social decline. The more sexually permissive a society becomes, Unwin says, the less creative energy it exhibits and the slower its movement toward rationality, philosophical speculation, and advanced civilization.

Harvard sociologist Pitirim Sorokin agrees with Unwin that sexual restraints promote cultural progress; in *The American Sexual Revolution* he contends that immoral and antisocial behavior increases with cultural permissiveness toward the erotic subarts. In an article in the *New York Times* magazine entitled "Why I Dislike Western Civilization," May 10, 1964, Arnold Toynbee argued that a culture which postpones rather than stimulates sexual experience in young adults is a culture most prone to progress.

In another article in the *New York Times* magazine, Bruno Bettelheim, the noted psychoanalyst, recently observed: "If a society does not taboo sex, children will grow up in relative sex freedom. But so far, history has shown that such a society cannot create culture or civilization; it remains primitive." Sorokin asserts, ". . . There is no example of a community which has retained its high position on the cultural scale after less rigorous sexual customs have replaced more restricting ones."

Many social scientists doubt that contemporary research skills are capable of either affirming or denying these charges. The Middle American, then, can hardly be blamed for concluding that, in the absence of scientific proof one way or the other, majority views should prevail. In *The Common Law,* the late Oliver Wendell Holmes, celebrated Justice of the United States Supreme Court, declared that "the first requirement of a sound body of law is that it should correspond with the actual feelings and demands of the community, whether right or wrong." And Justice John M. Harlan, in Alberts v. California, declared, "The state can reasonably draw the inference that over a long period of time the indiscriminate dissemination of materials, the essential character of which is to degrade sex, will have an eroding effect on moral standards." Harlan has thus established the crucial link between dubious practices and reasonable law.

But should majorities deprive minorities of free expression, whatever their fears may be? When the First Amendment says, "Congress shall make no law . . . abridging freedom of speech or press," should it not mean what it says—no law?

The First Amendment does not really mean "no law" and never has. We have had a score of respectable laws abridging freedom of speech and press, some dating back to the earliest days of our republic. A few of these forbid libel, perjury, contempt of court, incitement to violence, disrespect toward commanding officers, and copyright violation. The First Amendment itself limits free expression; by implication, the "establishment of religion" clause forbids the advocacy of religious doctrines in public schools. The true meaning of the First Amendment is that Congress may place no *unreasonable* restraints on freedom of speech and press. Our entire history attests to this view.

The drafters of the Constitution probably and properly intended an absolute ban on efforts by the Government to forbid the dissemination of any political, economic, religious, or social ideas. John Stuart Mill and others have made an overwhelming cogent case for such freedom; no equally persuasive case has been made for the unlimited freedom of commercial entertainment. There is a right, therefore, to advocate the most disgusting forms of sexual perversion—so long as the proponent is clearly attempting to persuade rather than to entertain commercially. But the commercial entertainment cannot logically claim the same constitutional protection as normal political discourse.

To the extent that entertainment and persuasion are combined, the case for constitutional protection is proportionately enhanced. But no one has yet demonstrated that the effective dissemination of ideas demands the use of pornographic techniques. The latter are conceivably of peripheral persuasive value but surely no more than that. The marginal loss of free speech involved in sensible pornography legislation, as with other reasonable restrictions on free speech, is more than counterbalanced by the protection of children and the creation of an environment, especially for children, which is more conducive to responsible sex behavior.

The ACLU takes no absolutist position on the First Amendment, but it does oppose limitations on speech and press unless it can be proved that a given expression creates a clear and present danger that it will trigger an act which society has a right to forbid. The ACLU is also convinced that no scientifically valid proof exists that the consumption of pornography produces criminal behavior.

Obviously, the ACLU wants society to consider only short-term effects since it regards long-term effects as unknowable. The truth is that short-term effects are also unknowable. The difficulties of delving into the depths of human motivations and sorting out from the richly tangled psychic undergrowth those strands which "cause" a criminal act are so formidable that root causes or even the relative importance of contributory factors may never be satisfactorily established.

Unhappily, all of the major premises on which our society rests derive from the realm of intuition—the viscera. Can anyone *prove* that the family is a desirable institution? That higher education promotes human welfare?

That technology makes men happier? That love is better than hate? That democracy is superior to dictatorship? None of these is provable. But this does not stop us from acting on our best judgment, knowing that all human judgment is fallible. If, then, the regulation of pornography comes down to a matter of visceral hunches, why should not the majority of viscera prevail?

Is "pornography" such an imprecise term that it lacks sufficient clarity to meet the "due process" test?

Current state laws could be updated and made more explicit if they were refined to forbid actual or simulated exhibitions of sexual intercourse or sexual perversion on stage or screen—or pictorial representations thereof in other media—when such exhibitions or pictorial representations are primarily intended for commercial entertainment rather than for education.

If the emerging vogue for making a fast buck by portraying such scenes on stage and screen is not an example of moral degradation, that term must be bereft of all meaning. There are limits of human decency, and these limits are being transgressed more blatantly year after year in the shameless commercial exploitation of man's baser instincts. Admittedly a few playwrights or motion picture directors may be able to handle these scenes in a sensitive and illuminating manner, but for every artist who can do so, a hundred entrepreneurs will use such themes in a fashion which can only cheapen and coarsen sex. The interests of the general American public are considerably more important than gratifying the erotic-esthetic yearnings of the avant-garde.

It should be noted that statutory-judicial definitions or pornography are rather vague. But the same applies to numerous other laws. The Sherman antitrust law forbids monopolies. What is a monopoly? When one firm—or an oligopoly—controls 30% of the output in a field? Fifty percent? Seventy-five percent? Ninety percent? No one knows, and the Supreme Court has never been able to tell us.

What is an "unfair trade practice"? What is a merger which "substantially" reduces competition? What is "negligent" manslaughter? When is guilt proved beyond a "reasonable" doubt?

In terms of imprecision, then, pornography statutes are no more defective than many other well-accepted and adjudicable laws. At one end of their administered continuum, it is clear that a publisher or dealer has not broken the law and no one will take him to court. At the other end, he has so clearly broken the law that he will not bother to appeal the case. But movement toward the center leads to more difficult decisions, until a middle zone is reached in which it is anyone's guess whether the courts will find the defendant guilty. Decisions in this zone inevitably entail a certain amount of arbitrariness and raw subjectivity. Yet those indignant over the lack of specificity in obscenity laws are quite complacent about vagueness in laws they approve.

It is often argued that judges have no special expertise on sexual proprieties. True enough, but if they can bring no special wisdom to bear, they are likely to bring moderation to bear. And that is no mean asset. Furthermore, citizens will accept decisions by judges which they would not so readily accept from others. In brief, entrusting these decisions to the judiciary is a good practical solution to the problem.

Since negative judicial decisions on pornography are sure to be subjected to scathing attacks by civil libertarians—as judges well know—there is much more likelihood of judicial leniency than of excessive restraint. Perhaps it is best to err on the side of leniency, while imposing sufficiently severe penalties where guilt is found to discourage those who specialize in exploring and exploiting the margins of decency.

It is easy to produce a long list of worthwhile books which have been banned and to make censors look ridiculous in the light of modern opinion. But each generation has a right to set its own standards, and if pornography criteria change from time to time, the same is true of legal criteria in other fields. A thousand examples could be cited, including such notable constitutional clauses as "equal protection of the laws" and "the establishment of religion."

Of course, critics are inclined to evaluate censorship solely by its "failures," the banning of works of genuine merit. But it is unfair to exhibit the "failures" of censorship without considering the other side of the coin. If all of the loathsome materials which officials have confiscated and the law has discouraged were balanced against the mistakes, the over-all results would look much less damning of censorship than many English professors would have us believe.

Opponents of pornography censorship sometimes contend that the state should not try to be the moral custodian of the people. Nor should a majority seek to impose its moral standards on a minority, it is said.

Yet *every* criminal law represents a moral judgment. And laws typically constitute a coercion of the minority by the majority. Presumably bigamists resent laws against bigamy, polygamists oppose laws against polygamy, and sexual exhibitionists dislike laws against indecent exposure. Their objections are not decisive once society regards these restrictions as reasonable. The same is true of pornography laws.

If the home, the church, and the school provided adequate sex education and moral training, there would be less need for pornography laws. But the law must deal with social realities, not Utopian visions. Since millions of children receive virtually no moral training or sex education, the nation is obliged to rely partly upon law for their protection.

Those who say, "Don't tell *me* what I can see or read," are consulting their impulses rather than the larger interests of society. A socially responsible person will forego the indulgence of a desire if the policy permitting that indulgence jeopardizes the well-being of others.

Most of us, it should be emphasized, welcome today's freedom to discuss sexual questions and seek greater sexual satisfactions through increased education and scientific knowledge. Nor will the censorship envisaged herein interfere with this solubrious development. It is a mistake, however, to believe that the commercial exploitation of sex frees us from crippling inhibitions and promotes a healthy attitude toward sex. Pornography is more likely to deposit ugly images in the consciousness or subconsciousness of the young than it is to contribute toward the information of a wholesome attitude toward sex.

The New York Academy of Medicine declared in 1963 that reading salacious literature "encourages a morbid preoccupation with sex and interferes with the development of a healthy attitude and respect for the opposite sex." Certainly if young people are stimulated to experiment with forms of perversion before they understand their implications, traumatic experiences may occur which leave them psychologically scarred for life. Parents who strongly oppose the introduction of unsolicited pornography into their homes display an eminently sensible attitude toward the protection of their children.

Sexually abnormal persons who "need" pornography probably need psychiatric care even more. However, since they are unlikely to get the latter, it would probably be unwise to try to eliminate all pornography. If dealers do not solicit or sell to children, do not advertise their wares, and limit their sales to adults who seek them out, perhaps it is best to leave such traffic alone. Sometimes it is prudent to temper the administration of law with a realistic regard for human weakness. The Greek rule applies—"nothing too much."

Are pornography laws unenforceable? Do they tend to make pornography more attractive, since it becomes forbidden fruit?

Enforcement is admittedly difficult. We have not been able to prevent drunken driving, either, or supermarket theft, or income tax evasion, but we do not proceed to make them legal. Instead, we seek more effective enforcement measures.

Laws may make pornography somewhat more attractive to certain persons; so do laws against vandalism and speeding and heaven knows how many other misdeeds. In any case, the repeal of pornography laws would not eliminate the social disapproval associated with the behavior involved. This social disapproval would continue the "forbidden fruit" effect, even in the absence of law.

As for oft-cited Denmark, which has repealed all prohibitions against written pornography (and against pictures sold to persons over sixteen years old), the trial period is far too short to enable us to draw any firm conclusions. Certain kinds of pornography have experienced declining sales; other kinds are flourishing even more. *Newsweek* has called Copenhagen "a veritable showcase of pornography," bristling with shops specializing in every conceivable form of erotic lingerie, sadomasochistic devices, sexual

314

stimulators, and pornographic jewelry. This may be an appealing demonstration of the delights of a free and liberated society, but a dissenting view is also conceivable.

Paradoxically, the existence of censorship probably assures greater freedom in America than its absence. Morris Ernst, the noted civil liberties lawyer, in *Censorship: The Search for the Obscene,* agrees that the decline of governmental censorship has led to an increase in private vigilantism. If, somehow, the tiny minority (Gallup estimates about 6%) which wants no censorship were to have their way, it would be an open invitation for vigilante groups to take over. Outraged at the irresponsibles, the Middle American would employ extralegal pressures as a substitute for law. And a sorry substitute they would be. Controlling pornography by legal means and orderly institutions gives us the best assurance that society's concern will be dealt with in a civilized manner.

To those in the entertainment world, freedom is the supreme value. Whatever makes men more free is believed *ipso facto* good. But freedom is not, standing alone, the *summum bonum* of human society. If it were, we would need no government. Men once saw *laissez-faire* as the culmination of economic progress, only to discover that commercial greed was not quite an adequate guide for achieving human welfare. When freedom is not accompanied by a reasonable amount of self-restraint and social responsibility, it can become a destructive force. I see neither this self-restraint nor this sense of social responsibility being manifested in much of the entertainment world. The most profound (although often subliminal) message which much of modern music, movies, and literature convey to the young is, "Let 'er rip."

A society can tolerate only so much emotional turmoil, so much disruption, so many assaults upon its sensibilities and its mores. At some point, the public's patience becomes exhausted; it cries, "Enough." This dénouement may not be far off in America. When it comes, the entertainment industry should be assigned its full share of responsibility in the area of pornographic presentations for the general repression which follows. (Those who condone gross social injustices and those who employ violence for political ends admittedly deserve a larger share of blame.)

For the record, I find much to applaud in our revolutionary age: the refusal to support a senseless war; the challenge to the military budget and to certain military assumptions; the so-called "equality revolution"; the demand for justice to the blacks and the poor; the call for sweeping educational reforms; the insistence on higher standards of public morality. But the stresses and strains involved in these movements are hard enough for the body politic to bear. Add to these a dubious sexual revolution powerfully stimulated by the entertainment industry, and society may be bearing an overload of tension.

A final word. Maybe all the "dumb people" are not so dumb after all.

Maybe they are right in sensing that sex needs to be treated with some caution, that sexual privacy needs to be preserved from commercial contamination, that sexual relations must not be divested of all sanctity, all mystery, and reduced to the level of leer and titter.

It is a disturbingly democratic idea that the common man just might be smarter, now and then, than many of our avant-garde intellectuals.

Obscenity and Freedom of Expression

Harry M. Clor

A new consideration has been introduced into the long-standing controversy over moral censorship and freedom of expression. Most people who write and debate about these matters have now come to agree that we are living through moral changes of such a magnitude as to warrant the designation "sexual revolution." There is, of course, little agreement about the value of this "revolution"—its potentialities for good or evil in our lives. Such ethical questions, questions about what is good for us and what is bad for us as human beings, are difficult to resolve with any certitude. Yet we cannot avoid grappling with the ethical issues if we are to arrive at reasoned judgments about the controversy over obscenity and about the sexual revolution which is now inextricably involved in that controversy.

The sexual revolution (or "the moral and sexual revolution," as it is sometimes called) may be said to have two distinguishing features—one in the realm of expression and the other in the realm of conduct. In recent years we have been witnessing a rapidly accelerating trend toward increasingly candid, or blatant, presentations of sexual and related subjects in literature and the arts, in public displays and advertising, and in public discourse generally. And, in the realm of conduct, we have been witnessing a similar trend toward sexual freedom, or promiscuity, among the young and in large sections of adult society as well.

Harry M. Clor is professor and chairman of the Department of Political Science at Kenyon College. From 1969 through 1972 he was director of the Public Affairs Conference Center there. He obtained his B.A. at Lawrence College in Wisconsin in 1951 and his Ph.D. from the University of Chicago in 1967. He is a member of the NAACP and Freedom House and is a Phi Beta Kappa. He has written or edited several books focusing on civil disorder, censorship, freedom of expression, obscenity and public morality, and the concept of a "radical democracy."

317

Yet, in spite of this apparent moral and sexual revolution, the law continues to be concerned with the restraint of certain kinds of literature, motion pictures, and public performances as "obscene." The Supreme Court, in its Roth, Manual Enterprises, Jacobellis, and Fanny Hill decisions, has steadily and sharply confined the operation of obscenity laws. But the law may still act to prevent the commercial distribution of materials which, among other things, predominantly "appeal to prurient interests." It is an interesting question why legislative majorities (backed, according to most available evidence, by substantial popular majorities [1]) continue to pass and support such laws. It is highly probable that the expanding market and multitudes of willing customers for erotic literature are provided, in part, from among the popular majorities that regularly indicate their support for censorship. The advocate of the sexual revolution and his frequent ally, the ideological libertarian, are inclined to explain this paradox as a result of sheer hypocrisy. Large sections of the American public are unwilling to acknowledge in public the sexual passions they indulge in private. But a somewhat different explanation is possible. As a private individual, the average American may be quite susceptible to the allure of prurient appeals. But in his capacity as a citizen and member of the public, and when called upon to render a judgment in that capacity, he still clings to the belief that there is something wrong with blatant appeals to prurient interest.

But what could be the matter with a prurient appeal? If "prurience" means, as courts have said, an arousal of "lust," and lust means sexual desire, what could possibly be wrong with that? We have it not only from the moral revolutionaries but also from the highest medical authorities that sexual desire is quite normal and healthy, and that it is the repression thereof which is unhealthy and productive of troubles. Why, then, should we disapprove of literature that stimulates a desire without which, as Judge Jerome Frank has seen fit to remind us, the human race would not survive? [2] And should we not positively rejoice at the open and candid treatment of a subject so long shrouded in morbid secrecy?

Academic discussions of this issue frequently suffer from overabstraction; overabstraction in deference, perhaps, to what remains of nonrevolutionary morality. The following are some more-or-less (but not wholly) concrete examples of the literature now prevalent as a result of the new candor and the new freedom of expression.

The "adult book shops" now flourishing in many of our larger cities feature what is called "spreader" pictorial magazines. These involve total nudity, very explicit portrayal of the female sexual organs (usually with the

---

1. The Commission on Obscenity and Pornography believes it has evidence to the contrary. See Appendix to this essay.

2. Judge Jerome Frank, United States v. Roth.

legs spread wide apart), and naked men and women posed together in provocative postures that stop just short of actual intercourse. Some of the magazines specialize in homosexual or lesbian portrayals. Often a large number of the "adult" shops are clustered in a central section of the city, with window displays advertising quite openly what is to be found inside.

One of the many New York "exploitation film" theaters just off Times Square recently featured a movie called *The Morbid Snatch*. Two men conceive and execute a plan to capture a young girl, imprison her, and compel her to submit to sexual acts of various sorts. The girl is drugged, confined in a basement, stripped naked, and subjected to sexual intercourse, first with one of the men, then with a lesbian, and then with both the man and the lesbian simultaneously. Periodically, the camera focuses very closely upon the sexual organs of all participants. Periodically also the girl (whose age is, perhaps by intention, difficult to determine; she could be as young as sixteen or as old as twenty-five) is represented as responding erotically to these acts. The sexual scenes, and preparation for them, constitute practically the sole content and surely the sole interest of this film. A companion film about twenty minutes long consists of nothing but close-up shots of a nude woman masturbating. The "coming attractions" promise films devoted to rape, violence, mass orgies, and the intercourse of women with apes.

Finally, consider the now standard theme of a whole *genre* of contemporary paperback novelettes—the systematic violation, humiliation, and domination of women. There are several variations of this theme. A recent novel, *The Orgiasts*, features the gradual introduction of a respectable woman to the practices of a "sex club," and her eventual complete subjection to the will and desires of its members. The plot is typical: by a combination of seduction and compulsion, the woman is induced to desire her own subjection. This is how it is done. Stage one: seduction. Stage two: she begs to be violated. Stage three: she is drawn irresistibly into deviant practices with multiparticipation. Stage four: she has lost all will of her own and has become a tool at the disposal of the group. In conjunction with vivid description of the verbal side of this process, there is a detailed portrayal of its physical side—the woman's sexual organs and contortions while under the domination of passion.

Another variation on this theme involves heavy emphasis upon violence in connection with the sexual act—the explicit interweaving of brutality and sexuality. In this kind of scenario, the woman is literally beaten into submission and is vividly portrayed as desiring and inviting this treatment. A recent novelette carries this principle to its utmost logical conclusion; the hero seduces women, tortures them, and then kills them.

Let us return to the original question. What is wrong with appealing to prurient interests? What, if anything, is the matter with the literature described above? If there is nothing the matter with it, then reasonable men are not entitled to be shocked by its relatively sudden liberation from social and moral restraints. Now, the moralist is inclined to answer our question with terms such as "smut," "filth," and "moral pollution," and many citizens are inclined to simply leave it at that. But revulsion and outrage do not constitute arguments. Common decency might suggest an obvious answer, but we can no longer take the claims of common decency for granted. This is a profoundly skeptical age in which, with regard to moral matters at least, little can be taken for granted. The rising generation of youth and many of their teachers do not accept the traditional ethical assumptions. Today's intellectual climate imposes a heavy burden of argument upon anyone who would defend any aspect of traditional morality.

Our question has two dimensions and can be broken down into two distinct inquiries. First, one must explore the nature of a "prurient appeal" and the intrinsic qualities of materials describable as prurient. And then, one must consider what social harms, if any, can result from the widespread circulation of such materials. If it can be reasonably concluded that legitimate community interests are endangered by obscenity, then there is a further question to be asked. What may organized society do to protect these interests?

The reader will note that I have presented my examples of obscene literature in a certain order and progressive sequence. They constitute a continuum of prurient appeals, beginning with those that arouse "lust" but do not portray violence, and concluding with those clearly recognizable as outright sadism. The intermediate forms portray sexual acts involving some degree of compulsion or constraint, but they do not portray torture or murder, and the infliction of physical pain does not constitute their explicit erotic appeal.

Now some of my readers may wish to argue as follows. There is nothing wrong with the "adult" pictorial magazines or with any other erotic material that simply appeals to normal sexual desire, but sadism is justly condemned. If moral judgment is to be rendered upon literature, it should be rendered at that point in our continuum where violence enters and is made sensually alluring. This argument relies on the distinction between erotic literature which portrays and, hence, stimulates normal sexuality and that which portrays and, hence, stimulates some perverted, distorted, or ugly form of sexuality.

This distinction has some merits but it is inadequate. It is inadequate for description and evaluation of our literary examples, and it is inadequate as a psychological analysis of what is going on between the reader or viewer and the prurient materials. Whatever is the perversion, distortion, or ugliness of outright sado-masochistic pornography, that perversion, distortion, or ugliness is also present in the "adult" pictorials, in a film or highly specific description of people copulating (however normally), and in the seduction scenes of *The Orgiasts.* The last literary items in our spectrum represent only the most extreme and flagrant form of an appeal that was present in all the

320

items and which is present in all literature properly called "obscene."

We are on the way to understanding the nature of that appeal when we consider how the woman in the "spreader" pictorial is presented to the viewer. First of all, and most obviously, she is presented naked. What is normally concealed, and exposed only in private situations, is wholly exposed and placed conspicuously on public display. Secondly, she is presented as nothing more than an object for the gratification of the viewer's passions. She is not a woman but a plaything. All the indicators of human personality have been removed from the picture. What the observer sees is a person who has been stripped down to a mere body at his disposal. It can even be said that the body itself has been stripped down to a sexual organ; it is not the human body but an organ upon which the eye of the viewer is focused.[3]

Essentially the same kind of voyeurism is solicited by the typical exploitation film and pornographic novel. The viewer of *The Morbid Snatch* is invited to enjoy the spectacle of a young woman reduced, as it were, to her parts and to a helpless object of manipulation. In *The Orgiasts* this appeal is made more explicit. The woman is represented as desiring her denigration to a passive tool, and the reader is thus made more consciously aware of what it is that he is invited to enjoy. By the time we arrive at that kind of pornography which specializes in cruel violence or brutishness, we should not be at all surprised. For there is a certain violence and brutishness in all the forms of obscenity examined here. Aspects of life believed to be intimately private are intrusively invaded, and the dignity of human personality has been violated.

In the most general terms, obscenity is that kind of representation which makes a gross public display of the private physical intimacies of life, and which degrades human beings by presenting them as mere objects of impersonal desire or violence. There are various forms of obscene portrayals, but they all have one thing in common—graphically and in detail they reduce human life to a subhuman or merely animal level.

In the usual pornographic novel, love is reduced to sex, and sex is vividly reduced to the interaction of organs and parts of organs. The "characters" are not presented as persons; they are (or in the process of the plot they become) little more than sexual instruments, stimulating in a reader the desire for sexual instruments. This kind of literature is predominantly calculated to arouse depersonalized desire. This is what is really meant by "stimulating lust": the systematic arousal of passions that are radically detached from love, affection, personal concern, or from any of those social, moral,

---

3. It is a great mistake to regard such obscene portrayals as indistinguishable from nude paintings and sculpture that are products of genuine art. The viewer of a prurient pictorial is not invited to contemplate the beauty or form of the human body; nor is he stimulated to learn something about the human condition.

and aesthetic considerations that make human relations human. Persons then become *things* to be manipulated for the gratification of the manipulator. What is sometimes termed "the obscenity of violence" is only the logical conclusion of this way of viewing and representing human beings.

The foregoing description and judgment of obscenity has presupposed certain moral concepts. Expressions such as "the dignity of human personality" are in frequent use today, but we seldom explore with real care the meaning and implications of these concepts. More specifically, there is need for exploration of the relation between personal dignity and privacy, and between those feelings we call love or affection and privacy.

Imagine, hypothetically, a man who is required to perform every act of his life in public and in the nude. Would those observing his acts be able to respect him, and would he be able to form a concept of his own dignity? We may well speculate on why it is difficult to answer with a confident "yes." Our dignity, or sense of self-respect, appears to depend heavily upon there being some aspects of our lives that we do not share indiscriminately with others. A sense of self-respect requires that there be some things that are protected, shielded from the world at large, belonging to the individual alone or to his very special relationships. And it would seem that the body and some of its acts belong in this category, demanding a shield of privacy.

Our human dignity is often said to derive from the fact that we possess higher and rational faculties having primacy, or potential primacy, over the lower and merely animal appetites. It is the very essence of pornography that, in it, the lower appetites are rendered supreme. The more specifically human part of us is represented, to the extent that it is represented at all, as the slave of the passions. These passions are indeed powerful. In ordinary life we are assisted in controlling them by social conventions, such as clothing and various moral and aesthetic proprieties, including verbal proprieties. Without any of these conventions we would be constantly confronted with the animal side of our existence and reminded of its demands. The conventions, by partially concealing that side of our existence, serve to subordinate it; to put it in its proper place. Our hypothetical wholly-public man would be, like the characters in a pornographic novel, utterly without any of the protection which this concealment affords.

Man's dignity is often said to derive from his capacity for freedom of choice or for individuality. The characters in pornographic literature are without dignity because they are totally at the mercy of passions and physiological reactions. Indeed, pornographic literature is devoted to emphasizing, elaborating, and thrusting upon our attention those circumstances in which human freedom of choice is swallowed up in elemental deterministic processes. By relegating some of these processes to the private realm, by restricting their public appearance, social propriety serves to emphasize human responsibility. This privacy also protects our individuality. It is unlikely that any of us would ever become "individuals" if we had to do all of our acts, and particularly all of our physical acts, in public. For the physical is that aspect of each man which is the least individual, the least unique. Social proprieties render the purely physiological things less obtrusive in our lives, enabling us to concentrate upon the things that distinguish us as individuals. Thus, paradoxical as it may seem, the restraints of social convention make a contribution to the development of individuality.

It is an ancient teaching that the higher human faculties and dispositions are fragile; they require considerable support. As we all know, a totally naked person exposed to the gaze of strangers is a very vulnerable creature indeed. He is vulnerable because what is specifically human and individual in him is without external support, and its fragility, in the face of that which is not specifically human and individual, is all too evident. The pornographer knows this. And there is a form of obscenity that specializes in the satisfaction of its audience's desire to leer at the vulnerability of what is human and to enjoy scenes of dehumanization.

If personal dignity could not survive total publicity, neither could love and affection. Love, whatever else it may be, is an exclusive emotion. It involves the sharing of privileged or secret things, things which it has been thought proper to share only with a special person. In the world of pornography there are no privileged or secret things, and there are no special persons. All things are revealed to all men, and all persons are, equally, objects of pleasure or manipulation. The characters in a pornographic novel cannot be loved for the same reason that they cannot have individuality. They have nothing that they can call their own. They are physical actors only, and their physical acts are made the public property of anyone who chooses to observe them.

From the discussion of the obscene presented here, several conclusions follow. Obscenity is not simply a sexual phenomenon. There can be and there are nonsexual forms of obscenity. With regard to sexual obscenity, its distinguishing feature is not the arousal of erotic feelings, but the systematic arousal of depersonalized sexuality. D. H. Lawrence's *Lady Chatterley's Lover* undoubtedly stimulates some erotic feelings for their own sake and in abstraction from a concern for the two people whose dilemma is the subject of the novel. The appropriate reader (the one whom Lawrence addresses) is never invited to lose interest in Constance and Mellors as persons and as representatives of the human problem in the modern world.

In principle we can distinguish obscene portrayals of sex and violence from the artistry of a D. H. Lawrence or an Arthur Conan Doyle and from serious works presenting arguments or ideas about these matters. Obscene novels, magazines, and films do not make arguments or present ideas in any significant sense of these terms. They are primarily addressed to the passions, to appetites, and, probably, to primitive symbolic processes.

One may ask what all this has to do with the public interest. One might acknowledge that bad things occur in obscene literature without necessarily concluding that the circulation of that literature is harmful to society. And, perhaps, if there is any harm, it is amply compensated for by the greater freedom of expression for genuine art that we now enjoy.

Is organized society simply neutral toward the widespread circulation of materials with the character and appeal that is here called "obscene"? Public concern about obscenity is sometimes justified on the grounds that salacious literature directly promotes "antisocial conduct." With regard to the direct effects of salacious literature upon the conduct of adults, such evidence as we have is problematic, and informed opinion is divided.[4] While evidence does not preclude a reasoned judgment that exposure to obscenity is sometimes a factor in the causation of violent or indecent acts, the case for public concern about it cannot rest solidly on this consideration alone. The ultimate evils include influences upon the cultural and moral environment of a people and, hence, upon mind and character. The fact that influences of this kind are always too subtle for exact measurement does not relieve us of either the responsibility or the opportunity for reasoning about them.

Most thinking people assume most of the time (when they are not talking about censorship) that adults, as well as children, are significantly influenced by their cultural environment. It is not simply with a view to children, or to the prevention of "clear and present dangers," that we disapprove of vulgar or sensationalist newspapers, garish or lewd public displays, and ugly dwelling places. It is understood (and the understanding is frequently acted upon) that, in the long run if not immediately, these things affect our way of life. Books, newspapers, magazines, pictorial displays, motion pictures, television, and advertising constitute a substantial part of the cultural environment, having, over a period of time, cumulative effects upon the quality of social and individual life. And if we believe that beneficial consequences are possible from the improvement of these media, it is impossible to argue coherently that harmful consequences need not be feared from their degeneration.

The arts have influence upon ethics because they have influence upon the tastes and sensibilities that are important ingredients of moral character. That aesthetic sensibilities are ingredients of moral character is acknowledged whenever we speak of the "moral sentiments" or "finer feelings" of men. Our attitudes about what is good and bad, noble and base are related to our feelings about what is beautiful and ugly, fitting and unfitting. And the moral sentiments are shaped by the arts and the mass media as well as by formal education and parental training. Thus, if noble arts can promote humane sensitivity, debased and prurient arts can undermine humane sensitivity. An ugly, prurient culture contributes to the erosion of the "finer

4. For a survey of evidence and arguments on both sides of this question, see Harry M. Clor, *Obscenity and Public Morality: Censorship in a Liberal Society* (Chicago: University of Chicago Press, 1969), Chapter 4. Also, see Appendix to this essay.

feelings" concerning the sexual relation, the meaning of love, the worth of a human being.

It is no small matter what images of man the arts regularly set before us. And it is no small matter how the mass media in a modern society play upon the tastes and sensibilities of a people. The arts, for good or ill, are teachers. What if they would teach many that love is reducible to sex, that people are objects to be used for self-centered gratification, that moral restraints upon self-centered gratification are outmoded, and that there are no intimacies that one is bound to respect as sacred or private?

It will be argued that such an outcome is highly improbable because, after all, we are only talking about literary and artistic expression, and expression is something quite different from conduct. This sharp distinction between expression and conduct, upon which the libertarian relies so heavily, is highly questionable in a number of respects. As has been noted, the sexual revolution is acknowledged, by supporters and opponents alike, to be a movement toward relaxation of traditional restraints on both expression and conduct. The new freedom with which sexual matters are treated in the arts and the media has been accompanied by corresponding liberties in sexual behavior. We do, after all, have an increase in such conduct as "wife-swapping" and "sex clubs," and in premarital and extramarital experimentation of all sorts—at the same time that these things are more openly discussed, exploited, advertised, and justified in various media of communication. These observations are not intended to imply a one-way causal relationship, with the arts as sole or primary determinant of social behavior. All that is claimed here is that "expression" is a significant factor in the shaping of attitudes, values, dispositions, and ultimately conduct.

It would be surprising if this were not so. It would be surprising if man, the speaking and image-making animal, were to be as impervious to words and images as some libertarian arguments imply.

If it is a matter of some importance what images the arts convey in society, it is also a matter of some importance what images society allows them to convey. Enlarged communal toleration of obscene expression probably has as much effect upon attitudes and inclinations as the expression itself. Most people tend to take their moral bearings from the community in which they live. This is hardly a condemnation of mankind. There are few moral philosophers among us, and genuinely independent thinking, like all forms of excellence, is a rare phenomenon. Thus, the opinions of the average citizen will be influenced by the fact that certain things are not permitted to be published, shown on the screen, or displayed in a store window because they are thought to be indecent. When the indecent things are subsequently allowed and the citizen begins to encounter them again and again, his first responses may be shock and outrage. But, in time, is he not likely to conclude that his community has changed its standards of decency and now regards as proper what it previously condemned as improper? He is not adept at making the refined distinction between what is permitted to be circulated or displayed in society and what is believed to be proper for circulation and display. And this distinction might be a bit too refined for correspondence with social reality. Why should the citizen struggle to maintain private values involving the discipline of his passions, when society's values appear to be changing radically in the direction of permissiveness? With the collapse of communal support for his old decencies, he may be left in a state of moral confusion, or he may adjust to the new opinions.

For good or ill, the community as a whole is a moral educator.[5] It educates most forcefully by what it allows and does not allow to appear in public. For what appears, and is permitted to appear, openly in public acquires, inevitably, a stamp of legitimacy. The publication of "high pornography" such as *Fanny Hill* has, evidently, some effect upon people's attitudes toward and toleration for prurient appeals. Fanny Hill's liberation from the law in 1966 has been relentlessly followed by the liberation and public display of much low pornography.[6] But there is a greater impact when total nakedness appears on the stage, when sexual intercourse appears on the screen, and when these things are flagrantly advertised on the marquees of theaters.

The Times Square area of New York, with its many exploitation theaters and "adult" book shops, is itself something of an education. The teaching seems to be this: the values implicit in these prurient displays are as legitimate and worthy as those implicit in the artistic dramatic productions that you can find right across the street or in the serious literature on display in the old-fashioned bookstore down the block. Indeed, the teaching continues, there is no distinction between prurient appeals and serious art, between the indecent and the decent. It is all a matter of personal taste. All tastes are equal, the teaching concludes, and "anything goes"—anything that people like or can be induced to like.

In total absence of restraints by organized society, this degeneration of ethical and aesthetic culture could conceivably be carried to great lengths. Does the community have to put up with it?

5. It will be said that the family and the school are the primary educators. This is true, but how are they educated? What determines the character of the family and the school?

6. It is also interesting to note that the relaxation of restraints on outright pornography has been followed by relaxation of standards concerning presentation of sexual and related matters in advertising, on television, and in the respectable press. One now finds in highly reputable newspapers the kind of advertisements for salacious motion pictures that, only a few years ago, would have been confined to the "girly" or sensationalist publications. Though it is difficult to be certain about causal sequences, it may be one consequence of the liberation of pornography that vulgarity becomes more prevalent and more acceptable in respectable media.

The censorship of obscenity rests upon two presuppositions: (1) that its unrestrained circulation endangers values and qualities of character that are indispensable for responsible citizenship and decent social relations; (2) that in society's effort to preserve values and qualities that are important to it, there is a legitimate role for the law. These presuppositions are not unreasonable.

Liberal democracy and the constitutional system of government depend, for their vitality if not for their sheer survival, upon the character of citizens. A political order that relies heavily upon citizen responsibility and judgment requires citizens who respect each other and who are capable of self-discipline. A society of thoroughgoing hedonists, with each individual given over to self-indulgent gratifications, would not generate mutual respect and the capacity for self-discipline.

Beyond these political concerns, civil society has an interest in the maintenance of, at least, that level of moral sensibility that is implied in the term "decency." It need not be argued at length why the community is interested in the vitality of the monogamous family. But there are other interests as well. A society worth living in will provide for such restraint of the elemental passions and appetites of man as is necessary to enable his higher aspirations to emerge and develop. A society worth living in is one in which love, friendship, and regard for the mystery of personality are encouraged, receiving some support against the forces that threaten them. A society that fails to make the distinction between what is higher or more human and what is lower or less human is not satisfying the needs of its members. Eventually, it will lose the respect and the allegiance of many.

These requisites for political responsibility and for decency in our relations with each other are what people usually have in mind when they speak of "civility." Without that moderation and self-restraint that we call civility, it is most difficult to maintain self-government in either the public or the private sphere of life.

Civility is not an inevitable or spontaneous product of unorganized social relations. It is a fragile product of organized effort. Its emergence and preservation always presupposes the existence of rules—rules that are enforced against uncivil behavior and, sometimes, against uncivil expression.

Obscenity is only one form of uncivil expression, though it is related to other forms.[7] Laws against obscenity constitute some of the community's rules of civility. They affirm that the society has a standard of decency and indecency—a public morality. The majority of us usually require some guidance from communal standards. And it would seem that no community of men can do without a public morality. By means of laws against the more

7. Consider, for example, the employment of obscenity in New Leftist political vituperation.

extreme forms of obscenity, we are reminded, and we remind ourselves, that "We, the People" have an ethical order and moral limits. The individual is made aware that the community in which he lives regards some things as beyond the pale of civility. This educative function of obscenity laws is ultimately more significant than their coercive function.

It is not the case that, through censorship, government is announcing to the citizens that "papa knows best" in matters ethical and literary. To represent the control of obscenity as a mere dictate of government officials is to present a false picture of the situation. Obscenity laws are made in deliberative assemblies by the representatives of the people, and they are scrutinized by the representatives of the Constitution. This procedure involves both democratic and deliberative elements. Properly conducted, it is a procedure by which the community (including the people in their capacity as citizens—not merely private individuals) determines what values ought to have the status of public moral standards.

If that entity designated "the people of the United States" is, in any true sense, a community, then it cannot be indifferent toward things that vitally affect its way of life. A movement of the magnitude of the sexual revolution affects the way of life of the people of the United States. It is a matter of public, as well as private, concern. Sexuality and the modes of controlling and directing it have far-reaching ramifications in many areas of life and morality.

It is quite true that many things which are matters of public concern are not appropriate subjects for legal regulation. Society may attempt to deal with aspects of the sexual revolution by methods other than law. But, with regard to obscenity, it is doubtful that the other methods can be effective without some support from law.

These arguments for the legitimacy of the legal control of obscenity have not been specifically addressed to the protection of children. I have been concerned with the larger and more controversial questions about public morality. But we might well consider whether, in the total absence of a public morality, it would be possible to protect children from obscenity. In an obscenity-saturated cultural environment, what good would it do to make laws forbidding the sale of prurient literature to children? In a nation of thoroughgoing hedonists, one in which "anything goes" in the adult world, it would be absurd to try to prevent the young from being exposed to prurience. And the hedonists would not long continue the effort to do so.

I have been contending that laws against obscenity serve a necessary function for society and for individuals. But how is this function reconcilable with the First Amendment's command that government "shall make no law ... abridging the freedom of speech, or of the press"?

As Justices Black and Douglas periodically remind us, the language of the First Amendment is absolute: it says "no law." But the First Amendment does not define "freedom of speech" and "freedom of the press." Nor does it specify just what constitutes an "abridgment" of these freedoms. These matters require interpretation. In the course of its interpretations, the Supreme Court has managed to find that various forms of verbal and written communication do not belong to that "freedom of speech and press" of which the Amendment speaks.

The labor laws of the country can constitutionally restrict an employer's right to say certain things to his employees during a collective bargaining election or unionization drive. In 1942, a unanimous Supreme Court (including Justices Black and Douglas) held that the First Amendment does not apply to "purely commercial advertising."[8] And laws against libel and slander continue to be regarded as constitutional. These and other exclusions from the apparently absolute language of the First Amendment have been made, or can only be justified, on the basis of inquiry into the purpose of the Amendment. One cannot escape the task of considering what objectives and what values the First Amendment is designed to promote.

Traditionally, it has been assumed that the First Amendment is designed to protect "the free exchange of ideas." Its central aim is to ensure and promote free discussion, inquiry, and argument on all matters of public concern.[9] This includes matters political, economic, ethical, and aesthetic. But obscenity, as I have defined it, is not an exchange of ideas; it is not some form of discussion about social or moral issues. It is true, as I have argued, that obscenity can affect moral values and attitudes. But it does not do so by making an argument about values and attitudes.

The First Amendment encompasses imaginative literature as well as the more abstract forms of communication. One of the most explicit statements we have of the ends of "freedom of speech and press" is that presented in a letter written by the Continental Congress in 1774 to the inhabitants of Quebec:

The last right we shall mention regards the freedom of the press. The importance of this consists, besides the advancement of truth, science, morality, and arts in general, in its diffusion of liberal sentiments on the administration of government. . . .[10]

It is reasonable to suppose that this statement of "free press values" includes imaginative literature. But it is not reasonable to suppose that it includes obscenity. Sado-masochistic novelettes, exploitation films, and Times Square pictorials are not imaginative literature; they do not address the mind of the reader or viewer. If it can be said that the purpose of the

---

8. Valentine v. Chrestensen, 316, U.S. 52 (1942).
9. Roth v. United States, 354, U.S. 476 (1957).
10. Cited in Roth v. United States, at 484.

First Amendment is to foster the pursuit of learning, the development of morality and art, and the debate of public issues, it can also be said that "prurient appeals" do not serve that purpose. Indeed, they undermine that purpose. For a prurient appeal bypasses the higher and rational faculties of man, arousing and manipulating the lower and subrational dispositions.

The First Amendment encompasses all "speech" that seriously addresses the mind of man. It protects such speech either absolutely or by some variety of clear-and-present-danger principle. The First Amendment protects my right to make an argument for any kind of morality or immorality, and to do so in literary form. But it does not protect my effort to manipulate the passions of others. What, after all, has the First Amendment to do with expression that is devoted merely to stimulation or gratification of appetites for no educational or artistic end?[11] In my judgment, this is the fundamental distinction by which legislators should be guided in framing statutes and by which courts should be guided in determining legal definitions of obscenity.

There are always practical problems, however, concerning that kind of "borderline" prurient material which can lay some claim to literary or intellectual qualities. Judgments on this borderline are often difficult and tenuous. And where there is real doubt, the First Amendment surely requires that the benefit of the doubt be given to freedom of expression. But it is debatable whether First Amendment values are served by the protection of materials overwhelmingly prurient in theme and impact which happen to contain some small measure of ideational or artistic content.

The plurality opinion in the Supreme Court's Fanny Hill decision declares that material, however prurient and offensive it may be as a whole, cannot be censored unless it is "*utterly*" without redeeming social value."[12]

Elsewhere I have suggested a legal formula for weighing and balancing the literary or intellectual qualities of a work against its prurient appeals. This "balancing" approach would have to include special provisions for protection of serious literature. It should be provided that in borderline cases the consideration of redeeming social importance shall always predominate. And it might be a further condition that works clearly acknowledged by the literary community as possessing *a high degree* of aesthetic worth are abso-

11. It is worth noting that, in order to bring motion pictures within the First Amendment, the Burstyn decision found it necessary to speak of the movies as "an organ of public opinion" and "a significant medium for the communication of ideas." Joseph Burstyn, Inc. v. Wilson, 343 U.S. 495 (1952), at 500.

12. Memoirs v. Massachusetts, 383 U.S. 413 (1966) at 419-20. *Editor's note:* The "utterly without redeeming social value" clause as a test for pornography was made obsolete by a Supreme Court ruling in June 1973 (Miller v. California). See the chapter by Paul J. McGeady, "Obscenity Law and the Supreme Court," in this volume.

lutely protected, regardless of their prurient effect on the average man. . . . [13]

Other problems of legal and social policy remain to be resolved. Motion pictures and public performances present a particular difficulty. It is not clear how the prevailing legal tests of obscenity, developed primarily in cases concerned with written materials, ought to be applied to visual and live performances. Viewing a film in public is a different kind of experience from reading a book in private. The law should take account of the difference.

For reasons already suggested, prurience that occurs in public is of greater concern to the community than prurience that occurs in more private situations. While the law can legitimately prevent commercial distribution of *The Orgiasts,* it is more important to control motion pictures, public displays, and overt pandering. This is more important not simply because such public obscenity may be offensive to unwilling observers, but also because it is the kind of obscenity that is most corrosive of public morality. Explicit adjustments in the law are necessary to provide adequately for these considerations.

Quite properly, adjustments in the law are made partly with a view to contemporary circumstances and opinion. These things can change. But the underlying issue does not change. Our community has an interest in the maintenance of a public morality which must be reconciled with its interest in freedom of expression. The problems involved in the reconciliation of these two needs of our society lie at the root of all the dilemmas with which the censorship of obscenity confronts us.

There is a way to avoid the problems and the dilemmas. Denying that there are really two public interests to be reconciled, the ultralibertarian clings to the absolutist interpretation of the First Amendment. Let us see where this leads.

In his dissenting opinion in the *Ginzburg* and *Mishkin* cases, Justice Douglas says:

The First Amendment allows all ideas to be expressed—whether orthodox, popular, offbeat, or repulsive. I do not think it permissible to draw lines between the "good" and the "bad" and be true to the Constitutional mandate to let all ideas alone. [14]

Justice Douglas is not using the term "idea" in any precise sense. The materials at issue in the Mishkin case had been found by New York to be well within the state's fairly rigorous definition of "hard-core pornography." Speaking for the Court majority, Justice Brennan found that Mishkin's sadistic novelettes were devoted to depiction (pictorial as well as written) of

---

13. See Clor, *Obscenity and Public Morality,* pp. 273-74.
14. Ginzburg v. United States, 383 U.S. 463 (1966) at 419-92.

"scantily clad women being whipped, beaten, tortured or abused."[15] The "ideas" here are difficult to discover, unless by "idea" is meant anything that might be expressed in words and pictures. Justice Douglas' First Amendment, then, is not concerned with ideas, but with anything that can be called "expression." And the Constitution of the United States is neutral toward the character of expression; it makes no distinction between good and bad expression, and it forbids the law to do so.

Why this Constitutional solicitude for mere "expression," regardless of its nature or worth? One begins to suspect that the solicitude is not entirely of Constitutional origin.

Justice Douglas has seen fit to attach to his Fanny Hill opinion an appendix embodying the arguments of a Universalist clergyman in defence of the morality of Fanny Hill. The Reverend John Graham is enthusiastic about the ethical insight of Fanny and her author "that self-expression is more human than self-control." Says the Reverend Graham:

To be alive and sensitive to life means that we have to choose what we want. There is no possible way for a person to be a slave and free at the same time. Self-control and self-expression are at opposite ends of the continuum. As much as some persons would like to have both, it is necessary to make a choice, since restraint and openness are contradictory qualities. To internalize external values denies the possibility of self-expression. We must decide what we want when it comes to conformity and creativity. If we want people to behave in a structured, predictable manner, then the ideal of creativity cannot have meaning.[16]

I have quoted this passage for several reasons. It is a succinct and remarkably straightforward statement of the ethic which is at the root of much contemporary libertarianism. And it conveys a number of beliefs that infuse the sexual revolution and are influential among the young. Finally, it is a most explicit challenge to the ethical premises of this essay.

The Reverend Graham must be given his due. He rebels against "conformity"—a lifeless, rigidly mechanical submission of the individual to externally imposed conventions. This kind of conformity cannot be too often protested against. But the Reverend Graham's protest goes much farther than this. It is, evidently, an emphatic rejection of any conformity whatever. The individual is not to adopt any social customs or any standards of value except those that he has spontaneously chosen for himself.

External restraints upon the individual, and, indeed, his self-restraint as well, are rejected in the name of a supreme good—self-expression. What is

15. Mishkin v. New York, 383 U.S. 502 (1966) at 505.
16. Memoirs v. Massachusetts, 383 U.S. 413 (1966), at 439.

this and why is it such a good thing? One might say that it is useful for getting rid of tensions and preventing neuroses, but it cannot, on such grounds, be declared to have moral priority over all those human concerns for the sake of which we exercise self-restraint. It is reasonable to say that self-expression is a fine thing when one has something worthwhile to express. But an ethic that makes self-expression the most important concern cannot promise that expressions will be worthy, for it cannot oblige or teach its sovereign individual to make them worthy.

Self-control is not an end in itself, but it is every bit as human as self-expression. Many human things depend upon it. Without the capacity to order our desires and resist, when necessary, the demands of our elemental nature, we could not direct our energies to ends that intelligence dictates. The higher human activities require concentrated effort, and that requires discipline. And genuine freedom of choice presupposes self-control. The act of choosing is dependent, in large measure, upon the control that the rational faculties can exercise over the irrational. And love, as we know it, depends upon self-restraint and upon sensitive self-limitation. Love is an exclusive passion, involving a concentration of emotion or concern upon one person. It is difficult to see how it could be compatible with unlimited sexual freedom. It certainly is not compatible with the employment of people as sheer objects of gratification. We may wonder how a person wholly devoted to self-expression and unable to submit to certain proprieties could be capable of love or affection.

To engage in any meaningful self-expression one must have a "self" to express. And, as Nietzsche taught, one does not develop a "self," or become an individual, without hard work and long discipline.[17] But the new morality appears to teach the opposite: we can have all good things without hard work and discipline. All that is needed is the relaxation of external restraints and liberation of the individual to spontaneously express whatever is in him. In this doctrinal glorification of spontaneity, there is no principle whatever by which self-expression can be distinguished from sheer self-indulgence.

An ethic of self-expression need not result in unlimited sexual freedom and the wholesale dissolution of civility in self-indulgence. But when this result is avoided, it is probably because the ethic of self-expression has been resisted and modified by a countervailing ethic. And the countervailing ethic cannot be expected to maintain itself without any attention from educational and other social institutions.

17. Nietzsche wrote: "The essential thing in heaven and earth is, apparently . . . that there should be long obedience in the same direction; there thereby results, and has always resulted in the long run, something which has made life worth living; for instance, virtue, art, music, dancing, reason, spirituality. . . . *Beyond Good and Evil*, in *The Philosophy of Nietzsche* (New York: Random House, 1966, p. 477.

The most thoughtful proponents of the sexual revolution do not advocate or welcome unlimited sexual freedom. They seek a proper balance between individual spontaneity and restraint in the sexual relation, and they believe that this can be promoted by the new permissiveness.[18] But a proper balance requires that there be guidelines and standards that sometimes take the form of rules, customs, and conventions. Guidelines and standards can also take the form of models of excellence—models of the better and the worse, the noble and the base, in sexual, moral, and aesthetic matters. But neither rules nor models of excellence can long survive in those places where nothing is taught and preached but liberation.

The total triumph of an ethic of self-expression would constitute a national catastrophe, endangering not just morality but freedom itself. The freedom to express ourselves is rendered meaningless when it becomes its own end and the only end. For, then, we lose the capacity to distinguish between a free exchange of ideas and an outburst of passion, between a genuine search for truth and an appeal to sensuality, between the art that ennobles and the pornography that debases. In such a climate of moral and aesthetic indifference, freedom of expression loses its justification. And the consequences of its abuse may then become too great for the community to bear.

These larger ethical and cultural issues are beyond the reach of the law. They are questions of education in the broadest sense. We need a countervailing ethic.

18. For example, see Richard F. Hettlinger, *Living with Sex: The Student's Dilemma* (New York: The Seabury Press, 1966).

Appendix: Commentary on the Report
of the Commission on Obscenity and Pornography*

After two years of inquiry, the Commission on Obscenity and Pornography issued its 640 page Report on September 30, 1970. The Report cannot be adequately analyzed and evaluated in a few pages of commentary. But since its conclusions are strikingly at variance with statements made in my essay above, and since some of its findings are at variance with statements by authors in this volume on both sides of the censorship controversy, some attention to it here is indispensable.

The Commission consisted of eighteen members—seventeen appointed by President Johnson and one by President Nixon. Twelve members of the Commission voted for its fundamental recommendation "that federal, state, and local legislation prohibiting the sale, exhibition, or distribution of sexual materials to consenting adults should be repealed." (U.S. Government Printing Office edition, p. 51. All citations here refer to this edition.) Six members dissented. The Commission majority recommended that obscenity statutes designed specifically to protect the young should be retained but with an important proviso: "that only pictorial materials should fall within prohibitions upon sale or commercial display to young persons" (p. 58). Thus the legal restriction of obscene books, pictorials, and motion pictures is to be totally abolished for adults, and restriction of obscene books and other textual materials is to be totally abolished for children.

These policy recommendations are based, essentially, on two conclusions: (1) "Extensive empirical investigation, both by the Commission and by others, provides no evidence that exposure to or use of explicit sexual materials plays a significant role in the causation of social or individual harms such as crime, delinquency, sexual or nonsexual deviancy, or severe emotional disturbances" (p. 52), and (2) "Public opinion in America does not support the imposition of legal prohibitions upon the rights of adults to read or see explicit sexual materials" (p. 53).

Most of the empirical investigations relied upon were those undertaken specifically for the Commission during the two years of its life. The investigations employed these research methods: surveys (using questionnaires or interviews) in which various samples of people were asked to report on their sexual behavior or attitudes and on the amount of their exposure to erotic materials; comparison of groups of delinquents and sex offenders with nondelinquents and nonoffenders with regard to their exposure to pornography; controlled experiments in which volunteers were exposed to a variety of

---

*Editor's note: While Clor's commentary on the report of the Commission is somewhat repetitive of that of others in this volume, it is valuable here for precisely that reason: a consensus exists among some literate and "thinking" people.

erotic books, pictures, and films and then tested for their responses; and statistical studies of the incidence of sex crimes in the United States and Denmark during the past decade when erotica has been widely available.

Interpreting the results of this research, the Commission drew the following conclusions. Exposure to erotic materials produces psychosexual stimulation in most people (females as well as males), but it does not produce any significant changes in either sexual behavior or moral attitudes. Experience with pornography, or erotica, is widespread among American youth, but there is no significant statistical difference between juvenile delinquents and nondelinquents in this regard. Sexual offenders have generally encountered erotica later in life than nonoffenders. In Copenhagen reported sexual offenses have decreased since the repeal of legal restrictions on obscenity. In the United States the incidence of sex offenses has increased in the past ten years but not as much as robbery and narcotics violations. There is evidence to suggest that "explicit sexual materials" may be useful for purposes of sexual education or entertainment and that repeated exposure to such materials results in satiation and loss of interest.

The validity, the meaning, and the general significance of these findings are already subjects of considerable debate. The Report's conclusions about the harmlessness of obscenity have been challenged on two different kinds of grounds. Some social scientists criticize the Commission for inaccurate or ideologically biased interpretation of its research findings; others deny that the type of research employed can yield answers to the crucial questions about effects of literature and the arts on human beings. A report filed by three dissenting Commissioners includes a detailed critical analysis by Professor Victor B. Cline, a clinical psychologist (pp. 390-412).* Quoting directly from many of the Commission's empirical studies, Cline presents evidence contradicting some of the Commission's interpretation and reporting of the results. He asserts:

A number of the research studies upon which the Report is based suggest significant statistical relationships between pornography, sexual deviancy, and promiscuity. Yet, some vital data suggesting this linkage are omitted or "concealed." Findings from seriously flawed research studies or findings which do not follow from the data are sometimes presented as fact without mentioning their very serious limitations (p. 390).

Other scholars have been critical of the Commission's exclusive reliance upon statistical and "behavioral science" techniques of analysis. (See James Q. Wilson, "Violence, Pornography and Social Science," elsewhere in this volume; Herbert L. Packer, "The Pornography Caper," *Commentary,* Volume

*Editor's note: *See also* Cline's chapter, "Another View: Pornography Effects, the State of the Art," in this volume.

51, Number 2, February, 1971; and the comments of Sheldon and Eleanor Glueck, recognized authorities on juvenile delinquency, interviewed in *U.S. News and World Report,* January 25, 1971.) Since fundamental issues are involved, this debate can be expected to continue for a long time. When the ten volumes of "Technical Reports" (containing detailed descriptions of all the research) are published, it will be easier than it is now to assess the allegations about concealed evidence and distortion of findings. But on the basis of the Commission's long summary of its research, we can identify some substantial defects.

The experimental studies did not (and could not) explore the *long-range* effects of frequent exposure to the obscene. The Commission was in existence for only two years, and less time than that was available for the actual conduct of research. Typical of the Commission's studies were those in which volunteers were shown two erotic films and asked to fill out questionnaires about their sexual behavior prior to the experiment and in the days or weeks following it. Most of the subjects did not report changes in their sexual behavior, and the changes reported were insubstantial. Other research involved exposure to obscene materials ninety minutes a day for three weeks or once a week for four weeks. Before and after the exposure, subjects were given tests designed to measure sexual attitudes. The investigation usually found that most people's attitudes had not changed and that such changes as did occur were insignificant. These results are not surprising. It would be more surprising if an individual's patterns of sexual behavior could be altered by a couple of erotic films or if basic attitudes would be revised as a result of three weeks of experimental exposure to erotic materials. Most thoughtful proponents of censorship are not really concerned about such direct and immediate effects as this research was presumably testing for.

The real issues concern the consequences of many years of indulgence in obscene literature and arts, or, more exactly, the consequences of growing up in a community in which grossly obscene arts are highly prevalent, readily accessible, and sanctioned by the law. The Commission's work throws less light on the basic issues than its majority seems to believe. More light could possibly result from studies covering much longer time periods. But even these could not be expected to yield conclusive proof; findings would remain problematic because of certain limitations inherent in an experimental-science approach to the larger human and social questions.

Necessarily, all of the Commission's experimental studies were conducted with volunteers, usually college students. We do not know if the persons who choose to participate in such experiments are sufficiently typical of the general population to warrant inferences from the responses of the former to those of the latter. In addition, many of these investigations were at least somewhat dependent upon the subjects' own testimony (in interviews or questionnaires) about their experiences with erotic literature or their sexual conduct—normal and abnormal, marital or extramarital. Some of the studies relied heavily upon such "self-reporting" about intimate matters. While the Commission made efforts to test the reliability of this information, there is no way to be certain of its reliability. Further, because of public attitudes (mistaken in the Commission's view) against exposing children to pornography, there were no experiments involving children; indeed, there was little research of any kind involving them.

The Commission acknowledges the limitations referred to above (although the acknowledgment does not appear to affect its confidence in the conclusions drawn). But the Report does not reflect awareness of certain other difficulties—difficulties concerning the effects of the experimental situation itself upon participants. A laboratory situation is a highly artificial one; it is not a "real-life" situation. And it would seem that the more rigorously scientific the experiment is, the more artificial and unlike ordinary experience it is. How can the Commission be as certain as it seems to be that responses of participants are not decisively influenced by their awareness of the fact that they are being tested for their responses and, in general, by the circumstances of the experiment?

For example, the Commission employed one study to test the theory that the result of frequent indulgence in obscenity is not stimulation and attraction but satiation and boredom. The subjects were twenty-three university students each of whom spent ninety minutes a day alone in a room with a variety of erotic materials. The subject was observed through a one-way window, and his psychosexual stimulation was tested by several devices. . . . Remarkably, the observations and tests indicated a declining interest in the pornography (and in the study as well) as the experiment continued. The Report solemnly concludes that "the results obtained from both physiological measures and reported levels of psychosexual stimulation support the hypothesis that repeated exposure to sexual stimuli results in decreased responsiveness" (p. 181). Of course, such a conclusion need not be drawn from this experiment—unless one is very anxious to draw it. One might just as well conclude that arousal from pornography is diminished by electrodes and systematic observation and that science and eros do not mix.

The factors that shape the life experience, dispositions, and attitudes of a human being are extremely complex, subtle, and interrelated. Is it realistic to suppose that two discrete factors—amount of indulgence in sexual literature and specific sexual behavior (or attitudes)—can be separated out of this human mosaic and the relationship between them precisely determined? And if the crucial question is not simply the influence of the erotic books one has read upon his sexual conduct but the influence of the cultural environment, public attitudes, and laws upon his view or feelings about human life, then the methodological problems become insuperable. If we cannot put a whole human life into the laboratory and proceed rigorously to distinguish and measure its parts, even less could we put a community's culture in the laboratory and proceed analytically to measure its broad effects.

338

The Commission has attempted to deal with these problems [to the extent that it was aware of them] by supplementing its experimental research with statistical correlations between exposure to obscenity and delinquency, sexual deviancy, moral attitudes, and moral character. Hence the findings that juvenile delinquents have not, generally, consumed more erotica than nondelinquents and that moral character is statistically unrelated to amount of indulgence in erotica. Assuming that the Commission has properly defined "delinquency" and correctly interpreted its data (arguable points), there remains the problem of the validity of the "self-reported" information upon which this kind of study so heavily relies. And statistical correlations or noncorrelations do not definitively prove or disprove causal relationships. Further, even if it has been shown that obscenity is not an important "cause" of juvenile delinquency or sexual deviancy, this would not establish its harmlessness to mind and character. The Commission, however, believes that it has established that, also—with the aid of a psychological test designed to assess the elements of moral character. In its sole study employing this test the Commission concludes that "moral character was statistically unrelated to the amount of exposure to erotica" (p. 202). Despite the importance of this one study for the report's conclusions, we are told remarkably little about it. We are told very little about the criteria of good and bad character employed and nothing about the techniques used to determine the character of the persons studied. In the absence of further description of the study (and in view of continuing disputes over the measurement of such human qualities as "intelligence"), we may continue to doubt that the subtleties of moral character are measurable by psychological tests and questionnaires.

Thus there are good reasons for believing that the great questions of cause and effect in human affairs will not be finally resolved for us with scientific certitude. Whatever contribution "behavioral research" may make to our understanding, the causes of far-reaching social movements and profound moral consequences will always be sufficiently intricate and ambiguous to allow for differences of interpretation. As James Q. Wilson has observed: "The irony is that social science may be weakest in detecting the broadest and most fundamental changes in human values, precisely because they are broad and fundamental" ("Violence, Pornography, and Social Science").

If it is illusory to believe that the most fundamental changes in human values can be conclusively explained by scientific data, it is equally illusory to believe that they can be analyzed wholly in that spirit of scientific detachment which prevails, for example, in a physics laboratory. Where issues are both intractable and controversial, and where plausible alternative viewpoints are always possible, our interpretations are necessarily subject to the influence of ideological or philosophic predispositions. It would be difficult to argue that, in interpreting and organizing its data, the Obscenity Commission has been wholly uninfluenced by ideology. Throughout the report one finds discrepancies or ambiguities in the facts presented and conclusions drawn from them. And where alternative interpretations of data are possible, the report unfailingly chooses the libertarian one; that is, an interpretation in accord with the libertarian view of the controversy over obscenity censorship. The following are just three examples.

The Commission finds that there has been a decline in the number of reported rapes in Copenhagen during the period in which pornography has been widely available (pp. 230-232). In his dissenting analysis Professor Cline presents rape statistics which challenge this finding; statistics derived from the same research that the Commission used (pp. 398-400). The implication in the Commission's report of the Denmark studies is that pornography has no causal connection with sex crimes or that its effect is to reduce sex crimes. But the statistical data about the United States seem to point in the opposite direction. The Commission grants that in the United States "both the availability of erotic material and the incidence of sex offenses increased over the past decade," although the increase in certain nonsexual offenses has been greater. The figures show a 50% increase in adult arrests for forcible rape and 60% for commercialized vice. But the Commission is not impressed with the significance of this finding. We are told: "If the heightened availability of erotica were directly related to the incidence of sex offenses, one would have expected an increase of much greater magnitude than the available figures indicate" (p. 229).

In the "satiation" study discussed above, the Commission claims to have discovered evidence to support the thesis that regular exposure to obscenity results in loss of interest. But other research conducted for the Commission has produced evidence clearly to the contrary. Studies of the patrons of adult bookstores and movie theaters indicate that large numbers of people patronize these establishments quite regularly (several times a week or more). And the report itself states that "somewhere around one-fifth to one-quarter of the male population of the United States has somewhat regular experience with sexual materials as explicit as intercourse" (p. 122). These studies, of course, were not testing for "satiation"; they were conducted for other purposes. But nowhere does the report call the reader's attention to the fact that it contains evidence sharply contrary to its conclusions about satiation or boredom.

As a result of its public opinion survey, the Commission triumphantly reports that 61 or 62% of American adults "believe that sexual materials provide information about sex" (pp. 157, 356). This point is presumably addressed to the question of "redeeming social importance." In the places where this result is reported we are not told what the respondents mean by "information" or how they evaluate that "information." But elsewhere in the report (as part of an argument that good "sex education" is preferable to censorship), the Commission finds that "in the opinion of most adults, especially most professional people, learning about sexuality . . . from pornographic or explicit sexual materials may lead to misconceptions, myths, and distortions and is not the preferred or ideal way to learn about sex" (p. 270). Now what, exactly, is it that most American adults believe about the informational value of pornography?

This leads me to the broader question about public attitudes toward censorship of obscenity. The Commission believes it has found that the majority of Americans do not support any legal restrictions on the right of adults to read or view "explicit sexual materials." Thus far, this is the only public opinion research to have produced that result. (A Gallup poll in 1969 found that 85% of the adult population "favor stricter laws on pornography," and a Harris poll in the same year found that 76% "want pornography literature outlawed" and 72% believe "smut is taking the beauty out of sex.")

It is not easy to assess the evidence that the Commission provides in support of its conclusions about public opinion. The evidence is not presented in a very coherent manner. Diverse statistical figures are scattered throughout the report, with apparent discrepancies between some of the "findings" and others and no explanation of the discrepancies. Frequently the reader is not told what was the precise question put to respondents in the attitude surveys. Of course, in any public opinion poll the exact wording of the question is extremely important. (It would make some difference, for example, whether people are asked, "Do you believe that some kinds of pornography should be totally outlawed?" or "Do you believe that adults should be legally prevented from viewing erotic materials that they wish to view?") And finally, it seems that some of the results are not presented in the majority report at all.

At one point in the report it is revealed that "68% of the sample felt that 'some people should not be allowed to read or see some' sexual materials," but that "51% of the population would be inclined to sanction availability of erotic materials if it were clearly demonstrated that such materials had no harmful effects on the user" (p. 157). Is this the crucial evidence on the basis of which the Commission has drawn its conclusions? We do not know; we are not told just what body of survey evidence has led the Commission to its confident assertions about public opinion. But it might be noted that 51% is not a very large majority willing to abandon all censorship (assuming that is what they would be willing to do) "if it were clearly demonstrated" that pornography is harmless. Perhaps the Commission believes that it has made the clear demonstration. But, evidently, the respondents were not asked what they would consider proof of the harmlessness of obscenity.

Elsewhere in the report we are told that "indeed, a majority of American adults (almost 60%) believe that adults should be allowed to read or see anything they want to" (p. 352), but that only "29% believed it all right to admit adults to movies showing sex activities which include whips, belts, or spankings" (p. 353). Apart from the discrepancy (which the report attempts to explain away), what of the ambiguity and possible predisposition of the response by the language "allowed to read or see"? At any rate, the responses to that question appear to conflict with responses to other questions in the same survey. Professor Cline (but not the majority report) presents this finding: "(Abelson, 1970) 88% of a national sample would prohibit sex scenes in movies that were put in for entertainment; but only 50% say that no one should be admitted to movies depicting sexual intercourse" (p. 402).

What are we to make of all this? Perhaps the ten volumes of "Technical Reports" will resolve it all, but this is much to be doubted. What is much less to be doubted is that libertarian ideology has presided over the doings of the Obscenity Commission. Among the libertarian beliefs apparently held by the majority of Commissioners are these: that precious freedoms would be endangered by laws restricting children's access to textual pornography (p. 58); that "pornography is in the eye of the beholder" (p. 210); that literature and the arts are merely "entertainment" or "amusement" and that the distinction between great literature (or "fine art") and pornography is reducible to the distinction between some people's amusements and other people's amusements (p. 360). These and similar propositions are asserted with scarcely any supporting argument.

But the fact that ideology has presided over the doings of this particular national Commission is not the most important fact. The most important consideration is what the Commission's work has to tell us about the limitations of behavioral social science as a resolver of controversial questions in public policy. It will be unfortunate if people conclude that the obscenity problem has now been resolved because now, at last, we have the "scientific facts." It would be even more unfortunate if people accept the implicit claims that the Commission has made for the primacy of its behavioralist methodology over other ways of thinking about social problems.

I find nothing in the Commission's work that requires abandonment of the proposition I asserted several years ago in *Obscenity and Public Morality:*

Such effects as these (the effects of the cultural environment upon the quality of life) are . . . most difficult to measure, and surely they cannot be predicted with scientific accuracy. It is with regard to this kind of cause-and-effect relationship that the limits of scientific and specialized expertise become most evident. It cannot be demonstrated by any kind of experimentation exactly how or to what extent good and bad literature affects the moral and intellectual life of a community. When this kind of problem is reached, science tends to give way to social philosophy and to sober reflection upon common experience" (p. 172).

There are opposing social philosophies and different ways of interpreting common experience, and these are the crucial battlegrounds.

Comments and Conclusions

Some of the writers in this section conclude that a line should be drawn somewhere between the extremes of total license on the one hand and a repressive censorship on the other. But each writer would probably draw the line at a different place for every issue upon which he was required to make a judgment, as would, perhaps, everyone in our society.

Whatever limit is placed on speech and artistic expression should reflect the consensus of a majority of our citizenry. And wherever that limit is, it will disappoint individuals at both extremes—the anxious censor and the radical libertarian. But if one considers the other alternatives—a dictatorial society with a one-man oligarchic rule or an absolute anarchy where our freedoms are also in jeopardy, majority rule becomes the sensible middle course.

And while some would argue that the majority should never be allowed to impose their will on a dissident minority, especially regarding free speech, there is a tenured judiciary who have done a reasonably good job historically of keeping transient majority passions from oppressing the minority while at the same time protecting majority rights. Undoubtedly, mistakes will be made. But with our systems of government and law, these mistakes can, as in the past, be modified and rectified.

AN OVERVIEW

*Give me the liberty to know, to
    think,
to believe, and to utter freely,
according to conscience,
above all other liberties.*
                    John Milton

A Summing Up

Victor B. Cline

A review of all the papers and evidences in this volume suggests the possibility of harms associated with exposure of humans to significant amounts of media violence as well as to certain kinds of pornography. Indeed, on the basis of a great deal of scientific evidence presented here, it would be difficult to deny such an assertion. If this is true, does society have the right to limit, control, censor, or forbid some of their presence in the various media? Various legalities and previous precedents suggest yes. But do we really want to? Wouldn't the price be too great? Are the harms or risks really of that magnitude? What about alcohol, pot, and gambling? There are risks here, too. And we've tried in a variety of ways to censure, prohibit, and control these, but with only varying success. Even excessive consumption of salt or sugar in the diet, for certain people, can cause serious health problems. Should these be banned, then?

As long as we live in a pluralistic society, we may not reasonably expect any overwhelming consensus on most of these issues. Undoubtedly, heated debate will continue unabated, as in the days of Socrates, no matter what the legislatures do or do not do and no matter how the courts respond to varieties of statutes and laws, old or new. Tensions and disputations over where to "draw the line" will probably always exist.

Some middle ground may ultimately be the most reasonable and judicious approach to media violence, pornography, and similar issues. However, we as a society don't have to be so foolish or masochistic as to allow the psychopathic and sick among us to use the media to destroy or harm us. Most of us should be able to learn from the lessons of history (which the psychopath can't) that the disasters of Auschwitz and the deaths of ten million Jews *began first in people's minds.* The nihilism of German philosophers became imminent in the SS (*Schutzstaffel,* or Hitler's elite guard). The fanatical amorality of German youth (greatly abetted by the media) was the reservoir from which the SS and the SA (*Sturm Abteilung,* or storm troopers) were recruited. Our cultural experience does affect us for better or worse. Would anybody, as David Holbrook (1973) notes, allow children to chant in class:

Keeping company with evil people can be just as harmful as eating a poisonous mushroom. One may even die. And do you know who are these evil people, these poisonous mushrooms of mankind? Yes, Mummy, I know it—they are Jews (Nazi textbook).

There are limits. Using democratic processes and procedures we should have the courage to set them in our own self-interest. And I think it would not be too difficult to set limits which would still protect the basic freedoms of expression and the dissemination of ideas.

When we think about book burning and the suppression of free thought in other societies, an extreme reaction-formation sets in with some of us. We become so fearful that this could occur here that we see, for example, the spectacle of literary critics perjuring themselves, denying under oath that something is obscene or pornographic because they fear that censorship of pornography may be extended to literature. As Van den Haag points out, "A witness is not entitled to deny that he saw what he did see, simply to save the accused from a punishment he dislikes. A critic who is capable of making the distinction has no business testifying that he is not."[1]

The notion that we have only two alternatives, total license or a repressive censorship that would destroy all of our hard won freedom, is irresponsible. A third alternative does exist—a limited, rational type of control endorsed by the majority in our society and subject to adjustment, modification, or repeal at any time through the usual processes of democratic government. That there might be an occasional abuse of these controls is no different than that the occasional innocent man is sent to jail; and that this occurs is not a good argument for abandoning all laws covering criminal misconduct. Society recognizes that any system of law or government will have its occasional inequities and abuses. But these are subject to appeal and rectification and the laws of modification.

There is no historical instance where control of obscene or violent media materials has endangered other freedoms. And the fact that freedom has been circumscribed in other countries, as in Communist Russia, modern Greece, or Saudi Arabia is irrelevant to this issue.

Some civil libertarians have correctly noted that most of those individuals who are for placing limits on erotica are remarkably silent about violence in our media. This silence is both an incongruity and an irony. If society

---

1. From "The Case for Pornography Is the Case for Censorship and Vice Versa," *Esquire,* May, 1967.

wishes, both erotica and violence could be reasonably controlled. But how could this be accomplished without curtailing the free exchange of ideas, whether they be conventional or heretical? Perhaps the "things" that harm most in media violence and pornography are the specific, explicit modelings of antisocial acts. It is actually the *style* more than the *content* of the idea that offends or harms. For example, the early Greeks had a great deal of violence and some eroticism in their plays. Yet few, if any, child psychologists would consider these plays damaging to the psyche of any child or even of an adult observer (in fact, children would most likely be bored by such plays). Why? Because the violence almost always occurs off stage. Shakespeare and the Holy Bible also have frequent instances of sex and violence. Yet nobody in this century has suggested that they should be censored or restricted to anybody of any age. The reason, again, has to do with the style or the specific technique of presentation, not the intellectual content. Shakespeare presented fifty-two violent deaths onstage and sixty-four behind the scenes in all of his works. These deeds do not occur for themselves or obsessively but are entirely subordinate to the plots, as psychiatrist Frederic Wertham has noted. Similarly, eroticism and violence in the Bible grow out of a larger narrative and are in balance with the other natural events in the lives of the people described. They occur in the context of the ebb and flow of more complete relationships between men and women, with antecedent events as well as consequences. There is not an obsessive or perverse preoccupation or a single-minded, detailed magnification of these events. Most pornography, on the other hand, is false and untrue in its depiction of real life or human sexuality. It is sex miseducation for the most part, presenting sex out of its human context as a series of depersonalized orifices and organs. Nearly all of pornography is sex without commitment, tenderness, love, responsibility, civility, and the texture of more complete human relationships.

Many television broadcasters have found it possible to broadcast R and even X-rated films by the simple expedient of editing small portions of certain scenes which go beyond certain customary limits of candor. However, the intellectual content or message of the film remains intact and unchanged—in no way affected. Thus, true freedom of speech is relatively unaffected by these minor stylistic changes.

Author-writer Max Lerner, who testified in defense of the publication of Henry Miller's *Tropic of Cancer* has declared himself for limited censorship. In his view, freedom operates best when we can set up safeguards against the destructiveness of those who don't care about freedom but advocate freedom so that they can exploit it. There are individuals who will be hurt if there are no restraints at all against what is depicted in our media: children who are forced by social pressures into an unhealthy sexual precocity, adults who are psychologically disturbed, and others who are walking a thin line in their search for selfhood and might easily be pushed over into a whirling confusion about their sexual identity. As justice Oliver Wendell Holmes once put it, "A line there must be."

However, the word *censor* has come to have a number of very negative and odious associations. It has become an epithet that has a power to impugn and to malign motives and character similar to such terms as *anti-Semite, Bircher,* and *pinko* or *red.* It is a remarkably powerful "put down" word with which to assail one's adversaries. It conjures up unpleasant images of a book burner, of the authoritarian personality who is going to control our thinking and tell us what we can or cannot read or say or see. It arouses significant and powerful emotional responses in many people.

Yet the very newspaper or magazine editors—who write editorials and articles condemning citizens' "decency groups" and others who express concern about the content of adult books, TV, theater, and cinema, branding them as censors and prudes—themselves daily edit (a polite word for censor) what will be presented in their particular media. When the librarian decides what books will or will not be stocked in the library, he calls it "selecting." Thus, determining who is a censor depends upon who is doing the name calling and whose ox is being gored.

I frankly am not too concerned how an editor edits. If his prose becomes too purple, too paranoid or slanted, I'll switch to another publication (as, in time, will most readers). His publication's survival in the free marketplace will depend in part on and will require of him reasonable responsibility.

The kind of censorship that would probably be most dangerous in a free society would involve establishing a board of censors or a government agency or even the Post Office which would have the power to dictate what one could or could not print, publish, distribute, and exhibit. Even the most concerned "decency" and "morality" groups in the United States are opposed to this. If, however, one publishes slanderous, libelous material, he should be liable for prosecution. Or, despite freedom of the press, if one prints counterfeit money he will be prosecuted. And if one prints, publishes, distributes, or exhibits that which can be defined as obscene under the law, he also is liable for prosecution. Thus the distinction between *law enforcement* and the *prior restraint* type of censorship is vital to our understanding of the issue. And if laws which control or restrict pornography and media violence are seen as onerous and unwanted, they should be repealed, as any other unwanted law, according to usual democratic procedures and processes. Thus, prior restraint of media materials should be looked at askance. Law enforcement, however, is legitimate and should not be considered as censorship—at least in the narrow definition. Organizations like the American Civil Liberties Union or the Citizens for Decent Literature should (and do) have the right in open discussion to debate and propagandize on these issues before the electorate, who eventually should decide through their legislators "where to draw the line"—if at all.

Legitimate forms of censorship occur all the time everywhere. Every newspaper and television network edits vast amounts of material daily. Sacred community cows are protected; people's feelings are considered. A lot of this involves editing to "good taste," but it is still censorship of a kind and probably appropriate in most instances—not governmental, but private.

All societies have some laws which restrict that which is shown or exhibited to the general public. Even in Sweden and Denmark, where a remarkable freedom exists in the presentation of erotic materials, a pragmatic control, or censorship, does exist governing the amount and quality of violence permitted in the mass media. This liberality in the sexual area and strict constraint in the violence area represents, in fact, an informal consensus of the people regarding these matters. And freedom of speech is in no way jeopardized there even though controls are placed on the depiction of excessive violence in the mass media.

Some have commented that what is obscene is essentially in the eye of the beholder. What is "dirty, disgusting, and pornographic" to one may be seen as beautiful and esthetically pleasing to another. Thus, obscenity begs definition since it is unique to the individual beholder. This, of course, is both true and not true. Yes, individuals will vary in their esthetic response to written and visual erotic materials; and some persons, because of their particular sexual neuroses, will object even to underwear ads in the Sears-Roebuck catalog. But as juries have demonstrated literally thousands of times over the years, community standards do exist, and when these standards are exceeded, juries bring home unanimous verdicts that certain materials are offensive, shocking, and obscene. And while some literary critics, lawyers, artists, and other professional people claim they cannot make the distinction between say, art and pornography, this is usually because they do not wish to, because they regard pornography as legitimate or fear that censorship of pornography may be extended to art or literature.

The argument, frequently raised, that it is the responsibility of the parents (not the community)[2] to control or "censor" the materials their children might be exposed to, is not as easy or practical as it sounds. In this permissive age where children have access to cars at an early age, where they have considerable money and mobility, control over what they are exposed to is difficult at best or impossible. Many parents have found this out to their dismay when they have learned that their son or daughter has been using sophisticated drugs for (sometimes) several years without their knowledge. If the whole environment becomes polluted, many kinds of parental controls become extremely difficult. Where the family is emotionally or

---

2. In 1973, interestingly, the West German government (Bundesrat) modernized its sex laws and codes but in so doing banned hard-core pornographic films and literature depicting acts of sadism, bestiality, and child molest; it also punishes "glorification of brutality and incitement to racial hatred on TV" with stiff fines and prison terms of up to a year.

psychologically disrupted, the problem becomes even more difficult. Throwing the full responsibility on the parents for determining what their children are exposed to is, in this day, naive and almost impossible. Parents need the help of the community with its various protective agencies and resources.

This raises the question of who is responsible for those children (or adults) who lack healthy models, who are damaged, or who have minimal internal controls. Does society have a responsibility to protect them through its legal codes? A specific sample of this problem in the area of violence is highlighted in the Final Report (1969) of the National Commission on the Causes and Prevention of Violence:

We believe it is reasonable to conclude that a constant diet of violent behavior on television has an adverse effect on human character and attitudes. Violence on television encourages violent forms of behavior, fosters moral and social values about violence in daily life which are unacceptable in a civilized society. Further, television may reduce or even counteract parental influence. Moreover, television is a particularly potent force in families where parental influences and primary group ties are weak or completely lacking, notably in low income areas or where violent lifestyles are common. In these instances, television does not displace parental influence; it fills a vacuum. The strong preference of low income teenagers for crime, action, and adventure stories means that they are constantly exposed to the values of violent television programs without social importance, especially in the light of the large amount of time low income youngsters spend with television and the high credence they place in what they watch. The television experience of these children and adolescents reinforces a distorted, pathological view of society.

The Violence Commission's study found that in every major city the district which had the lowest level of education, the highest rate of unemployment, the poorest housing, and the highest degree of poverty was also the district with the highest rate of violent crimes. These areas also had the most persistent television viewers. Here the distinction between the use of violence on television and that in real life is less than it is in other areas.[3]

---

3. One interesting strategy used to reduce violence programming on TV was initiated by a citizens' group, the Los Angeles based National Association for Better Radio and Television. When one Los Angeles television station's license came up for renewal—a station that had been a major offender in airing violent TV programs during prime children's viewing hours—NAFBRAT filed a voluminous and heavily documented petition to the FCC suggesting that their license not be renewed. The outcome was that the TV station agreed to eliminate some of its programs and shift the airing times of others if the petition were withdrawn. This has set an interesting precedent which could be used successfully in some of the other major television markets.

So whether we are talking about sex or violence and its expression, some individuals in our society are more susceptible than others to the things they are exposed to via the media. Since frequently sex and violence are combined in much popular literature and motion pictures, this combination could have harmful consequences.

Jimmy Walker, a former mayor of New York, once quipped that no girl was ever ruined by a book. This comment, plus some others, helped kill some pending obscenity control legislation in the New York legislature. While this is a slightly humorous remark, of course, we know it really isn't true. The Protestant Reformation was ignited by a written proclamation. Our whole educational system is dedicated to the proposition that books or the knowledge in them can change lives and affect our personal decisions. The printed word has laid the foundations for revolutions (e.g., Karl Marx's *Das Kapital*); it has helped change the course of elections and governments; it has even possibly converted or corrupted many people to entirely new ways of living. We have good evidence, as previously mentioned, that pornography does have the power to provoke and arouse sexual feelings in the viewer or the reader. In some it may merely titillate, in others it may elicit feelings of guilt or revulsion, while in others it might provoke antisocial sexual behavior or help condition them into deviancy.

A single book written by Ralph Nader, *Unsafe at Any Speed,* set in motion a whole series of events leading to legislation which is now undoubtedly saving thousands of lives yearly on the highway and which put General Motor's Corvair out of business. Ironically, later tests of the Corvair suggested that much of what Nader had to say was in error. But the book, in error or not, so caused Corvair sales to decline as to make marketing the car unprofitable.

An occasional argument used in defense of obscenity and pornography as well as movie and TV violence is that "We wouldn't sell it if there weren't people to buy it; we only give the public what it wants." The problem with this argument is that there is no kind of social evil that one cannot find a market for. But this does not mean that society has to tolerate it if it does not wish. Theater owners say, "We lose money on family pictures; it's sex and violence that sells." This statement is both true and untrue. Of the twenty films which are all-time money makers, the majority are in the G or GP category. A "family picture" will not sell, however, if it is poorly conceived and produced or if it happens not to strike a certain note or a popular chord with the movie-going public.

Psychiatrist Max Levin (April, 1966) has responded to the assertion made by the Kronhausens and many others that there is "no proof" that pornography produces crime and antisocial behavior by calling this claim naive and deceptive (earlier chapters have also dealt with this issue):

The present is the result of the past. What we do or think at a given moment is the culmination of our whole life history up to that point. When a man commits a crime, he is responding not only to the situation of the moment but to all the events of his life, to the conditions of his childhood, to all the traumatic experiences he has undergone from the day he was born. In a few instances it is fair to assume a direct connection between obscene literature and a sex crime. But in most cases it would be a thankless job to try to allocate responsibility among the many factors, remote and immediate, that might have affected his behavior. But there is another and more important reason to dismiss the argument of "no proof." A test of pornography that focuses on the rate of crime is the wrong test. There is overt behavior and implicit or internal behavior. Crime is overt behavior. A man's overt behavior may be impeccable in that he never commits a crime, he never assaults anyone, yet his internal behavior may be destructive in that he assaults himself with his distorted notions of sex and his disturbed sex fantasies, and, in the process, he victimizes those whose lives are intertwined with his, most of all his wife and children. It is probably no exaggeration to say that sexual and marital maladjustments cause a sum total of human suffering greater than cancer and heart disease. The number of people who commit rape is small, whereas the number of those who suffer from sex problems is enormous. This, then is the real test of pornography: does it disturb and pervert the feelings and attitudes that people have in the realm of sex. Does it foster an unhealthy conception of the role that sex plays in life. A man and a woman vow to love and cherish each other to the end of their days, but they end up as enemies. Hostilities in marriage are a complex matter, and it cannot always be defined in simple terms, but in many cases it stems from confused sexual attitudes. Sex ought to be the supreme expression of love and tenderness, but so often it is no more than a vehicle for the acting out of sadistic impulses. A husband, for example, fails to satisfy his wife and a study of his problem reveals that he fancies the sex act not as an act of love, but as a vent for his aggressive impulses.

A Conclusion

Victor B. Cline

We might ask, when does something become obscene? When does it cross that line where society might legitimately object? The debate in the pornography area has been going on for some years and has—with the recent Supreme Court decisions—culminated in the decision that pornography consists of a prurient (abnormal or shameful) interest in sex, a lack of serious literary, artistic, political, or scientific value, and a patent offensiveness (as defined by the particular local law). When material meets these tests it is by law obscene in most communities.

Let me propose a possible alternate fourfold test that would include violence as well. A coalescence of at least three out of the four elements would be required in the determination of objectionable material:

1. The material models antisocial behavior (torture, rape, etc.).

2. The sex or violence is presented out of context, unrealistically or obsessively.

3. A shock or trauma is provided to the sensibilities of the average viewer (exceeds community standards). A jury can decide this.

4. The purpose and/or effect is the stimulation of sexual lust/anger.

Violence or sex depicted responsibly in the natural context of human experience would not be affected by this test. Great artistic freedom would exist, but material that is exploitive or destructive would be limited. In no way would the expression of *ideas,* regardless of worth or nonworth, heretical or conventional, be limited.

This leads to the next question many people are bothered by—"Who is to judge?" Who is to be the "censor"—granted some of this material may be harmful? Who is to say how much is too much, where to draw the line, or where that point is where one exceeds contemporary community standards? The answer is simple: If a law has been breeched—a jury. If someone is offended, he brings charges. He indicates that he thinks the laws covering

355

this sort of thing have been violated. A jury representing a sampling of the community is called. They examine the evidence and the testimony and they decide. This has been done thousands of times over many centuries in free countries. It's not perfect, but it's better than any other method available. The advantage of the jury in determining community standards is that twelve people cancel out the effect of each person's individual sexual neurosis or personal bias and give a fairly true reflection of current contemporary community standards. And the requirement of a unanimous verdict for conviction by twelve or even eight people means, practically, that the material has to be patently offensive. And what will be termed patently offensive will vary over time and from community to community. It will also differ for adults and children. But this line still needs to be drawn for the same reason we need to control airborne pollutants, excessive noise, heroin traffic, and other social dangers—for the welfare of the citizenry.

Where an individual judge is required to rule on whether a particular motion picture or book is obscene, we are faced with the same psychological dilemma as where an individual vice squad officer or Mrs. Grundy becomes the arbiter of the community's morals. All are locked in by their particular biases, unique culture, and personal history. The judge can just as easily have a sexual neurosis which will affect his decision as will any paid small-town censor. There may be some real problems in the tendency of higher courts (judges) overturning decisions arrived at by local juries where, at least, the individual biases and unique sexual hang-ups of the jurors might cancel each other out and who also represent a fair sampling of the community, assuring arrival at a community standard. One California judge has the remarkable record of never letting an obscenity trial come before a jury. He throws them out of court on one technicality after another. The judge, however, has no one to cancel out his biases and prejudices. Hence, in a psychological sense, he is probably less suited than a jury to make such a judgement, which involves values and consent of the governed as much as any clear legally defined concept of what is obscene or not. And to pretend that all judges have some standard measuring stick in assessing obscene material is unrealistic and naive.

Columnist J. L. Jones (*Deseret News*, March, 1968) has expressed this same notion:

Judges who are less judges than activists, who are concerned less with law than with means of bringing about what they consider desirable end results are naturally a threat to the system of checks and balances. By novel interpretations of the Federal Constitution they amend, in effect, the Constitution itself, and thus invade this ancient right of the state legislatures. By interpreting the intent of lawmakers far beyond the law's wording, they really write new law and thus move into the field of legislation.

Even liberal and activist Justice Black, according to Jones, has expressed concern here:

Too often judges forget that they have taken an oath to support the Constitution as it is, not as they think it should be. There is a tendency now among some to look to the judiciary to make all major policy decisions of our society under the guise of determining constitutionality. The belief is that the Supreme Court will reach a faster and more desirable resolution of our problems than the legislative or executive branches of government. I would much prefer to put my faith in the people and their elected representatives to choose the proper policies, leaving to the courts questions of constitutional interpretation and enforcement. I strongly believe that the public welfare demands that constitutional cases must be decided according to the terms of our Constitution itself and not according to the judges' views of fairness, reasonableness or justice. . . . I fear the rewriting of the Constitution by judges under the guise of interpretation.

As it is now, the real possibility exists that the censor (or anticensor) of the future will be a corps of judges who may well spend a great deal of their time in private screening rooms deciding what movies the public can and cannot see. And of course this is no different than when the sheriff's deputy alone made the decision. The costumes they wear are different, but the humanness and imperfection of the men remain the same.

In conclusion, then, we must draw the kind of line just discussed for the following reason. Both pornography and media violence assault taboos with persuasive force, especially taboos involving sexuality and injury/assault on fellow humans—taboos that are intrinsic to social order. George Elliot (1965:60) has suggested that since Western society is founded on the family as an essential social unit, nihilists and totalitarians must always attack the family as their enemy. And those who attack the family as an institution are enemies of our kind of society. The totalitarian would substitute the state for the family; the nihilists would dissolve both the state and the family in the name of unrestricted gratification of natural appetites, sexual and aggressive. To effect this dissolution, nihilists assault taboos, both because taboos restrain appetite and because they are an integral part of civilized order. And since of all taboos, the sexual ones are most important, pornography becomes for the nihilists important as an instrument of dissolution. The same is true for personal aggression and violence.

Elliot comments, "If one is for civilization, for being civilized, for even our warped but still possible society in preference to the anarchy that threatens from one side or the totalitarianism from the other, then one must be willing to take a middle way and to pay the price for responsibility. To be civilized, to accept authority, to rule with order, costs deep in the soul, and not the least of what it costs is likely to be some of the sensuality of the irresponsible."

Some have argued, as Elliot notes, that since guilt reduces pleasure in sex, the obvious solution is to abolish all sexual taboos and liberate pornography, which in turn would supposedly free the human spirit—and body. This is a cheery optimistic view, not unlike the sweet hopefulness of the oldfashioned anarchists who thought that all we had to do in order to attain happiness was to get rid of governments so that we might all express our essentially good nature unrestrained. But sexual anarchism, or the aggressive impulse turned loose, like political anarchism before it, is a "lovely" but fraudulent daydream. Perhaps, before civilization, savages were noble, but if there is anything we have learned in this century, it is that those who regress from civilization become ignoble beyond all toleration. They may aspire to innocent savagery, but what they achieve too often is brutality and loss of their essential humanity.

References

Elliot, G.
   1967   Harper's, May.

Holbrook, D.
   1973   The Case against Pornography. New York: The Library Press.

Kronhausen, E., and P. Kronhausen
   1959   Pornography and the Law: The Psychology of Erotic Realism. New York: Ballantine Books.

Levin, M.
   1966   "A doctor discusses pornography." Current Medical Digest, April.

To Establish Justice, to Insure Domestic Tranquility.
   1969   Final report of the National Commission on the Causes and Prevention of Violence. New York: Award Books.

Index

Eysenck, Hans, 147, 203, 231-32

F

Falsehood
    defamatory, 63
    protection of demonstrable, 66
    right to publish, 64
Fanny Hill, 28, 30, 38-39, 54, 326
Fanny Hill case (Memoirs of a Woman of Plea-
        sure v. Attorney General of Massa-
        chusetts), 84, 88-95, 102, 105,
        318, 326
Fantasy-reality distinction, 131-37
A Farewell to Arms, 25
FBI (Federal Bureau of Investigation), 2, 193
Federal Communications Commission, 178,
    193, 290-91, 295
Ferguson, Ernest B., 1
Feshback, Seymour, 179, 298-99, 303
Fielding, Henry, 47
First Amendment. *See also* Freedom of the
        press, Freedom of speech
    exceptions to, freedoms, 2, 7-9, 63-77, 195
    freedoms, 1-2, 80, 328-32
    historical significance of the, 64-65
Forever Amber, 276
Fortas, Justice Abe, 88, 91
Fortune and Men's Eyes, 39, 45
Four-letter words
    as freedom of speech, 40-41
    use of, in literature, 26, 47-48
Fourteenth Amendment, 95, 195
Frank, Justice Jerome, 318
Freedom
    necessity of limits to, 267-68
    security of, assumed, 65
Freedom of assembly, 68
Freedom of expression
    censorship versus, 1, 3-7, 23
    limits to, 7-9, 23
    versus public morality, 36-37
Freedom of the press
    historical significance of, 64-65
    restrictions of, 23
    versus government regulation, 76-77, 79-80
Freedom of speech
    approved restrictions of, 7-9
    censorship versus, 2
    historical significance of, 64-66
    "individual interest" in, 65
    necessary restrictions of, 66-68
    "social interest" in, 65
Freud, Sigmund, 171, 175

G

Galvanic skin response (GSR), 149-54
Genitals
    display of, in pornographic literature, 93, 95

injury to, in the mass media, 24
mutilation of, in desensitization films, 149
Genovese, Kitty, 147
Ginzburg v. New York, 31-32, 331
Gitlow v. New York, 66, 72
Goal achievement, 118, 135-37
Goldberg, Justice, 89
Gottfried, Martin, 38-39
Government, proper role of, 35-36
Goya, Francisco, 16, 21
Graham, Reverend John, 332
Greenwood, Edward D., 205-6, 216, 247,
    245-51
"Gresham's Law" in art and ethics, 17, 54-55

H

Habituation to violence, 147-54
Hair!, 32
Hand, Justice Learned, 64, 67-68, 85
Harlan, Justice John M., 69, 99, 310
Hawthorne, Nathaniel, 25-26
Heller v. New York, 105
Hemingway, Ernest, 25-26
Hero worship
    and the idealization of violence, 164
    demise of, in Hollywood, 224
Hicklin Test of obscenity, 85-86
Hill, Morton A., 90, 247-48
Hill-Link Minority Report of National Obscen-
        ity and Pornography Commission,
    90, 104-5, 248
Holmes, Justice Oliver Wendell, Jr., 66-68, 72,
    74-75, 310
Homer, 16
Homosexual magazines, 30
Homosexuality, 214, 218
    role of pornography in promoting, 214-15,
    218, 272, 276
Horror shows, 160-61
Human sexuality, change in social attitudes
    toward, 2
Humanity, cultural idealizations of, 20-21

I

I Am Curious (Yellow), 29
"I Love Lucy," 117
Idealization of violence, 164, 166
Imitative learning
    of aggressive behavior, 114-22, 130-32,
    134-39
    of sexual behavior, 207-8
Incitement to violent resistance, application of
        the "clear-and-present-danger" test
    to, 66-67
Indifference to acts of brutality. *See* desensiti-
    zation
Infantile sexuality, 50
Interstate Circuit v. Dallas, 31
"Invisible hand" doctrine, 29